RETRACING THE PAST

Readings in the History of the American People

Volume II

SINCE 1865

Fifth Edition

Gary B. Nash
University of California, Los Angeles

Ronald Schultz
University of Wyoming

Longman

New York San Francisco Boston
London Toronto Sydney Tokyo Singapore Madrid
Mexico City Munich Paris Cape Town Hong Kong Montreal

Vice President and Publisher: Priscilla McGeehon
Acquisitions Editor: Ashley Dodge
Executive Marketing Manager: Sue Westmoreland
Project Coordination, Text Design, and Electronic Page Makeup: Stet, Inc.
Cover Design Manager: Wendy Fredericks
Cover Designer: Laura Shaw
Cover Illustration: Aaron Birnbaum, *Summer Scene*, 1975 (oil on wood with found frame),
  © K. S. Art/Art Resource, NY Private Collection.
Manufacturing Buyer: Roy Pickering
Printer and Binder: Hamilton Printing Company
Cover Printer: The Lehigh Press

For permission to use copyrighted material, grateful acknowledgment is made to the copyright holders on the chapter opening pages, which are hereby made part of this copyright page.

Library of Congress Cataloging-in-Publication Data

Please visit out website at http://www.ablongman.com

ISBN 0-321-10138-3

1 2 3 4 5 6 7 8 9 10—HT—04 03 02

CONTENTS

PART TWO

A Modernizing People   90

PART THREE
A Resilient People   190

PREFACE

This two-volume reader has been constructed as a supplement to the many American history survey textbooks currently in use in the United States and elsewhere. The essays have been selected with three goals in mind: first, to blend political and social history; second, to lead students to a consideration of the roles of women, ethnic groups, and laboring Americans in the weaving of the nation's social fabric; and third, to explore life at the individual and community levels. The material is also intended to introduce students to the individuals and groups that made a critical difference in the shaping of American history or whose experience reflected key changes in society.

A few of the individuals highlighted are famous—James Madison, Abraham Lincoln, and Lyndon Johnson, for example. A number of others are historically visible but are not quite household names—George Whitefield, Tecumseh, and John Muir. Some will be totally unknown to students, such as George Robert Twelves Hewes, a Boston shoemaker who participated in some of the most important events of the American Revolution; Absalom Jones, who bought his way out of slavery and became a leader of Philadelphia's free African American community after the Revolution; and Lozen, an Apache women who functioned as an important war leader in the last decades of the nineteenth century. Often the focus is on groups whose role in history has not been adequately treated—the Chinese in the building of the transcontinental railroad, the grassroots black leaders during Reconstruction, and the rising African American middle and underclasses of the post–Civil Rights era.

Some of these essays take us inside American homes, farms, and factories, such as the essays on working women and their families in New York City before the Civil War and the people of Butte, Montana, who welcomed newly available radios into their homes during the 1920s and 1930s. Such essays, it is hoped, convey an understanding of the daily lives of ordinary Americans, who collectively helped shape their society. Other essays deal with the vital social and political movements that transformed American society: the debate over the Constitution in the 1780s; reform in the antebellum period; populism and progressivism in the late nineteenth and early twentieth centuries; and the rise of economic uncertainty and political conservatism in our own time.

Accessibility has been a guiding concern in preparing this edition of *Retracing the Past*. Consequently, we have introduced several important changes to make the readings more accessible and useful to student readers and more effective in the classroom. First, we have added new readings that reflect current scholarship and current student interests. For example, the first volume opens with James Axtell's depiction of the first encounters between Europeans and Native Americans in the sixteenth and seventeenth centuries, while the second volume closes with Juliet B.

Schor's trenchant analysis of overworked Americans in the late twentieth century. We have edited each of the readings to make them more straightforward and understandable to students and, in addition, have included glossaries at the end of each reading to help students better identify the people and terms discussed in the essays.

One of the most important changes in this edition is the inclusion of thought-provoking questions at the end of each essay. These questions—**implications**—ask students to move from the local and personal focus of the essays to consider the broader implications of what they have read, placing the essays in the wider perspective of the American past. Another important change has been the inclusion of primary documents to introduce each reading. These documents, often taken from sources used in the essays themselves, enliven the past, make the experiences of the American people more concrete, and set the stage for the readings that follow. Finally, like its predecessor, this edition includes a brief introductory essay—Sources and Interpretations—that provides students with a strategy for reading these documents and the essays that follow in a way that is both efficient and effective. This strategy has been used at the University of Wyoming for a decade with excellent results, and we think it will work equally well in any college or high school classroom. In sum, we think these changes in the fifth edition of *Retracing the Past* will make this a more approachable and therefore more useful reader and will make the American past an engaging and rewarding subject for a new generation of students.

Acknowledgments

In developing this volume of readings, the editors have been well-advised by the following academic colleagues, who reviewed the previous edition and read preliminary tables of contents:

Kathleen Carter
High Point University

Marianne Bumgarner-Davis
Johnson C. Smith University

Chad Berry
Maryville College

Adam Howard
University of Florida

Sharon A. Roger Hepburn
Radford University

Juli Jones
St. Charles County Community College

Jessica Gerard
Southwest Missouri State

Kathryn Ratcliffe
Marlboro College

Margaret Jacobs
New Mexico State University

Charlotte Haller
Drake University

David M. Head
John Tyler Community College

Jana S. Pisani
Texas A&M International

Gary B. Nash
Ronald Schultz

INTRODUCTION

Sources and Intrepretations

People often think that history is mostly about facts: Who invented the cotton gin? Where was the nation's first capital? When did women secure the vote? But, while no historian would dispute the importance of facts, historical writers are much more concerned with interpretation, that is, with giving facts historical meaning. In practice, historians normally spend very little time debating the facts of a particular historical process or event; instead they typically differ about what those established facts mean. Take, for example, a letter written by an early nineteenth-century New England farmer outlining his plan to purchase land on the western New York frontier. One historian might recall what she has read about the family-centeredness of New Englanders and find in the letter a father's concern to place each of his sons on freehold land, thus allowing them to re-create his own life as an independent family farmer. On the other hand, the contents of the same letter might lead another historian to remember the economic position of early American farmers and conclude that the father was purchasing land for speculation, hoping to sell the land at a higher price once settlers entered the region. Or a third historian might integrate both of these views and infer from the letter that the farmer's main aim was family continuance but that he was not above a little speculation along the way. In all of these cases, the historians have no dispute with the source (the letter) itself but draw very different and potentially conflicting conclusions from it.

This example points to one of the fundamental features of historical interpretation: the essential ambiguity of sources. Like the farmer's letter, no document or physical artifact is ever perfectly clear to the reader or observer. Instead, it requires the exercise of historical judgment—re-creating the context in which the source was produced and making collateral connections between it and other sources from the same time and place—to give it meaning. It is the historian's job to interrogate a source by asking a series of questions, most importantly, Who produced the source? What was their purpose in doing so? For whom was the source intended? How was the source received and how was it used? Historians employ this basic arsenal of questions when analyzing a source, and only when the source has been internally scrutinized and these questions answered satisfactorily can the source be used to build an interpretation.

Facts and interpretations are thus closely linked and historians acknowledge this linkage by dividing their materials into two groups: primary sources and secondary interpretations. Primary sources are items produced during the time period being investigated. These items might be written documents—such as letters, diaries, travel accounts, or contemporary books—or they might be statistical compilations—such as census tabulations, business records, or tax lists. They might even be material artifacts—such as houses, home furnishings, or clothing—that have survived from the period in question. It is from the broad array of such primary sources that historians draw the facts they will use in constructing interpretations of past events and processes.

History is a discipline that builds on the work of others, and historians continually measure the primary source data they gather against existing interpretations of their subject. These interpretations (sometimes called secondary sources) most commonly appear as articles in professional journals and as monographs which deal with a specific aspect of the period in question, say an essay about agricultural change in the early republic or a book about the origin of Jim Crow laws in the post–Reconstruction South. Historians use secondary sources to help them place their primary materials in context and to give those materials a wider meaning. In turn, they use primary sources to question the conclusions drawn by other writers. By utilizing primary sources and secondary interpretations in this way, historians advance historical understanding through a process of successive interrogation and refinement. Written history is thus a continuous dialogue between the past and the present, a dialogue that is always ongoing and provisional and one that is never final or complete.

As you read each of the essays in *Retracing the Past*, you will first encounter "Past Traces," a brief selection of primary documents drawn from the time period of the essay. The purpose of these documents is two-fold: first, to give you a sense of the lives and concerns of ordinary people in a particular time period and, second, to involve you in the process of historical evaluation and interpretation. For example, in the opening essay of this volume you will find a letter written by a former slave, answering his exmaster's request that he return with his family to work as an employee on his old plantation. Read with care and imagination, the letter tells us much about the attitudes that slaves held about slavery and slave owners. We learn, for example, that slaves recognized the importance of their labor and the value it generated. If we look a little further, we also learn that slaves, like many other subordinate people, were adept at using irony as a symbolic assertion of their humanity and power. By offering to return to the South if properly compensated for his and his family's previous labor, this former slave assumes the upper hand and, at the same time, reminds his exmaster that he has not forgotten the fact of exploitation under the slave regime. These are just a few of the things that can be learned from the primary documents that follow; there are many others as you will discover. As you read the documents, you will begin to ask your own questions and form your own interpretations. Most importantly, in learning to read the documents for their diverse meanings, you will already be thinking like a historian.

Following the documents, you will find six essays of historical interpretation. In each, a historian has consulted primary and secondary sources and constructed an interpretation that explains what he or she thinks the sources reveal about an individual or group of people in the chronological period in question. Thus in "Messenger of the New Age," Mary Murphy uses letters from listeners of radio station KGIR in Butte, Montana, to measure the impact that the new medium of radio had on one American community. In doing so, Murphy uses her sources to question historians who claim that during the Great Depression of the 1930s Americans were left with few national resources to cope with the disruptions that economic downturn brought to their lives. This, then, is the procedure of the working historian, a procedure that depends on the mutual interrogation of primary sources and secondary interpretations in the process of reaching historical conclusions.

Reading with Purpose

One of the unusual aspects of written history is that, like literature, it is often read by nonhistorians for no other purpose than simple relaxation and pleasure. Thus, while few people will spend their leisure hours reading a new book on the biochemistry of enzymes, many nonspecialists will read the latest book about the American Civil War. This difference between a work of chemistry and a work of history lays a trap that often snares student readers. The chemistry book will most likely be read pragmatically, that is, it will be read in order to gain specific information about enzymes that can be used later in an experimental or classroom application. The history book, on the other hand, will more likely be read without any expectation of future use or application.

Each of the historical essays that follow can be read as an interesting story in its own right, whether about southern slave resistance, the Populist critique of big business, or the youth culture of the 1960s. As such, each essay invites a casual rather than a pragmatic reading. Yet, most history courses will ask for exactly that: a purposeful, pragmatic, and analytical reading that goes beyond the story line and focuses instead on what the essay and its evidence tell us about a person (or group of people) and their times. In his essay about slave resistance, for example, Peter Wood uses newspapers and contemporary journals to reveal ways in which southern slaves contested the terms of their enslavement and put the lie to slaveholder attempts to dehumanize their bondsmen and women. It is a compelling story in its own right, but in a college classroom or discussion section you would be expected to gain more from Wood's essay than a casual reading would allow. At a minimum, you would be expected to recount the main and subsidiary points of his essay and be able to say something about how the essay adds to our understanding of southern society in the colonial period.

How, then, does one avoid the pitfalls of a casual reading of an essay and grasp its most salient points? One of the most effective ways to accomplish this is to read each essay with a structured set of questions in mind, that is, to read with a purpose. There are five basic questions you should ask yourself as you read the essays in *Retracing the Past*.

First, you should be able to identify the main subject of the essay and place that person or group in the context of their times. Some questions you might wish to ask include: Who are the most important people in the essay? Is the essay about an individual or group? What are the most important characteristics of this person or group for an understanding of the essay? What is their class? Their race? Their gender? Their occupation? Where did the events discussed in the essay take place? When?

Second, since history deals with human predicaments, you should be able to identify the major problem or problems faced by the subject of the essay. What did the subject hope to accomplish? What was the most important obstacle(s) or impediment(s) standing in the way of the fulfillment of the subject's desires? What was the source of this impediment(s)? Was it individual and personal or structural and impersonal?

Third, because people respond to their predicaments in many different ways, you should be able to locate major actions undertaken by the subject to solve the problem(s). How did the subject go about trying to solve the problem(s)? Does the person or group solve the problem alone? Who provides help? What help was given? Why was it given?

Fourth, since some actions lead to successful conclusions and others do not, make a judgment about the ultimate resolution of the actions taken by the people in the essay. Did they achieve what they set out to accomplish? Or did they realize only some of their goals? If they solved their problem(s), what allowed them to do this? If the problem remained unsolved, why wasn't it solved? What obstacles prevented a solution? What was the person's or group's response to the lack of a solution?

Lastly, since each essay in *Retracing the Past* is a case study of a larger historical process, you should be able to place the subject's problem and its resolution into the larger context of the historical period in question. What ideas do you think the author wanted to convey in his or her article? How does the essay relate to other course materials, such as lectures, multimedia presentations, or points made in your textbook and other readings? Do the points made in the essay agree or disagree with other interpretations you've heard or read about in the course? How do they agree or disagree? If they disagree, which interpretation do you accept? Why?

By asking these questions as you read the essays in *Retracing the Past*, you will be engaged in reading pragmatically. This purposeful way of reading will help you to understand and enjoy the essays more fully and, at the same time, will actively engage you in the process of historical interpretation, thus helping you draw your own conclusions and form your own arguments about the historical period in question.

RETRACING THE PAST

PART ONE

An Industrializing People

The post–Civil War decades witnessed the rapid expansion of heavy industry, large-scale immigration and urbanization, the effective completion of western settlement, and the continued subordination of African Americans, not only in the South but in northern and western cities as well. But while the economic success of the late nineteenth century meant prosperity for some, it also meant wrenching changes in the lives of ordinary people, many of whom became disenchanted with the nation's new urban-industrial order.

The end of the Civil War posed one of the most critical questions in American social relations. The Thirteenth, Fourteenth, and Fifteenth Amendments to the Constitution had promised ex-slaves citizenship and civil rights and guaranteed freedmen the right to vote. But constitutional doctrine was one thing and social practice another. In "African-Americans in Public Office during Reconstruction," Eric Foner reveals the vital role of African American leaders in shaping social and political relations in the postwar South. Much of the local character of southern politics before 1877, he argues, derived from the active participation of ex-slaves in the formal political process.

In 1865, the United States spanned some 3,000 miles between its Atlantic and Pacific coasts, yet the cheapest and most effective form of transportation between East and West remained the arduous ocean route around the southern tip of South America. In 1863, the Civil War Congress sought to bind the nation together more effectively by authorizing the construction of a transcontinental railroad. Working feverishly from bases in California and Nebraska, Chinese and Irish immigrants forged a rail link that made rapid settlement of the western territories a practical possibility. In "The Chinese Link a Continent and a Nation," Jack Chen takes us into the world of Chinese workers who, using an unsurpassed knowledge of explosives learned in their native land, risked life and limb to blast a path for the Central Pacific Railroad through the granite mountains of the Sierra Nevada range. Christine Stansell, on the other hand, reconstructs the lives of "Women on the Great Plains" of Kansas, Nebraska, and the Dakotas. She finds that while some women welcomed resettlement as an adventure and a chance for a better life, most found western life something to be endured in the hope that the trappings of "civilization" would quickly follow along the rails stretching from the East.

One consequence of rapid economic growth at the close of the nineteenth century was growing unrest among the nation's family farmers. Finding themselves forced into cycles of overproduction to pay for mechanized farm implements and trapped by railroad conglomerates who overcharged to ship their goods to market, American farmers increasingly turned to politics for a solution to their problems. In "The Southern Populist Critique of American Capitalism," Bruce Palmer explores the ideas behind the Populist movement and its political arm, the Peoples' party. He discovers that, far from being a backward-looking movement, Populism combined traditional agrarian values with a modern acceptance of the marketplace. Populism, he shows, was a creative attempt to preserve long-held ideals in the face of the realities of the modern world.

The rapidly changing world of the industrial Northeast created both unparalleled opportunities for wealth and unprecedented examples of poverty and social dislocation. In this fluid world, the promise of upward mobility held a special appeal, as evidenced by the enormous popular success of Horatio Alger's rags-to-riches tales. In over a hundred short novels, Alger portrayed fictional characters who started low in life but rose to the heights of wealth. In "Of Factories and Failures," Carol Nackenoff reexamines the Alger stories in light of the growing importance of large factories in American working life. Alger, she argues, portrayed factory labor as a sure path to failure and warned his readers about the snares of dependent wage work. For Alger, respectable work was the key to success.

The closing decades of the nineteenth century witnessed the final phase of a century-long process of government-sponsored Indian removal. Employing an army composed of battle-hardened Civil War veterans, the federal government sought to clear the Great Plains and Southwest of its native residents and move them onto isolated reservations. Native American resistance to this process took many forms, ranging from cultural revitalization to armed conflict. In, "Lozen: An Apache Woman Warrior," Laura Jane Moore shows that Native American resistance was complex and depended on female as well as male leaders.

PAST TRACES

One of the most important results of the Civil War was the freedom gained by southern slaves. In the decade following the defeat of the Confederacy, hundreds of thousands of freed men and women migrated throughout the South searching for land, work, and relatives lost through prewar sale. Some former slaves, however, took an even bolder step, leaving the South altogether and traveling west in search of cheap farmland or north seeking industrial employment. While most faced difficult years adjusting to the world of free labor and white prejudice, none would have exchanged their life of freedom for the days of bondage.

In this document, a letter from an ex-slave to his former master, we can read the emotional force of freed people's hatred of slavery as well as the sharp mind and poignant wit of the author. Finding the tables turned, the former slave underlined his newfound status as a free man, using the pretext of a reply to his ex-master's offer of work, to point out the exploitation he and his wife endured under the slave regime.

As is often the case in reconstructing the history of ordinary people, we know little about the author of this letter beyond what can be inferred from the letter itself. He was literate, an unusual condition for slaves, but we don't know whether he became literate before or after he became free. Likewise, we don't know whether he was one of the thousands of ex-slaves who searched for their spouses and loved ones at the end of the Civil War, or whether he married after he became free. But, whatever his personal history might have been, we can be certain that he possessed crucial skills and abilities that his former master wanted very much to regain.

Jourdon Anderson, A Letter "To My Old Master . . . ," (c. 1865)
To My Old Master, Colonel P. H. Anderson
Big Spring, Tennessee

Sir: I got your letter, and was glad to find that you had not forgotten Jourdon, and that you wanted me to come back and live with you again, promising to do better for me than anybody else can. I have often felt uneasy about you. I thought the Yankees would have hung you long before this, for harboring Rebs they found at your house. I suppose they never heard about your going to Colonel Martin's to kill the Union soldier that was left by his company in their stable. Although you shot at me twice before I left you, I did not want to hear of your being hurt, and am glad you are still living. It would do me good to go back to the dear old home again, and see Miss Mary and Miss Martha and Allen, Esther, Green, and Lee. Give my love to them all, and tell them I hope we will meet in the better world, if not in this. I would have gone back to see

4

you all when I was working in the Nashville Hospital, but one of the neighbors told me that Henry intended to shoot me if he ever got a chance.

I want to know particularly what the good chance is you propose to give me. I am doing tolerably well here. I get twenty-five dollars a month, with victuals and clothing; have a comfortable home for Mandy—the folks call her Mrs. Anderson—and the children—Milly, Jane, and Grundy—go to school and are learning well. The teacher says Grundy has a head for a preacher. They go to Sunday school, and Mandy and me attend church regularly. We are kindly treated. Sometimes we overhear others saying, "Them colored people were slaves" down in Tennessee. The children feel hurt when they hear such remarks; but I tell them it was no disgrace in Tennessee to belong to Colonel Anderson. Many darkeys would have been proud, as I used to be, to call you master. Now if you will write and say what wages you will give me, I will be better able to decide whether it would be to my advantage to move back again.

As to my freedom, which you say I can have, there is nothing to be gained on that score, as I got my free papers in 1864 from the Provost-Marshal-General of the Department of Nashville. Mandy says she would be afraid to go back without some proof that you were disposed to treat us justly and kindly; and we have concluded to test your sincerity by asking you to send us our wages for the time we served you. This will make us forget and forgive old scores, and rely on your justice and friendship in the future. I served you faithfully for thirty-two years, and Mandy twenty years. At twenty-five dollars a month for me, and two dollars a week for Mandy, our earnings would amount to eleven thousand six hundred and eighty dollars. Add to this the interest for the time our wages have been kept back, and deduct what you paid for our clothing, and three doctor's visits to me, and pulling a tooth for Mandy, and the balance will show what we are in justice entitled to. Please send the money by Adam's Express, in care of V. Winters, Esq., Dayton, Ohio. If you fail to pay us for faithful labors in the past, we can have little faith in your promises in the future. We trust the good Maker has opened your eyes to the wrongs which you and your fathers have done to me and my fathers, in making us toil for you for generations without recompense. Here I draw my wages every Saturday night; but in Tennessee there was never any pay-day for the Negroes any more than for the horses and cows. Surely there will be a day of reckoning for those who defraud the laborer of his hire.

In answering this letter, please state if there would be any safety for my Milly and Jane, who are now grown up, and both good-looking girls. You know how it was with poor Matilda and Catherine. I would rather stay here and starve—and die, if it come to that—than have my girls brought to shame by the violence and wickedness of their young masters. You will also please state if there has been any schools opened for the colored children in your neighborhood. The great desire of my life now is to give my children an education, and have them form virtuous habits.

Say howdy to George Carter, and thank him for taking the pistol from you when you were shooting at me.

From Your Old Servant,
Jourdon Anderson

—*Source:* L. Maria Child, *The Freedmen's Book* (1865).

5

1

African Americans in Public Office During the Era of Reconstruction: A Profile

Eric Foner

The end of the Civil War in 1865 raised the question of the position of freedpeople in American society. Now that they were no longer slaves, would black Americans be allowed the same rights as white citizens? Should black males be allowed to vote? To serve on juries? To hold office? To own property? The Fourteenth and Fifteenth Amendments to the Constitution provided one answer to these questions: They gave to freedmen all of the rights of American citizenship, including the right to vote.

But constitutional principle was one thing and southern practice another. Through intimidation and violence, southern whites sought to maintain the old system of racial domination and white supremacy that had prevailed in the prewar South. Throughout the region, blacks were beaten for attempting to vote, black political leaders were assassinated, and the Ku Klux Klan was organized with the object of keeping blacks "in their place." By the late 1860s it was clear that white southerners were determined to prevent any change in their system of racial privilege and power.

The history of Reconstruction was not only a story of black suppression and white domination, however. Wherever they could, freedpeople reestablished the family and kinship ties they had lost during slavery. Meanwhile, thousands of ex-slaves flocked to urban areas in search of employment, and others purchased land and livestock in order to establish their economic independence. Most importantly, with citizenship rights guaranteed by the Constitution and the Union Army, southern blacks eagerly embraced politics as a means to gain an equal place for themselves in American society. From a series of black political conventions held in the early years of Reconstruction emerged a group of black officeholders who spoke for the rights of freedmen to not only economic opportunity and political and legal equity, but also the possession of confiscated Confederate land. In this essay, Eric Foner tells the story of these political leaders and in the process reveals the hopes and dreams of freedpeople as well as the limits of black Reconstruction.

....

Reconstruction, which began during the Civil War and ended in 1877, was a time of momentous change in American political and social life. In the aftermath of slavery's demise, the federal government guaranteed the equality before the law of all citizens, black as well as white. In the South, former masters and former slaves struggled to shape the new labor systems that arose from the ashes of slavery, and new institutions—black churches, public schools, and many others—redefined the communities of both blacks and whites and relations between them. But no development during the turbulent years that followed the Civil War marked so dramatic a break with the nation's traditions, or aroused such bitter hostility, as the appearance of large numbers of black Americans in public office only a few years after the destruction of slavery.

Before the Civil War, blacks did not form part of America's "political nation." Black officeholding was unknown in the slave South, and virtually unheard of in the free states. Four years before the outbreak of civil war, the Supreme Court decreed in *Dred Scott v. Sanford* that no black person could be a citizen of the United States. In 1860, only five Northern states, all with tiny black populations, allowed black men to vote on the same terms as white.

During Presidential Reconstruction (1865–67), when President Andrew Johnson gave the white South a free hand in governing the region, voting and elective office in the South continued to be restricted to whites, although a handful of blacks were appointed to local offices and federal patronage posts. Black officeholding began in earnest in 1867, when

Congress, in the Reconstruction Act, ordered the election of new Southern governments under suffrage rules that did not discriminate on the basis of race. This inaugurated the era known as Radical Reconstruction. The right to vote for black men was extended throughout the nation in the Fifteenth Amendment, ratified in 1870. By 1877, when the last Radical Reconstruction governments were overthrown, approximately 2,000 black men had held federal, state, and local public offices, ranging from member of Congress to justice of the peace. Although much reduced after the abandonment of Reconstruction, black officeholding continued until the turn of the century, when most Southern blacks were disenfranchised. The next large group of black officials emerged in urban centers of the North, a product of the Great Migration that began during World War I. Not until the passage of the Voting Rights Act of 1965 did significant numbers of black Southerners again hold public office.

Although blacks held office in every part of the old Confederacy during the Reconstruction (as well as in Missouri and the nation's capital), the number varied considerably from state to state. Factors that explain the pattern of black officeholding include the size of a state's black population, the length of time that Reconstruction survived, attitudes of white Republicans toward blacks exercising political power, and the structure of state and local government. Of the eleven former Confederate states, blacks in 1870 comprised nearly 60 percent of the population in South Carolina; over half in Mississippi and Louisiana; between

40 and 50 percent in Alabama, Florida, Georgia, and Virginia; over one third in North Carolina; and between one quarter and one third in Arkansas, Tennessee, and Texas. Since in most states there were few white Republican voters, and these in any case often proved reluctant to vote for black candidates, almost all black officials represented localities with black majorities. Thus, it is not surprising that South Carolina, Mississippi, and Louisiana had the largest number of black officeholders, and Arkansas, Tennessee, and Texas relatively few. South Carolina was the only state where blacks comprised a majority of the House of Representatives throughout Reconstruction, and about half of the state Senate between 1872 and 1876. South Carolina and Louisiana, in addition, possessed large communities of free blacks, many of them educated, economically independent, and well-positioned to demand a role in government from the outset of Reconstruction. Mississippi's black leadership took longer to demand a significant share of political power, but by the early 1870s, blacks there had significantly increased their representation in the legislature and on county boards of supervisors throughout the plantation belt. Black officials in these three states account for more than half of those elected during Reconstruction.

Nowhere in the South did blacks really control state government, and nowhere did they hold office in numbers commensurate with their proportion of the total population, not to mention the Republican electorate. Nonetheless, the fact that over 1,400 blacks occupied positions of political authority in the South represented a stunning departure in American government. Moreover, because of the black population's concentration, nearly all these officials served in or represented plantation counties, home of the wealthiest and, before the Civil War, most powerful Southerners. The spectacle of former slaves representing the South Carolina rice kingdom and the Mississippi cotton belt in state legislatures, assessing taxes on the property of their former owners, and serving on juries alongside them, epitomized the political revolution wrought by Reconstruction.

Black officials served at every level of government during Reconstruction. Two sat in the United States Senate (Hiram Revels and Blanche K. Bruce of Mississippi) and 14 in the House of Representatives. For the first time in American history, the nation had black ambassadors: Don Carlos Bassett in Haiti, and J. Milton Turner in Liberia. Blacks also held numerous federal patronage appointments, including postmaster, deputy U.S. Marshall, treasury agent, and clerks in federal offices.

In December 1872, P. B. S. Pinchback became governor of Louisiana when he succeeded Henry C. Warmoth, who had been suspended because of impeachment proceedings. Pinchback served until the inauguration five weeks later of William P. Kellogg. A century and a quarter would pass until C. Douglas Wilder of Virginia, elected in 1989, became the next black American to serve as governor. Twenty-five major state executive positions (lieutenant governor, treasurer, superintendent of education, secretary of state, and state commissioner) were occupied by blacks during Reconstruction, and one, Jonathan J. Wright of South Carolina, sat on a state supreme court. Of the approximately 1,000 delegates to the constitutional conventions of 1867–69 that created new structures of government for the Southern states, 267 were black (they comprised a majority of the delegates in South Carolina and Louisiana). And during Reconstruction, 683 black men sat in the lower house of state legislatures (four serving as Speaker of the House), and 112 in state senates.

In virtually every county with a sizable black population, blacks held some local office. At least 110 served as members of the boards that governed county affairs, variously called the county commission, board of supervisors, board of police, or police jury; of these, the largest number served in Mississippi, South Carolina, and North Carolina. There were at least 41 black sheriffs (most in Louisiana and Mississippi), and 25 deputy sheriffs. Five held the office of mayor, and 132 served on city councils and boards of aldermen. Among the other important county and local offices occupied by blacks were 17 county treasurers, 31 coroners, and 35 tax collectors. At least 78 blacks served on local school boards, 109 as policemen or constables, and 228 as justice of the peace or magistrate.

The backgrounds of black officeholders reflect the often neglected diversity of the black population in mid-nineteenth century America. Nearly half (324) of those for whom information is available had been born free. Another fifty-four were former slaves who, by manumission, purchase, or escaping to the North, gained their liberty before the Civil War. Fewer than 300,000 free blacks lived in the South in 1860. But they clearly enjoyed far greater opportunities to obtain education, accumulate property, and observe public affairs. South Carolina and Louisiana were the homes of the South's wealthiest and best-educated free black communities, and about half the officeholders known to have been free served in these two states. In Louisiana, where the New Orleans free community had agitated incessantly for civil rights and the vote from the moment federal forces occupied the city during the Civil War, the freeborn far outnumbered former slaves in political office.

Many of the freeborn officeholders were men of uncommon experiences and abilities. Andrew J. Dumont, born free in Louisiana, had emigrated to Mexico, and served there as an army officer under Emperor Maximillian, before returning home, where he was elected to the state house and senate. Ovid Gregory of Alabama, a member of the constitutional convention and legislature, was fluent in Spanish and French and had traveled widely in the United States and Latin America before the Civil War. Deputy Sheriff James H. Jones of Wake County, North Carolina, had worked as coachman and personal servant for the Confederacy's President, Jefferson Davis,

during the Civil War. Jones helped the Confederate president escape from Richmond in April 1865, and three decades later drove the funeral car when Davis' body was interred in a Virginia cemetery.

Many of these freeborn officeholders had held themselves aloof from the plight of slaves before the Civil War. Twenty-two had themselves been slaveholders, nearly all in South Carolina and Louisiana. A few held slaves by necessity, owning a relative who, according to state law, could not be freed without being compelled to leave the state. Others were craftsmen whose slaves worked in their shops, or entrepreneurs who purchased slaves as an investment. One, Antoine Dubuclet, Louisiana's Reconstruction treasurer, was a sugar planter who had owned over 100 slaves.

On the other hand, a number of free blacks who became officials had placed themselves in considerable danger before the war by offering clandestine assistance to slaves. James D. Porter, a member of Georgia's legislature during Reconstruction, had operated secret schools for black children in Charleston and Savannah. Although a slaveholder himself, William Breedlove, who served in Virginia's constitutional convention, had been convicted during the Civil War of helping slaves escape to Union lines. Another freeborn Virginian, William Hodges, who served as superintendent of the poor for Norfolk county during Reconstruction, had been arrested around 1830 for providing slaves with forged free papers, leading to the persecution of his entire family and their flight to the North.

No fewer than 138 officeholders lived outside the South before the Civil War. Most were born in the North (where about 220,000 free blacks lived in 1860), but their numbers also included free Southerners whose families moved to the North, free blacks and privileged slaves sent North for education, a few immigrants from abroad, and fugitives from bondage. A majority held office in Louisiana, Mississippi, or South Carolina where opportunities were greatest for aspiring black political leaders from outside the state. Although these black "carpetbaggers" have received far less attention from historians than their white counterparts, they included individuals with remarkable life histories. Mifflin Gibbs, for instance, a native of Philadelphia, traveled to California in 1850 as part of the gold rush, established the state's first black newspaper, moved to British Columbia in 1858 to engage in railroad and mining ventures, and eventually made his way to Arkansas, where he became a judge, attorney, and longtime power in the Republican party.

Ten black officials are known to have escaped from slavery before the Civil War. Half had been born in Virginia, where proximity to the North made flight far easier than from the Deep South. Fugitive slaves who returned South during or after the Civil War included some of Reconstruction's most militant black leaders. Daniel M. Norton, who, with his brother Robert (also a Reconstruction office-holder) escaped from Virginia around 1850, returned to the Hampton area in 1864. The following year, he was "elected" as local blacks' representative on a Freedmen's Bureau court but denied his place by the Bureau. Embittered by this experience, Norton formed an all-black political association that became the basis of a career in York county politics lasting forty years. Another Virginia fugitive was Thomas Bayne, who failed in one escape attempt in 1844, and finally reached the North in 1855. Returning to Norfolk at the end of the Civil War, Bayne immediately became involved in the movement for black suffrage, and chaired a mass meeting one of whose resolutions declared, "traitors shall not dictate or prescribe to us the terms or conditions of our citizenship." Described by one newspaper as an "eloquent and fiery orator," Bayne became the most important black leader at the Virginia Constitutional Convention of 1867, advocating, among other things, an overhaul of the state's antiquated taxation system to shift the tax burden from the poor to large landowners.

Among the most radical of all black office-holders was Aaron A. Bradley, once the slave of Francis Pickens, South Carolina's Civil War governor. Born around 1815, Bradley escaped during the 1830s to Boston, where he studied law and became an attorney. He returned to Georgia in 1865, and emerged as an articulate champion of black suffrage and land distribution. Early in 1866, after helping to organize freedmen who resisted the restoration of land to their former owners, and delivering a speech containing disparaging remarks about Abraham Lincoln and Secretary of War Edwin M. Stanton, Bradley was expelled from Georgia by the Freedmen's Bureau. He soon returned, however, and in 1867 held a "confiscation-homestead" meeting in Savannah. He went on to serve in the constitutional convention and state senate.

Despite the prominence of those born free or who in one way or another acquired their freedom before 1860, the majority of black office-holders had remained slaves until sometime during the Civil War. A number had occupied positions of considerable privilege, enabling them to have access to education, despite laws barring such instruction. Several were sons of their owners and treated virtually as free; others, even when not related by blood, were educated by their masters or other whites. Blanche K. Bruce, the future Senator from Mississippi and possibly his owner's son, was educated by the same private tutor who instructed his master's legitimate child. Alabama legislator John Dozier had been owned by a Virginia college president and acquired an extensive education, including a command of Greek. Théophile L. Allain, who served in both houses of the Louisiana legislature, accompanied his planter father on a trip to Europe and was educated by private tutors. Ulysses S. Houston, a member of Georgia's legislature, was taught to read by white sailors while working as a slave in Savannah's Marine Hospital.

Some black officials had previously been allowed to sell their own labor and accumulate property, like Reconstruction Congressman Benjamin S. Turner, who operated a hotel and livery stable in Selma, Alabama, while still a slave. William A. Rector, a Little Rock city marshall had been owned by Chester Ashley, U. S. Senator from Arkansas, and as a youth played in "Ashley's Band," a traveling musical troupe composed of the Senator's slaves. (Rector was the only one to escape death when a steamboat on which the band was sailing exploded.)

In a few cases, the actions of privileged slaves and their owners reflected a shared sense of mutual obligation. Walter F. Burton, a Texan sheriff and tax collector during Reconstruction, remained devoted to his owner, who had taught him to read and write and sold him several plots of land after the Civil War. Mississippi legislator Ambrose Henderson, who had been able to sell his own labor as a slave barber, rescued his owner when the latter was wounded in the Confederate army. Meshack Roberts, who later served in the Texas House of Representatives, protected his master's family while the owner fought in the Civil War, and later received from him a gift of land in appreciation for his loyalty.

As the experience of a number of black Reconstruction officials illustrates, however, the status of even the most privileged slave was always precarious. The death of a paternalistic owner was often a time of disruption for his slaves, even those he had fathered. Future Florida constitutional convention delegate and Senator Robert Meacham was the son of his owner. According to Meacham, his father "always told me that I was free." But after his father's death, Meacham was forced to work as a slave for his own aunt. Especially when the inheritance of property (including property in slaves) was involved, the master's sense of obligation frequently followed him to the grave. John Carraway, who served in Alabama's constitutional convention and legislature, was the son of a planter and a slave mother, and was freed in his father's will. Yet, according to Carraway, white "guardians" sold

his mother "all for the purpose of getting possession of the property left us by my father." Carraway remained free but was forced to leave the state. Reconstruction Congressman John R. Lynch's Irish-born father arranged in his will for the freedom of Lynch and his slave mother. But the white trustee in charge of the arrangement forced Lynch to remain in bondage. Thomas M. Allen, a Charleston slave, was freed along with his mother and brother in the will of his owner-father. But, as Allen later related, his father's relatives "stole" the members of his family, sold them to Georgia, and seized the money bequeathed to them. Allen remained a slave until the end of the Civil War. During Reconstruction, he served in Georgia's legislature.

Some Reconstruction officials had experienced first hand the worst horrors of slavery. Congressmen Jeremiah Haralson and John A. Hyman had both been sold on the auction block, where, as Hyman put it, he was treated "as a brute." Richard Griggs, Mississippi's Commissioner of Immigration and Agriculture, was sold 18 times while a slave; at one point, Griggs was owned by Nathan B. Forrest, the Confederate general responsible for the murder of black soldiers in the Fort Pillow massacre, and a founder of the Ku Klux Klan. William H. Heard, a deputy United States marshall and a bishop in the African Methodist Episcopal church, was sold twice before the Civil War, and saw his mother used as a "breeder." Florida legislator John Proctor was the son of a free black man who had bonded himself to purchase the freedom of his slave wife, defaulted, and had his wife and children repossessed. Virginia constitutional convention delegate John Brown, a slave in Southampton county, saw his wife and two daughters sold to Mississippi, and the sister, two daughters, and a son of Charles L. Jones, who held the same position in South Carolina, were sold at auction in Charleston. It should not be surprising that in the black political ideology that emerged after the Civil War, slavery was remembered not as a time of mutual rights and responsibilities, but as a terrible injustice, a stain upon the conscience of the nation.

The 1,465 blacks who served as officials during Reconstruction followed a wide range of occupations, from apothecary to woodfactor, chef to gardener, insurance agent to "conjurer." Taken together, the black officials present a picture that should be familiar to anyone acquainted with the political leadership that generally emerged from nineteenth-century lower-class communities in times of political crisis—artisans, professionals, small property-holders, and laborers. For some, their prominence in Reconstruction was an extension of leadership roles they had occupied in the slave community. Henry W. Jones, a slave preacher and later a delegate to the South Carolina constitutional convention of 1868, had been "a ruling spirit among his race before the war," according to a Charleston newspaper. T. Thomas Fortune later explained how the political role of his father, Emanuel Fortune, a Florida constitutional convention delegate and legislator, was rooted in events antedating the Civil War:

> It was natural for him to take the leadership in any independent improvement of the Negros. During and before the Civil War he had commanded his time as a tanner and expert shoe and bootmaker. In such life as the slaves were allowed and in church work, he took the leader's part. When the matter of the Constitutional Convention was decided upon his people in Jackson County naturally looked to him.

Like Fortune, a large number of black officeholders had been enslaved artisans whose skill and relative independence (often reflected in command over their own time and the ability to travel off the plantation) accorded them high status in the slave community. Others were free blacks who had followed skilled trades before the Civil War. Among artisans, carpenter (125), barber (50), blacksmith (47), mason (37), and shoemaker (37) were the crafts most frequently represented.

Another large occupational grouping consisted of professionals. There were 237 ministers among the Reconstruction officials (many of whom held other occupations as well, since it was difficult for black congregations to support their pastors). Most were Methodists and Baptists, with a handful of Presbyterians, Congregationalists, and Episcopalians. "A man cannot do his whole duty as a minister except he looks out for the political interests of his people," said Charles H. Pearce, who had purchased his freedom in Maryland as a young man, served as an African Methodist Episcopal preacher in Canada before the Civil War, came to Florida as a religious missionary, and was elected to the constitutional convention and state senate.

Many of Reconstruction's most prominent black leaders not only emerged from the church, but had a political outlook grounded in a providential view of history inspired by black Christianity. The cause of the Civil War, declared James D. Lynch, a minister and religious missionary who became Mississippi's secretary of sate during Reconstruction, was America's "disobedience," via slavery, to its divine mission to "elevate humanity" and spread freedom throughout the globe. Justice for the former slaves, Lynch continued, could not be long delayed, because "Divine Providence will wring from you in wrath, that which should have been given in love."

Teachers accounted for 172 officeholders, some of whom not only established schools for black children on their own initiative immediately after the Civil War, but used their literacy to assist the freed people. William V. Turner, a former slave, established a school in Wetumpka, Alabama, served as agent in northern Alabama for the black-owned Mobile *Nationalist*, and brought cases of injustice against blacks in the local courts to the attention of the Freedmen's Bureau. Turner went on to serve as a registrar and member of the state legislature. Other educators included Francis L. Cardoza, the Reconstruction secretary of state and treasurer of South Carolina, who had lived in the North and Europe before the war, and returned to his native Charleston where he served as a teacher for the American Missionary Association and helped to establish the Avery Normal Institute. The training of black teachers, Cardoza wrote, was "the object for which I left all the superior advantages and privileges of the North and came South."

Of the 83 officials who edited and published newspapers, a few, like South Carolina trial justice Martin R. Delany and Isaac D. Shadd, Speaker of the House in Mississippi, had acquired journalistic experience in the North before the Civil War. (Delany published *The Mystery* in Pittsburgh during the 1840s, and Shadd, with his sister Mary Ann, edited the *Provincial Freeman* in Canada in the following decade.) Those who operated newspapers during or after Reconstruction included Florida Congressman Josiah T. Walls, owner of the Gainesville *New Era*; Richard Nelson, a Texas justice of the peace, who established the Galveston *Spectator*, the state's first black newspaper; and James P. Ball, clerk of the district court in Concordia parish, Louisiana, who edited the *Concordia Eagle*. Sixty-nine black officeholders were attorneys, seven were musicians, five were physicians, and one practiced dentistry.

Businessmen comprised another large group of officeholders, the majority (104) of whom were small shopkeepers and grocers. Fifty-two earned their livings as merchants, and there was a scattering of building contractors, saloonkeepers, and hotel owners. Not surprisingly, farmers constituted the largest occupational category, accounting for 294 officials. Unfortunately, the census of 1870 did not distinguish between farm owners and tenants, so it is not known how many worked for their own land. An additional 32 were planters, who owned a significant amount of acreage. Finally, there were 115 laborers, most of whom worked on farms, but a few worked as factory operatives and unskilled employees in artisan shops and mercantile establishments.

Information about ownership of property is available for 928 black officials. Of these, 236 were propertyless, while 352 owned real estate

and personal property amounting to under $1,000. Three hundred thirty-nine held property valued at over $1,000, a considerable sum at a time when the average non-farm employee earned under $500 per year and Southern farm wages ranged between $10 and $15 per month. Of these wealthiest black officials, a majority had been born free or became free before the Civil War. Nearly half held office in South Carolina and Louisiana, states with relatively large populations of propertied freeborn blacks. At least 94, however, had remained slaves until the Civil War and acquired their wealth during Reconstruction. Holding office, for many blacks, was a surer way to advance their economic standing than laboring in the postwar Southern economy. The thirteen dollars per diem earned by members of the Louisiana constitutional convention, or the seven dollars per day plus mileage paid to North Carolina legislators, far outstripped the wages most blacks could ordinarily command, and offices like sheriff garnered far higher rewards in commissions and fees.

The black political leadership included a few men of truly substantial wealth. Antoine Dubuclet owned over $200,000 worth of property on the eve of the Civil War. Florida Congressmen Josiah T. Walls, a former slave, prospered as a planter during Reconstruction, and Mississippi Senator Blanche K. Bruce acquired a fortune in real estate. When he died in 1898, Bruce was worth over $100,000. Ferdinand Havis, a former slave who served on the Pine Bluff, Arkansas board of aldermen and in the state legislature, owned a saloon, whiskey business, and 2,000 acres of farm land. Toward the end of the century, Havis described himself in the city directory simply as a "capitalist." William J. Whipper, a South Carolina legislator and rice planter, was said to have lost $75,000 in a single night of poker. Pinckney B. S. Pinchback, who served briefly as Louisiana's governor, operated a commis-sion brokerage and parlayed inside information about state expenditures into a fortune in government bonds. (Despite earlier historians' charges of widespread corruption during Reconstruction, Pinchback is one of relatively few black officials against whom charges of malfeasance in office can in fact be documented.)

Most black propertyholders, however, were men of relatively modest incomes, and often precarious economic standing. Like their white counterparts, black small farmers, tenants, artisans, and small businessmen were subject to the vagaries of the post-Civil War economy. Among Reconstruction officeholders, at least 24 black entrepreneurs, mostly grocers and small merchants, are known to have gone out of business during the depression of the 1870s. Even Dubuclet suffered financial reverses; when he died in 1887, his estate was valued at only $1,300. Black professionals often found it difficult to make ends meet, since whites shunned them and few blacks were able to pay their fees. Talented professionals like Robert B. Elliott, a congressman and lawyer from South Carolina, sometimes had to request small loans from white politicians to meet day-to-day expenses. Unlike white counterparts, moreover, black officials who operated businesses found themselves subjected to ostracism by their political opponents, often with devastating effect. Georgia Congressman Jefferson Long, a tailor, had commanded "much of the fine custom" of Macon before embarking on his political career. But as another black official recalled, "Long's stand in politics ruined his business with the whites who had been his patrons chiefly." Most truly wealthy blacks avoided politics, and black politicians, even those who owned property, relied heavily on office for their livelihood.

Ridiculed by their opponents as incompetent and corrupt, most black officials proved themselves fully capable of understanding public issues and pursuing the interests of their constituents and party. To be sure, slavery, once described by its apologists as a "school" that introduced "uncivilized" Africans into Western culture, was hardly intended as a training ground for political leaders. Looking back on the post-emancipation years, James K. Green, who served in Alabama's constitutional convention and legislature, remarked:

> I believe that the colored people have done well, considering all their circumstances and surroundings, as emancipation made them. I for one was entirely ignorant; I knew nothing more than to obey my master; and there were thousands of us in the same attitude . . . but the tocsin of freedom sounded and knocked at the door and we walked out like free men and met the exigencies as they grew up, and shouldered the responsibilities.

As Green suggested, there was something remarkable about how men, who until recently had been excluded from the main currents of American life, "shouldered the responsibilities" of Reconstruction lawmaking. It would be wrong, however, to assume that the black officials were mainly unschooled.

Remarkably, in a region where before the Civil War it was illegal to teach slaves to read and write, and where educational opportunities for free blacks were in many areas extremely limited, the large majority of black officials were literate. Of the 1,126 for whom information is available, 933, or 83 percent, were able to read and write. Of these, 339 had been born or become free before the Civil War, and 273 were former slaves. Some slaves, as has been related, were educated by their owners or sympathetic whites. Others were taught to read and write by a literate slave, often a relative, or, like George W. Albright, a Mississippi field hand who went on to serve in the state Senate, became literate "by trickery." Albright listened surreptitiously as his owner's children did their school lessons in the kitchen, where his mother worked. A number of literate officials learned to read and write in the Union army, and others studied during and after the Civil War in schools established by the Freedmen's Bureau or Northern aid societies. Albright himself attended a Reconstruction school for blacks run by a Northerner, married a white instructor from the North, and became a teacher.

However acquired, the ability to read and write marked many black officials as community leaders. Former slave Thomas M. Allen explained how he became a political organizer in rural Jasper county, Georgia, and was chosen to sit in the legislature:

> In all those counties of course the colored people are generally very ignorant; . . . but some know more about things than the others. In my county the colored people came to me for instructions, and I gave them the best instructions I could. I took the New York Tribune and other papers, and in that way I found out a great deal, and I thought they had been freed by the Yankees and Union men, and I thought they ought to vote with them; go with that party always.

Those officials who could not read relied on associates or relatives who could. "I have a son I sent to school when he was small," said Georgia legislator Abram Colby. "I make him read all my letters and do all my writing. I keep him with me all the time."

At least 64 black officeholders attended college or professional school either before or during their terms of public service. Thirty-four studied in the South: 25 at the black colleges established immediately after the Civil War, including Howard, Lincoln, Shaw, and Straight Universities, and Hampton Institute, and nine at the University of South Carolina when it admitted black pupils between 1873 and 1877. Twenty-seven received their higher education in the North, 14 at Oberlin College. Four officials had studied abroad: Francis L. Cardoza, who received a degree from the University of Glasgow; Louisiana legislator Eugéne-Victor Macarty, a musician who graduated from the Imperial Conservatoire in Paris; James W. Mason, an Arkansas sheriff whose father, a wealthy planter, sent him to college in France; and Martin Becker, a native of Surinam and member of South Carolina's constitutional convention, who appears to have attended college in Holland or Germany. Black college graduates included Mifflin Gibbs, who received a degree from Oberlin's law department in 1870, and his brother Jonathan, who graduated from Dartmouth College in 1852 after being refused

admission to 18 colleges in the North because of his color. Among other officeholders who had at least some higher education were Benjamin A. Boseman, a member of South Carolina's legislature, who had graduated from the Medical School of Maine; John W. Menard, who attended Iberia College in Ohio before the Civil War and went on to hold several posts in Florida Reconstruction; and Louisiana officials C. C. Antoine, Robert H. Isabelle, Joseph Lott, Louis A. Martinet, and Victor Rochon, all of whom attended Straight University during the 1870s.

Given the almost universal prohibition on blacks voting and holding office before the Civil War, few Reconstruction officials had experience in public service. Two, John M. Langston and Macon B. Allen, had held public office in the North before the Civil War. Allen was appointed justice of the peace in Middlesex county, Massachusetts in 1848, and Langston in 1855 apparently became the first black American to hold elective office when he was chosen township clerk in Brownhelm, Ohio, a stronghold of abolitionism. Immediately after the war, Thomas Bayne was elected to the New Bedford, Massachusetts, city council, and beginning in 1866, Mifflin Gibbs served two terms on the city council of Victoria, British Columbia. William H. Grey, the leading black spokesman at the Arkansas constitutional convention, had learned legislative procedures while attending sessions of Congress with his antebellum employer, Virginia Congressman Henry A. Wise. Among other Reconstruction officials with experience in public affairs were the nine who had worked at newspapers before or during the Civil War.

Thirty-one officials, either natives of the North or men who had migrated or escaped from the slave South, were involved in the movement for the abolition of slavery and equal rights for Northern blacks before the Civil War. Fugitive slaves Thomas Bayne and Aaron A. Bradley worked with the antislavery movement in Massachusetts, and the freeborn

Hodges brothers—Charles, William, and Willis, whose family had been forced to flee Virginia—were active in the abolitionist crusade and the movement for black suffrage in New York State. John and Matthew Leary, North Carolina officeholders, had a brother, Lewis S. Leary, who was killed in 1859 while fighting alongside John Brown at Harper's Ferry. O. S. B. Wall, the first black justice of the peace in the nation's capital, and Andrew J. Chestnutt, a town commissioner in Cumberland county, North Carolina, had participated in violent encounters in Ohio that prevented fugitive slaves from being returned to the South. Five officials, including brothers Abraham and Isaac Shadd, had been active in the abolitionist movement while living in Canada, and eight, including the "father of black nationalism," Martin R. Delany, in the 1850s had advocated black emigration from the United States. Delany traveled to Africa seeking a homeland for black Americans, and George T. Ruby, born in New York City and brought up in Portland, Maine, had journeyed to Haiti as an emigration agent and newspaper correspondent before coming South to teach and work for the Freedmen's Bureau. Ruby went on to serve the Texas constitutional convention and senate.

At least 129 officeholders were among the 200,000 African American black men who served in the Union army and navy during the Civil War. Military service was a politicizing experience, a training ground for postwar black leadership. Many not only received schooling in the army, but for the first time became involved in political activism. Such men included several officers of Louisiana regiments who protested discriminatory treatment by white counterparts, and the nine Reconstruction officials who served in the famous 54th and 55th Massachusetts regiments, which for many months refused their salaries to protest the government's policy of paying black soldiers less than white.

Another stepping stone to office was the Freedmen's Bureau, the federal agency estab-

lished in 1865 to oversee the transition from slavery to freedom, for which 46 black officials worked in some capacity immediately after the war. Another path to political prominence was organizational work with the Republican party. In 1867, the Republican Congressional Committee employed 118 speakers, 83 of them black, to lecture in the South. Of the blacks, 26 went on to hold Reconstruction office. Many other officials were members of black fraternal societies like the Masons, and emerged from the black church and other positions of leadership within the slave community.

It is difficult to gauge with precision how much political power black officeholders exercised. The phrase "Black Reconstruction" originated as a Democratic effort to arouse the resentments of white voters, even though political power generally remained in white hands. Even in Louisiana, with its articulate and well-organized black leadership, a group of prominent black officeholders, including the state's lieutenant governor and treasurer, complained in 1874 of their systematic exclusion from "participation and knowledge of the confidential workings of the party and government." Black officials never controlled Reconstruction. But, as DuBois indicated when he adopted the term "Black Reconstruction" to describe the era, blacks were major actors of the Reconstruction drama, and their ascent to even limited positions of political power represented a revolution in American government and race relations.

In the early days of Radical Reconstruction, blacks often stood aside when nominations for office were decided upon, so as not to embarrass the Republican party in the North or lend credence to Democratic charges of "black supremacy." In South Carolina, Francis L. Cardozo and Martin R. Delany, promoted, respectively, for the lieutenant governership and a Congressional seat in 1868, declined to run, citing the need for "the greatest possible discretion and prudence." In the first state governments established after the advent of black suffrage, blacks held no important positions in six states, and occupied only the largely ceremonial post of secretary of state in Florida, Mississippi, and South Carolina. In Louisiana alone, where Oscar J. Dunn was elected lieutenant governor in 1868 and Antoine Dubuclet treasurer, did blacks hold more than one major post from the beginning of Reconstruction.

It did not take long for black leaders, and voters, to become dissatisfied with the role of junior partners in the Republican coalition, especially since the first governors of Republican Reconstruction seemed to devote greater energy to attracting white support than addressing the needs of black constituents. By the early 1870s, prominent black leaders in many states were condemning white Republican leaders who, in the words of Texas state senator Matthew Gaines, set themselves up as "the Big Gods of the negroes." Gaines organized a Colored Men's Convention to press for more black officeholders. By this time, black officeholding was already waning in Virginia and Tennessee, where coalitions of Democrats and conservative Republicans had come to power in 1869, and in Georgia, where Democrats overthrew Republican rule in 1871. Elsewhere, however, black leaders not only assumed a larger share of offices, but led successful efforts to repudiate the conservative policies of the early governors, often engineering their replacement by men more attuned to blacks' demands. During the 1870s, blacks in five states occupied powerful executive positions as lieutenant governors, treasurers, and superintendents of education. Blacks served, moreover, as Speakers of the House in Mississippi and South Carolina.

Even more remarkable was the growing presence of blacks in county and local offices scattered across the South. Most local officials were white, but the high concentration of the black population, a legacy of the plantation system, meant that most former slaves encountered at least some local black officials during Reconstruction. (The Mississippi counties and Louisiana parishes that elected black sheriffs,

for example, accounted for a considerable majority of these states' black populations.) John R. Lynch later recalled how, when he served as a justice of the peace, freedmen "magnified" his office "far beyond its importance," bringing him cases ranging from disputes with employers to family squabbles. With control over such matters as public expenditures, poor relief, the administration of justice, and taxation policy, local officials had a real impact on the day to day lives of all Southerners. On the Atlanta city council, William Finch pressed for the establishment of black schools and the hiring of black teachers, and lobbied effectively for street improvements in black and poor white neighborhoods. Other officials tried to ensure that blacks were chosen to serve on juries, and were employed, at the same wages as whites, on pubic projects.

Only a handful of black officials, including former slave Aaron A. Bradley, were actively involved in efforts to assist freedmen in acquiring land, or advocated confiscation of the land of ex-Confederates. Many black officials fully embraced the prevailing free labor ethos, which saw individual initiative in the "race of life," not public assistance, as the route to upward mobility. Free blacks from both North and South, many of whom had achieved astonishing success given the barriers erected against them, expressed most forcefully the idea of competitive equality. "Look at the progress of our people—their wonderful civilization," declared freeborn North Carolina registrar George W. Brodie. "What have we to fear in competition with the whites, if they give us a fair race?"

A considerable number of black officeholders made efforts to uplift the conditions of black laborers in other ways. William H. Grey of Arkansas purchased a plantation in order to sell it in small plots to sharecroppers. Benjamin S. Turner introduced a bill in Congress for the sale of small tracts of land to Southern freedmen, and several officials, including Matthew Gaines of Texas and Abraham Galloway, who served in the constitutional convention and state senate of North Carolina, urged heavy taxation of unoccupied land, to force it onto the market. At least 58 black officials attended statewide labor conventions, encouraged the formation of agricultural labor unions, or sponsored legislation to assist farm laborers. Other local officeholders, as planters persistently complained, sided with employees in contract disputes, failed to enforce vagrancy laws, and refused to coerce freedmen into signing plantation labor contracts.

Even the most powerful African American officials were not immune to the numerous indignities and inequalities to which blacks were subjected in the post-Civil War South. Despite national and state civil rights laws, many common carriers and places of business either refused to serve blacks, or relegated them to inferior accommodations. A common experience was being refused service in a first class railroad car or steamboat cabin, and being forced to ride in the "smoking car" or on deck. Edward Butler, a member of Louisiana's Senate, was beaten and stabbed by a riverboat crew while seeking admission to the first class cabin. In speeches supporting Charles Sumner's Civil Rights Bill in 1874, black Congressmen related the "outrages and indignities" to which they had been subjected. Joseph Rainey had been thrown from a Virginia streetcar, John R. Lynch forced to occupy a railroad smoking car with gamblers and drunkards, Richard H. Cain and Robert B. Elliott excluded from a North Carolina restaurant, James T. Rapier denied service by inns at every stopping point between Montgomery and Washington. Such incidents were not confined to the South. In 1864, Robert Smalls, a military hero soon to become a major political leader in Reconstruction South Carolina, was evicted from a Philadelphia streetcar, provoking a mass protest that led to the desegregation of the city's public transportation.

Like Smalls, many black officials resisted their exclusion from access to public facilities. Mifflin Gibbs and Arkansas legislator W. Hines Furbush successfully sued a Little Rock saloon for refusing to serve blacks, and in Louisiana, Charles S. Sauvinet, the sheriff of Orleans parish, took a saloonkeeper to court after being denied service, and was awarded $1,000. South Carolina Supreme Court Justice Jonathan B. Wright won $1,200 in a lawsuit after being ejected from a first-class railroad car. When Eugéne-Victor Macarty was refused a seat at the New Orleans Opera House in 1869, he sued and organized a black boycott, which lasted until the theater was integrated in 1875.

Given such experiences, and the broad aspiration widely shared in the black community to construct a color-blind society from the ashes of slavery, black officials devoted considerable effort to the passage of national and state civil rights legislation. "Sir," North Carolina legislator Thomas A. Sykes wrote Charles Sumner, "if I am a free citizen of this 'grand Republic,' why am I denied privileges which are given to my white brother, although he might be the basest culprit on earth?" It was the insistence of black legislators that led Florida, Louisiana, Mississippi, South Carolina, and Texas to enact laws during Reconstruction requiring equal treatment by railroads and places of public accommodation.

The frequent denial of equal access to public facilities, however, was hardly the most serious danger confronting black officials during Reconstruction. It is difficult to think of any group of public officials in American history who faced the threat of violence as persistently as Reconstruction's black officeholders. No fewer than 156 officials—over ten percent of the total—were victimized by violence, generally by the Ku Klux Klan, White League, and other paramilitary criminal organizations allied with the Democratic party. Their number included 36 officials who received death threats, 45 of whom were driven from their homes, and 41 shot at, stabbed, or otherwise assaulted. Thirty-four black officeholders were actually murdered, most during Reconstruction, but a few after the South's "Redemption."

Violence was an endemic feature of post-Civil War Southern society, directed against anyone who challenged inherited norms of white supremacy. The targets included laborers who refused to work in a disciplined manner or sought to acquire their own land, teachers and others who worked to uplift the former slaves, Union League officials, and Republican party organizers. No state was immune from political violence, but the targeting of public officials was concentrated in four states—Georgia, Louisiana, Mississippi, and South Carolina—which together accounted for nearly 80 percent of the known victims. All were centers of Klan or White League violence in the late 1860s and early 1870s and all except Georgia were the scene of exceptionally violent Redemption campaigns as Reconstruction drew to a close.

From constables and justices of the peace to legislators and members of constitutional conventions, no black official was immune from the threat of violence. Those murdered included eight constitutional convention delegates and twelve legislators, the most prominent of whom was Benjamin Randolph, killed in 1868 while serving as chairman of the Republican state executive committee in South Carolina. Numerous Mississippi officials were threatened or driven from their homes during the 1875 campaign in which Democrats regained control of the state, and at least five were murdered, including state senator Charles Caldwell, who was lured to his assassination by a white "friend" a few weeks after the election. Andrew J. Flowers, a justice of the peace in Tennessee, was whipped by the Ku Klux Klan because, in his words, "I had the impudence to run against a white man for office, and beat him. . . . They said they had nothing particular against me . . . but they did not intend [to allow] any nigger to hold office in the United States."

Abram Colby, a member of Georgia's legislature, was beaten "in the most cruel manner" by Klansmen in 1869. His offense, reported the local agent of the American Missionary Association, was that he had gone to Atlanta to request protection for the former slaves, "and [they] had besides . . . many old scores against him, as a leader of his people in the county." Richard Burke, a minister and teacher in Sumter county, Alabama who served in the state House of Representatives, was murdered in 1870. Burke, his former owner told a Congressional committee, "had made himself obnoxious to a certain class of young men by having been a leader in the Loyal League and by having acquired a great influence over people of his color," but the immediate cause of his death was a report that he had delivered a speech stating that blacks had the same right to carry arms as whites.

In Edgefield county, South Carolina, violence was pervasive throughout Reconstruction. Local political leader Lawrence Cain in 1868 appealed to Governor Robert K. Scott for protection: "If we cannot get this we will all be killed or beat . . . to death. There cannot pass a night but what some colored man are killed or runned from his house." Eight years later, during South Carolina's violent Redemption campaign, threats of murder prevented Cain himself from campaigning. One letter warned him: "If you want to rule a country, you must go to Africa." The roster of black officials victimized by violence offers a striking insight into the personal courage required to take a position of prominence in Reconstruction politics, and the corruption of public morality among those who called themselves the region's "natural rulers."

Southern black officeholding did not end immediately with the overthrow of Reconstruction. Although the Redeemers in several states moved to restrict black voting, gerrymander districts, and reduce the number of elective positions in predominantly black counties, blacks continued to serve in state legislatures and local positions, and a handful even managed to win election to Congress. Many others occupied patronage posts distributed by Republican administrations in Washington.

The nation's longest-serving black official was Joseph H. Lee, a Reconstruction legislator who served as customs collector at Jacksonville, Florida from the 1880s until 1913. The number of black officeholders was reduced substantially after Reconstruction, but until disfranchisement had been completed around the turn of the century, enclaves of local black political power existed in most of the Southern states. Ferdinand Havis remained the "boss" of Jefferson county, Arkansas long after Reconstruction, and Norris W. Cuney was the most powerful black politician in late nineteenth-century Texas, his machine resting on his post as collector of customs at Galveston. Daniel M. Norton's political organization in Hampton, Virginia survived into the twentieth century, as did his tenure as justice of the peace. Robert Smalls won election to Congress in the 1880s, served as collector of customs at Beaufort until 1913, and represented his county in South Carolina's constitutional convention of 1895, where he spoke out eloquently against the disfranchisement of black voters.

Of Reconstruction's black officials, 285 are known to have occupied some public office, elective or appointive, after Redemption. But if black officeholding survived the end of Reconstruction, it did so in a profoundly altered context. Local officials confronted hostile state governments and national administrations at best indifferent to blacks' concerns, and black lawmakers found it impossible to exert any influence in Democratic legislatures. Most black officials now depended for their influence on the goodwill of prominent Democrats, connections with white Republicans, and the patronage largess of the federal government, rather than the backing of a politically mobilized black community.

One indication of the limiting of options after Reconstruction was the revival of interest in emigration among Southern blacks. "Let us go where we can grow lawyers, doctors, teachers," said Davidson county commissioner Randall Brown after Democrats ended Tennessee's brief period of Reconstruction. Let us go "where we can be representatives, Congressmen, judges and anything else." Twenty-nine Reconstruction officials supported post-Reconstruction emigration projects, particularly the Liberia movement that flourished in South Carolina in 1877 and 1878, and the Kansas "Exodus" of 1879. Harrison N. Bouey, a probate judge in Edgefield county during South Carolina's Reconstruction, concluded "that the colored man has no home in America," and helped organize the Liberia emigration movement. Bouey himself left for Liberia in 1878, returned to the United States as a Baptist religious missionary a few years later, and then sailed again for Africa, where he died in 1909. Aaron A. Bradley, the militant spokesman for Georgia's freedmen, helped publicize the Kansas Exodus, and died in St. Louis in 1881.

Many officeholders, although not involved in emigration projects, left the South after the end of Reconstruction. A number, including Pinchback, Bruce, and John R. Lynch, moved to Washington, D.C., where they held federal appointments and became part of the city's black elite. Legislator Thomas Walker, driven from Alabama during the state's violent election campaign in 1874, ended up in Washington, where he became a successful lawyer and real estate broker. William Thornton Montgomery, who had been treasurer of Warren county, Mississippi, moved to Dakota territory, where he lived among Scandinavian immigrants and became the largest black farmer in the northwest. His enterprise failed, however, and he died in poverty in 1909. Alabama Congressman Jeremiah Haralson farmed in Louisiana and Arkansas, and engaged in coal mining in Colorado. In 1916, he was reported to have been "killed by wild beasts."

Many black "carpetbaggers" returned to the North. After being ousted from the legislature and jailed by Georgia's Redeemers, Tunis G. Campbell moved to Boston, where he devoted his remaining years to church work. James P. Ball left Louisiana for Montana and then Seattle, where he worked as a photographer, newspaper editor, and lawyer.

The majority of Reconstruction officials remained in the South, many seeking careers in the black church, education, and journalism. Edward Shaw, the militant county commissioner of Shelby county, Tennessee, who had fought for more positions for blacks from the white political machine of Memphis, left politics in disgust and devoted the remainder of his life to the black Masons and church work. Former South Carolina Congressman Richard H. Cain became president of Paul Quinn College in Waco, Texas, and then a bishop of the African Methodist Episcopal church. After Reconstruction, William E. Johnson, a South Carolina legislator, helped to found the Independent A. M. E. Church, and preached that Christ, Mary, and Joseph were black Africans. Joseph T. Wilson edited a number of newspapers and published a volume of poetry and other books. Jeremiah J. Hamilton, a Reconstruction legislator in Texas, published until the twentieth century a succession of newspapers in Austin.

A number of Reconstruction officials prospered in business and the professions after leaving politics. Former Speaker of South Carolina's House Samuel J. Lee was the state's leading black lawyer until his death in 1895. Matthew M. Lewey, a Reconstruction postmaster and mayor, became president of the Florida State Negro Business League, and James C. Napier, who had been Davidson county claims commissioner, headed the National Negro Business League and became a friend and political ally of Booker T. Washington. Alabama senator Lloyd Leftwich acquired an Alabama plantation that remained in his family's hands into the 1960s.

Other officeholders found their economic standing severely diminished by the elimination of politics as a livelihood. Henry Turpin, former Virginia legislator, worked as a sleeping car porter, and his Louisiana counterpart

Moses Sterrett was employed as janitor of the Caddo parish court house. Alonzo Ransier, who had been South Carolina's lieutenant governor, was employed as a night watchman at the Charleston Custom House and as a day laborer for the city. His Reconstruction successor, Richard H. Gleaves, spent his last years as a waiter at the Jefferson Club in Washington, D.C. Prince Rivers, a member of South Carolina's Reconstruction constitutional convention and legislature, worked as a coachman, as he had while a slave. Robert B. Elliott, unable to earn a living as a lawyer "owing to the severe ostracism and mean prejudice of my political opponents," held minor patronage posts and died penniless in New Orleans. Former fugitive slave Thomas Baynes abandoned politics after Reconstruction and in 1888 entered Virginia's Central State Lunatic Asylum, where he died. In the asylum's records, his disease was said to have been caused by "religion and politics."

While many black officeholders scattered after the end of Reconstruction, some continued in various ways to work for the ideals of civil rights and economic uplift that had animated the post-Civil War era. Lewis Lindsay, an advocate of land confiscation while serving in the Virginia constitutional convention in 1868, became a leader in Richmond's Knights of Labor, and Cyrus Myers, a member of the Mississippi constitutional convention, became prominent in the effort to have Congress provide pensions to former slaves, at one point bringing a petition with 6,000 signatures to the nation's capital. J. Milton Turner, who had served as Missouri's assistant superintendent of education, devoted his career to winning for Cherokee freedmen a share of the funds appropriated by Congress to the Cherokee nation, finally winning his prolonged court battle in 1895.

A number of Reconstruction officeholders reemerged in the Populist movement. When a Populist Republican coalition in the mid-1890s ousted the Democrats in North Carolina from power, Reconstruction officials J. P. Butler, formerly mayor of Jamesville, and Richard Elliott, who had served in the legislature, were again elected to office. John B. Rayner, who held several local posts in Tarboro, North Carolina during Reconstruction, became the leading black Populist of Texas, and at the end of his life collected "Wise Sayings," intending to publish them, including "When wealth concentrates, poverty radiates," and "God does not intend for one part of his people to feel that they are superior to another part."

When the Southern states, around 1890, began to enact laws mandating racial segregation, veterans of Reconstruction were involved in opposition. Winfield Scott, who had served on Little Rock's city council, took part in an 1891 protest meeting against an Arkansas law requiring segregation in transportation, and in Louisiana, several former Reconstruction officials helped to create the New Orleans Citizens Committee, which filed the court challenge that gave rise to *Plessy v. Ferguson*. The civil rights impulse of Reconstruction also survived in other careers. Daniel A. Straker, a customs collector in Charleston during the 1870s, moved from South Carolina to Detroit, where he served as an attorney in civil rights cases, won election as a municipal judge, and took part in the movement that led to the formation of the NAACP. George W. Albright, who moved with his wife, a white teacher, to Chicago, Kansas, and Colorado after the end of Reconstruction in Mississippi, lived into the 1930s. At the age of 91, he was interviewed by the *Daily Worker*, and praised the Communist party for nominating a black man, James W. Ford, for vice president. Former Mississippi Congressman John R. Lynch wrote *The Facts of Reconstruction* and a series of articles exposing the shortcomings of historical scholarship of the early twentieth century. At a 1930 Negro History Week celebration in Washington, Lynch said, "we must make paramount the enforcement of the Fifteenth Amendment."

Today, of the nation's approximately 350,000 elected officials, some 7,000 (or two percent) are black Americans, including 436 state legislators (the majority in states of the North and West), and mayors of some of the nation's largest cities. It is safe to say, however, that nowhere do black officials as a group exercise the political power they enjoyed in at least some Southern states during Reconstruction.

Reconstruction's black leaders, to be sure, faced political dilemmas in some ways similar to those of their counterparts today. With the black vote concentrated in a single party, it could essentially be taken for granted by white allies, while opponents saw no need to address black concerns. Neither during the first Reconstruction nor the civil rights era, often called the Second Reconstruction, did black officials find a way to translate political equality into meaningful long-term economic advancement for the mass of the black community. Nonetheless, the overthrow of Reconstruction was a disaster for black America. It delayed for nearly a century the nation's effort to confront the social and racial agenda generated by the destruction of slavery.

The accomplishments of this nation's first generation of black officeholders were a remarkable part of America's first experiment in interracial democracy. The nation's failure to make good on the promise of equality reminds us that rights, once won, may be taken away, that even when rights are enshrined in the Constitution and laws, their survival requires continuing struggle.

GLOSSARY

Freedmen's Bureau: The Bureau of Freedmen, Refugees, and Abandoned Lands, a federal agency charged with reconstructing American society following the Civil War, especially concerned with integrating ex-slaves into postwar society.

Redeemers: Southern Democratic politicians who used their power to end Reconstruction in their individual locales.

Carpetbagger: A Northerner who went into the South after the Civil War to seek political or financial advantage.

Populist Party: Political party that sought to represent the interests of farmers and laborers in the 1890s, advocating increased currency issue, free coinage of gold and silver, public ownership of railroads, and a graduated federal income tax.

IMPLICATIONS

In this essay, Foner provides a profile of African American officeholders following the Civil War and recounts their attempts to use the political arena to address the problems faced by freed people during Reconstruction.

Why do you think these African American politicians had only limited impact on postwar politics? What were the limits of their power in Reconstruction America?

PAST TRACES

No sooner had word of the 1848 California gold strikes reached the southern Chinese port of Guangzhou than thousands of young men left their homes in the surrounding countryside and booked passage on merchant ships bound for the United States. Their aim was to work the gold mines for a few years, save money, and return to their homes and families richer for the experience. Once in California, however, the Chinese found themselves driven from the gold fields by white racism and forced to seek whatever employment they could find. By the 1860s, many had found work building the western half of the transcontinental railroad. In this document, Lee Chew, one of these immigrants, recounts his life as a Chinese immigrant. Like most of his cohorts, Chew's brief sojourn in America turned into a life-long stay.

Lee Chew, Life of a Chinese Immigrant (1903)

The village where I was born is situated in the province of Canton, on one of the banks of the Si-Kiang River. It is called a village, altho it is really as big as a city, for there are about 5,000 men in it over eighteen years of age—women and children and even youths are not counted in our villages. . . .

. . . I heard about the American foreign devils, that they were false, having made a treaty by which it was agreed that they could freely come to China, and the Chinese as freely go to their country. After this treaty was made China opened its doors to them and then they broke the treaty that they had asked for by shutting the Chinese out of their country. . . .

The man had gone away from our village a poor boy. Now he returned with unlimited wealth, which he had obtained in the country of the American wizards. After many amazing adventures he had become a merchant in a city called Mott Street, so it was said. . . .

Having made his wealth among the barbarians this man had faithfully returned to pour it out among his tribesmen, and he is living in our village now very happy, and a pillar of strength to the poor.

The wealth of this man filled my mind with the idea that I, too, would like to go to the country of the wizards and gain some of their wealth, and after a long time my father consented, and gave me his blessing, and my mother took leave of me with tears, while my grandfather laid his hand upon my head and told me to remember and live up to the admonitions of the Sages, to avoid gambling, bad women and men of evil minds, and so to govern my conduct that when I died my ancestors might rejoice to welcome me as a guest on high.

My father gave me $100, and I went to Hong Kong with five other boys from our place and we got steerage passage on a steamer, paying $50 each. . . .

. . . Of the great power of these people I saw many signs. The engines that moved the ship were wonderful monsters, strong enough to lift mountains. When I got to San Francisco, which was before the passage of the Exclusion act, I was half starved, because I was afraid to eat the provisions of the barbarians, but a few days' living in the Chinese quarter made me happy again. . . .

The Chinese laundryman does not learn his trade in China; there are no laundries in China. . . . All the Chinese laundrymen here were taught in the first place by American women just as I was taught.

When I went to work for that American family I could not speak a word of English, and I did not know anything about house work. The family consisted of husband, wife and two children. They were very good to me and paid me $3.50 a week, of which I could save $3. . . .

In six months I had learned how to do the work of our house quite well, and I was getting $5 a week and board, and putting away about $4.25 a week. I had also learned some English, and by going to a Sunday school I learned more English and something about Jesus, who was a great Sage, and whose precepts are like those of Kong-foo-tsze.

It was twenty years ago when I came to this country, and I worked for two years as a servant, getting at least $35 a month. I sent money home to comfort my parents. . . .

When I first opened a laundry it was in company with a partner, who had been in the business for some years. We went to a town about 500 miles inland, where a railroad was building. We got a board shanty and worked for the men employed by the railroads. . . .

We were three years with the railroad, and then went to the mines, where we made plenty of money in gold dust, but had a hard time, for many of the miners were wild men who carried revolvers and after drinking would come into our place to shoot and steal shirts, for which we had to pay. One of these men hit his head hard against a flat iron and all the miners came and broke our laundry, chasing us out of town. They were going to hang us. We lost all our property and $365 in money, which a member of the mob must have found.

Luckily most of our money was in the hands of Chinese bankers in San Francisco. I drew $500 and went East to Chicago, where I had a laundry for three years, during which I increased my capital to $2,500. After that I was four years in Detroit. I went home to China in 1897, but returned in 1898, and began a laundry business in Buffalo.

The ordinary laundry shop is generally divided into three rooms. In front is the room where the customers are received, behind that a bedroom and in the back the work shop, which is also the dining room and kitchen. The stove and cooking utensils are the same as those of the Americans. . . .

I have found out, during my residence in this country, that much of the

Chinese prejudice against Americans is unfounded, and I no longer put faith in the wild tales that were told about them in our village, tho some of the Chinese, who have been here twenty years and who are learned men, still believe that there is no marriage in this country, that the land is infested with demons and that all the people are given over to general wickedness.

I know better. Americans are not all bad, nor are they wicked wizards. Still, they have their faults, and their treatment of us is outrageous. . . .

The reason why so many Chinese go into the laundry business in this country is because it requires little capital and is one of the few opportunities that are open. . . .

There is no reason for the prejudice against the Chinese. The cheap labor cry was always a falsehood. Their labor was never cheap, and is not cheap now. It has always commanded the highest market price. But the trouble is that the Chinese are such excellent and faithful workers that bosses will have no others when they can get them. If you look at men working on the street you will find an overseer for every four or five of them. That watching is not necessary for Chinese. They work as well when left to themselves as they do when some one is looking at them. . . .

From *The Independent*,
54 (2818), February 19, 1903,
417–423.

2

The Chinese Link a Continent and a Nation

Jack Chen

It is a historical commonplace that America is a nation of immigrants. From the original settlers of Jamestown in 1607 to the Hispanic and Asian immigrants of the 1990s, new Americans have loomed large in the national experience. But while immigration has always played an important role in American life, its impact was perhaps greatest during America's industrial revolution of the nineteenth century. From the 1820s, when 100,000 men, women, and children entered the United States, to the first decade of the twentieth century, when 8.2 million landed on American shores, more than thirty-three million immigrants came to the United States and helped build it into the world's premier industrial power.

Among these millions of immigrants, one group has received scant attention—the Chinese peasants, almost entirely males, who came to America as contract laborers to provide agricultural labor for California's central valley and to build railroads and levees in the West. Unlike European immigrants who arrived as free men and women in New York and other eastern cities, the Chinese who landed in San Francisco were bound to the mercantile companies that acted as labor contractors and had advanced them the cost of their fare. Under this contract system, one of the Six Companies in San Francisco negotiated with an employer to provide workers at an agreed-upon rate. The Companies were then responsible for the supply, supervision, and discipline of the contract laborers.

As Jack Chen shows in this essay, these Chinese contract laborers braved the harshest of conditions to fulfill their contract to build America's first transcontinental railroad. Employing skills in excavation and the use of explosives, which they had brought from China, these Chinese workers carved a path through the solid granite of the Sierra Nevada range that opened the West to the remainder of the nation.

The expansion of the railroad system in the United States was astonishingly swift. England had pioneered the building of railways and for a time was the acknowledged leader in the field, but from the moment the first locomotive was imported into the United States in 1829 the farsighted saw railways as the obvious solution for transport across the vast spaces of the American continent. By 1850, 9,000 miles of rails had been laid in the eastern states and up to the Mississippi. The California Gold Rush and the opening of the American West made talk about a transcontinental line more urgent. As too often happens, war spurred the realization of this project.

The West was won. California was a rich and influential state, but a wide unsettled belt of desert, plain, and mountains separated it and Oregon from the rest of the states. As the economic separation of North and South showed, this situation was fraught with danger. It could lead to a political rift. In 1860, it was cheaper and quicker to reach San Francisco from Canton in China—a sixty-day voyage by sea—than from the Missouri River, six months away by wagon train. The urgent need was to link California firmly with the industrialized eastern states and their 30,000 miles of railways. A railway would cut the journey to a week. The threat of civil war loomed larger between North and South over the slavery issue. Abraham Lincoln's Republican administration saw a northern transcontinental railway as a means to outflank the South by drawing the western states closer to the North. In 1862, Congress voted funds to build the 2,500-mile-long railway. It required enormous resourcefulness and determination to get this giant project off the drawing boards. Not much imagination was required to see its necessity, but the actual building presented daunting difficulties. It was calculated that its cost would mount to $100 million, double the federal budget of 1861.

It was Theodore Judah, described by his contemporaries as "Pacific Railroad Crazy," who began to give substance to the dream. An eastern engineer who had come west to build the short Sacramento Valley Railroad, he undertook a preliminary survey and reported that he had found a feasible route crossing the Sierra by way of Dutch Flat. But the mainly small investors who supported his efforts could not carry through the whole immense undertaking. With rumors of civil war between North and South, San Francisco capitalists, mostly Southerners, boycotted the scheme as a northern plot, and pressed for a southern route. Then the Big Four, Sacramento merchants, took up the challenge: Leland Stanford as president, C. P. Huntington as vice-president, Mark Hopkins as treasurer, and Charles Crocker, in charge of construction, formed the Central Pacific Railway Company. Judah was elbowed out.

The Big Four came as gold seekers in 1849 or soon after but found that there was more money to be made in storekeeping than in scrabbling in the rocks in the mountains. As Republicans, they held the state for the Union against the secessionists. Leland Stanford, the first president of the Central Pacific, was also the first Republican governor of California.

The beginnings were not auspicious. The Union Pacific was building from Omaha in the East over the plains to the Rockies, but supplies had to come in by water or wagon because the railways had not yet reached Omaha. The Civil War now raged and manpower, materials, and funds were hard to get. The Indians were still contesting invasion of their lands. By 1864, however, with the Civil War ending, these problems were solved. The UP hired Civil War veterans, Irish immigrants fleeing famine, and even Indian women, and the line began to move westward.

The Central Pacific, building eastward from Sacramento, had broken ground on January 8, 1863, but in 1864, beset by money and labor problems, it had built only thirty-one miles of track. It had an even more intractable manpower problem than the UP. California was sparsely populated, and the gold mines, homesteading, and other lucrative employments offered stiff competition for labor. Brought to the railhead, three out of every five men quit immediately and took off for the better prospects of the new Nevada silver strikes. Even Charles Crocker, boss of construction and raging like a mad bull in the railway camps, could not control them. In the winter of 1864, the company had only 600 men working on the line when it had advertised for 5,000. Up to then, only white labor had been recruited, and California white labor was still motivated by the Gold Rush syndrome. They wanted quick wealth, not hard, regimented railway work. After two years only fifty miles of track had been laid.

James Strobridge, superintendent of construction, testified to the 1876 Joint Congressional Committee on Chinese Immigration: "[These] were unsteady men, unreliable. Some would not go to work at all. . . . Some would stay until pay day, get a little money, get drunk and clear out." Something drastic had to be done.

In 1858, fifty Chinese had helped to build the California Central Railroad from Sacramento to Marysville. In 1860, Chinese were working on the San Jose Railway and giving a good account of themselves, so it is surprising that there was so much hesitation about employing them on the Central Pacific's western end of the first transcontinental railway. Faced with a growing crisis of no work done and mounting costs, Crocker suggested hiring Chinese. Strobridge strongly objected: "I will not boss Chinese. I don't think they could build a railroad." Leland Stanford was also reluctant. He had advocated exclusion on the Chinese from California and was embarrassed to reverse himself. Crocker, Huntington, Hopkins, and Stanford, the "Big Four" of the Central Pacific, were all merchants in hardware, dried goods, and groceries in the little town of Sacramento. Originally, they knew nothing about railroad building, but they were astute and hard-headed businessmen. Crocker was insistent. Wasted time was wasted money. The CP's need for labor was critical.

The men they already had were threatening a strike. Finally fifty Chinese were hired for a trial.

BUILDING THE TRANSCONTINENTAL RAILROAD

In February 1865, they marched up in self-formed gangs of twelve to twenty men with their own supplies and cooks for each mess. They ate a meal of rice and dried cuttlefish, washed and slept, and early next morning were ready for work filling dump carts. Their discipline and grading—preparing the ground for track laying—delighted Strobridge. Soon fifty more were hired, and finally some 15,000 had been put on the payroll. Crocker was enthusiastic: "They prove nearly equal to white men in the amount of labor they perform, and are much more reliable. No danger of strikes among them. We are training them to all kinds of labor: blasting, driving horses, handling rock as well as pick and shovel." Countering Strobridge's argument that the Chinese were "not masons," Crocker pointed out that the race that built the Great Wall could certainly build a railroad culvert. Up on the Donner Pass today the fine stonework embankments built by the Chinese are serving well after a hundred years.

Charles Nordhoff, an acute observer, reports Strobridge telling him, "[The Chinese] learn all parts of the work easily." Nordhoff says he saw them "employed on every kind of work. . . . They do not drink, fight or strike; they do gamble, if it is not prevented; and it is always said of them that they are very cleanly in their habits. It is the custom, among them, after they have had their suppers every evening, to bathe with the help of small tubs. I doubt if the white laborers do as much." As well he might. Well-run boarding-houses in California in those days proudly advertised that they provided guests with a weekly bath.

Their wages at the start were $28 a month (twenty-six working days), and they furnished all their own food, cooking utensils, and tents.

The headman of each gang, or sometimes an American employed as clerk by them, received all the wages and handed them out to the members of the work gang according to what had been earned. "Competent and wonderfully effective because tireless and unremitting in their industry," they worked from sun-up to sun-down.

All observers remarked on the frugality of the Chinese. This was not surprising in view of the fact that, with a strong sense of filial duty, they came to America in order to save money and return as soon as possible to their homes and families in China. So they usually dressed poorly, and their dwellings were of the simplest. However, they ate well; rice and vermicelli (noodles) garnished with meats and vegetables; fish, dried oysters, cuttlefish, bacon and pork, and chicken on holidays, abalone meat, five kinds of dried vegetables, bamboo shoots, seaweed, salted cabbage, and mushroom, four kinds of dried fruit, and peanut oil and tea. This diet shows a considerable degree of sophistication and balance compared to the beef, beans, potatoes, bread, and butter of the white laborers. Other supplies were purchased from the shop maintained by a Chinese merchant contractor in one of the railway cars that followed them as they carried the railway line forward. Here they could buy pipes, tobacco, bowls, chopsticks, lamps, Chinese-style shoes of cotton with soft cotton soles, and ready-made clothing imported from China.

On Sundays, they rested, did their washing, and gambled. They were prone to argue noisily, but did not become besotted with whiskey and make themselves unfit for work on Monday. Their sobriety was much appreciated by their employers.

Curtis, the engineer in charge, described them as "the best roadbuilders in the world." The once skeptical Strobridge, a smart, pushing Irishman, also now pronounced them "the best in the world." Leland Stanford described them in a report on October 10, 1865, to Andrew Johnson:

As a class, they are quiet, peaceable, patient, industrious, and economical. More prudent and economical [than white laborers] they are contented with less wages. We find them organized for mutual aid and assistance. Without them, it would be impossible to complete the western portion of this great national enterprise within the time required by the Act of Congress.

Crocker testified before the congressional committee that "if we found that we were in a hurry for a job of work, it was better to put on Chinese at once." All these men had originally resisted the employment of Chinese on the railway.

Four-fifths of the grading labor from Sacramento to Ogden was done by Chinese. In a couple of years more, of 13,500 workers on the payroll 12,000 were Chinese. They were nicknamed "Crocker's Pets."

APPRECIATING CHINESE SKILLS

The Chinese crews won their reputation the hard way. They outperformed Cornish men brought in at extra wages to cut rock. Crocker testified,

They would cut more rock in a week than the Cornish miners, and it was hard work, bone labor. [They] were skilled in using the hammer and drill, and they proved themselves equal to the very best Cornish miners in that work. They were very trusty, they were intelligent, and they lived up to their contracts.

Stanford held the Chinese workers in such high esteem that he provided in his will for the permanent employment of a large number on his estates. In the 1930s, some of their descendants were still living and working lands now owned by Stanford University.

The Chinese saved the day for Crocker and his colleagues. The terms of agreement with the government were that the railway companies would be paid from $16,000 to $48,000 for each mile of track laid. But there were only so many miles between the two terminal points of the projected line. The Union Pacific Company, working with 10,000 mainly Irish immigrants and Civil War veterans, had the advantage of building the line through Nebraska over the plains and made steady progress. The Central Pacific, after the first easy twenty-three miles between Newcastle and Colfax, had to conquer the granite mountains and gorges of the Sierra Nevada and Rockies before it could emerge onto the Nevada-Utah plains and make real speed and money. The line had to rise 7,000 feet in 100 miles over daunting terrain. Crocker and the Chinese proved up to the challenge. After reaching Cisco, there was no easy going. The line had to be literally carved out of the Sierra granite, through tunnels and on rock ledges cut on the side of precipices.

Using techniques from China, they attacked one of the most difficult parts of the work: carrying the line over Cape Horn, with its sheer granite buttresses and steep shale embankments, 2,000 feet above the American River canyon. There was no foothold on its flanks. The indomitable Chinese, using age-old ways, were lowered from above in rope-held baskets, and there, suspended between earth and sky, they began to chip away with hammer and crowbar to form the narrow ledge that was later laboriously deepened to a shelf wide enough for the railway roadbed, 1,400 feet above the river.

The weather, as well as the terrain, was harsh. The winter of 1865–1866 was one of the severest on record. Snow fell early, and storm after storm blanketed the Sierra Nevada. The ground froze solid. Sixty-foot drifts of snow had to be shoveled away before the graders could even reach the roadbed. Nearly half the work force of 9,000 men were set to clearing snow.

In these conditions, construction crews tackled the most formidable obstacle in their path: building the ten Summit Tunnels on the twenty-mile stretch between Cisco, ninety-two miles from Sacramento and Lake Ridge just west of Cold Stream Valley on the eastern slope of the summit. Work went on at all the tunnels simultaneously. Three shifts of eight hours each worked day and night.

The builders lived an eerie existence. In *The Big Four*, Oscar Lewis writes,

> Tunnels were dug beneath forty-foot drifts and for months, 3,000 workmen lived curious mole-like lives, passing from work to living quarters in dim passages far beneath the snows surface. . . . [There] was constant danger, for as snow's accumulated on the upper ridges, avalanches grew frequent, their approach heralded only by a brief thunderous roar. A second later, a work crew, a bunkhouse, an entire camp would go hurtling at a dizzy speed down miles of frozen canyon. Not until months later were the bodies recovered; sometimes groups were found with shovels or picks still clutched in their frozen hands.

On Christmas Day, 1866, the papers reported that "a gang of Chinamen employed by the railroad were covered up by a snow slide and four or five [note the imprecision] died before they could be exhumed." A whole camp of Chinese railway workers was enveloped during one night and had to be rescued by shovelers the next day.

No one has recorded the names of those who gave their lives in this stupendous undertaking. It is known that the bones of 1,200 men were shipped back to China to be buried in the land of their forefathers, but that was by no means the total score. The engineer John Gills recalled that "at Tunnel No. 10, some 15–20 Chinese [again, note the imprecision] were killed by a slide that winter. The year before, in the winter of 1864–65, two wagon road repairers had been buried and killed by a slide at the same location."

A. P. Partridge, who worked on the line, describes how 3,000 Chinese builders were driven out of the mountains by the early snow. "Most . . . came to Truckee and filled up all the old buildings and sheds. An old barn collapsed and killed four Chinese. A good many were frozen to death." One is astonished at the fortitude, discipline, and dedication of the Chinese railroad workers.

Many years later, looking at the Union Pacific section of the line, an old railwayman remarked, "There's an Irishman buried under every tie of that road." Brawling, drink, cholera, and malaria took a heavy toll. The construction crew towns on the Union Pacific part of the track, with their saloons, gambling dens, and bordellos, were nicknamed "hells on wheels." Jack Casement, in charge of construction there, had been a general in the Civil War and prided himself on the discipline of his fighting forces. His work crews worked with military precision, but off the job they let themselves go. One day, after gambling in the streets on payday (instigated by professional gamblers) had gotten too much out of hand, a visitor, finding the street suddenly very quiet, asked him where the gamblers had gone. Casement pointed at a nearby cemetery and replied, "They all died with their boots on." It was still the Wild West.

It is characteristic that only one single case of violent brawling was reported among the Chinese from the time they started work until they completed the job.

The Central Pacific's Chinese became expert at all kinds of work: grading, drilling, masonry, and demolition. Using black powder, they could average 1.18 feet daily through granite so hard that an incautiously placed charge could blow out backward. The Summit Tunnel work force was entirely composed of Chinese, with mainly Irish foremen. Thirty to forty worked on each face, with twelve to fifteen on the heading and the rest on the bottom removing material.

The Donner tunnels, totaling 1,695 feet, had to be bored through solid rock, and 9,000 Chinese worked on them. To speed the work, a new and untried explosive, nitroglycerin, was used. The tunnels were completed in November 1867, after thirteen months. But winter began before the way could be opened and the tracks laid. That winter was worse than the preceding one, but to save time it was necessary to send crews ahead to continue building the line even while the tunnels were being cut. Therefore, 3,000 men were sent with 400 carts and horses to Palisade Canyon, 300 miles in advance of the railhead. "Hay, grain and all supplies for men and horses had to be hauled by teams over the deserts for that great distance," writes Strobridge. "Water for men and animals was hauled at times 40 miles." Trees were felled and the logs laid side by side to form a "corduroy" roadway. On log sleds greased with lard, hundreds of Chinese manhandled three locomotives and forty wagons over the mountains. Strobridge later testified that it "cost nearly three times what it would have cost to have done it in the summertime when it should have been done. But we shortened the time seven years from what Congress expected when the act was passed."

Between 10,000 and 11,000 men were kept working on the line from 1866 to 1869. The Sison and Wallace Company (in which Crocker's brother was a leading member) and the Dutch merchant Cornelius Koopmanschap of San Francisco procured these men for the line. Through the summer of 1866, Crocker's Pets—6,000 strong—swarmed over the upper canyons of the Sierra, methodically slicing cuttings and pouring rock and debris to make landfills and strengthen the foundations of trestle bridges. Unlike the Caucasian laborers, who drank unboiled stream water, the Chinese slaked their thirst with weak tea and boiled water kept in old whiskey kegs filled by their mess cooks. They kept themselves clean and healthy by daily sponge baths in tubs of hot water prepared by their cooks, and the work went steadily forward.

Crocker has been described as a "hulking, relentless driver of men." But his Chinese crews responded to his leadership and drive and were caught up in the spirit of the epic work on which they were engaged. They cheered and waved their cartwheel hats as the first through train swept down the eastern slopes of the Sierra to the meeting of the lines. They worked with devotion and self-sacrifice to lay that twenty-odd miles of track for the Central Pacific Company in 1866 over the most difficult terrain. The cost of those miles was enormous—$280,000 a mile—but it brought the builders in sight of the easier terrain beyond the

Sierra and the Rockies. Here costs of construction by veteran crews were only half the estimated amount of federal pay.

By summer 1868, an army of 14,000 railway builders was passing over the mountains into the great interior plain. Nine-tenths of that work force was Chinese. More than a quarter of all Chinese in the country were building the railway.

By September 1868, the track was completed for 307 miles from Sacramento, and the crews were laying rails across the plain east of the Sierra. Parallel with the track layers went the telegraph installers, stringing their wires on the poles and keeping the planners back at headquarters precisely apprised of where the end of the track was.

THE GREAT RAILWAY COMPETITION

On the plains, the Chinese worked in tandem with all the Indians Crocker could entice to work on the iron rails. They began to hear of the exploits of the Union Pacific's "Irish terriers" building from the east. One day, the Irish laid six miles of track. The Chinese topped this with seven. "No Chinaman is going to beat us," growled the Irish, and the next day, they laid seven and a half miles of track. They swore that they would outperform the competition no matter what it did.

Croaker taunted the Union Pacific that his men could lay ten miles of track a day. Durant, president of the rival line, laid a $10,000 wager that it could not be done. Crocker took no chances. He waited until the day before the last sixteen miles of track could be laid and brought up all needed supplies for instant use. Then he unleashed his crews. On April 28, 1869, while Union Pacific checkers and newspaper reporters looked on, a combined gang of Chinese and eight picked Irish rail handlers laid ten miles and 1,800 feet more of track in twelve hours. This record was never surpassed until the advent of mechanized track laying. Each Irishman that day walked a total distance

of ten miles, and their combined muscle handled sixty tons of rail.

So keen was the competition that when the two lines approached each other, instead of changing direction to link up, their builders careered on and on for 100 miles, building lines that would never meet. Finally, the government prescribed that the linkage point should be Promontory, Utah.

On May 10, 1869, the two lines were officially joined at Promontory, north of Ogden in Utah. A great crowd gathered. A band played. An Irish crew and a Chinese crew were chosen to lay the last two rails side by side. The last tie was made of polished California laurel with a silver plate in its center proclaiming it "The last tie laid on the completion of the Pacific Railroad, May 10, 1869." But when the time came it was nowhere to be found. As consternation mounted, four Chinese approached with it on their shoulders and they laid it beneath the rails. A photographer stepped up and someone shouted to him "Shoot!" The Chinese only knew one meaning for that word. They fled. But order was restored and the famous ceremony began; Stanford drove a golden spike into the last tie with a silver hammer. The news flashed by telegraph to a waiting nation. But no Chinese appears in that famous picture of the toast celebrating the joining of the rails.

Crocker was one of the few who paid tribute to the Chinese that day: "I wish to call to your minds that the early completion of this railroad we have built has been in large measure due to that poor, despised class of laborers called the Chinese, to the fidelity and industry they have shown." No one even mentioned the name of Judah.

The building of the first transcontinental railway stands as a monument to the union of Yankee and Chinese-Irish drive and know-how. This was a formidable combination. They all complemented each other. Together they did in seven years what was expected to take at least fourteen.

It was heroic work. The Central Pacific crews had carried their railway 1,800 miles through the Sierra and Rocky mountains, over sagebrush desert and plain. The Union Pacific built only 689 miles, over much easier terrain. It had 500 miles in which to carry its part of the line to a height of 5,000 feet, with another fifty more miles in which to reach the high passes of the Black Hills. With newly recruited crews, the Central Pacific had to gain an altitude of 7,000 feet from the plain in just over 100 miles and make a climb of 2,000 feet in just 20 miles.

All this monumental work was done before the age of mechanization. It was pick and shovel, hammer and crowbar work, with baskets for earth carried slung from shoulder poles and put on one-horse carts.

For their heroic work, the Chinese workmen began with a wage of $28 a month, providing their own food and shelter. This was gradually raised to $30 to $35 a month. Caucasians were paid the same amount of money, but their food and shelter were provided. Because it cost $0.75 to $1.00 a day to feed a white unskilled worker, each Chinese saved the Central Pacific, at a minimum, two-thirds the price of a white laborer (1865 rates). Chinese worked as masons, dynamiters, and blacksmiths and at other skilled jobs that paid white workers from $3 to $5 a day. So, at a minimum, the company saved about $5 million by hiring Chinese workers.

When the task was done, most of the Chinese railwaymen were paid off. Some returned to China with their hard-earned savings, and the epic story of building the Iron Horse's pathway across the continent must have regaled many a family gathering there. Some returned with souvenirs of the great work, chips of one of the last ties, which had been dug up and split up among them. Some settled in the little towns that had grown up along the line of the railway. Others took the railway to seek adventure further east and south. Most made their way back to California and took what jobs they could find in that state's growing industries, trades, and other occupations. Many used their traditional and newly acquired skills on the other transcontinental lines and railways that were being swiftly built in the West and Midwest. This was the start of the diaspora of the Chinese immigrants in America.

Ironically, the great railway soon had disastrous results for the Chinese themselves. It now cost only $40 for an immigrant to cross the continent by rail and a flood of immigrants took advantage of the ease and cheapness of travel on the line the Chinese had helped to build. The labor shortage (and resulting high wages) in California turned into a glut. When the tangled affairs of the Northern Pacific line led to the stock market crash of Black Friday, September 19, 1873, and to financial panic, California experienced its first real economic depression. There was devastating unemployment, and the Chinese were made the scapegoats.

The transcontinental lines on which [the Chinese] worked "more than any other factor helped make the United States a united nation," writes the *Encyclopaedia Britannica* ["Railways"]. They played a major role in building the communications network of iron roads that was the transport base of American industrial might in the twentieth century.

Speaking eloquently in favor of the Chinese immigrants, Oswald Garrison Villard said,

> I want to remind you of the things that Chinese labor did in opening up the Western portion of this country. . . . [They] stormed the forest fastness, endured cold and heat and the risk of death at hands of hostile Indians to aid in the opening up of our northwestern empire. l have a dispatch from the chief engineer of the Northwestern Pacific telling how Chinese laborers went out into eight feet of snow with the temperature far below zero to carry on the work when no American dared face the conditions.

And these men were from China's sun-drenched south, where it never snows.

In certain circles, there has been a conspiracy of silence about the Chinese railroadmen and what they did. When U.S. Secretary of Transportation John Volpe spoke at the "Golden Spike" centenary, not a single Chinese American was invited, and he made no mention in his speech of the Chinese railroad builders.

GLOSSARY

California Gold Rush: Discovery of gold in 1849 that brought a flood of migrants to California, whose population mushroomed from 15,000 to nearly 300,000 between 1849 and 1856.

Irish "terriers": Irish railroad workers known for their speed in track-laying.

Iron Horse: Railroad locomotive.

IMPLICATIONS

Chen's account of Chinese railroad workers raises the issue of racism and financial interest in nineteenth-century America. Do you think Crocker's decision to employ Chinese workers to build his portion of the transcontinental railroad shows him to be less racist than most of his fellow white Californians? What does this essay say about the relationship between self-interest and racism?

PAST TRACES

Western historians have long dealt with the distance between myth and reality in the history of their region. One of the most persistent western myths is one that claims that male and female roles became more equal on the western frontier. The reality, however, was often very different. As a number of historians have recently shown, traditional gender roles were often reinforced on the westward journey and men and women usually recreated their eastern roles as they settled in the West. In these excerpts from the diary of her westward journey, Lydia Rudd reveals the harsh realities of western migration and settlement.

Lydia Allen Rudd, Diary of Westward Travel (1852)

May 6 1852 Left the Missouri river for our long journey across the wild uncultivated plains and unhabitated except by the red man. As we left the river bottom and ascended the bluffs the view from them was handsome! In front of us as far as vision could reach extended the green hills covered with fine grass. . . . Behind us lay the Missouri with its muddy water hurrying past as if in great haste to reach some destined point ahead all unheeding the impatient emigrants on the opposite shore at the ferrying which arrived faster than they could be conveyed over. About half a miles down the river lay a steamboat stuck fast on a sandbar. Still farther down lay the busy village of St. Joseph looking us a good bye and reminding us that we were leaving all signs of civilised life for the present. But with good courage and not one sigh of regret I mounted my pony (whose name by the way is Samy) and rode slowly on. In going some two miles, the scene changed from bright sunshine to drenching showers of rain this was not quite agreeable for in spite of our good blankets and intentions otherwise we got some wet. The rain detained us so that we have not made but ten miles today. . . .

May 7 I found myself this morning with a severe headache from the effects of yesterday's rain. . . .

There is a toll bridge across this stream kept by the Indians. The toll for our team in total was six bits. We have had some calls this evening from the Indians. We gave them something to eat and they left. Some of them [had] on no shirt only a blanket, whiles others were ornamented in Indian style with their faces painted in spots and stripes feathers and fur on their heads beeds on their neck brass rings on their wrists and arms and in their ears armed with rifles and spears.

May 8 . . . We have come about 12 miles and were obliged to camp in the open prairie without any wood. Mary and myself collected some dry weeds and grass and made a little fire and cooked some meat and the last of our supply of eggs with these and some hard bread with water we made our supper.

May 9 . . . We passed a new made grave today . . . a man from Ohio We also met a man that was going back: he had buried his Wife this morning She died from the effects of measels we have come ten miles today encamped on a small stream called Vermillion creek Wood and water plenty Their are as many as fifty waggons on this stream and some thousand head of stock It looks like a village the tents and waggons extend as much as a mile. . . .

Some are singing some talking and some laughing and the cattle are adding their mite by shaking their bells and grunt[ing]. Mosquitoes are intruding their unwelcome presence. Harry says that I must not sit here any longer writing but go to bed for I will not want to get up early in the morning to get breakfast.

May 10 I got up this morning and got breakfast and before sunrise we had eat in spite of Harry's prophecies to the contrary. . . .

May 11 We had a very heavy fog this morning which cleared up about noon. Our men are not any of them very well this morning. We passed another grave to day which was made this morning. The board stated that he died of cholera. He was from Indiana. We met several that had taken the back track for the states homesick I presume let them go. We have passed through a handsome country and have encamped on the Nimehaw river, the most beautiful spot that ever I saw in my life. I would like to live here. As far as the eye can reach either way lay handsome rolling prairies, not a stone a tree nor a bush even nothing but grass and flowers meets the eye until you reach the valley of the river which is as level as the house floor and about half a mile wide, where on the bank of the stream for two or three rods wide is one of the heaviest belts of timber I ever saw covered with thick foliage so thick that you could not get a glimpse of the stream through it. You can see this belt of timber for three or four miles from the hills on both sides winding through the prairie like some huge snake. We have traveled twelve miles. . . .

May 12 . . . Our men not much better.

May 13 . . . Henry has been no better to day. Soon after we stopped to night a man came along with a wheel barrow going to California: he is a dutchmann. He wheels his provisions and clothing all day and then stops where night overtakes him sleeps on the ground in the open air. He eats raw meat and bread for his supper. I think that he will get tired wheeling his way through the world by the time he gets to California.

May 14 Just after we started this morning we passed four men dig[g]ing a grave. They were packers. The man that had died was taken sick yesterday noon and died last night. They called it cholera morbus. The corpse lay on the ground a few feet from where they were dig[g]ing. The grave it was a sad sight. . . .

On the bank of the stream waiting to cross, stood a dray with five men harnessed to it bound for California. They must be some of the persevering kind I think. Wanting to go to California more than I do. . . . We passed three more graves this afternoon. . . .

Sept. 5 Traveled eighteen miles today encamped on a slough of powder river poor camp not much grass water nor wood. I am almost dead tonight. I have been sick two or three days with the bowel complaint and am much worse tonight.

Sept. 6 We have not been able to leave this miserable place today. I am not as well as yesterday and no physician to be had. We got a little medicine from a train tonight that has checked the disease some, the first thing that has done me any good.

Sept. 7 . . . I am some better today so much so that they ventured to move me this for the sake of better camp. Mrs. Girtman is also sick with the same disease. Our cattle are most all of them ailing-there are two more that we expect will die every day. . . .

Oct. 8 started early this morning without any breakfast for the very good reason that we had nothing to eat still three miles from the falls safely landed about eight o'clock tired hungry and with a severe cold from last nights exposure something like civilization here in the shape of three or four houses there is an excuse here for a railroad of a mile and half on which to convey bag[g]age below the falls where they can again take water for the steamboat landing. Harry packed our bag[g]age down the railroad and the rest of us walked the car is drawn across the railroad by a mule and they will car[r]y no persons but sick. We again hired an Indian with his canoe to take us from the falls to the steamboat landing ar[r]ived about sundown a great many emigrants waiting for a chance to leave the steamboat and several flat boats lying ready to start out in the morning encamped on the shore for the night.

October 9–October 13 . . .

October 14 . . . I am so anxious to get some place to stop and settle that my patience is not worth much.

October 15–18 . . .

October 19 . . . We have had a very bad day today for traveling it has rained nearly all the time and it has rained very hard some of the time and we have had a miserable road the rain has made the hills very slippery and had to get up and down we have made but eleven miles of travel encamped on the prairie no water for our stock and not much for ourselves.

October 21 . . .

October 22 . . . Traveled three miles this morning and reached the village of Salem it is quite a pretty town a much handsomer place than Oregon City and larger. . . .

I am afraid that we shall be obliged to pack from here the rest of our journey and it will be a wet job another wet rainy day I am afraid that the rain will make us all sick. I am already begin to feel the affects of it by a bad cold.

October 23 . . . We cannot get any wagon to take us on our journey and are obliged to pack the rest of the way Mr. Clark and wife have found a house to live in and employment for the winter and they will stop here in Salem. It took us until nearly noon to get our packs fixed for packing went about two miles and it rained so fast that we were obliged to stop got our dinner and supper in one meal cooked in a small cabin ignorant people but kind started again just.

October 24–25 . . . *October 26* . . . we reached Burlington about two o'clock. There is one store one blacksmith shop and tnree or four dwelling houses. We encamped close by found

Mr. Donals in his store an old acquaintance of my husband's. I do not know what we shall yet conclude on doing for the winter. There is no house in town that we can get to winter in. We shall probably stay here tomorrow and by the time know what we are to do for a while at least.

October 27 . . . Our men have been looking around for a house and employment and have been successful for which I feel very thankful. Harry has gone into copartnership with Mr. Donals in the mercantile business and we are to live in the back part of the store for this winter. Henry and Mary are going into Mr. D—house on his farm for the winter one mile from here. Mr. D— will also find him employment if he wants. I expect that we shall not make a claim after all our trouble in getting here on purpose for one. I shall have to be poor and dependent on a man my life time.

3

Women on the Great Plains, 1865–1890

Christine Stansell

In the generation after the Civil War, tens of thousands of families left the familiar surroundings of their eastern homes, kin, and friends to settle west of the Mississippi River. Although long considered the "Great American Desert," the midwestern prairies in fact contained some of the most fertile land in North America. But what drew these droves of settlers to the Dakotas, Kansas, and Nebraska was less a matter of high soil fertility than one of changes in federal land policy during the Civil War. With the issue of free soil versus slavery no longer inhibiting congressional debate, the Civil War Congress passed the Homestead Act in 1862. This act permitted any adult citizen or permanent resident to claim 160 acres of western federal land for a $10 filing fee and granted title to such persons after five years of successful residence. It was this prospect of free land that created a veritable land rush in the postwar era.

While the burdens of migration and resettlement fell on every homesteader, they fell especially hard on pioneer wives and mothers. Removal to the trans-Mississippi West meant severing connections with an intimate network of female friends and relatives who had provided not only companionship but assistance in childbirth, ill health, and times of stress. Isolated within the family group, homesteading women had only their own resources and the labor of their husbands and children to rely on as they engaged in the arduous task of farmmaking on the trackless prairies. As Christine Stansell reveals in this essay, resettlement on the Great Plains brought other problems as well, not the least of which was how to maintain familiar notions of womanliness while living in sod huts and working on the windswept prairies. While some wives welcomed the challenge, Stansell suggests that most simply endured, hoping life would be easier and more "womanly" for their daughters. This essay affords the opportunity to evaluate how much traditional values held by eastern women were changed by the frontier experience.

"Women on the Great Plains, 1865–1890." *Women's Studies*, 4 (1976), pp. 87–98. Reprinted by permission of the author.

In 1841, Catherine Beecher proudly attested to the power of her sex by quoting some of Tocqueville's observations on the position of American women. On his tour of 1831, Tocqueville had found Americans to be remarkably egalitarian in dividing social power between the sexes. In his opinion, their ability to institute democratic equality stemmed from a clearcut division of work and responsibilities: "in no country has such constant care been taken . . . to trace two clearly distinct lines of action for the two sexes, and to make them keep pace with the other, but in two pathways which are always different." In theory, men and women controlled separate "spheres" of life: women held sway in the home, while men attended to economic and political matters. Women were not unaware of the inequities in a trade-off between ascendancy in the domestic sphere and participation in society as a whole. Attached to the metaphorical bargain struck between the sexes was a clause ensuring that women, through "home influence," could also affect the course of nation-building. For Miss Beecher, domesticity was also imperial power: "to American women, more than to any others on earth, is committed the exalted privilege of extending over the world those blessed influences, which are to renovate degraded man, and 'clothe all climes with beauty.' "

Yet despite Beecher's assertions to the contrary, by 1841 one masculine "line of action" was diverging dangerously from female influences. Increasing numbers of men were following a pathway which led them across the Mississippi to a land devoid of American women and American homes. In the twenty-odd years since the Santa Fe trade opened the Far West to American businessmen, only men, seeking profits in furs or trading, had gone beyond the western farmlands of the Mississippi Valley; no women participated in the first stages of American expansion. Consequently, by 1841 the West was in one sense a geographical incarnation of the masculine sphere, altogether untouched by "home influence." Although in theory American development preserved a heterosexually balanced democracy, in actuality, the West, new arena of political and economic growth, had become a man's world.

In 1841, the first Americans intending to settle in the trans-Mississippi region rather than only trap or trade began to migrate over the great overland road to the coast. For the first time, women were present in the caravans, and in the next decades, thousands of women in families followed. Their wagon trains generally carried about one-half men, one-half women and children: a population with the capacity to reinstate a heterosexual culture. Only during the Gold Rush years, 1849–1852, were most of the emigrants once again male. Many of the forty-niners, however, chose to return East rather than to settle. In the aftermath of the Rush, the numerical balance of men and women was restored. By 1860, the sex ratio in frontier counties, including those settled on the Great Plains, was no different from the average sex ratio in the East.

Despite the heterosexual demography, however, the West in the years after 1840 still appeared to be masculine terrain. Everywhere, emigrants and travellers saw "such lots of men, but very few ladies and children." In mining camps, "representatives of the gentler sex were so conspicuous by their absence that in one camp a lady's bonnet and boots were exhibited for one dollar a look." Similarly, "the Great Plains in the early period was strictly a man's country." Even later, historians agree that "the Far West had a great preponderance of men over women," and that the absence of "mothers and wives to provide moral anchorage to the large male population" was a primary cause of its social ills. What accounts for the disparity between these observations and the bare facts of demography? In many frontier regions, women failed to reinstitute their own sphere. Without a cultural base of their own, they disappeared behind the masculine preoccupations and social structure which dominated the West. Despite their numbers, women were often invisible, not only in the first two decades of family settlement but in successive phases as well.

In this essay, I try to sketch out some ways of understanding how the fact of this masculine imperium affected women's experiences in the great trans-Mississippi migrations. The following pages are in no way a monograph but rather a collection of suggestions which I have developed through reading and teaching about the West, and which I hope will encourage others to begin investigating this neglected area. Western migration constituted a critical rite of passage in nineteenth-century culture; its impact still reverberates a century later in our own "Western" novels, movies, and television serials. Women's relationship to this key area of the "American experience" has remained submerged and unquestioned. There are only a few secondary books on women in the West, and the two best-known works are simplistic and sentimental. Few writers or scholars have attempted to look at frontier women in the light of the newer interpretations of women's history which have evolved over the last four years. There are a wealth of questions to investigate and a wealth of sources to use. To demonstrate how new analyses can illuminate conventional teaching and lecture material, I have chosen one clearly defined area of "pioneer experience," settlers on the Great Plains from 1865–1890. The half-dozen books I use here are nearly all published and readily available.

Until after the Civil War, emigrants usually travelled over the Great Plains without a thought of stopping. Explorers, farmers, and travellers agreed that the dry grasslands of the "Great American Desert"—the Dakotas, western Kansas, and western Nebraska—were not suitable for lucrative cultivation. In the late 60's, however, western land-grant railroads attempting to boost profits from passenger fares and land sales by promoting settlement in the region launched an advertising campaign in America and Europe which portrayed the Plains as a new Eden of verdant grasslands, rich soil, and plenteous streams. The railroad propaganda influenced a shift in public opinion, but technological advances in wheat-growing and steadily expanding urban markets for crops were far more significant in attracting settlers from Europe and the Mississippi Valley to the region. Emigrants came

to take advantage of opportunities for more land, more crops, and more profits.

Who decided to move to the new lands? In the prevailing American notions of family relations, decisions about breadwinning and family finances were more or less in the hands of the male. Of course, removal to the Plains was a significant matter, and it is doubtful that many husbands and fathers made a unilateral decision to pull up stakes. Unfortunately, no large body of evidence about the choice to migrate to the Plains has been found or, at least, utilized in scholarly studies. I have sampled, however, some of the more than seven hundred diaries of men and women traveling to California and Oregon twenty years earlier. These indicate that the man usually initiated a plan to emigrate, made the final decision, and to a greater or lesser degree imposed it on his family. Men's involvement with self-advancement in the working world provided them with a logical and obvious rationale for going West.

The everyday concerns of "woman's sphere," however, did not provide women with many reasons to move. In the system that Tocqueville praised and Beecher vaunted, women's work, social responsibilities, and very identities were based almost entirely in the home. Domesticity involved professionalized housekeeping, solicitous child-rearing, and an assiduous maintenance of a proper moral and religious character in the family. Clearly, women could keep house better, literally and metaphorically, in "civilized" parts, where churches, kinfolk, and women friends supported them. The West held no promise of a happier family life or a more salutary moral atmosphere. On the contrary, it was notoriously destructive to those institutions and values which women held dear.

The Plains region was an especially arid prospect for the transplantation of womanly values. Lonely and crude frontier conditions prevailed into the 90's; in some areas, the sparse population actually declined with time: "following the great boom of the 80's, when the tide of migration began to recede, central Dakota and western Nebraska and Kansas presented anything but a land of occupied farms." The loneliness which women endured "must have been such as to crush the soul," according to one historian of the region. Another asserts that "without a doubt" the burden of the adverse conditions of Plains life—the aridity, treelessness, heat, perpetual wind, and deadening cold—fell upon the women. Almost without exception, others concur: "although the life of the frontier farmer was difficult special sympathy should go to his wife" . . . "it is certain that many stayed until the prairie broke them in spirit or body while others fled from the monotonous terror of it." An observer who visited the Plains in the 50's found life there to be "peculiarly severe upon women and oxen." The duration as well as the severity of cultural disruption which Plains women experienced was perhaps without parallel in the history of nineteenth-century frontiers.

First of all, emigrant women did not move into homes like the ones they had left behind, but into sod huts, tarpaper shacks, and dugouts. Seldom as temporary as they planned to be, these crude structures still existed as late as the nineties. Most settlers lived in one room "soddies" for six or seven years: if luck left a little cash, they might move into a wooden shack. Thus a farmer's wife often spent years trying to keep clean a house made of dirt. The effort became especially disheartening in rainstorms, when leaking walls splattered mud over bedclothes and dishes: "in those trying times the mud floors were too swampy to walk upon and wives could cook only with an umbrella held over the stove; after they were over every stitch of clothing must be hung out to dry." Dry weather gave no respite from dirt, since dust and straw incessantly sifted down from the walls. Housekeeping as a profession in the sense that Catherine Beecher promulgated it was impossible under such circumstances. Soddies were so badly insulated that during the winter, water froze away from the stove. In summer, the paucity of light and air could be stifling.

Often there was simply no money available to build a decent house. Drought, grasshoppers, or unseasonable rains destroyed many of the har-

vests of the 80's and 90's. Even good crops did not necessarily change a family's living conditions, since debts and mortgages which had accrued during hard times could swallow up any profits. But in any case, home improvements were a low priority, and families often remained in soddies or shacks even when there was cash or credit to finance a frame house. The farmer usually earmarked his profits for reinvestment into the money-making outlay of better seeds, new stock, machinery, and tools. Farm machinery came first, labor-saving devices for women last: "there was a tendency for the new homesteader to buy new machinery to till broad acres and build new barns to house more stock and grain, while his wife went about the drudgery of household life in the old way in a little drab dwelling overshadowed by the splendour of machine farming." Washers and sewing machines graced some farms in the 80's, but "for the most part . . . the machine age did not greatly help woman. She continued to operate the churn, carry water, and run the washing machine—if she were fortunate enough to have one—and do her other work without the aid of horse power which her more fortunate husband began to apply in his harvesting, threshing, and planting."

Against such odds, women were unable to recreate the kinds of houses they had left. Nor could they reinstate the home as a venerated institution. A sod house was only a makeshift shelter; no effort of the will or imagination could fashion it into what one of its greatest defenders eulogized as "the fairest garden in the wide field of endeavour and achievement." There were other losses as well. Many feminine social activities in more settled farm communities revolved around the church, but with the exception of the European immigrant enclaves, churches were scarce on the Plains. At best, religious observance was makeshift; at worst, it was non-existent. Although "it is not to be supposed that only the ungodly came west," one historian noted, "there seemed to exist in some parts of the new settlements a spirit of apathy if not actual hostility toward religion." Circuit-riders and evangelical freelancers drew crowds during droughts and depressions, but during normal times, everyday piety was rare. Few families read the Bible, sang hymns, or prayed together: "when people heard that a family was religious, it was thought that the head of the household must be a minister."

Women were also unable to reconstitute the network of female friendships which had been an accustomed and sustaining part of daily life "back home." Long prairie winters kept everyone housebound for much of the year. During summers and warmer weather, however, men travelled to town to buy supplies and negotiate loans, and rode to nearby claims to deliver mail, borrow tools, or share news. "As soon as the storms let up, the men could get away from the isolation," wrote Mari Sandoz, Nebraska writer and daughter of a homesteader: "But not their women. They had only the wind and the cold and the problems of clothing, shelter, food, and fuel." On ordinary days men could escape, at least temporarily, "into the fields, the woods, or perhaps to the nearest saloon where there was warmth and companionship," but women had almost no excuses to leave. Neighbors lived too far apart to make casual visiting practicable; besides, a farmer could seldom spare a wagon team from field work to take a woman calling. Hamlin Garland, who moved to the Plains as a young boy, remembered that women visited less than in Wisconsin, his former home, since "the work on the new farms was never-ending": "I doubt if the women—any of them—got out into the fields or meadows long enough to enjoy the birds and the breezes."

In most respects, the patterns of life rarely accommodated women's needs. Plains society paid little mind to women, yet women were essential, not incidental, to its functioning. Without female labor, cash-crop agriculture could never have developed. A man could not farm alone, and hired help was almost impossible to come by. Ordinarily, a farmer could count only on his wife and children as extra hands. On the homestead, women's responsibilities as a farmhand, not as a homemaker or a mother, were of first priority.

Women still cooked, sewed, and washed, but they also herded livestock and toted water for irrigation.

The ambitious farmer's need for the labor power of women and children often lent a utilitarian quality to relations between men and women. For this single settler, marriage was, at least in part, a matter of efficiency. Courtships were typically brief and frank. Molly Dorsey Sanford, a young unmarried homesteader in Nebraska territory, recorded in her diary over half a dozen proposals in a few years. Most of her suitors were strangers. One transient liked her cooking, another heard about a "hull lot of girls" at the Dorsey farm and came to try his luck, and an old man on the steamboat going to Nebraska proposed after an hour's acquaintance. Jules Sandoz, father of Mari Sandoz, married four times. Three wives fled before he found a woman who resigned herself to the emotionless regimen of his farm. Stolid and resilient, the fourth, Mari's mother, lived to a taciturn old age, but her daughter could not forget others of her mother's generation who had not survived their hasty marriages: "after his arrival the wife found that her husband seldom mentioned her in his letters or manuscripts save in connection with calamity. She sickened and left her work undone . . . so the pioneer could not plow or build or hunt. If his luck was exceedingly bad, she died and left him his home without a housekeeper until she could be replaced." With characteristic ambivalence, Sandoz added, "at first this seems a calloused, even a brutal attitude, but it was not so intended."

Instrumentality could also characterize other family relations. Jules Sandoz "never spoke well of anyone who might make his words an excuse for less prompt jumping when he commanded. This included his wife and children." Garland described himself and his fellows as "a Spartan lot. We did not believe in letting our wives and children know they were an important part of our contentment." Jules' wife "considered praise of her children as suspect as self praise would be." Preoccupied by her chores, she maintained only minimal relationships with her family and assigned the care of the younger children to Mari, the oldest daughter.

In the domestic ideology of the family, careful and attentive child-rearing was especially important. Unlike the stoic Mrs. Sandoz, the American women who emigrated were often openly disturbed and troubled by a situation in which mothering was only peripheral to a day's work, and keenly felt the absence of cultural support for correct child-rearing. Mrs. Dorsey, the mother of diarist Molly Sanford, continually worried that her children, exiled from civilization, would turn into barbarians. In towns like Indianapolis, the family's home, schools, churches, and mothers worked in concert. In Nebraska, a mother could count on few aids. The day the Dorseys reached their claim, Molly wrote, "Mother hardly enters into ecstasies . . . she no doubt realizes what it is to bring a young rising family away from the world . . . if the country would only fill up, if there were only schools or churches or even some society. We do not see women at all. All men, single, or bachelors, and one gets tired of them." Molly occasionally responded to her mother's anxiety by searching herself and her siblings for signs of mental degeneration, but Mrs. Dorsey's fears were never warranted. The children grew up healthy and dutiful: in Molly's words, "the wild outdoor life strengthens our physical faculties, and the privations, our powers of endurance." To her confident appraisal, however, she appended a cautionary note in her mother's mode: "so that we do not degenerate mentally, it is all right; Heaven help us." Mrs. Dorsey, however, could seldom be reassured. When a snake bit one of the children, "Poor Mother was perfectly prostrated . . . she sometimes feels wicked to think she is so far away from all help with her family." On her mother's fortieth birthday, Molly wrote, "I fear she is a little blue today. I do try so hard to keep cheerful. I don't know as it is hard work to keep myself so, but it is hard with her. She knows now that the children ought to be in school. We will have to do the teaching ourselves." Without help from the old networks of kin and institutions, a mother could not be assured of success in fending off such dangers.

As Mrs. Dorsey saw her ideas of childrearing atrophy, she also witnessed a general attenuation of the womanliness which had been central to her own identity and sense of importance in the world. Her daughters particularly taxed her investment in an outmoded conception of womanhood. Molly, for instance, was pleased with her facility in learning traditionally male skills. "So it seems I can put my hand to almost anything," she wrote with pride after helping her father roof the house. Mrs. Dorsey regarded her daughter's expanding capacities in a different light. When Molly disguised herself as a man to do some chores, "it was very funny to all but Mother, who fears I am losing all the dignity I ever possessed." Molly was repentant but defensive: "I know I am getting demoralized, but I should be more so, to mope around and have no fun."

Mrs. Dorsey's partial failure to transmit her own values of womanhood to her daughter is emblematic of many difficulties of the first generation of woman settlers. Women could not keep their daughters out of men's clothes, their children in shoes, their family Bibles in use, or their houses clean; at every step, they failed to make manifest their traditions, values, and collective sensibility. It was perhaps the resistance of the Plains to the slightest feminine modification rather than the land itself which contributed to the legend of woman's fear of the empty prairies: "literature is filled with women's fear and distrust of the Plains . . . if one may judge by fiction, one must conclude that the Plains exerted a peculiarly appalling effect on women." The heroine of Rolvaag's *Giants in the Earth* echoed the experience of real women in her question to herself: "how will human beings be able to endure this place? . . . Why, there isn't even a thing that one can *hide behind!*" The desolation even affected women who passed through on their way to the coast. Sarah Royce remembered shrinking from the "chilling prospect" of her first night on the Plains on the Overland Trail: "surely there would be a few trees or a sheltering hillside. . . . No, only the level prairie. . . . Nothing indicated a place for us—a cozy nook, in which for the night we might be guarded."

Fright was not a rarity on the Plains. Both men and women knew the fear of droughts, blizzards, and accidental death. Yet the reported frequency of madness and suicide among women is one indication that Dick may have been right in his contention that "the real burden . . . fell upon the wife and mother." Men's responsibilities required them to act upon their fears. If a blizzard hung in the air, they brought the cattle in; if crops failed, they renegotiated the mortgages and planned for the next season. In contrast, women could often do nothing in the face of calamity. "If hardships came," Sandoz wrote, "the women faced it at home. The results were tersely told by the items in the newspapers of the day. Only sheriff sales seem to have been more numerous than the items telling of trips to the insane asylum."

Men made themselves known in the acres of furrows they ploughed up from the grassland. Women, lacking the opportunities of a home, had few ways to make either the land or their neighbors aware of their presence. The inability of women to leave a mark on their surroundings is a persistent theme in Sandoz's memoirs. When Mari was a child, a woman killed herself and her three children with gopher poison and a filed down case knife. The neighbors agreed that "she had been plodding and silent for a long time," and a woman friend added sorrowfully, "If she could'a had even a geranium, but in that cold shell of a shack. . . ." In Sandoz's memory, the women of her mother's generation are shadows, "silent . . . always there, in the dark corner near the stove."

I have emphasized only one side of woman's experience on the Plains. For many, the years brought better times, better houses, and even neighbors. A second generation came to maturity: some were daughters like the strong farm women of Willa Cather's novels who managed to reclaim the land that had crushed their mothers. Yet the dark side of the lives of the first women on the Plains cannot be denied. Workers in an enterprise often not of their own making, their labor was essential to the farm, their womanhood irrelevant. Hamlin Garland's *Main Travelled Roads*, written in part as a condemnation of "the futility of woman's life on a farm," elicited this response from his mother: "you might have said more but I'm glad you didn't. Farmer's wives have enough to bear as it is."

GLOSSARY

Catherine Beecher: Early advocate of domesticity as an empowering ideology, epitomized in her *Treatise on Domestic Economy*.

Alexis de Tocqueville (1805–1859): French social philosopher best known for his *Democracy in America* (1835).

Willa Cather (1873–1947): American author best known for her novels about frontier life.

Ole Edvart Rolvaag (1876–1931): Norwegian-born American writer whose novels—especially the trilogy beginning with *Giants in the Earth*—concern the lives of Norwegian settlers of the American West.

Gold Rush: The California Gold Rush of 1849.

IMPLICATIONS

In this essay, Stansell points to the importance of women's work in the making of Plains society. In what ways do you think these women maintained the eastern ideals of domesticity? What do you think were the greatest pressures working to change women's roles in the West?

PAST TRACES

The economic changes that swept through American society at the close of the nineteenth century disrupted the lives of urban and rural residents alike. On America's farms, mechanization, competition, monopoly, and overproduction made agrarian life ever more precarious. Faced with the decline of their long-established way of life, farmers throughout the country joined the Populist movement and its political arm, the People's party. In this document, the national platform of the People's party, we see a clear statement of the wrongs felt by American farmers and their plan to restore their traditional independence and security.

The Omaha Platform of the Populist Party (1892)

Preamble

The conditions which surround us best justify our cooperation; we meet in the midst of a nation brought to the verge of moral, political, and material ruin. Corruption dominates the ballot-box, the Legislatures, the Congress, and touches even the ermine of the bench. The people are demoralized; most of the States have been compelled to isolate the voters at the polling places to prevent universal intimidation and bribery. The newspapers are largely subsidized or muzzled, public opinion silenced, business prostrated, homes covered with mortgages, labor impoverished, and the land concentrating in the hands of capitalists. The urban workmen are denied the right to organize for self-protection, imported pauperized labor beats down their wages, a hireling standing army, unrecognized by our laws, is established to shoot them down, and they are rapidly degenerating into European conditions. The fruits of the toil of millions are boldly stolen to build up colossal fortunes for a few, unprecedented in the history of mankind and the possessors of these, in turn, despise the Republic and endanger liberty. From the same prolific womb of governmental injustice we breed the two great classes—tramps and millionaires. . . .

Assembled on the anniversary of the birthday of the nation, and filled with the spirit of the grand general and chief who established our independence, we seek to restore the government of the Republic to the hands of the "plain people," with which class it originated. We assert our purposes to be identical with the purposes of the National Constitution; to form a more perfect union and establish justice, insure domestic tranquillity, provide for the common defense, promote the general welfare, and secure the blessings of liberty for ourselves and our posterity. . . .

Platform

We declare, therefore—

First.—That the union of the labor forces of the United States this day consummated shall be permanent and perpetual; may its spirit enter into all hearts for the salvation of the Republic and the uplifting of mankind.

Second.—Wealth belongs to him who creates it, and every dollar taken from industry without an equivalent is robbery. "If any will not work, neither shall he eat." The interests of rural and civil labor are the same; their enemies are identical.

Third.—We believe that the time has come when the railroad corporations will either own the people or the people must own the railroads. . . .

FINANCE.—We demand a national currency, safe, sound, and flexible issued by the general government only, a full legal tender for all debts, public and private. . . .

1. We demand free and unlimited coinage of silver and gold at the present legal ratio of 16 to 1.
2. We demand that the amount of circulating medium be speedily increased to not less than $50 per capita.
3. We demand a graduated income tax.
4. We believe that the money of the country should be kept as much as possible in the hands of the people, and hence we demand that all State and national revenues shall be limited to the necessary expenses of the government, economically and honestly administered.
5. We demand that postal savings banks be established by the government for the safe deposit of the earnings of the people and to facilitate exchange.

TRANSPORTATION.—Transportation being a means of exchange and a public necessity, the government should own and operate the railroads in the interest of the people. The telegraph and telephone, like the post-office system, being a necessity for the transmission of news, should be owned and operated by the government in the interest of the people.

LAND.—The land, including all the natural sources of wealth, is the heritage of the people, and should not be monopolized for speculative purposes, and alien ownership of land should be prohibited. All land now held by railroads and other corporations in excess of their actual needs, and all lands now owned by aliens should be reclaimed by the government and held for actual settlers only.

Expressions of Sentiments

1. RESOLVED, That we demand a free ballot, and a fair count of all elections, and pledge ourselves to secure it to every legal voter without Federal intervention, through the adoption by the States of the unperverted Australian or secret ballot system.
2. RESOLVED, That the revenue derived from a graduated income tax should be applied to the reduction of the burden of taxation now levied upon the domestic industries of this country.
3. RESOLVED, That we pledge our support to fair and liberal pensions to ex-Union soldiers and sailors.
4. RESOLVED, That we condemn the fallacy of protecting American labor under the present system, which opens our ports to the pauper and criminal classes of the world and crowds out our wage-earners; and we denounce the present ineffective laws against contract labor, and

demand the further restriction of undesirable emigration.

5. RESOLVED, That we cordially sympathize with the efforts of organized workingmen to shorten the hours of labor, and demand a rigid enforcement of the existing eight-hour law on Government work, and ask that a penalty clause be added to the said law.

6. RESOLVED, That we regard the maintenance of a large standing army of mercenaries, known as the Pinkerton system, as a menace to our liberties, and we demand its abolition. . . .

7. RESOLVED, That we commend to the favorable consideration of the people and the reform press the legislative system known as the initiative and referendum.

8. RESOLVED, That we favor a constitutional provision limiting the office of President and Vice-President to one term, and providing for the election of Senators of the United States by a direct vote of the people.

9. RESOLVED, That we oppose any subsidy or national aid to any private corporation for any purpose.

4

The Southern Populist Critique of American Capitalism

Bruce Palmer

The last decade of the nineteenth century was a time of upheaval in a century marked by unprecedented change. In the Northeast, mammoth factories and the immigrants who labored in them dominated the cities of America's industrial heartland. Throughout the country, an ever-growing network of railroads connected even outlying regions to the burgeoning metropolises of the nation. And in these metropolises, financial and industrial cartels, monopolies, and holding companies exercised an economic and political influence unparalleled in American life.

Facing these changes were workers and farmers. American workers responded to the growing power of industrial capitalism with the collective power of their numbers and struggled with their employers over control of the workplace and the process of production itself. For their part, the small farmers of the South, Midwest, and Far West responded by forming local organizations to fight discriminatory railroad freight rates and to challenge the power of eastern banks to yoke them to a cycle of unending indebtedness.

Beginning in the late 1880s, these farm protests took on a national political focus. Dissatisfied with inaction and outright hostility on the part of both national parties, southern and midwestern farmers created a series of Farmers' Alliances and eventually the Populist or People's Party. The Populists quickly became one of the greatest social and political reform movements in American history. At the heart of the movement was their belief in the importance of small family farms and their concern about the threat that an eastern "moneyed interest" posed to this agrarian institution. Their rallying cry became "man over money," and by 1892, the People's party had elected governors in Kansas and North Dakota and dominated all levels of politics in Colorado. Although the Populists met the fate of all third parties in American politics — being absorbed into the easy-credit, free-silver wing of the Democratic party represented by William Jennings Bryant—their protest served notice to both parties that the needs of American family farmers could not be ignored.

In this study of populism, Bruce Palmer investigates the ideas behind the movement. He finds that both traditional agrarian ideals and a modern appreciation of the marketplace animated the thoughts of Populist leaders, rank and file members, and the platform of the People's party.

....

For the Southern Populists any properly ordered society required what might best be called balance, though they most often used the words "harmony," "equilibrium," and sometimes "homogeneity." "When He multiplied the loaves and the fishes," wrote a North Carolina Allianceman, "none went away hungry. God does not create disparities." "Despite their positions at opposite ends of the Populist political spectrum in the South, North Carolina Populist Senator Marion Butler and radical Texas organizer H. S. P. "Stump" Ashby could agree that in a society properly ordered "the merchant and farmer, lawyer and artisan . . . [would] dwell together, not as warring enemies, but as kind friends, joining willing hands in the beneficent work of production. "Rather than serve as a battleground on which selfish people fought each other for personal advantage, society should be the arena in which everyone worked together for what most benefited each—the production of tangible wealth.

The distance between the ideal and the actual social order, those real disparities which existed in America, made this idea pivotal in the Southern Populist demand for reform. L. L. Polk, president of the National Farmers' Alliance and Industrial Union for a little less than three years, noted that the country had not witnessed the "peace, contentment and plenty" that should have been expected from America's tremendous post-1865 expansion in railroads, manufacturing, towns, and cities. Instead, the result had been hard times. "The greatest industrial revolution of the ages" had one more goal to reach: "To restore and maintain that equipoise between the great industrial interests of the country which is absolutely essential to a healthful progress and to the development of our civilization." A balanced and harmonious development did not mean America's thousands of homeless and hungry families, thousands dressed in rags. America's social development, concluded Helen W. Post, a *People's Party Paper* contributing editor, "is deformity, monstrosity; it is not symmetry; it is dropsy and not good healthy substance; and it means premature death."

At the center of the Southern Populists' notion of social balance lay their concept of the "middle class": "the great and noble middle farming and laboring class" to which a Georgia Populist declared the southern reformers themselves belonged. This class consisted solely of the producers of tangible wealth and drew its members neither from the rich nor the poor. These people provided "the bone and sinew of the country," those who supported the government, "the bulwark of any social system." But in America these people of "moderate means" were fast disappearing, wrote a Texas Populist, "leaving only the two classes, the two extremes, the very rich, who live in idleness, extravagance and luxuriousness, and the destitute poor, who are compelled with their families to labor incessantly for a subsistence."

More clearly than anything else this growing imbalance signaled a major injustice in American society. God had made the bounty available and ruled that it be distributed properly, to all people. "Larger equity in the division of labor—in the distribution of the products of labor, must obtain," wrote a North Carolina Populist. "Anything short of this is contrary to the teachings of the Holy Writ." At issue were not the productive abilities of

American farmers and laborers. "There is plenty of wealth in this country," wrote a Georgia Populist. "It is not that we are kicking about. The trouble is that the people who produce all this great wealth are robbed of it by bad laws made in the interest of an idle, do-nothing class of people." To correct the situation the producers demanded enjoyment of the fruits of their own toil, fruits which heretofore the Rockefellers, Carnegies, Goulds, and others had stolen from them to create their gigantic fortunes.

The worsening depression of the 1890s substantiated the Southern Populists' fear that social and economic disaster would follow the growing injustice. Nor was the issue at hand purely secular. The wealthy few's accumulation of riches, stolen from the producers, flew in the face of a righteous and wrathful God. "False systems," created by "false legislation," meant that labor no longer enjoyed what it produced, millions of children starved, and thousands of women were forced into prostitution. It was the work of the Devil, and the millionaires were warned by Arkansas editor W. S. Morgan that "it is only a matter of time when [the people] will turn upon you and rend you. Again we say, beware. Get back to the righteousness of God." Whether the problem was a secular or a moral and religious one, however, the result was the same. "Millionaires make paupers," declared a Texas Populist; "paupers make anarchists and anarchists destroy nations."

Southern Populists often drew on a specific Biblical image, the Belshazzar story, to express their sense of outrage at the material and moral disaster they saw flowing from the growing maldistribution of wealth. One part of the image juxtaposed riches and poverty to emphasize the injustice of the widening chasm between rich and poor. Watson in early 1892. described a postelection dinner of the Georgia Democratic leaders in Atlanta using the image to make his point, contrasting the elaborate preparations and food inside the hotel with the "millions of toilers going to rest in their squalid homes, amid all the gloom, the cold and the hunger of their hard lot." The second element of the image made the threat to the wrongdoers explicit. Disaster awaited the rich who robbed and plundered the producing masses. Blind to what was happening, they wined and dined on their last evening, Watson wrote, "the tread of Cyrus and his Persians without. The pampered Aristocrats will listen to no warning, until Daniel strides into the Hall and the laugh of the voluptuary freezes on the lips of the quaking coward." The situation could not continue. Retribution would be had, justice be done.

The Southern Populists, however, did not always picture the danger from growing extremes of wealth in such stark terms. The maldistribution also caused disorders and immorality on a lower but increasing level of intensity. The extremes of wealth and poverty bred disease, vice, and sensuality—the extremes of human personal and social behavior. The producing middle class—quite literally in the middle between rich and poor, debauched and degraded, idler and slave—furnished the moderate virtues which sustained a harmonious and balanced society. The same class which concentrated wealth was destroying had, as Populists, to save the country from both the rich and poor by restoring the proper distribution of wealth. Politically this achievement required returning equality to the social order. Inherited from the Jacksonians, the motto which ran at the head of Watson's *People's Party Paper* from 1891 through 1896 read "Equal Rights to All, Special Privileges to None." His southern brethren agreed completely with him on his choice. They did not intend, as a North Carolina editor pointed out, an actual material equality for everyone, for "people are not born equals, neither physically, mentally nor morally." They did share "natural rights" to life, liberty, and happiness, however, which implied "a right to the means of comfortable existence, the right to the conditions that produce happiness."

To what area did this demand for equal rights refer? "The Omaha platform has but one principle," wrote a Georgia Populist, F. J. Ripley, "that wealth belongs to him who creates it, rather than to those who by chicanery, legislation and fortuitous circumstances manage to get possession of it." The platform favored the distribution of "wealth, prosperity and happiness," and opposed their concentration; it called for "such legislation as will give every man a fair chance to obtain and retain a competency." If that fair chance were provided, observed a North Carolina editor, there would be but one class, "those who do honest work and enjoy the fruits of their labor. Of course some of these will be richer than others in worldly goods, for God has given to some men more talents than to others, but all of this class will be equally as rich in contentment and happiness." No one who worked would be poor. The major problem of imbalance in society be solved, social and economic justice served.

Their religious experience gave the Southern Populists, like most Americans, a tool for explaining and understanding American society. One of the best examples of its usage appeared in the southern reformers' attempt to deal with their own relation to American politics in the 1890s. An Alabama Allianceman, in mid-1892, expressed his hopes and concern for the reform movement with an elaborately mixed metaphor built around the flight of the Jews from Egypt. "The children of Israel," he wrote, had at last escaped Egypt, and would regain the promised land if they did not hesitate at the Red Sea or linger to hear "the syren [sic] song of the money power Delilah, and the lying entreaties or menaces of the Benedict Arnolds of American Independence, and the Judases to the cause of justice, liberty and righteousness." Although they had turned toward the land of milk and honey, the reformers, open to the blandishments and threats of their enemies and faced with the seeming impossibility of defeating them, had yet to win their struggle. The metaphor served to define, in terms the Populists' listeners would understand, the difficulty of the reform struggle, the

enemies it confronted, and the promise victory held. And it gave all the importance that only the guiding hand of God could provide for the faithful.

Often their choice of terms indicated that the Southern Populists perceived the mission of their party as analogous to the task of religious salvation. Many believed, with one Georgia Populist, that "the People's Party is the political Savior of this country." The southern reformers often used Christ to link religious salvation with Populism. Their Christ was not, however, a savior who told people to repent of this world to win salvation in the next. "Christ did not come, as our theological quacks are so fond of saying, to prepare men for another world," wrote a Texas Populist, "but to teach them how to rightly live in this." Christ was a reformer and a radical. The Southern Populist demand for equal rights to all and special privileges to none urged nothing new. "Years ago the Man of Galilee used it," wrote Watson, "as the chief plank in His platform. 'Whatsoever ye would that I do unto you do ye even so unto them.'" Like the Populists, Christ was born a workingman, a producer, and His Sermon on the Mount, argued a North Carolina Populist editor, showed that He understood that "the unduly rich were the worst sort of criminals, because it is they who are responsible for the social conditions which make all other crimes possible or necessary."

The Southerners took their religion seriously. They took literally what they heard from the pulpit or read in their Bibles about the wrongs of oppression and the responsibility of all for their neighbors. The Populists, a Texas reformer asserted, "led mainly by men who are Christians in principle, but like the late Judge Nugent, not members of any so-called orthodox church," were "leading the industrial millions out of slavery into freedom. The church that professes to be the light of the world under Christ is not doing it. We plead for the rights of man and the old-fashioned gospel of the brotherhood of humanity as Christ preached it and lined [sic] it." In this real sense, for many southern reformers the Populist party obviously came very close to replacing the church, at least in this world. As the use of the religious metaphors and imagery indicated, for these the authority of the church in society belonged to the People's party.

While their own experience taught them about the injustice of a growing maldistribution of wealth, the Southern Populists often used religious metaphors and imagery to organize and articulate that experience, to give it more universal meaning, and to explain both the process and solutions they proposed utilizing to eradicate that social and economic injustice. The southern reformers, of course, had another frame of reference available—their Jeffersonian and Jacksonian intellectual and political heritage—which they often closely tied to their moral and religious referents. One Alabama editor called Populism "the morals of Christ and the politics of Thomas Jefferson." The religious framework lent divine sanction to the Jeffersonian and Jacksonian formulations, while Jeffersonian and Jacksonian ideas often served to particularize God's commandments as they affected politics, economics, and society.

The Southern Populists cited not only God's commandments but Jefferson's authority for the injustice of and solutions to the great inequalities of wealth in American society. Not only was equal rights to all and special privileges to none a Jeffersonian doctrine, but so was the idea to which the Southern Populists tied it, equal opportunities for each person in the race of life. The notion of Jeffersonian simplicity highlighted for the Southern Populists the evils of the growing extremes of wealth. Regarding the costly paraphernalia and the elaborate ceremony surrounding President Cleveland and his entourage, Populists in North Carolina, Georgia, and Texas could only regret the passing of the "days of Jeffersonian simplicity." The concentration of wealth from which this extravagance flowed threatened to destroy American society. The extravagance itself signaled impending destruction. Jeffersonian simplicity, in the same way, reflected the ideal society out of which it grew, a society balanced and homogeneous, where all enjoyed a relatively equal amount of the total wealth of the country.

The analysis of society based on the function of tangible production allowed the Southern Populists to elaborate an ideal society which consisted of the interaction of several groups—working people, manufacturers, bankers, merchants, and some professionals. Religious metaphors and images affected the range of this elaboration little, although they helped to explain some of it. The Southern Populists drew most of the content of this ideal society from their own rural and reform experience, although they often interpreted it through the metaphors and images their Jeffersonian and Jacksonian heritage provided them. While their background as post-Civil War southern farmers taught them, with the sharp lessons of experience, that the most central injustice in American society was the growing maldistribution of wealth, they used their religious heritage, and the metaphors and images offered, to explain the extent and import of this injustice, to predict what would happen if the wrong were not righted, and to explain the importance of the means to be used by the reform movement in correcting it. As their religious heritage had played a secondary role in their elaboration of a producer-oriented society, so their Jeffersonian and Jacksonian heritage, while it identified some of the more particular elements of society that needed change, played a secondary role in explaining what had gone wrong with America. It was contact with the specific society around them, however, that forced the Southern Populists to make the choices which ultimately governed their reform program.

As late nineteenth-century Southerners, the Populists encountered a conception of the proper economic and social order which owed little to Jefferson and Jackson. When the South emerged in the late 1870s from the turmoil of Reconstruction and depression, among some young urban Southerners talk began of a way to solve the problems of southern backwardness, poverty, and the region's burdens of race and sectional isolation. Henry Grady, Richard Edmonds, Henry Watterson, Daniel Tompkins, and others like them outlined a plan for sectional development which they called the New South and which Paul Gaston has noted "bespoke harmonious reconciliation of sectional differences, racial peace, and a new economic and social order based on industry and scientific, diversified agriculture—all of which would lead, eventually, to the South's dominance in the reunited nation."

In the 1880s a small but vigorous southern "new middle class" adopted this creed as its own, and as this commercial, professional, and land-owning class grew stronger in the cities and towns of the South, the New South gospel matured with it. Although in order to win political control in most southern states the new middle class had to wait for the Populists and the Redeemers to destroy each other, by the 1890s their creed of industrialization and urbanization had spread widely in the small towns and cities of the South. The New South advocates were the middle class regional representatives of America's maturing industrial society. They rode to sectional power on the direct penetration of American capitalism into the southern towns and countryside, and the New South creed furnished them with an ideology to explain and justify both their struggle and their victory. The Populists, challenging the Redeemers and the Redeemers' temporary middle-class allies in the 1890s, also had to confront the New South creed.

Although the New South advocates paid only spotty, and usually critical, attention to the farmers, Southern Populists did not remain entirely immune to the plans and promises of the new order. Walter Hines Page had a wider readership in North Carolina than many historians have credited him with. "We regret," wrote a North Carolina Allianceman, "that we have a good many old fogies in the State, but are glad that North Carolina is keeping up with what is known as the New South." They often supported the New South's largest advertising vehicle, the local, state, or regional fair. Almost every Southern Populist newspaper, and all the major ones, at one time or another carried a column from the *Manufacturers' Record*, a Baltimore-based paper and major exponent of the New South gospel, noting the start of manufacturing and other enterprises in their states, and sometimes in the whole South. On rare occasions editorial paragraphs distinctly reminiscent of the heyday of Grady and Dawson appeared in southern reform papers. In an otherwise critical response to an editorial in the Brooklyn *Eagle* praising the North, the *Progressive Farmer* in 1892 commented that Northerners were, in fact, "full of business; they read, they study, they plan. They put business into politics, where we of the South put sentiment. We must change. We must have some business ideas. Our people must read and get posted." The *Farmer* continued the advice, four years later urging farmers to visit "some prosperous manufacturing establishment" to learn techniques of regularity and efficiency.

Like most Southerners, the Populists uncritically accepted certain other accoutrements of the New South order which were often alien to their rural-centered life. The business college was one, and while the reformers frequently opposed them, even land development and town building schemes, close to the heart of the New South gospel of progress, could get support. Watson's paper in early March 1892 began carrying a full-page advertisement offering land for sale in Nantahala, a town planed for western North Carolina. Although he was careful to observe that such "town-booming" schemes could be risky, Watson also noted that "more fortunes have been made out of new built towns of late years than in any other way." Having found that the officers and stockholders were "substantial," "cautious," and "reliable" Georgia businessmen and that a demand existed for Nantahala's mineral and timber resources, Watson in an editorial praised it as "one of the very best investments now offered" and "a grand opportunity." Three years later he gave editorial support to a similar development in Atlanta, a "speculation" in town lots in Inman Park that would beat "even farm lands" for investment.

Nor was Watson alone in his advocacy. The county-city booster edition of the Dallas, Georgia, *Herald* could have been primed in any town or county weekly within the last ninety years. For the growth it promised, Populist editors in North Carolina and Texas urged their readers to fight for railroads through their counties and towns. The Ozark, Alabama, *Banner-Advertiser* mounted a two-year campaign of varying intensity, starting in early 1895, to get a cotton factory started in the town. W. S. Morgan constantly advertised benefits and desirability of Arkansas for farming and business. Progress, development, and town growth sometimes mattered as much to these Populist papers as they always did to their many Democratic, New South rivals.

But while they supported the New South goals of progress and prosperity—few Southerners would not have done so—and even some of that creed's techniques, the Southern Populists were never happy with the new society envisaged by the New South adherents. In the heart of the northern Alabama coalfields, location of one of the proudest examples of the New South, Birmingham, an Alabama Populist editor wondered whether the new era would blend with the old to prevent "the undesirable surroundings too often produced in a 'development' whose only object is the sordid desire for the accumulation of wealth." Even the *Progressive Farmer*, which generally responded more positively than other Populist papers to New South sentiments, knew the reality of the New South. "A few cities like Atlanta,

Birmingham, Chattanooga and other smaller places have grown up quite rapidly, factories have multiplied with gratifying rapidity," wrote the editor in 1893, "but the great agricultural sections of the South have made no progress." A very few farmers had prospered, but most of them were worse off than in 1880. Until the farmers benefited the "New South" would remain "rather more vapor than anything else." The New South was an urban and industrial ideal, the ideology of a new southern small town and city merchant and professional class which led the opposition to the Alliance and later to Southern Populism.

The Southern Alliance and its Populist issue spoke, as much as any group in the late Nineteenth century, for the victims of the penetration of Northern industrial and finance capitalism into the South. The new southern middle class climbed to power on that penetration, and used the New South gospel of urban and industrial development to sell the new order and to justify their efforts toward political and social dominance. Despite some talk of making the farmer an efficiency expert, the Southern Populists knew that a victory for this class and its creed would come at their expense. They did not object to southern prosperity; they found advantage to the producers in the development of manufacturing and processing industries. But they wanted everyone to benefit, and had second thoughts about the effects of New South boosterism and development on the rural society to which they remained firmly attached. They wholeheartedly endorsed economic development for the South, objecting only to what now appear to be the necessary concomitants of that development. They never succeeded, however, in separating the one from the other. By accepting the same basic economic system which the New South advocates did, the Southern Populists chose to fight on territory not only far more familiar to their New South opponents, but also where they were outmanned and completely outgunned. The choice made, the reformers were bound to lose.

That they made this choice was evident whenever the Southern Populists discussed the kind of economic system America ought to have. Almost all of them accepted what they understood to be the basic American economic system—a simple market society with private property, profit, and economic competition among small producers. The Populists, wrote a Virginia Populist editor, were not "destroyers of private property" and did not desire "to uproot the existing order of things and start a brand new arrangement of our own." Populists elsewhere echoed his demurrer. At issue was not private ownership of wealth and property but their concentration in a few hands. A wider distribution of private property through equalization of opportunities would correct this basic injustice.

Since a chance to accumulate wealth remained important to their argument, most southern reformers, although they equivocated about it, could not spurn economic competition. The Populist party, stated Watson, "stands for the doctrine that the whole world's stock of wealth and opportunity belongs to all mankind—to be won or lost on the basis of merit and demerit." Accumulated wealth should not be permitted to protect itself from the risks of "competition" through legislation giving special privileges to the wealthy few. Other southern reformers agreed." Marion Butler, defending government ownership of the railroads, argued that the men who wrote the Constitution "took the position that any business that affected all or a great portion of the people, under circumstances where there could be no successful competition by men of small capital, was a *government function* and should be owned and operated by the government, at cost, for the benefit of all the people alike." He justified an apparent violation of America's economic system in terms of preserving one of its essential qualities. According to Judge Nugent, the Populists wanted a society where "strictly public or social functions shall be turned over to the government, and the private citizen left in undisturbed freedom to achieve

his own destiny in his own way by the exercise of his own individual skill and industry, and the legitimate investment of his own capital." The Southern Populists accepted competition between small, individual, relatively equal economic units and, within this context, the individual accumulation of wealth.

The southern reformers' attitude toward socialism provided a counterpoint to their adherence to a private enterprise market economy. When they spoke as producers or as landowners or aspiring landowners, most of them wanted no part of what they felt to be the socialists' commitment to ending private ownership of property and profits. This opposition was a good deal more vocal during the 1893 and 1896 debate between the right and left wings of the party, although so few reformers advocated socialism, before 1895 that there is little reason to suspect large numbers of Populists had suddenly deserted it. Certainly Watson had not. A committed though more articulate Lockean than most other Southern Populists, he maintained that the Populist party protected those who profited justly from their exertions and skills by supporting "the constitutional rights of the individual—individual liberty, individual enterprise, and individual property. She (the party) does not believe in Socialism, with all its collective ownership of land, homes, and pocketbooks." An Alabama Populist found communism "fascinating" but "impracticable" and "evidently unwise" because it was based on a yet unreachable "individual perfection." Without the incentive provided by profit and private ownership, people, no longer driven by their material self-interest, would stop working, production would cease, and society would" collapse.

A just and equitable society did not require eliminating the existing economic order. While the unequal distribution of wealth was the "menacing evil of the times," the way to distribute it more evenly, argued Judge Nugent, was not to grant every person an equal share, but to give everybody "fair opportunities for the exertion of their faculties." The creation of a "community" with "no material waste, no check in production" and a general sharing among the producers of the wealth they created required only the destruction of "monopoly in these things which productive labor must have for practical use. Protect these things from the speculative greed of men, disembarrass trade of arbitrary legal interference, give free play to competition within the proper sphere of individual effort and investment, and steadily oppose those extreme socialistic schemes which ask by the outside pressure of mere enactments or systems to accomplish what can only come from the free activities of men—do these things and you will have achieved the real genuine and lasting reforms which labor and capital equally need, and which, in fact, are the only practicable reforms lying within range of party action." Socialism could not accomplish what control and reform of the existing economic system would. With the assurance of profits and private ownership and some governmental control, "individual effort and investment" would assure ceaseless production and a fair distribution to all who worked.

When not talking about practical political and economic problems, however, the Southern Populists, antimonopoly greenbackers and financial reformers alike, often had positive things to say about socialism. Many agreed with the Alabama editor who thought socialism too ideal to be a workable way of organizing society, with the qualification that "if the whole world should be converted to practical Christianity . . . thus rendering socialism possible, so much the better." Some even felt that there might be some good in the doctrine in the here and now. This was particularly true of the antimonopoly greenback Populists. One Texan maintained that although the People's party was not socialist, its platform did contain "a few of the underlying principles of socialism," a necessity for destroying "the infernal industrial monopolistic system which we have upon us." Such principles included demands for a national currency, an income tax, a postal savings bank, and government ownership of the railroad, telephone, and telegraph systems. "There is socialism in all governments that are not purely despotic," stated the editors of the *Arkansaw Kicker.*

In fact, two Austin, Texas, Populist papers openly adopted socialism during the period—the *People's Advocate* and the *Argus.* Neither paper stopped backing Populist candidates. The editor of the *People's Advocate,* G. W. Mendell, in 1894 served as chairman of the Travis County (Austin) People's party executive committee. The call to socialism, the call to get rid of private property, proceeded from the same perceptions of the ills in existing society that other Populists held—millions unable to work, the growing chasm between the poor masses who produced the wealth and the wealthy few who consumed it, the same contrasts of poverty amid plenty, starvation alongside wealth. The *Argus,* discussing the Pullman strike and its lessons, shared with Watson, Marion Butler, Judge Nugent, and the rest of the Southern Populists the idea that government ownership would solve the railroad crisis. Unlike them, however, it extended the reasoning behind such a solution and came up with something a little different. If the government had owned and operated the coal mines, the railroads, the oil wells, the sugar refineries, and the banks, then coal millionaires, Pullman, Gould, Rockefeller, Havemeyer, a sugar Senate, and a financial panic would not have been possible. "The only remedy, the only means of abolishing wage-slavery, poverty, and the unendurable despotism of the money kings is the collective ownership of all the means of production and distribution." These papers, with a slight extension of Southern Populist ideas, became socialist, albeit very moderate. Both papers, however, continued to advocate the whole panoply of Populist reform, including the Omaha platform.

The ease with which it was ideologically possible to move to socialism meant that the Southern Populists often had to make a conscious decision to avoid it. In some cases political expediency helped draw the line. As Watson pointed out, "do you believe that the People's party in Georgia would have a corporal's guard left, if it were generally understood among Populists that the platform opposed individual ownership of homes and money?" There was, however, more to it, as Watson's statement itself hinted. Their desire for a better society could propel them in the opposite direction. "Every living man who has a spark of human sympathy in his chest is socialistic to some extent," wrote W. S. Morgan in the *National Reformer*. "Socialism, in its literal sense, means a better state of society, and as the world gets better it 'drifts' nearer to socialism." Their experience with poverty and exploitation, combined with a sense of human sympathy reinforced by their religious background and tradition, tended to push the Southern Populists toward some sort of socialism as the only decent and humane alternative to the society they found around them. But their political heritage and their class position as landowners or aspiring landowners suggested both the decency and possibility of a market society of independent producers. The latter influence, reinforced by political considerations of the kind Watson stated so bluntly, prevented them from moving into socialism, a move which would seem to have been an easy one for them to make, given their adherence to government ownership of various large industries and a basic commitment to a society made more decent by a more equitable distribution of wealth. Some of the Southern Populists, though, particularly the antimonopoly greenback radicals, came close.

Anarchy, socialism's nineteenth-century radical American counterpart, had no appeal at all, although the reformers used the term quite as often, applying it most frequently to those whom they regarded as the most serious enemies of the social order, the anarchistic politicians, plutocrats, and corporations." Their condemnation of anarchy or anarchists concentrated on the order imposed on society by its laws. The Southern Populists, believing as they did in the importance of private prop-

erty, had no reason to regard with equanimity the social upheaval anarchy promised. The producing middle classes, wrote a North Carolina Populist in 1892, "are not enemies of law and order, they do not envy or hate those who have acquired property by honest methods." The reformers carefully supported strict adherence to the law, good or bad, until it was changed. Walter E. Grant, running for Congress on the Populist ticket in Virginia's third congressional district, told the voters that despite inequitable laws his party did "not blame anyone for using the law to accumulate a large fortune;" the Populists would, if necessary, "aid him in keeping whatever he has lawfully acquired."

Because they associated the rule of law with a stable, orderly society, the Southern Populists often expressed concern over the violence of labor strikes. Few of them, however, censured strikes quite as completely as did the North Carolina Populists, who announced in their 1894 platform: "We sympathize with the oppressed everywhere, but we are opposed to all lawless combinations of men, whether representing capital or labor. We believe in peace and strict obedience to law." The platform urged that, instead, labor use the ballot to defeat monopoly peacefully. The political orientation of the Knights of Labor and its minimal strike activity in the state during the late 1880s and early 1890s, the financial reform stance of most of the state Populist leadership, and fusion with the Republicans had much to do with the attitude of the North Carolina party. In Texas, Alabama, and Georgia, Populists more often directed their antistrike hostility at the owners and the capitalists.

On the other hand, most Southern Populists advised laboringmen to vote right instead of striking. This was not the case usually only where the Populists had some contact with working people and strikes. In Alabama, in the Birmingham area, Populists worked in 1894 to keep the miners' strike going at least through the fall elections. In Texas the massive 1886 railroad strike played a role in energizing the

Alliance radicalism which led to the Omaha platform and the Populist party. Connections like these made the attitudes of some Southern Populists toward working people more complex.

In general, however, most Southern Populists regarded strikes and labor violence with concern. Part of the reason was their lack of contact with industrial labor and the absence of a thorough education in working class problems such as the mass of Texas Alliancemen received in 1886. They also differed with working people on how best to win the goals labor wanted. "Quicker than dynamite, more effective and more lasting than revolution, more far-reaching in its sweep than strikes, and more terrible to plutocracy than all is the ballot," argued the socialist editor of the Austin *Argus*. This advice had a strong element of practicality, for strikes often seemed to work badly for the strikers. Nevertheless, the Southern Populists, even those who had a better understanding than most of their brethren of the working people's lot, often failed to appreciate either the desperation of strikers like those at Pullman or the tactical pressures which labor union leaders like Debs faced when a strike broke out. In neither case did the participants have much choice. Certainly the option of ballot or strike was not available in the spring of 1894 to workers living in Pullman, Illinois.

Both of these commitments—to America's basic economic order and to a stable, orderly society—also revealed a side of Southern Populism about which we have not spoken. Their conception of themselves as the middle class was not rooted exclusively in their Jeffersonian-Jacksonian heritage. The economic revolution after the Civil War created, even in the South of the 1890s, a new kind of middle class. Ragged Dick and Andrew Carnegie often replaced the yeoman farmer and Daniel Boone as cultural heroes. Independence shaded into cleverness in the search for the main chance; simple abundance became the security of success, hard work acquired over-

tones of diligence and tenacity in search of profits; and a business education became more important than a farm upbringing for social mobility. This new urban middle class, a white-collar, professional, clerical, storekeeper, management middle class, had its own ethos of success and failure which the Southern Populists did not escape any more completely than they did other parts of the middle class' New South creed. While they questioned the actual existence of equal opportunity for success, the reformers shared with most other Americans a firm belief in the beneficial effect of such equal opportunity for all who would work. The concern for law and order, the careful opposition to socialist and anarchist, was more familiar in the late nineteenth century than in Jeffersonian or Jacksonian America. The yeoman farmer and artisan worried about threats to private property from anarchist and labor violence far less than did the new middle class, or the Southern Populists. Jeffersonians and. Jacksomans would not have given corporations, finance capitalism, and town-booming quite as clean a bill of health as the Southern Populists sometimes did, even though the latter's certificate always contained many more qualifications than those handed out by most of their contemporaries.

At times the religious metaphors and imagery used by the Southern Populists reflected a more recent middle-class concern for purity than did the Biblically based religious morality of a younger America. An Alabama Populist spoke of the need for "wholesome" reform legislation. A favorite crusade of this new middle class, the prohibition movement, occasionally touched the Southern Populist party around its edges, although demon rum never became an important party issue. Another North Carolina man identified himself as a "Bryan Populist" for three reasons, the first being that, like himself, Bryan was a good moral man, affiliated with the church, and did not smoke, chew, swear, or drink. The Southern Populists rarely denied the propriety of prohibition. Many obviously felt that temperance might be a good, if not important, ingredient in a better society.

The Southern Populists' concern with respectability also disclosed some affinity with the new middle classes. The complaint against the influence of riches in society, especially in regard to personal integrity and character, was rather widespread. "Honest labor," blessed by God, and not the accumulation of money, made men "truly great," wrote a Texas reformer. "Therefore, men should seek rather to be upright, honest and true rather than to be rich." The increasing importance of money in determining one's respectability furnished another excellent example of the evils of the growing maldistribution of wealth. But the concern with this change, although rare, also reflected the impact on the Southern Populists of the social code of new middle class society, where men were respectable as often as independent, pure-minded as often as rational, and as virtuous in the service of blue laws as in the preservation of republican government. The Populist did "not wish to be rich," maintained a North Carolina reformer, "but only want a reasonable chance that we may be able to go decent and respectable and educate our children. Surely no enemy could say anything against such doctrine as this." No one could; the wish was only for a decent life. A more even distribution of wealth and the opportunity to enjoy the fruits of their toil, however, promised not only a more productive, harmonious, and balanced society, but also an increased portion of a new town and city middle class respectability.

Finally, the Southern Populists also shared with other nineteenth-century Americans, including their new middle class, success-oriented contemporaries, a belief in the social and personal value of industry and frugality. "Nothing in this life can be gained without hard work. . . . If you are industrious, your work, even though hard, will be a pleasure." But the Southern Populists, having experienced for a generation the seemingly inexorable advance of rural poverty, knew that the exist-

ing organization of society failed to reward properly hard work and frugality. A Georgia Populist speaker in 1892. pointed out that in the last twenty-five years Georgia farmers had grown millions of dollars worth of cotton, yet remained poor. The farmers were "intelligent, economical and industrious," but under the existing system these qualities went unrewarded. Since the seventeenth century hard work and saving had been supposed to guarantee at least a fair share of wealth to those who practiced them diligently. When the Southern Populists found this ideal at odds with reality, however, rather than question their own personal worth, as the success ethic and their middle class contemporaries told them to do, they questioned the organization of society and found it unbalanced and unjust, favoring not those who worked but those who were clever enough to get more than they needed without working.

The Southern Populists found themselves in a difficult situation in the 1890s. They and those around them were sliding quickly into a poverty and dependence from which it became more and more difficult to escape. At the same time certain aspects of the new world encroaching upon their lives—machinery, railroads, economic development, and new markets—seemed beneficial, apparently representing possible gains for them and their neighbors. In response to the unfavorable elements of this new American industrial society, the Southern Populists tried to elaborate a social order which would preserve what they wanted to keep and get rid of what they did not. In doing so they drew on the material available to them—-their rural Southern experience, their evangelical Protestant heritage, and their Jeffersonian–Jacksonian tradition. Of course, these elements supplied the basis for their critique of the new world they faced as well as their response to it.

Sometimes the Southern Populists' and heritage distorted their perceptions of capitalist America, particularly when, as in the case of manufacturers or the new industrial labor, these two things gave them no way develop an accurate analysis of this new society. On the other hand, in some cases their class position or contemporary experience overrode the dictates of their heritage, as occurred in their response to the New South gospel or in their affinity for a socialist ideal of society. In the areas of conflict between their heritage and their experience lay the sources of change in the Southern Populists' response to American industrial and financial capitalism.

GLOSSARY

Farmers' Alliance: Organization of farmers created in 1880. By 1882, it counted 100,000 members in eight state alliances and 200 local alliances. The Alliance was the forerunner of the Populist Party.

People's Party: An alternative name for the Populist Party.

Panic of 1893:   Financial panic that led to one of the nation's worst economic depressions, 1893–1897.

IMPLICATIONS

In this essay, Palmer notes that while the Populists criticized the drift of modern capitalist society, they did not propose eliminating the marketplace or commercial transactions. What do you think was the true aim of the Populists? To restore the rural past? To limit the impact of industrial society? Or to reform American society?

PAST TRACES

One of the most popular writers of turn-of-the-century America, Horatio Alger, Jr., built his reputation on providing formulaic novels depicting upward social mobility and the way to attain it. This reading begins with a selection from one of Alger's most mature novels. As the title suggests, upward mobility was never easy, and young men (women were excluded from Alger's world) needed to be wary of the many traps laid by modern society that could prevent their climb "up the ladder" of success.

Horatio Alger, Jr., Bound to Rise, Or, Up the Ladder (1900)

Chapter IX
In Search of Work

When Harry awoke the next morning, after a sound and refreshing sleep, the sun was shining brightly in at the window. He rubbed his eyes, and stared about him, not at first remembering where he was. But almost immediately recollection came to his aid, and he smiled as he thought of the eccentric old man whose guest he was. He leaped out of bed, and, quickly dressing himself, went downstairs. The fire was burning and breakfast was already on the table. It was precisely similar to the supper of the night previous. The old man sat at the fireside smoking a pipe.

"Good-morning," said Harry. "I am up late."

"It is no matter. You have a long journey before you, and it is well to rest before starting."

"Breakfast is ready," said the old man, hospitably.

Harry made a hearty breakfast. When it was over he rose to go.

"I must be going," he said. "Thank you for your kind entertainment. If you would allow me to pay you."

"I do not keep an inn," said the old man, with dignity.

Shaking the old man by the hand, he made his way across the fields to the main road. Looking back from time to time, he saw the old man watching him from his place in the doorway, his eyes shaded by his hand.

"He is the strangest man I ever saw," thought Harry. "Still he treated me kindly."

When he reached the road he saw, just in front of him, a boy of about his own age driving half a dozen cows before him.

"Hello!" he cried, by way of salutation.

"Hello!" returned the country boy. "Where are you going?"

"I don't know. Wherever I can find work," answered our hero.

The boy laughed. "Dad finds enough for me to do. I don't have to go after it. Haven't you got a father?"

"Yes."

"Why don't you work for him?"

"I want to work for pay."

"On a farm?"

"No. I'll work in a shoeshop if I get a chance or in a printing office."

"Do you understand the shoe business?"

"No; but I can learn."

"Where did you come from?"

"Granton."

Here the boy reached the pasture to which he was driving the cows, and Harry, bidding him good-by, went on his way. He felt fresh and vigorous, and walked ten miles before he felt the need of rest. He felt hungry, and the provision which he brought from home was nearly gone. There was a grocery store close at hand, and he went in, thinking that he would find something to help his meal. On the counter he saw some rolls, and there was an open barrel of apples not far off.

For four cents Harry made quite a substantial addition to his meal. As he left the store and walked up the road, with a roll in his hand, and eating an apple, he called to mind Benjamin Franklin's entrance of Philadelphia with a roll under each arm.

"I hope I shall have as good luck as Franklin had," he thought.

Walking slowly, he saw, on a small building which he had just reached, the sign, "Post Office."

"Perhaps the postmaster will know if anybody about here wants a boy," Harry said to himself.

He entered, finding himself in a small room, with one part partitioned off as a repository for mail matter. He stepped up to a little window, and presently the postmaster, an elderly man, presented himself.

"What name?" he asked.

"I haven't come for a letter," said Harry.

"What do you want, then?" asked the official.

"Do you know of anyone that wants to hire a boy?"

"Who's the boy?"

"I am. I want to get a chance to work."

"What kind of work?"

"Any kind that'll pay my board and a little over."

"I don't know of any place," said the postmaster, after a little thought.

"Isn't there any shoeshop where I could get in?"

"That reminds me—James Leavitt told me this morning that his boy was going to Boston to go into a store in a couple of months. He's been pegging for his father, and I guess they'll have to get somebody in his place."

Harry's face brightened at this intelligence.

"That's just the kind of place I'd like to get," he said. "Where does Mr. Leavitt live?"

"A quarter of a mile from here—over the bridge. You'll know it well enough. It's a cottage house, with a shoeshop in the back yard."

"Thank you, sir," said Harry. "I'll go there and try my luck."

"Wait a minute," said the postmaster. "There's a letter here for Mr. Leavitt. If you're going there, you may as well carry it along. It's from Boston. I shouldn't wonder if it's about the place Bob Leavitt wants."

"I'll take it with pleasure," said Harry.

It occurred to him that it would be a good introduction for him, and pave the way for his application.

He walked up the street, crossing the bridge referred to by the postmaster, and looked carefully on each side of him for the cottage and shop. As he neared the shop he heard a noise which indicated that work was going on inside. He opened the door and entered.

5

Of Factories and Failures:
Exploring the Invisible Factory Gates
of Horatio Alger, Jr.

Carol Nackenoff

Books promising to reveal the way to wealth have a long history in American culture, beginning with Benjamin Franklin's pamphlet by that title, which was published in 1747. Appealing to those with few family and social connections and to those with limited access to education, these guidebooks to prosperity held out the promise of lifting "self-made men" out of poverty and poorly paid employment into the world of independent wealth and respectability. While these manuals for success had little actual effect in a society in which social mobility had been sharply limited since the mid-eighteenth century, they nonetheless appealed to a wide readership of citizens who believed passionately in the American myth of success.

Among the most famous and popular of these handbooks for success were the 135 books penned by the late-nineteenth-century writer Horatio Alger, Jr. Following a prescribed formula, his "rags-to-riches" stories featured young boys of unimpeachable character ready to begin their journey through life with confident expectation. Like Christian in John Bunyan's perennially popular religious tract *The Pilgrim's Progress*, Alger's expectant lads confronted many temptations and a host of seedy characters intent on derailing their quest for success, but drawing on hard work and high moral principles, they always reached their final goal.

In this essay, Carol Nackenoff takes a fresh look at Alger's stories. Coupled with Alger's traditional advice to work hard and remain true to mainstream moral principles, she finds equally important advice to avoid the sort of factory work that was coming to dominate the age. Alger's message to American youth was clear: Factory work was unrespectable labor, and one could never pass through factory gates and find happiness and success inside.

....

What happens to the growing young boot-blacks, newsboys, and street urchins who surround the hero in Horatio Alger, Jr.'s Gilded Age tales? What lot falls to someone who does *not* succeed? What does success save Alger's heroes *from*? Such questions lead to a rather novel way of thinking about Alger's success formulas.

The Gilded Age characters of Horatio Alger, Jr. have long been treated as symbols of success, but that success is much misunderstood. A few astute readers have seen that, for Alger, the meaning of success is not identical with the acquisition of wealth. The stories stress the importance of morality, the prevalence of middle-class occupations and modest rewards, and the unattractiveness of selfish materialism. What has been less well recognized is Alger's rootedness in the economic transformations of the second half of the Nineteenth Century, and the role these transformations play in the definition of success.

It is my contention that, in Alger's fiction, economic success is measured against common and undesirable outcomes of the Gilded Age. The author of over one hundred juvenile tales arranged to rescue his characters from some of the worst consequences of an industrializing economy. Heroes acquire the ability to distance themselves from hardship, economic marginality, and instability which are ever-present in these novels. Failure is the backdrop against which success is defined in Alger's universe, and factory labor is clearly part of the lot one seeks to escape.

SAVED FROM THE FACTORY

In an Alger story serialized beginning December, 1892, Ben Bruce determines to leave the home of his mean stepfather. He meets a friend of his who is superintendent of a "factory for the manufacture of leather board." The superintendent asks the boy how he would like to work there. Ben Bruce, expressing a desire to secure a better education, nonetheless answers: "If the choice lies between working on a farm and working in your factory, I will work for you if I can get the chance." The starting wage is adequate, and the hero inquires whether he would be preparing himself for "higher" work; the superintendent answers in the affirmative. Just when it looks like they are about to strike a bargain, the dam which provides water power for the factory is blown up, apparently by two discharged workmen. Since the factory must be shut down until the dam is rebuilt, this ends the boy's hope of employment there. And so, Alger "blows up" this option rather than forsake Ben there. The boy is saved!

Though Alger frequently set his tales in late antebellum America, the factory was, even at that point, an inescapable presence in the northeastern landscape. Such boosters of industrialism as Edward Everett (for whom Alger would run errands as a Harvard freshman in 1848) could proclaim the factory at Lowell, begun in the second decade of the century, the "fulfillment of the American Revolution and a model of republicanism." But others were not so sanguine. Antebellum travellers to England worried over the poverty and moral debasement that accompanied industrialization and wondered whether they were looking at America's future and the demise of republican virtue. "The machine unmans the user," Emerson would write after his 1847 trip abroad. By the late 1830s, the vision of the American factory as a community was increasingly difficult to maintain in light of labor discontent, worker combinations, and emerging analyses of wage slavery.

The rare brick, furniture, or shoe manufactory in Alger stories still involved pre-industrial skilled craft work; mechanization had not appreciably altered the nature of work. At the outset of *Five Hundred Dollars* (serialized beginning 1889), Bert Barton is thrown out of work as a shoe pegger by the introduction of a machine. Though such effects of mechanization of a craft were hardly rare in the 1880s, this was an extremely rare occurrence in Alger's fiction.

A few Alger heroes begin work life in a factory, but circumstances (e.g., dullness in a trade; malicious intervention by the superintendent's son) quickly conspire to compel them to look for other work. One scholar notes:

> on the rare occasions when he [Alger] did [start a boy in a factory] he could only think to have the lad fired or laid off at the outset, as if desperate for some contrivance to expel him as quickly as possible into the world where a man could make his mark.

Alger's factory work is virtually never described. Often, the reader has no idea what is made, and is not taken into areas of production. The author exhibits little or no curiosity about this place of work. Robert Rushton, for instance, provides the chief support of his family by working in the factory in Millville. Beyond this, one learns only that the brick factory provided about the only avenue of employment to be had in town, that Robert was able to earn six dollars a week, and that tardiness resulted in a twenty-five cent docking.

Alger boys exit the factory; they do not seek to make their way within it. Heroes are not dependent upon factory work as the sole possible employment unless they confine their search to the local community in which they begin life. In Alger's city, there are other things to do.

When seeking work, the central character will often turn down manual labor or the opportunity to learn a craft or trade. The stinginess of the man to whom the hero would be apprenticed is sometimes adduced as the reason for refusal, or the boy might submit that he does not want to live away from his mother (which he inevitably chooses to do when he leaves for the city). Often he merely asserts that he doesn't believe he is cut out for certain types of work, or doesn't think he would like it. Alger heroes are clearly destined for another fate.

To what length Alger is willing to go to keep the boy afloat and away from the factory gates! The young hero may join a circus, or even whistle and give bird imitations on the stage for a living. When one nearly penniless boy claims to feel foolish playing the harmonica on stage for money, his companion replies: "it would be more ridiculous *not* playing for money. Whatever talents we possess our Creator meant us to exercise for our benefit and the pleasure of the community."

Alger's young boys not infrequently discover positions that do not pay a living wage, but they walk away. Even if they are hard up, they are never put into the position of having to accept anything that is offered. Something or someone intervenes to obviate the necessity of such a choice. Some choices are simply unacceptable. The factory, and working class jobs more broadly, fall into this category.

Once the boy gets to the city—which is most frequently New York—Alger provides quite a bit of detail about city sights, scenes, architecture, and prices. Some of these novels took the reader on a guided tour of Manhattan sights, with perhaps even an expedition by ferry to Brooklyn. More than one Alger enthusiast has claimed that these books were veritable Baedeker's guides. According to one:

> You could find out *what* to do, *where* to go, *how* to begin, and *how* to proceed in the city.... A young man from the country could brief himself on transportation around the city, the ways to obtain lodging and employment....

However, when Alger's heroes wander the streets in search of work, factories disappear. P.

T. Barnum's is there, but not its surroundings. One does not know who occupies factory positions or why but we know that heroes do not. To remove even the possibility of exchanging one's labor power for a wage in the factory, the factory must become invisible.

One of Alger's Chicago stories, *Luke Walton*, is deposited for copyright the same month and year that Carrie Meeber comes to Chicago in *Sister Carrie* (August, 1889). Luke sees many of the same new downtown sights Carrie does. Yet Dreiser's Carrie, who trudges the streets in search of work, could not avoid passing and viewing the manufacturing establishments on her long walk from home on the west side of the river to the downtown area. Unable to find a position as a shop girl, she eventually finds a poorly paid, unpleasant position manufacturing shoes. The factory girls she eventually leaves behind have little hope of betterment. Carrie could not help but see men toiling at heavy labor in the streets; poorly clad shop girls who worked so hard and had so little; the pale, ragged creatures in states of mental stupor who walked the streets or held out their hands for change. And yet, when Alger's newsboy walks home to his poor and unfashionable neighborhood, he does not seem to pass any factories or see the ways many people labor. Away from the bustling downtown commercial center, across the Chicago River, there is only the usual Alger drama.

One would hardly realize that Alger inhabited the same universe as Edward Bellamy, who published his extremely popular novel *Looking Backward* in 1888, purporting to solve the most pressing issue of the day—the labor problem. The era was notable for labor organization, strikes, and violence, but Alger allows almost no worker combinations on strikes to cross the pages of even his later novels. When one labor uprising is mentioned in *A Debt of Honor*, it is a passing reference by someone remote from the scene of action; the destruction of property noted above in *Ben Bruce* is extremely unusual.

Once jobs in factories, crafts, and trades drop from sight, career and earning trajectories of Alger characters do not mirror options in the economy. All his boys find employment in the white-collar workforce, though less than 20% of all workers are so employed by 1900. Boys are found earning at the high end of the scale for average weekly adult earnings during the period.

Engels had noted in 1845 that the structure of the city almost conspires to keep the manufacturing establishments and the squalid tenements of the poor out of view of the untroubled bourgeoisie, lining the streets with tidy shops and concealing what lies behind. Alger did see the tenements, and saw those left unemployed by panics and depressions; he even condemned those who did not see poverty or try to assist the worthy among the poor. But he did not see any pattern to poverty and unemployment among males that did not stem from character flaws. It is clear that, at least so far as concerns the factory, Alger's boys share the privileged gaze of the bourgeoisie.

FACTORIES AND FAILURE

This "blindness" is part of a pattern in Alger to go to great lengths to rescue heroes from the prospect of factory labor. Factory labor is something to be avoided or escaped. In part, this reflects the fact that Alger was the product of literary traditions which preceded realism. Though his most popular works tended to feature neglected street urchins of New York, he may well have believed some things were not the fit subject of discussion. William Dean Howells' literary realism had to do battle with an earlier faith; "in the strife-torn, graft-ridden years of the late Nineteenth Century, industrial society had understandably seemed to literary men an enemy, not a subject." The author E. C. Stedman, whom Alger greatly admired, expressed a wish to lift readers above the sordid details of contemporary life. Alger admired Howells, but his own literary work reflected more the views of the *Christian Union*:

> Realism . . . [seemed bent on] crowding the world of fiction with commonplace people whom one could positively avoid coming into contact with in real life; people without native sweetness or strength, without acquired culture or accomplishments, without the touch of the ideal which makes the commonplace significant and worthy of study.

Alger's heroes were always those exceptional boys, regardless of the economic circumstances in which they found themselves. The commonplace children were there, but not at center stage.

Alger did not think the factory offered a very good route of mobility. It did not nurture aspiration. Alger spent his youth in Marlboro, Massachusetts, which he remembered as engaging in shoe manufacturing. "Though diversified, the local economy was not immune to the cyclical fluctuations which plagued the shoe industry at large." Nearby towns, more dependent upon manufacture than Marlboro, suffered frequent cycles of boom and bust. When forced to shut down temporarily in a glutted market, an Alger shoemaker comments:

> That's the worst of the shoe trade. It isn't steady. When it's good everybody rushes into it, and the market soon gets overstocked. Then there's no work for weeks. If a man manages to save up a little money in good times, he has to spend it then. . . .

Alger's "experience" with manufacturing was that it did not provide a reliable income. Thus, heroes sought to escape business cycle fluctuations and discover steady work with reliable and rising wages. Boys sought careers at work.

Rosy depictions of factory opportunities were repeated throughout the century by industrialists and their supporters. They were even found in one advice manual Alger recommended to a young friend. Such depictions also provoked this 1889 response:

> If you tell a single concrete workman on the Baltimore and Ohio Railroad that he may yet be president of the company, it is not demonstrable that you have told him what is not true, although it is within bounds to say that he is far more likely to be killed by a stroke of lightning.

Alger seems to realize there is something in this position. He was not as positive as some of his contemporaries and at least a few later historians about opportunities in the nineteenth century factory. "We find that *many of our most conspicuous public men* have commenced their careers as newsboys," Alger was fond of repeating. He did not say "factory hands."

The bulk of evidence unturned by historians and sociologists would seem to be on his side. Scholars have tended to find that the route from shop hand to supervisor was neither quick nor terribly likely. There might be some upward mobility through positions, but downward mobility was perhaps as likely, and lateral movement from department to department was also common. Patronage was instrumental to advancement. A pioneer among these studies, examining mobility in Newburyport, Massachusetts, argues:

> Most of the social gains registered by laborers and their sons during these years were decidedly modest—a move one notch up the occupational scale, the acquisition of a small amount of property. Yet *in their eyes* these accomplishments must have loomed large.

Aside from the mobility issue, there were other reasons to bypass the factory. A significant element in Alger's elimination of this option lies in his distrust of capitalists. The term itself tends to connote for him selfish men who are unconcerned with the interests of their workers and who would readily exploit their dependence to depress their wages. They tend to worship money and ignore community. Capitalists lack respect for the exchange of equivalents, failing to pay labor at its value (whatever this means—Alger does not much trouble himself with the basis of wages or profits, but he believes workers deserve a living wage). They could choose to behave differently, but they have taken money out of proper perspective. Individuals who put money before people are anything but successes in Alger's universe, and he frequently arranges some sort of economic justice for them.

It is essential to Alger's formula for advancement that character be noticed. Character is the most valuable asset that the hero brings to the marketplace; its recognition becomes the means by which the boy rises. The factory system was surely not one to illustrate Alger's principle that, by application, hard work, cheerfulness, loyalty to one's employer, and honesty, any boy can hope to be noticed for his endeavors and advance. In the emerging industrial order, there was less opportunity for the individual to engage in personal contact with a boss, impress him, or employ his education or wits in new and different tasks. The factory wage labor system was impersonal, and offered workers limited scope within which to affect their destinies. The equivalents in market exchange were hides, not character.

It was not a world in which community of interest between employer and employee would endure. The boss who notices and rewards the trusted employee and who invites him home to dinner bridges the gap between social classes—in effect, negates the meaning of class. The only class worthy of mention is an aristocracy of character.

Factory labor was not likely to take a street-hardened hero without advantages and uplift him, exposing him to a better class of people who would encourage him to better himself. Without the human contact and example of men of good character, the factory would not nurture character or virtue. Even if indifferent workers might comply with factory discipline in order to keep their jobs, the work environment did not help make them men—it did not improve them, and hardened companions might even lead them astray. Those with power may well stand to affect the identity and morals of those over whom they exercise control. If capitalists and their factory agents do not stand for virtue, what will become of their employees?

Self-improvement was a moral imperative. Certain occupations were less desirable because they did not allow the youth to grow and improve by using his mind:

> Idealess occupations, associates, and books should be avoided, since they are not friendly to intelligent manhood and womanhood. Ideas make the wise man; the want of them the fool.

In the Harvard Unitarian tradition, "Man had both a mind (that is, a spirit) and a body, but his destiny clearly lay in developing the power of the former." Physical labor, while honorable, might not provide the opportunities necessary to development. Even if crafts or trades offered the prospect of steady work, there was perhaps inadequate opportunity for self-improvement; the case is similar to that of the factory.

Distaste for such labor was also linked to issues of power. The laborer tended to be subject to the close control of others and had little discretion. The Alger hero manages to find work in which he retains a great deal of control over his bodily movements and tasks, and in which mental and manual labor are not separated. Often, the employer sends the boy off as his agent in some business matter; the boy is highly independent and may even define the employer's interest in some cases.

Alger's guidance, however unwitting, is largely geared to escaping proletarianization. The successful attain middle class occupations and comforts while *avoiding* manufacturing establishment, crafts, and trades. Alger does not place his faith in opportunity in the growing productive sector, but with sectors engaged in the distribution and exchange of the new wealth of a capitalist economy. Merchandising, the growing trade sector, finance, banking, and real estate tend to provide the routes into middle class comforts for Alger's heroes.

Stories frequently end when the boy escapes economic marginalization. Beyond a "competence" and beyond comfort, money allowed one to help others. Success was measured by preservation and development of character, by escape from privation and insecurity, and by avoidance of the factory.

If a boy cultivates character and remembers duties and obligations, he is likely to improve his lot. Two benevolent merchants in New York who started out poor state the success formula and the nature of the aspirations particularly well:

> Most of the men in this city who have succeeded in business or in the professions started as poor boys. . . . There are the same chances now that there always were. Serve your employer well, learn business as rapidly as possible, don't fall into bad habits, and you'll get on.

CONCLUSION

Failure in Alger is linked with a transition from youth to adulthood without establishing secure, stable employment with opportunities for incremental advancement of one's wage. Failures continue not to know from whence their next meals come. Failures do not establish careers. Failures do not develop the personal relationship with employers that the hero does; they do not merit the attention of benefactors. Unconnected and alone, they are treated impersonally as labor. Those who do not succeed are buffeted about by the vicissitudes of the business cycle—cut adrift in times of depression without the means to fend for themselves. They have nothing to fall back on, and lack skills in high demand. Failures do not have bank accounts, and they do not own property. This certainly appears to describe the fate of those being incorporated into the industrial wage labor force.

It is against twin spectres of economic marginalization and proletarianization that economic success is defined. Both scenarios threaten the moral order. The Alger story takes a boy who has been cut adrift from the traditional economy and thus economically marginalized—and inserts him into the new economic world—bypassing the mines and factories.

The persisting invocation of the Alger story in American popular culture owes something to the continuing presence of outcomes and work environments to be avoided in an industrialized and deindustrializing economy. Employment instability, dead-end jobs, low wages, impersonalized work environments, and routinized activity are still present. A comforting measure of success lies in the fate one has eluded. In a world increasingly economically interdependent, the dream of interdependence and self-reliance—and of desirable, fulfilling work—may be all the more seductive.

GLOSSARY

Edward Everett (1794–1865): A clergyman, orator, educator, and diplomat whose many offices included U.S. representative from Massachusetts, minister to Great Britain, and secretary of state.

Ralph Waldo Emerson (1803–1882): One of America's most renowned writers and a central figure of American transcendentalism. His poems, orations, and especially his essays are regarded as landmarks in the development of American thought and literary expression.

P. T. Barnum (1810–1891): Early circus showman who established The Greatest Show on Earth in 1871 and in 1881 created the Barnum and Bailey Circus.

IMPLICATIONS

Nackenoff's essay raises the issue of social mobility in smokestack America. If, as she claims, Alger's stories warn the upwardly mobile against factory work, to what groups of Americans do you think Alger's stories appealed? Do you think people took Alger's advice to heart? Or did they simply read the stories for enjoyment?

PAST TRACES

Following the Civil War, the main focus of army activities turned to the western plains, where the army's new mission was to "protect" white immigrants and settlers and to move the 150,000 remaining Plains Indians onto government reservations. That Native Americans did not passively accept Washington's strategy is attested to by the numerous movements of cultural resurgence that punctuated the last decades of the nineteenth century. This reading is introduced by two documents, one stating the Native American position regarding ancient tribal lands and a second recalling the infamous army massacre of 300 Sioux men, women, and children following a cultural revival at Wounded Knee, South Dakota, in 1890.

Red Cloud (1890) and Flying Hawk (1936) on Wounded Knee

Red Cloud (1890)

I will tell you the reason for the trouble. When we first made treaties with the Government, our old life and our old customs were about to end; the game on which we lived was disappearing; the whites were closing around us, and nothing remained for us but to adopt their ways,—the Government promised us all the means necessary to make our living out of the land, and to instruct us how to do it, and with abundant food to support us until we could take care of ourselves. We looked forward with hope to the time we could be as independent as the whites, and have a voice in the Government.

The army officers could have helped better than anyone else but we were not left to them. An Indian Department was made with a large number of agents and other officials drawing large salaries—then came the beginning of trouble; these men took care of themselves but not of us. It was very hard to deal with the government through them—they could make more for themselves by keeping us back than by helping us forward.

We did not get the means for working our lands; the few things they gave us did little good.

Our rations began to be reduced; they said we were lazy. That is false. How does any man of sense suppose that so great a number of people could get work at once unless they were at once supplied with the means to work and instructors enough to teach them?

Our ponies were taken away from us under the promise that they would be replaced by oxen and large horses; it was long before we saw any, and then we got very few. We tried with the means we had, but on one pretext or another, we were shifted from one place to another, or were told that such a transfer was coming. Great efforts were made to break up our customs, but nothing was done to introduce us to customs of the whites. Everything was done to break up the power of the real chiefs.

Those old men really wished their people to improve, but little men, so-called chiefs, were made to act as disturbers and agitators. Spotted Tail wanted the ways of the whites, but an assassin was found to remove him. This was charged to the Indians because an Indian did it, but who set on the Indian? I was abused and slandered, to weaken my influence for good. This was done by men paid by the government to teach us the ways of the whites. I have visited many other tribes and found that the same things were done amongst them; all was done to discourage us and nothing to encourage us. I saw men paid by the government to help us, all very busy making money for themselves, but doing nothing for us. . . .

The men who counted (census) told all around that we were feasting and wasting food. Where did he see it? How could we waste what we did not have? We felt we were mocked in our misery; we had no newspaper and no one to speak for us. Our rations were again reduced.

You who eat three times a day and see your children well and happy around you cannot understand what a starving Indian feels! We were faint with hunger and maddened by despair. We held our dying children and felt their little bodies tremble as their soul went out and left only a dead weight in our hands. They were not very heavy but we were faint and the dead weighed us down. There was no hope on earth. God seemed to have forgotten.

Some one had been talking of the Son of God and said He had come. The people did not know; they did not care; they snatched at hope; they screamed like crazy people to Him for mercy they caught at the promise they heard He had made.

The white men were frightened and called for soldiers. We begged for life and the white men thought we wanted theirs; we heard the soldiers were coming. We did not fear. We hoped we could tell them our suffering and could get help. The white men told us the soldiers meant to kill us; we did not believe it but some were frightened and ran away to the Bad Lands. The soldiers came. They said: "don't be afraid—we come to make peace, not war." It was true; they brought us food. But the hunger-crazed who had taken fright at the soldiers' coming and went to the Bad Lands could not be induced to return to the horrors of reservation life. They were called Hostiles and the Government sent the army to force them back to their reservation prison.

Flying Hawk (1936)
This was the last big trouble with the Indians and soldiers and was in the winter in 1890. When the Indians would not come in from the Bad Lands, they got a big army together with plenty of clothing and supplies and camp-and-wagon equipment for a big campaign; they had enough soldiers to make a round-up of all the Indians they called hostiles.

The Government army, after many fights and loss of lives, succeeded in driving these starving Indians, with their families of women and gaunt-faced children, into a trap, where they could be forced to surrender their arms. This was on Wounded Knee creek, northeast of Pine Ridge, and here the Indians were surrounded by the soldiers, who had Hotchkiss machine guns along with them. There were about four thousand Indians in this big camp, and the soldiers had the machine guns pointed at them from all around the village as the soldiers formed a ring about the tepees so that Indians could not escape.

The Indians were hungry and weak and they suffered from lack of clothing and furs because the whites had driven away all the game. When the soldiers had them all surrounded and they had their tepees set up, the officers sent troopers to each of them to search for guns and take them from the owners. If the Indians in the tepees did not at once hand over a gun, the soldier tore open their parfleech trunks and bundles and bags of robes or clothes,—looking for pistols and knives and ammunition. It was an ugly business, and brutal; they treated the Indians like they would torment a wolf with one foot in a strong trap; they could do this because the Indians were now in the white man's trap,—and they were helpless.

Then a shot was heard from among the Indian tepees. An Indian was blamed; the excitement began; soldiers ran to their stations; officers gave orders to open fire with the machine guns into the crowds of innocent men, women and children, and in a few minutes more than two hundred and twenty of them lay in the snow dead and dying. A terrible blizzard raged for two days covering the bodies with Nature's great white blanket; some lay in piles of four or five; others in twos or threes or singly, where they fell until the storm subsided. When a trench had been dug of sufficient length and depth to contain the frozen corpses, they were collected and piled, like cord-wood, in one vast icy tomb. While separating several stiffened forms which had fallen in a heap, two of them proved to be women, and bugged closely to their breasts were infant babes still alive after lying in the storm for two days in 20° below zero weather.

I was there and saw the trouble,—but after the shooting was over; it was all bad.

6

Lozen: An Apache Woman Warrior

Laura Jane Moore

In 1893, Frederick Jackson Turner, a young historian at the University of Wisconsin, proclaimed the closing of the American frontier. The 1890 census, he argued, had revealed all of America to now be a settled land; the frontier that had defined America since the seventeenth century no longer existed. Turner advanced his thesis from the perspective of white America, making no connection in his thesis between the closing of the frontier and the final displacement of the Plains Indians, the last remaining large-scale contingent of Native Americans in the United States. What Turner had ignored was that the true meaning of the "closing" of the frontier had been the destruction through disease and warfare of the Plains and southwestern bands—the Sioux, Cheyennes, Crows, and Navahos—and their confinement on desolate and isolated reservations.

This, the final stage in a national program of western expansion and Native American displacement that had begun in the trans-Appalachian west during the 1780s, gained renewed force following the Civil War. In 1867, federal Indian policy turned increasingly toward forced segregation, federal supervision, and the forced education of children designed to suppress and eventually eradicate Indian culture and ways of life. Then, with the completion of the transcontinental railroad in 1869, settlers flooded the Plains and the Southwest, putting further pressure on the native residents. At the same time, the railroads also allowed soldiers to move rapidly and efficiently, enhancing their ability to enforce federal Indian policy. The arrival of the railroads and settlers dealt a final blow to the traditional Plains economy, as army-supported hunters nearly exterminated the buffalo, the Plains Indians' primary source of meat and leather. Where perhaps as many as 40 million buffalo had ranged the plains in the early nineteenth century, by 1895 fewer than a thousand remained.

Native American resistance had grown alongside this century-long program of displacement, beginning with the Miami and Shawnee defeat of General Josiah Harman's American army in 1790 and ending with the massacre at Wounded Knee,

South Dakota, in 1890. In those years, hundreds of young warriors had aggressively defended their people and their lands by a creative combination of military engagement and negotiation. In this essay, Laura Jane Moore tells the story of one of these warriors, the Apache war leader Lozen. Like most Native American warriors, Lozen chose the warrior's path early in life and endured privation and demanding training regimens in the process of becoming a full-fledged warrior. What made Lozen unusual—though not unique—was that she was a women. As Moore shows, Native American conceptions of gender were flexible enough to incorporate women warriors, shamans, and occasional chiefs into their communities.

....

During the waning days of the nineteenth-century Indian wars, five thousand American soldiers pursued a band of thirty-six Apache men, women, and children. Led by the chief Naiche and the shaman Geronimo, the group had holed up in the Sierra Madre mountains in northern Mexico. These Apaches never suffered a decisive defeat, but by the summer of 1886 they were tired of running and wanted to be reunited with their families back on the reservation. Two women assumed the dangerous mission of approaching United States troops in order to begin negotiations. While the American soldiers proudly recorded the names of the Apache men whom they met during these military campaigns, only Apache oral traditions identify Lozen and Dahteste as the "squaws" who played such an important role. Well suited to their task, the women were fighting members of the band, able to defend themselves and speak for their people. Each no doubt carried a knife, rifle, and cartridge belt, but since they were women, the soldiers did not assume that they posed much threat.

Both Lozen and Dahteste stepped outside the position usually occupied by Apache women, and both of them fought bravely in battles against U.S. and Mexican troops. Dahteste had found her way to warfare, as Apache women often did, by extending her role as a wife and accompanying her husband, Anandia, on raids and war expeditions. Lozen was more unusual. Probably in her forties in the 1880s, she had never married and had no children. Lozen's choice to opt out of the roles typically adopted by Apache women,

however, did not lead to her marginalization or degradation within her Apache community. Rather, she became one of the most revered Apache warriors of the late nineteenth century. As a woman warrior, she possessed qualities that Apaches associated with both men and women that, in their eyes, made her especially powerful. Convinced that she was responsible for much of their success against their enemies, her comrades and kin celebrated her spiritual power and physical prowess. Geronimo and the rest of the group knew they could trust her to represent them to the American soldiers.

Lozen's life exemplifies the permeability of gender roles in a complex Native American culture even when those roles seem to be rigidly defined. Anthropologists describe Apaches as having strict divisions between men and women who performed different work and even occupied separate space in dwellings. "The feeling is," explained one Apache, "that a man should go his way with his friends and a woman her way with her friends." This separation of the sexes was extreme enough that it made men and women quite shy in the presence of each others. Unmarried women, in particular, refrained from spending time with men. Moreover, kin relations imposed further expectations of avoidance. Once grown, brothers and sisters dodged each other's company. Since Apaches considered people whom Euro-Americans call cousins to be siblings, avoidance often extended to many people. "If we even spoke" to the adolescent girls, recalled one Apache man of his own youth, "we could do so only with a bush between us, and back to back."

In contrast to these rules, Lozen was an unmarried woman who rode with male warriors by the side of her brother, the chief Victorio. She was an important enough member of the fighting force that Victorio called her "my right hand. . . . Strong as a man, braver than most, and cunning in strategy." By adopting the unusual but respected role of a woman warrior, Lozen stood in a powerful cross-gender position from which she could act as "a shield to her people."

Lozen and Victorio were Chiricahua Apaches, one of seven different Apachean tribes that lived in the southwestern United States. In the mid-nineteenth century the Chiricahuas occupied an area west of the Rio Grande, including what is now southwestern New Mexico, southeastern Arizona, and part of the Mexican borderlands. The Chiricahuas were highly decentralized and did not necessarily recognize each other as related, even if anthropologists have identified them as the same cultural group. Four major bands of Chiricahuas occupied this area: the Chihene, the Bedonkohe, the Chokonen, and the Nednai. These bands were composed of local groups that in turn each consisted of ten to thirty extended families. Most activities, including marriages, were carried out within the local group. Raiding and war parties, for example, usually were composed of members of a family or local group. Within a local group, a leader or "chief" gained prominence and influence through personal traits of generosity, bravery, integrity, eloquence, and ceremonial knowledge. By 1870, Victorio had assumed a leadership role in one of these local groups, the Warm Springs Apaches.

Apaches organized their society around a sexual division of labor embodied in the matrilocal extended family. That is, when a man married a woman, they lived near her mother. Generally property also followed a matrilineal line. The women of an extended family worked together gathering and processing the wild plants that were an essential food source. Meanwhile, men of the same family hunted in pairs or small groups, providing the game that supplemented their diet. Despite the disruptions of reservations and warfare in the late nineteenth century, Apaches living on reservations maintained this social organization. For example, Charlie Smith remembered that sometime in the 1880s his family received permission from the Indian agent to travel to an area where there was a good piñon crop. In the morning "usually by twos, the men left to hunt. . . . The women also divided into small groups." They brought the young children along and followed trails of pack rats to their dens, where they could sometimes gather as many as two gallons of nuts from one nest. They also placed skins under piñon trees and beat the lower branches to gather more nuts. "When the men returned in the evening, the women dressed the game" and began the process of tanning the hides.

The sexual division of labor did not put women in a subordinate position to men, but instead led to complementary roles for women and men. Women controlled a family's economic activities and managed its wealth; men, more mobile in their responsibilities for hunting and raiding, took command of relations with those outside the group. With marriage, a man assumed obligations not only to his wife but to her extended family as well, obligations that divorce or a wife's death did not automatically terminate. Though marriage for Euro-American women meant economic and legal dependence in this period, in many ways it was the opposite for Apache women. Marriage did, however, lead Apache women to be assigned certain roles within the community, roles that an unmarried woman such as Lozen could eschew, especially the domestic tasks of food preparation, child care, and house building.

Lozen's orientation toward more typically male activities probably emerged during her childhood. When they were small, girls and boys played together and competed in foot races. When they were about six, however, the community began to separate them. During puberty, girls were initiated into womanhood and boys into manhood, and they then avoided each other's company except within strict limits. Lozen apparently did not make this transition, but instead continued to participate in the boys' activities. She was not castigated for her seemingly masculine skills. After all, girls were "urged to be strong and fast. It is simply accepted," the anthropologist Morris Opler explained, that some individuals "have carried the requirement further than is strictly necessary. The attitude of those discussing them is never one of ridicule or condemnation but rather one of admiration." Eventually even girls who excelled at masculine pursuits usually married and entered into typically female roles. Lozen, instead, remained unmarried and became a warrior. That this was the right choice for her may well have been confirmed during puberty.

When a girl began to menstruate, it was a cause for celebration. A crowd of relatives, friends, and members of neighboring communities attended an elaborate four-day ceremony in her honor. During the ceremony the girl became "White Painted Woman," the central Chiricahua deity, and emerged at the end as a woman. No moment so definite as a girl's first period signaled when a boy was ready to make the transition to adulthood. Instead, once he was strong enough, perhaps when he was about fifteen, he volunteered to become an apprentice warrior. He then had to participate in four raids during which he followed special rules, used a special apprentice's language, and was called "Child of the Water" after the son of White Painted Woman. Once he had successfully joined four raids, he was considered a full-fledged warrior.

We can only speculate, based on what we know of Chiricahua culture, about Lozen's youth and how she chose the route of the woman warrior. Perhaps not long after her puberty ceremony Lozen volunteered to become an apprentice warrior, and the men in her family, recognizing her unusual talents with horses and hunting, agreed. It is also likely that she acquired the spiritual power that contributed to her skill as a warrior during adolescence, another sign, perhaps, that she was well suited for the alternative life of a woman warrior.

Both men and women had access to the supernatural world that infused nature. Apaches tapped into this power through visions that sometimes occurred in dreams but often were brought on by fasting in isolation during a "vision quest." In such a vision a supernatural force visited, usually in the guise of an animal, and taught the person a ceremony by which he or she could call on the force for aid. This ceremonial knowledge or "power" was an individual's own, and it normally could not be passed on or shared. Still, Apaches understood that their power was to be used for the good of their community. Those who did not were witches. Apaches might go on vision quests in order to make contact with the supernatural world, but they could not choose winch "power" would visit them. Most of these powers involved healing. Some Apaches also could call on the supernatural world to help them diagnose illness, find lost objects, even withstand bullets.

Ceremonial knowledge was an essential complement to a warrior's physical skills and intelligence. Geronimo based his leadership role, for example, on his abilities as a shaman. He had the power to foretell the result of a battle and to "handle men." Another chief, Chihuahua, had "the Power over horses" so that he "could gentle and ride the wildest" and "heal them of sickness or wounds." The chief Nana's "Power was over ammunition trains and rattlesnakes." Even when he was over eighty and crippled, he could make a successful raid for ammunition when younger men failed.

Lozen had the ability, through ceremony, to ask for supernatural aid in locating the enemy. The power that she received related to warfare, and so it may have helped confirm her special standing as a woman warrior. She summoned this power through a ritual in which she stood with arms outstretched and palms up. As she turned slowly in a circle, she sang a prayer such as:

Upon this earth
On which we live
Ussen has Power
This Power is mine
For locating the enemy
Which only Ussen the great
Can show to me.

During this ceremony a tingling in her palms indicated the direction and distance to the enemy. If the enemy were very near, her palms would turn purple.

Lozen's ceremony illustrates central aspects of the Apache worldview. Her power stemmed from her relationship with the supernatural, called in this case Ussen, the life-giver. Through her individual vision quest she had obtained the ability to manipulate this power, which she used to help her community. In another of her prayers she sang, "Ussen has Power. Sometimes He shares it. . . . This Power he has given me [f]or the benefit of my people. . . . This Power I may use [f]or the good of my people."

Shamans whose ceremonial knowledge related to warfare, such as Lozen's, always accompanied war expeditions, which departed only after certain ritualistic dances and singing were held. While both women and men had equal access to the supernatural world, traditionally warfare was strictly in the male domain, an extension of men's roles in hunting and raiding from which women were normally excluded. This exclusion stemmed from women's reproductive abilities, which made them especially powerful but also potentially dangerous to men, particularly men at war. Because menstruation was so powerful and so uniquely female, it could also cause harm. Boys learned early that contact with menstrual blood would make their joints swollen and painful and that sex with a menstruating woman could lead to deformity. The bodily discharge that accompanied childbirth was equated with menstrual blood, so men were well advised to avoid it. In other words, at the moments when a woman was most a woman, at menstruation and childbirth, she was also most dangerous to men. The rheumatism or

deformed joints that resulted from such contact would, in turn, hinder a man's ability to perform his duties as a warrior and hunter. The necessary separation of the sexes, however, could be bridged by a woman warrior such as Lozen. Her skills as a warrior would not be compromised by contact with women, for she shared their unique powers as well. Her powerful cross-gender position combined the most respected aspects of Apache femininity and masculinity.

As a warrior, Lozen displayed impressive talent at the masculine pursuits of hunting, raiding, and warfare. While raiding was a means to obtain supplies and, like hunting, an economic activity, a war party exacted revenge when a member of the group was killed. Apaches explained that "it is the duty of a man to avenge injury to his relatives." Moreover, "when the enemy does something, there have got to be consequences. If there aren't, things get out of balance. Pretty soon everything is upset." Apaches went to war, therefore, to preserve a necessary balance. War parties also reflected Apaches' kin-based social organization: "The relatives of the father of the dead person or of his wife get it started and try to enlist as many as possible."

Although women did not typically participate in war parties, they were as concerned as men were with the importance of exacting revenge. Sometimes women called for the organization of war parties. Sometimes married women followed the expedition in order to provide domestic services such as cooking or dressing wounds. And occasionally women who had accompanied their husbands found themselves participating in the fighting. If her husband were killed, for example, a wife might take his place and personally assume the task of avenging his death. Indeed, it was far easier for women to cross into the men's domain than for men to assume typically female tasks. Whether warriors or not, women needed to be prepared to participate in skirmishes, to handle weapons, and to defend themselves and their families. But even if respected for fighting bravely beside her husband, a woman observed the strict rules that governed relations between the sexes while raiding or warring. Warriors practiced strict sexual abstinence before and during war expeditions because a woman's strength could impede a man's. "Women could go with their husbands, but they could not live together," one Apache later explained.

Women's ability to participate in raids and war parties may have increased in the late nineteenth century. After the United States won the Southwest from Mexico at midcentury and increasing numbers of Angles began passing through and settling there, the U.S. military waged a campaign to move the various Native American residents onto reservations. The land set aside for reservations was often far from traditional homelands, overcrowded with a conglomeration of traditionally hostile Indian groups, and incapable of supporting the numbers expected to live there. During the last few decades of the century, various bands alternatively fought and negotiated with U.S. troops, agreeing to live on reservation lands for a time and then leaving when their situation became untenable.

Apache groups that resisted reservation life had to be increasingly mobile to elude capture. Warfare severely circumscribed life for Apaches on the run. If families were to stay together, women and children often had little choice but to accompany warriors. Constant movement and the possibility of attack and capture made it difficult for women to perform their normal productive roles as gatherers and processors of food. Raiding instead became the main means of obtaining food and other supplies, especially the all-important horses and ammunition that were necessary to keep up the fight. Not only did women participate in raids and skirmishes themselves but they dug trenches and acted as lockouts and scouts. It was not easy to keep warriors' activities within war parties separate from the activities of women and children. Charlie Smith remembered that frequently "Geronimo had the women and children along. . . . If pursued he, as did all Apaches, tried to

protect them by sending them ahead; but ordinarily, when fighting occurred, it was because he laid an ambush, and every one of the band was there." He added that "some of the women were very good shots," Lozen most of all.

In 1870 the Warm Springs Apaches had agreed to live on a reservation called Ojo Caliente (Warm Springs) within their traditional lands in southwestern New Mexico. Because of bureaucratic complications between Washington, D.C., and the presiding military officers, along with the hostility of the local American and Mexican population, the site of the reservation kept changing. But the elder Warm Springs leader, Loco, and the younger and more hotheaded Victorio kept their bands settled and at peace with the American troops. Then in 1875 the American authorities began a new policy of trying to concentrate all Apaches on one reservation, called San Carlos, along the Gila River in eastern Arizona, far from where the Chiricahuas had agreed to live. Ace Daklugie, whose parents were Geronimo's sister, Ishton, and the Nednai chief, Juh, later claimed that it "was the worst place in all the great territory stolen from the Apaches." No one had lived there permanently before because there was no grass and no game, and the only vegetation was cacti. "The heat was terrible. The insects were terrible. The water was terrible. What there was in the sluggish river was brackish and warm. . . . Insects and rattlesnakes seemed to thrive there." James Kaywaykla, who was a few years younger than Daklugie, recalled the malaria, summer temperatures reaching well over a hundred degrees, and insects that "almost devoured the babies." At San Carlos, disease-ridden, inadequately supplied, and overcrowded with different Indian groups who were unfamiliar, suspicious, or even overtly hostile toward each other, Chiricahuas found themselves hungry, sick, and tense. The Warm Springs Apaches tried to live there for a time, but many found it intolerable. Loco and his followers, determined to pursue peace with the Americans, decided to remain, but at least three hundred others, including Victorio's band, left in 1877. Many of them were caught or killed; others made it across the border into Mexico.

Victorio's band eventually returned to their old reservation, Ojo Caliente, which the military had shut down, and indicated their willingness to surrender but not to live at San Carlos. Some of the Warm Springs group, following another chief, Nana, registered at the Mescalero reservation in New Mexico, while Victorio continued to pressure American officials to honor their promise of the Ojo Caliente land. Meanwhile, other Chiricahua leaders, including Juh and Geronimo, were arrested and imprisoned at San Carlos. In July 1879 the Warm Springs band heard a rumor that Victorio was to be arrested too, and the group again left the reservation and fled into the mountains. While family members hid in caves, Victorio and about sixty warriors attacked a contingent of cavalrymen near their old reservation. This battle opened a bloody war in which the Warm Springs Apaches fought to avenge the deaths of their kin and to live where they chose.

When the Apaches fled from the reservations, they left quietly at night in small scattered groups in order to evade pursuit. Their means of escape reflected their gender organization. Women took charge of helping young boys and girls and moved separately from the warriors. Kaywaykla's grandmother woke him one night and told him they were leaving. He had his emergency rations handy. At first she carried the sleepy boy on her back as they ran, and then they crawled slowly. Shielded from sight by mesquite and cactus, they froze when they heard a jingle of metal indicating that soldiers were nearby. They traveled carefully for a few days before they rendezvoused with the rest of their band on the banks of a swollen river.

While deeply ingrained ideas about the proper roles of women and men influenced this dangerous flight, the story also suggests the permeability of those roles. Kaywaykla's grandmother took charge of his safety because his mother accompanied her husband and the other warriors. When they reached the river, Kaywaykla's parents were there, as were the leaders Nana and Victorio. Kaywaykla spoke only briefly with his mother. When he later asked for her, his grandmother explained that "she rides with your father and Nana on another raid."

Meanwhile, the women and children needed to cross the river before the cavalry discovered them. Kaywaykla's grandmother tried to lead her horse into the water, but it balked. They seemed to be stuck in this dangerous position, between the rising water and the American soldiers who could find them there at any time. But then arrived "a magnificent woman on a beautiful black horse—Lozen, sister of Victorio. Lozen, the woman warrior!" She held her rifle over her head as she turned her horse into the torrent, and it began to swim against the current. The others followed across safely, with Lozen having to rescue just one horse and rider who began to wash downstream. On the other side of the river, Lozen gave Kaywaykla's grandmother instructions: "You take charge now," she said. "I must return to the warriors." She told the older woman to hurry to Salinas Peak, their "Sacred Mountain in the San Andres," taking only short stops along the way, and then to wait there for Nana. "We can spare no men," she explained, "but the young boys will obey your orders. . . . I go to join my brother." The success of this escape relied on Lozen's skill with horses, her physical strength, the trust that the other Apaches placed in her, and her ability to move between the worlds of women and warriors.

Normally only married women could ride with the warriors. But Lozen was not a normal woman. "No," Charlie Smith explained, "she never married. But to us she was as a Holy Woman and she was regarded and treated as one. White Painted Woman herself was not more respected." Kaywaykla agreed that although "she had not married, she went on the warpath with the men, which no woman other than the wives of warriors was permitted to do; and she was held in the greatest respect by them, much as though she were a holy person." He also remembered Lozen participating in the council of leaders as they deliberated about whether to return to the reservation or continue their fight. Lozen's position indicates that, even if men usually controlled politics, a person earned a place at the council fire not by one's biological sex, but by being a successful warrior, which required physical prowess, intelligence, and integrity. "No other woman" was "bidden to the council, but that was because no other had the skill as a warrior that Lozen did." Lozen's unusual position rested on a confluence to cultural, historical, and individual factors. Apache culture's flexibility allowed and even respected her unusual choice, and her physical and spiritual skills made her an asset to the beleaguered Chiricahuas, whose numbers in the 1870s and 1880s were depleted. Those skills were apparently extraordinary. "She could ride, shoot, and fight like a man; and I think she had more ability in planning military strategy than did Victorio," Kaywaykla recalled.

While Apache girls and boys, men and women, were expert riders, horses were especially associated with men and their roles in hunting, raiding, and warfare. Lozen was a renowned raider, thanks in large part to her skills with horses. She likely was the woman that cavalry officer John C. Cremony remembered "as one of the most dextrous horse thieves and horse breakers in the tribe, [who] seldom permitted an expedition to go on a raid without her presence." Ace Daklugie remembered her taking advantage of a melee between soldiers and Indians at San Carlos to grab some much needed ammunition. She and another warrior, Sanchez, "swooped down on the horse herd and drove a bunch off. They wanted especially the ammunition mules, for they had not yet been unloaded. . . . I do know that they got a good supply of ammunition." Kaywaykla, too, emphasized her ability to catch horses. She "was expert at roping. . . . No man in the tribe

was more skillful in stealing horses or stampeding a herd than she."

One particularly dramatic example of Lozen's talent, and how she chose to use it, occurred during the summer of 1880 while the Warm Springs band made its way into West Texas and then toward Mexico, pursued closely by American troops. Lozen dropped out of the main group in order to help a pregnant Mescalero Apache woman who had gone into labor. The two women hid just out of sight of the cavalry, and then Lozen helped the woman deliver her baby. They had not taken any horses, fearing that the soldiers would notice the tracks and realize that someone had separated from the group. They had limited food and no water, and the distance between water holes was too great to make on foot. When they spotted a herd of cattle, Lozen killed a longhorn with her knife, "a feat that few men would undertake," but they still could not travel far without water. They hid alongside the Rio Grande and observed a camp of Mexicans on the opposite bank. Lozen decided to steal one of their horses. She cut a strip from the longhorn's hide to fashion into a bridle, waited for nightfall, and swam across the rushing river. The men slept around the fire, white one guarded the horses hobbled not far away. She waited until the guard started toward the fire and then "crept softly" to the "powerful steed" she had selected. "When she bent to cut the hobbles it snorted and plunged. She leaped to its back and turned it toward the river. Bullets whizzed past her head as the horse slid down the bank and plunged into the water." She was scrambling up the opposite bank before the men could follow. By the time the sun rose, the two women, the infant, and their new horse were far away.

Their ordeal, however, had not yet ended. The American troops had received reinforcements, who were guarding every water hole and had inadvertently cut off the women's path back to their band. Lozen guided the woman and her newborn by a stealthy and circuitous route back to the Mescalero reservation, which took several more weeks and involved stealing another horse on the way.

Because Lozen was both a warrior and a woman, her cross-gender position made it possible for her to protect the Mescalero woman as a man normally would and to help her deliver her baby, which, because of the association with menstrual blood, would have been perilous for a man. Lozen, like many women, had ceremonial healing powers and may have known some of the ritual with which Apaches greeted a new life. At the same time, her skill as a warrior shielded the woman who was forced to give birth under particularly dangerous and unusual circumstances.

While Lozen and the new mother sneaked past enemy lines and made their way slowly to the Mescalero reservation, U.S. troops chased Victorio, Nana, and the rest of the band into Mexico. Previously, the Americans had not been able to follow them over the border, but Mexico and the United States had just instituted a treaty by which American troops were allowed to enter Mexican territory in pursuit of hostile Indians. The Apaches, low on ammunition, food, and water, camped on the slopes of a three-peak mountain range called Tres Castillos that rose out of the parched desert in the Mexican state of Chihuahua. Here their extraordinary ability to evade their pursuers finally failed. Mexican forces, who were the first to find them, attacked at dawn on October 15. At the end of this bloody battle, perhaps eighty Apaches lay dead and about seventy more, including Kaywaykla's grandmother, were captured and marched to the Mexican city, Chihuahua, where they were sold into slavery. Among the dead was Victorio.

"Many of the old Apaches," Ace Daklugie explained, "are convinced that, had [Lozen] been with Victorio at Tres Castillos, there would have been no ambush." She was missed not so much for her fighting skills—the band was outnumbered and trapped among the boulders on the mountain slope, an impossible situation for the best warrior—as for her ceremonial power to locate the enemy. If she had been there, they believed, she would have anticipated the attack, and they could have escaped.

Lozen learned of her people's demoralizing defeat and her brother's death when she reached the Mescalero reservation. Leaving the mother and infant there, she headed south to find the remnants of the band, which was still unwilling to return to reservation life. An older chief, Nana, had been on a raid for ammunition during the battle and now led the group as it avenged Victorio's death.

Meanwhile, other Chiricahuas, including Geronimo, were living restlessly at San Carlos. There the "repugnant natural conditions" were exacerbated by "intrigue, intertribal rivalries, incompetent and corrupt agents, and conflict between civil and military officials." Moreover, land-hungry, Indian-hating white settlers ringed its boundaries. Tensions were already high when, in August 1881, the army tried to arrest a Western Apache shaman whose preaching seemed to the officials to have dangerously antiwhite overtones. Fighting broke out between the army and the shaman's followers, and the shaman, his wife, and several other Apaches were shot and killed. Lozen may have been visiting the reservation, as one Apache placed her theft of the ammunition laden mules at this time. About seventy Chiricahuas, including Geronimo and other leaders, broke out and headed for Mexico.

They arrived in the Sierra Madre mountains, where the elderly Nednai Apache leader, Juh, was now living. He welcomed straggling groups of recalcitrant Apaches including Nana's Warm Springs band. Juh, too, had given up his attempt, to live at San Carlos and had escaped to the Sierra Madres where his people had lived for generations. The mountains provided an impregnable natural fortress. Various leaders from different Apache bands, local groups, and tribes deferred to Juh. When he died suddenly, Naiche, the son of Cochise (a respected Apache leader who had been killed some years earlier), assumed the role of chief, but Geronimo, by virtue of his military leadership and stronger spiritual power, increasingly became the most important leader.

The Apaches used their natural fortress as a base from which to launch daring raids. In the spring of 1882 Geronimo led sixty warriors back to San Carlos where they killed the police chief and enticed several hundred more Chiricahuas to join them in Mexico. In response the American troops launched an all-out offensive, led by General George Crook, to recapture and subdue the last of the in Apaches once and for all.

Crook was never able to administer a decisive defeat, but thanks to Apache scouts working for the U.S. army, he was able to keep the "hostiles" on the run. Constant pursuit and the coming winter made the reservation seem more appealing. It was the summers at San Carlos that the Chirtcahuas feared the most, when the heat and malaria-carrying mosquitoes were most dangerous. Winter in the mountains could be harsh, especially when they were so short on supplies. And so, according to Apache memory, Lozen and Dahteste began the negotiations for their people's return. The Apaches reached a deal by which about three hundred of the renegade Chiricahuas moved to an area called Turkey Creek near Fort Apache, on much more appealing land north of San Carlos. Kaywaykla, now old enough to be a young warrior himself, remembered his people settling happily at Turkey Creek and planting successful crops.

But the old reservation tensions resurfaced almost immediately. The agents heard whisperings of insurrection, and the Indians heard rumors that their leaders were to be arrested and imprisoned at Alcatraz Island in San Francisco Bay. Moreover, the military took it upon themselves to interfere more than ever before in the Apaches' family life, policing domestic conflicts normally regulated through the 'kin-based community structure. In May of 1885, fearing arrest, Geronimo and Naiche fled the reservation once again with approximately 140 followers including Lozen and about forty other warriors. The majority of Chiricahuas remained at San Carlos. Those who escaped leaded back to the fortress of the Sierra Madres. And once again, they left in small groups, the women leading the children. Most of the soldiers pursued the warriors, but a number of women and children were shot or recaptured. General Crook, with his Apache scouts, pursued them for almost a year until a woman, probably Lozen, brought word that again they were ready to negotiate.

Crook met with them on March 25, 1886. Once again, he had administered no decisive defeat so the Chiricahuas were in a strong negotiating position. The Apaches' desire to restore ties of kin and community motivated them to reach an agreement. According to the new deal, the renegades would go to prison in the east for two years, after which they would be permitted to live freely with their families at Turkey Creek. The Indians retained their arms as they began to move north toward the border, but they remained suspicious. While the majority of the group continued on with the troops, Geronimo and Naiche changed their minds and took off again with a handful of their followers. Lozen, as usual, was at their side.

As it turned out, Geronimo and his followers were right to be suspicious of the terms of their surrender. Crook's superiors, General Philip Sheridan and President Grover Cleveland, repudiated the arrangements that Crook had made. They had no intention of releasing these infamous Apache warriors after two years. In anger and embarrassment, Crook resigned, while his replacement, General George Miles, led an augmented force of 5,000 soldiers against the thirty-six men, women, and children who bad returned once more to the Sierra Madres. And, again, the American troops, despite their numbers and constant replenishment of supplies, could not defeat the Apaches.

In late August 1886, Lozen and Dahteste, for the final time, assumed the task of opening negotiations. For several days, Lieutenant Charles B. Gatewood, with whom the Apaches had dealt before, and two Apache scouts called Martine and Kayitah followed the women into the mountains, toward the hidden camp. The scouts, carrying a white flag, went ahead up the steep and winding trail. The warriors observed the scouts climb, first with field glasses and then, as the two men got closer, with bare eyes, and they recognized them. The fugitives debated whether or not to shoot them, but decided to admit them to the camp only because Martine was a Nednai and related to one of the warriors.

Geronimo and Naiche's band thought they were in a strong position to negotiate their return to Turkey Creek to join their families, but they were stunned by the news that all the Chiricahuas had been rounded up and sent to Florida. The prisoners included those who had remained in good faith on the reservation the whole time and even the Apache scouts who had served in the U.S. army. The very scouts who had found their hiding place and who had been promised land at Turkey Creek would, it turned out, be imprisoned in Florida. No Chiricahuas would remain in the Southwest. If they wanted to rejoin their kin, this last free group had to go east as well. They agreed to surrender personally to General Miles and, on September 3, 1886, laid down their arms for the last time. Five days later they were train-bound for Florida, and the Indian wars ended.

On the way to Florida, the train stopped near the Nueces River in Texas where a photographer captured a group of the Apaches sitting in front of a railroad car. Naiche, as the chief, sits in the center of the front row, with Geronimo in the place of honor at his left. Lozen is there too, in the only photograph ever taken of her. She is to Geronimo's left, a place reserved for one's second in command, but behind him as well, with women and girls on either side of her. Her face is calm, although her brow is furrowed. None of the captives betray their feelings to the photographer, but Lozen's stance, leaning slightly forward, seems a ready and restless pose, as though she

remains prepared to protect either the girls who hide slightly behind her shoulders or to join the warriors in front of her.

Crowded into Florida's Fort Marion and Fort Pickens, accustomed to the dry climate of their homeland, the Chiricahuas suffered in Florida's heat and humidity. Tuberculosis, malaria, and smallpox took a heavy toll. By 1890, 119 of the 498 Chiricahuas who had been shipped to Florida had died. Their condition, especially the treatment of scouts who had served the American military faithfully, caused a public outcry led by General Crook. In 1887 and 1888, they were moved to the Mount Vernon barracks near Mobile, Alabama, which turned out to be just as miserable and unhealthy, and then, in 1894, to Fort Sill in Oklahoma. Finally, in 1913 the remaining Chiricahua Apaches were given their freedom and the choice of land near Fort Sill or a reservation in south-central New Mexico that they would share with the Mescalero Apaches. While some remained in Oklahoma, the majority returned to New Mexico, where their descendants still live. It was far too late, however, for Lozen. She had survived as far as Alabama, but there, like so many of those she had fought with and for, she succumbed to the "coughing sickness" and died of tuberculosis.

The story of the Apache Indian wars is often told as a heroic struggle among men with legendary names: Geronimo, Victorio, Crook, Miles. It is too easy to forget that at the heart of the wars lay the battle to preserve families, communities, and a culture—and that whole families and communities participated actively in the struggle and suffered immensely in the end. Apaches fought to live on land from which not only their sustenance but also their identity derived, an identity grounded in matrilocal extended families and a complementary sexual division of labor. Throughout this devastating period, Apache culture's strength lay in part in its flexibility. War parties continued to reflect traditional Apache social organization as they were structured around kin relationships and community bonds and called up in order to avenge the deaths of relatives. At the same time the all-out warfare of the late nineteenth century meant that women had difficulty practicing their normal economic roles and instead followed, and sometimes joined, their husbands at war. As wives these women brushed against a permeable gender boundary that Lozen, an unmarried woman warrior, was able to cross.

Lozen forswore Chiricahua gender norms. But although she did not marry, did not have children, did not perform women's typical tasks and instead excelled at masculine pursuits, her community perceived her as neither a threat nor a deviant. Quite the contrary, it celebrated her powerful cross-gender position.

Women warriors may have been unusual in Apache history, but they were also admired, even revered, and Lozen remains emblematic of that tradition. Almost invisible to the American authorities, her reputation and daring exploits survived in Chiricahua oral memory. That there was a place for such a woman within Apache society and that she was committed to using her exceptional position for the good of that society illustrate Apache culture's strength and complexity as it adapted to the dire circumstances of the late nineteenth century. When Lozen declined to live the life of a typical Apache woman, she did not deny the viability of her culture; instead, she spent her life defending it.

GLOSSARY

Apache: A Native American people inhabiting the southwest United States and northern Mexico. Various Apache tribes offered strong resistance to encroachment on their territory in the latter half of the nineteenth century. Present-day Apache populations are located in Arizona, New Mexico, and Oklahoma.

Alcatraz: A rocky island in San Francisco Bay. It was a military prison from 1859 to 1933 and a federal prison until 1963. It is now a tourist attraction.

IMPLICATIONS

Lozen's story raises important issues about Indian resistance and gender roles in Native American society. What do you think made it possible for women to assume such seemingly male roles as war leaders in Indian society? How do you think white Americans would have interpreted the existence of woman warriors such as Lozen?

PART TWO

A Modernizing People

Although the United States entered the twentieth century as one of the world's most advanced industrial nations, many Americans retained their traditional social and religious values and an isolationist view of the world. Between 1900 and 1940, however, intense social change and the worst economic depression in the nation's history forced many ordinary people to question these traditional values and brought others to embrace new, "modern" ways of life and thought. The tension between tradition and modernity thus became an integral part of everyday life in the early-twentieth-century world.

The early twentieth century witnessed the first sustained migration of African Americans from the rural South into the nation's northern and southern cities. Since there were few urban jobs for black men before World War I, the first wave of migrants was composed mostly of African American women, who moved to the cities in order to find work as domestics and laundresses. As Jacqueline Jones argues, these women formed "A Bridge of Bent Backs and Laboring Muscles" that linked their new urban lives with the lives of family members who remained in the rural South. The result was the creation of migration routes that would lead tens of thousands of African Americans to northern industrial centers in the second and third decades of the century.

While cities were the most obvious areas in need of reform during the early decades of the century, numerous problems also existed in rural areas and in the nation's rapidly vanishing wilderness. As the pressure of burgeoning population gradually transformed the natural landscape into farms, ranches, and cities, some reformers wondered about the health of nature itself. Would the heedless destruction of natural resources eventually strip the nation of its scenic resources? And would there be anything left of the country's magnificent wilderness for future generations to enjoy? As Peter Wild argues in "John Muir: The Mysteries of Mountains," it was to ensure the preservation of the nation's natural beauty that reformers such as John Muir fought for the creation of national parks and forests as places where the pristine beauty of nature would be left undisturbed by the consuming forces of modernization.

The urban centers that attracted rural migrants were also the homes of millions of immigrants who had come from Europe and Latin America to work in the nation's new industrial enterprises. Poor, unskilled strangers in an unfamiliar country, most of these immigrants lived close to the margins of subsistence and relied on relatives and ethnic political machines to secure jobs, housing, and relief in hard times. The poverty, poor public health, and political corruption that accompanied immigration, industrialization, and rapid urban growth prompted middle- and upper-class reformers to seek novel solutions to this unprecedented cluster of social problems. Under the banner of Progressivism, these reformers established commissions to investigate the causes of poverty, founded settlement houses to integrate immigrants into American society, and lobbied legislatures for political reforms. As Jeffrey P. Moran argues in "Modernism Gone Mad," the continued failure of Progressive reforms to ameliorate conditions in Chicago led many reformers to adopt sex education among the young as a new mechanism of urban improvement.

Reformers were not the only ones who felt ambivalent about change in twentieth-century America. Ordinary people, too, felt the contradictory attractions of tradition and modernity in their everyday lives. In "Messenger of the New Age," Mary Murphy reveals the magnetic appeal of radio to ordinary citizens during the 1920s. Network entertainment programs, national and international news, and advertising spots opened new worlds to millions of listeners, who embraced the new medium with the same enthusiasm they showed for the motion picture theaters that had begun to appear in their local communities.

The Great Depression burned itself into the minds of all who lived through it. In "What the Depression Did to People," Edward R. Ellis captures the human meaning of the Depression and recounts the myriad ways in which ordinary people coped with this unprecedented crisis in their daily lives.

Sacrifice on the battlefield was taken for granted by all Americans during World War II, but sacrifice on the home front was a different matter. As Mark H. Leff shows in "The Politics of Sacrifice on the American Home Front," ordinary men and women readily accepted the need for personal sacrifice, but at the political and business level, interest groups battled continuously to minimize the extent of their own losses. Like the internment of Japanese Americans, sacrifice on the home front was a thoroughly political process.

PAST TRACES

In the wake of the Civil War and Reconstruction, southern planters struggled to adjust to the changed circumstances of their lives. Foremost among these concerns was the supply of labor: now that slaves were free, who would work their fields and process their cotton? The answer throughout the South was to contain the social and political power of freedmen through the creation of Black Codes and the use of intimidation and to keep their former slaves as a usable labor force by trapping them in sharecropping contracts. This essay is introduced by Senate testimony describing the exploitative realities of the sharecropping system.

James T. Rapier, The Agricultural Labor Force in the South (1880)

A. Well, sir, there are several reasons why the colored people desire to emigrate from Alabama; one among them is the poverty of the South. On a large part of it a man cannot make a decent living. Another is their want of school privileges in the State: and there is a majority of the people who believe that they cannot any longer get justice in the courts; and another and the greatest reason is found in the local laws that we have, and which are very oppressive to that class of people in the black belt.

Q. State what some of them are.—A. First, we have only schools about three months in the year, and I suppose I need not say anything more on that head. In reference to the poverty of the soil, 33 to 40 per cent of the lands in Alabama is about all on which a man can make a living.

Q. Do you mean the parts that are subdued?—A. Yes, sir; the arable land. The average is one-third of a bale of cotton to the acre, not making three bales to the hand; and a hundred bushels of corn to the hand, on an average. Then take the price of cotton for the last two years; it has not netted more than $45 to $47.50 to the bale; and I suppose it would not be amiss for me to state something of the plans of working the land in Alabama.

Mr. Vance. It will be very proper.

The Witness. The general plan is that the landlord furnishes the land and the teams and feed for the teams and the implements, for which he draws one half of the crop. I remarked that the three bales of cotton and a hundred bushels of corn is about all that you can make to a hand. We allow in Alabama that much, for that is as much as a man can get out of it, and that is not enough to support his family, including himself and the feed of his family; $95 to $100 is as much as a hand can make, and that is not enough to feed any man in a Christian country. . . .

A. . . . Now, it is very clear that a man cannot live on such terms, and hence the conclusion of many of these people, that there is not a decent living for them in that State. They are like the white people, and their living no better. Numbers of them, probably not less than 20,000 whites, have left Alabama since the war and gone to Texas to better their condition, and the blacks are doing the same thing, and that is the whole there is of it. So far as the negroes are concerned now they have a high desire to submit their fate to their own keeping in another country. Now here is one of the laws which also affects us, to which I will call attention. It is found in the acts of Alabama for 1878–79, page 63, act No. 57, section 1.

Section 1. *Be it enacted by the general assembly of Alabama*, That section 4369 of the Code be, and the same is hereby, amended so as to read as follows: Any person who shall buy, sell, receive, barter, or dispose of any cotton, corn, wheat, oats, pease, or potatoes after the hour of sunset and before the hour of sunrise of the next succeeding day, and any person who shall in any manner move, carry, convey, or transport, except within the limits of the farm or plantation on which it is raised or grown, any seed cotton between the hours of sunset and sunrise of the next succeeding day, shall be guilty of a misdemeanor, and, on conviction, shall be fined not less than ten nor more five hundred dollars, and may also be imprisoned in the county jail, or put to hard labor for the county, for not more than twelve months. But this section shall not effect the right of municipal corporations to establish and regulate under their charters public markets within their limits for the sale of commodities for culinary purposes, nor the right of any proprietor or owner of any plantation or premises to sell on such plantation or premises the necessary grain and provisions for the subsistence of man and beast for the night to traveling or transient persons, or for the use of agricultural laborers in his own employment on such plantation or premises: *Provided*, That the provisions of such section shall not apply to any person carrying seed cotton to a gin for the purpose of having the same ginned.

Now, the effect of this upon the labor of the South is this: A great many laborers work by the month, but all of them are under contract. If I live three miles from a store, and I must work from sunup to sundown, I cannot go where I can do my trading to the best advantage. A man is prevented, no matter whether his family is sick from sundown to sunrise, from going and selling anything that he has, as the landlord will not give them time between sunrise and sundown.

Q. What was the purpose of this law?—A. It was, as appears from the debates, to keep the negroes from going to stores and taking off seed cotton from the plantation. Certainly it was to have that effect, but it goes further and prevents a man from selling what he has raised and has a right to sell. If a man commits a crime he ought to be punished, but every man ought to have a right to dispose of his own property.

Q. Is there any particular limitation of time to which this law applies?—A. No, sir.

Q. It runs all the year round?—A. Yes, sir.

Q. After the division of the crops as well as before?—A. Yes, sir; it operates so that a man cannot sell his crop at all in many cases.

Q. Do you say that the landlord will not let him sell his crop or that he can prevent it?—A. I say he will not let him do it, because the landlord will not let him take two or three hours out of the time due him in the day to sell it, and the law prevents him from selling at night.

Q. You say the effect of it is not to let him sell his crop at all?—A. I do; for if a man agrees to work from sunup to sundown he is made to do it. I work them that way myself, and I believe all the rest do. . . .

Q. It shall not be lawful to buy or sell seed cotton?—A. Yes, sir.

Q. At any time?—A. Yes, sir; night or day.

Q. From nobody?—A. From nobody.

Q. White or black?—A. White or black; but you see it applies wholly to black counties.

Q. But there are some white people there, are there not?—A. Yes, sir; but I do not know many who raise seed cotton.

Q. I thought something, may be, was left out of that act?—A. No, sir; that is to say, the gist of the matter is this: I may raise as much cotton as I please in the seed, but I am prohibited by law from selling it to anybody but the landlord, who can buy it because he has advanced to me on the crop. One of the rules is this: I have people working for me to day, but I give them an outside patch. If a man makes outside 1,200 pounds of seed cotton, which is worth $2.50 per 100 pounds, he cannot sell it unless to me. I may say I will give him $1.50 per 100 pounds for it, and he will be forced to take it; but I cannot sell it again unless I have a merchantable bale, which is 500 pounds, or 450 pounds by the cotton congress.

Q. Then the effect of that law is to place all the seed cotton into the hands of the landlord?—A. Yes, sir.

Q. He is the only purchaser who is allowed by law to buy it?—A. Yes, sir; nobody else can buy it. . . .

Q. I thought the law said that grand larceny should consist of as much as $235 worth?—A. No, sir; you have not got it right yet. Two ears or a stalk of corn is a part of an outstanding crop, and any man who sells any part of an outstanding crop can be prosecuted and convicted of grand larceny. . . .

The Witness. The point is this: Under the laws of Alabama the probate judge, the clerk, and the sheriff have had the drawing of jurors, and have had since Alabama was admitted as a State: but this bill comes in and covers those counties where the Republicans are likely to have a majority, and where they would draw the jurors. The proper heading of the law might have been, "An act to keep negroes off the juries." I want to state that it is the general opinion of the colored people in Alabama, and I will say of some of the judges, that it is a difficult matter for a colored man to get justice when there is a case between him and a white man. I will cite one of those cases: There was a case in Montgomery in which Judge J. Q. Smith presided. It was a civil suit. A white man had a black man's crop attached, and he had lost it. The colored man sued him on the attachment bond, and employed Judge Gardiner to defend or prosecute it for him. Soon after the case was given to the jury they brought in a verdict for the defendant. Judge Gardiner moved for a new trial, on the ground that the verdict was not in accordance with the facts; and the judge said, "I have observed that where an issue is between a white and a black man before a jury the verdict is almost invariably against the black man. The grounds on which the judge said he would not grant a new trial would be because he thinks the next verdict would not be different from that rendered, and as I do not think there would be a different verdict, I decline to give the new trial."

7

A Bridge of Bent Backs and Laboring Muscles: The Rural South, 1880–1915

Jacqueline Jones

In the years immediately following the Civil War, southern planters faced an uncertain future. The Union victory ended the slave labor system that planters had relied on since the seventeenth century, and while they were able to forestall a congressional attempt to dispossess former slave owners of their land, that land was useless without the labor necessary for growing and harvesting the cotton, sugar, and tobacco crops that were the source of planter profits. Faced with an immediate and pressing need for low-cost labor, between 1865 and 1880 landowners throughout the South turned to sharecropping and debt peonage as a means to secure a continued supply of agricultural labor. By the end of Reconstruction in 1877, the majority of former slaves, although legally free, were again under the control of white planters.

The working lives of these black sharecroppers were little different from their existence under slavery. This was especially true of freedwomen, who continued to be bound to the double duties of field and household labor long after the end of slavery. Until they abandoned sharecropping and moved northward to take up independent work as laundresses and domestics during World War I, these southern black women lived lives of toil and persistent expectation. Like every member of sharecropping households, women labored long hours to help families survive; but as Jacqueline Jones reveals in this essay, they also lived with the hope that their labor would permit their children to escape the economic and social bondage of postwar southern society.

For black women in the rural South, the years 1880 to 1915 spanned a period between the Civil War era and the "Great Migration" northward beginning with World War I. Although the physical dimensions of their domestic chores and field work had not changed much since slavery, women during this period toiled with the new hope that their sons and daughters would one day escape from the Cotton South. Maud Lee Bryant, a farm wife in Moncure, North Carolina, spent long days in the fields chopping cotton, wheat, and tobacco, and long nights in the house, washing dishes and clothes, scrubbing floors, and sewing, starching, and ironing. She later recalled, "My main object of working was wanting the children to have a better way of living, that the world might be just a little better because the Lord had me here of something, and I tried to make good out of it, that was my aim." Thus the substance of rural women's work stayed the same compared to earlier generations, while its social context was transformed by the promise, but not necessarily the reality, of freedom.

Black sharecroppers, with the "proverbial unacquisitiveness of the 'rolling stone,'" remained outside the mainstream of liberal American society during the years from 1880 to 1915. Their quest for household and group autonomy, like the heavy iron hoes they carried to the cotton fields, represented the tangible legacy of slavery. In an industrializing, urbanizing nation, the former slaves and their children were concentrated in the rural South, and their distinctive way of life became increasingly anomalous within the larger society. Caught in the contradiction of a cash-crop economy based upon a repressive labor system, black households achieved neither consumer status nor total self-sufficiency. Consequently, the lives of black women were fraught with irony; though many had planted, chopped, and picked their share of cotton over the years, they rarely enjoyed the pleasure of a new cotton dress. Though they labored within an agricultural economy, they and their families barely survived on meager, protein-deficient diets. Within individual black households, this tension between commercial and subsistence agriculture helped to shape the sexual division of labor, as wives divided their time among domestic responsibilities, field work, and petty moneymaking activities.

The postbellum plantation economy required a large, subservient work force that reinforced the racial caste system but also undermined the economic status of an increasing number of nonelite whites. By the end of the nineteenth century, nine out of ten Afro-Americans lived in the South, and 80 percent of these resided in rural areas, primarily in the formerly slave Cotton Belt. Blacks represented one-third of the southern population and 40 percent of its farmers and farm laborers, but by no means its only poverty-stricken agricultural group. Up-country yeomen farmers were gradually drawn away from livestock and food production and into the commercial economy after the Civil War. In the process they lost their economic independence to a burgeoning system of financial credit. Yet on a social hierarchy that ranged from planters at the top to small landowners in the middle and various states of tenancy at the bottom—cash renters, share tenants, sharecroppers, and wage laborers—blacks monopolized the very lowliest positions. In 1910 fully nine-tenths of all southern blacks who made their living from the soil worked as tenants, sharecroppers, or contract laborers. Most barely eked out enough in cotton to pay for rent, food, and supplies. They did not own their own equipment, nor could they market their crop independent of the landlord. As the price of cotton declined precipitously near the end of the century, landlords began to insist on a fixed amount of cash—rather than a share of the crop—as payment for rent. Thus individual black households had to bear the brunt of a faltering staple-crop economy.

The black women who emerged from slavery "knew that what they got wasn't what they wanted, it wasn't freedom, really." So they constantly searched for freedom, moving with their families at the end of each year to find better soil or a more reasonable landlord; or, bereft of a husband and grown sons, traveling to a nearby town to locate gainful employment; or raising chickens so they could sell eggs and send their children to school. These women partook of the uniqueness of rural, late-nineteenth-century Afro-American culture and at the same time bore the universal burdens and took solace from the universal satisfactions of motherhood. They were the mothers and grandmothers of the early-twentieth-century migrants to northern cities, migrants who as young people had been reared in homes with primitive hearths where women of all ages continued to guard the "embers of a smoldering liberty."

THE TRIPLE DUTY OF WIVES, MOTHERS, DAUGHTERS, AND GRANDMOTHERS

For black Americans, the post-Reconstruction era opened inauspiciously. According to Nell Irvin Painter, between 1879 and 1881 as many as twenty thousand rural blacks fled the "young hell" of the Lower South in search of the "promised land" of Kansas. Around this millenarian migration coalesced the major themes of Afro-American history from 1880 to 1915: the forces of terrorism and poverty that enveloped all rural blacks, and the lure of land, education, and "protection for their women" that made them yearn for true freedom. "Rooted in faith and in fear," the Kansas fever exodus consisted primarily of families headed by former slaves desperate to escape neoslavery. Together with their menfolk, then, black women did their best to minimize the control that whites sought to retain over their lives—a "New South" mandate succinctly summarized by the governor of North Carolina in 1883: "Your work is the tilling of the ground, . . . Address yourselves to the work, men and women alike."

In order to understand the roles of black women as workers and household members, it is necessary to examine the methods used by whites to supervise and restrict the options of the family as an economic unit. Although granted relatively more overall freedom than their slave parents, black men and women in the late nineteenth century had only a limited ability to make crucial decisions related to household and farm management. The nature of the sharecropping system meant that economic matters and family affairs overlapped to a considerable degree. Under optimal conditions, each family would have been able to decide for itself how best to use its members' labor, and when or whether to leave one plantation in search of better land or a more favorable contractual arrangement. These conditions rarely pertained in the Cotton South.

By the early twentieth century, some plantations were so large and efficiently managed they resembled agricultural industrial establishments with hired hands rather than a loose conglomeration of independently operated family farms. The degree to which a household was supervised determined its overall status in southern society, and blacks were systematically deprived of self-determination to a greater degree than their poor white counterparts. For example, in an effort to monitor their tenants' work habits, large cotton planters often employed armed "riders" who were "constantly traveling from farm to farm." As agents of the white landowner, these men kept track of the size of each black family and had the authority to order all "working hands" into the fields at any time. Riders dealt with recalcitrant workers by "wearing them out" (that is, inflicting physical punishment). Indeed, a government researcher noted that southern sharecroppers in general were "subjected to quite as complete supervision by the owner, general lessee or hired manager as that to which the wage laborers are subjected on large farms in the North and West, and indeed in the South." The more tenants a planter had, the larger his profit; hence he would more readily withhold food from a family of unsatisfactory workers, or deny its children an opportunity for schooling, than turn them off his land.

The planter thus sought to intervene in the black farmer's attempt to organize the labor of various family members. Usually the father assumed major responsibility for crop production, and he relied on the assistance of his wife and children during planting and harvesting. But, reported Thomas J. Edwards in his 1911 study of Alabama sharecroppers, if the father failed to oversee the satisfactory completion of a chore, then "the landlord compels every member of his family who is able to carry a hoe or plow to clean out the crops." Some very small households counted on relatives and neighbors to help them during these times; others had to pay the expense of extra laborers hired by the landlord to plow, weed, or chop the cotton on their own farms.

Ultimately a white employer controlled not only a family's labor, but also its "furnishings" and food. By combining the roles of landlord and merchant-financier, he could regulate the flow of both cash and supplies to his tenants. Annual interest rates as high as 25 percent (in the form of a lien on the next year's crop) were not unusual, and tenants had little choice but to borrow when they needed to buy seed, fertilizer, and clothes for the children. Some white men, like the planter who forbade sharecroppers on his land to raise hogs so that they would have to buy their salt pork from him, effectively reduced the opportunities for families to provide for their own welfare in the most basic way. To escape this vicious cycle of dependency required a good deal of luck, as well as the cooperation of each household member. The hardworking Pickens family of Arkansas, overwhelmed by debt in 1888, tried desperately to free themselves. Recalled William, the sixth of ten children: ". . . in the ensuing winter Mother cooked and washed and Father felled trees in the icy 'brakes' to make rails and boards [to sell]." Their landlord removed temptation by closing the neighbor-

hood school. Referring to that time, William Pickens remembered many years later that "very small children can be used to hoe and pick cotton, and I have seen my older sisters drive a plow."

Since tenant–landlord accounts were reckoned at the end of each year, sharecroppers had to remain on a farm until they received payment for their cotton (usually in December) or until they had discharged their debt to their employer. The tendency of families to move whenever they had the opportunity—up to one-third left for another, usually nearby, plantation at the end of any one year—caused apprehension among planters who wanted to count on a stable work force for extended periods of time. In the end the very measures used to subordinate black farmers served as an impetus for them to migrate—to another county, a nearby town, or, after 1916, a northern city. But until alternative forms of employment became available (the lack of free land and transportation halted the exodus to Kansas after a couple of years), most sharecroppers continued to move around to some extent within the plantation economy, but not out of it. Consequently, the annual December trek of sharecropping families from one plantation to another constituted a significant part of Afro-American community life. Some families "were ever on the move from cabin to cabin," prompting the story about the household whose chickens "regularly presented themselves in the dooryard at Christmastime with their legs crossed for tying up before the next morning. . . ." Within such a circumscribed realm of activity, even a neighboring plantation seemed to beckon with opportunity, or at least the possibility of change.

As productive members of the household economy, black women helped to fulfill the economic as well as the emotional needs of their families, factors to consider whenever a move was contemplated. These needs changed over the life course of individual families and clans. So too did the demands upon women fluctuate in the cabin and out in the cotton field, from season to season and from year to year. Thus the responsibilities of wives and mothers reflected considerations related to their families' immediate daily welfare, the fortunes of their kinfolk, and the staple-crop planting and harvesting cycle. Within this constantly shifting matrix of obligations, black women performed housekeeping and childcare tasks, earned modest sums of cash, and worked in the fields.

It is useful to begin a discussion of the farm wife's daily routine with the experience of a young married couple. She and her husband began their life together with very little in the way of material possessions, and they often had to make do with the "sorriest land"— "Land so doggone thin . . . 'it won't sprout unknown peas.'" At least for the first few years, each new baby (there would probably be five or six who would survive infancy) meant an extra mouth to feed and body to clothe while the number of available "hands" in the family stayed the same. Consequently a young wife had to divide her time between domestic tasks and cotton cultivation, the mainstay of family life; she did "a man's share in the field, and a woman's part at home." As Rossa B. Cooley reported of a South Carolina Sea Island family, "Occupation: Mother, farming and housework. Father, farming."

The primitive conditions under which these women performed household chores means that the term housework—when used in the traditional sense—is somewhat misleading. The size and rudeness of a sharecropper's dwelling made it extremely difficult to keep clean and tidy. Constructed by the white landowner usually many years before, the one- or two-room log or sawn-lumber cabin measured only fifteen or twenty square feet. It lacked glass windows, screens to keep out bugs and flies, running water, sanitary facilities, artificial illumination, cupboard and shelf space, and adequate insulation as well as ventilation. Most of the daily business of living—eating, sleeping, bathing— took place in one room where "stale sickly odors" inevitably accumulated. The ashes from

a smoky fire used to prepare the evening meal had barely cooled before the children had to "bundle themselves up as well as they might and sleep on the floor in front of the fireplace," while their parents shared a small bed in the same room. Each modest addition to the cabin increased a family's living space and relative comfort—a lean-to, chicken coop–like kitchen; a wooden floor; efficient chimney; sleeping loft for the children; closets and cupboards; or an extra bedroom.

Farm wives had little in the way of time, money, or incentive to make permanent improvements in or around a cabin the family did not own and hoped to leave in the next year or two anyway. One Alabama mother summed up her frustration this way: "I have done dug holes in de ya[r]d by moonlight mo' dan o[n]ce so dat whah I stay at might hab a rose-bush, but I nebber could be sho' whose ya[r]d it would be de nex' yeah." Yet many women remained sensitive to their domestic environment; if they could not always find time to clean up the mud tracked in from outside each day, still they rearranged the house "very nice to meet the great Easter morning," white-washed it for a Christmas celebration, dug up flowers in the woods to plant in the yard, or attached brightly colored pictures to the inside walls.

Most families owned few pieces of heavy furniture; modest earnings were often invested in a mule, ox, plow, or wagon rather than domestic furnishings. In any case, a paucity of goods was appreciated when the time came to pick up and move on to another place. Sharecroppers' households also lacked artifacts of middle-class life, such as a wide variety of eating and cooking utensils, books, papers, pencils, bric-a-brac, and clocks. Black rural women relied on very few pieces of basic equipment in the course of the day; these included a large tub in which to bathe the youngsters and scrub the clothes, a cooking kettle, and a water pail. Their material standard of living was considerably lower than that of mid-century western pioneer families.

The round of daily chores performed by a sharecropper's wife indicates that the arduousness of this way of life bore an inverse relation to its "simplicity." She usually rose with the roosters (about 4 A.M., before other members) to prepare breakfast over an open fire—salt pork (sliced thin and then fried), molasses and fat on cornbread. She either served the meal in the cabin or took it out to family members who were by this time already at work in the field.

During the planting season she joined her husband and children outside at tasks assigned on the basis of sex and age. For example, a typical division of labor included a father who "ran furrows" using a plow drawn by a mule or oxen, a small child who followed him dropping seeds or "potato slips" on the ground, and "at each step the mother covering them with a cumbersome hoe or setting out the plants by piercing holes in the ground with a sharp stick, inserting the roots, and packing the earth with deft movements of the hand." Although she knew as much about the growing cycle as her husband, she probably deferred to his judgment when it came to deciding what she needed to do and when. More than one black person remembered a mother who "done anything my daddy told her to do as far as cultivatin a crop out there. . . ."

Harvest time consumed a substantial portion of each year; two to four cotton pickings lasted from August to December. Like planting techniques, picking had remained the same since the earliest days of slavery, and young and old, male and female, performed essentially the same task. During this period in particular, the Cotton South was remarkable for its resistance to technological innovations compared to the industrial section of the Northeast, or commercial agriculture in the Midwest, a fact that weighed heavily on the shoulders of rural black women. Cotton picking was still such a labor-intensive task, few tenant-farm wives could escape its rigors. The importance of this operation to the well-being of the family—the greater the crop, the more favor-

able their economic situation at the end of the year—necessitated the labor of every able-bodied person and took priority over all but the most vital household chores.

In the sharecropping family, children were a distinct economic asset. In 1880 nine out of ten southern black wives between the ages of twenty-one and thirty had at least one child aged three or under. Just as the agricultural system helped to influence family size, so the growing season affected an expectant mother's ability to refrain from field work. In 1918 a Children's Bureau report noted that "to some extent, the amount of rest a mother can have before and after confinement is determined by the time of year or by the stage of cotton crop upon which depends the livelihood of the family." The birth of a child represented the promise of better times in terms of augmenting the household's labor supply, but for the time being it increased the workload of other family members and placed additional physical demands on the new mother herself.

Compared to slave women, sharecroppers' wives had more flexibility when it came to taking care of their children during the day. Some women managed to hoe and keep an eye on an infant at the same time. But many, like the mother who laid her baby to sleep on a nearby fence rail, only to return and find "a great snake crawling over the child," found it difficult to divide their attention between the two tasks. Slightly older children presented problems of a different sort. For instance, the mother of five-year-old John Coleman had to choose between leaving him to his own devices while she worked in the field—he liked to run off and get into mischief in the creek—and coaxing him to help alongside her, "thinning the cotton or corn . . . picking cotton or peas." At the age of six or seven oldest siblings often remained at home to watch over the younger children while their mother labored "in the crop."

In preparation for the main meal of the day (about 11 A.M.), a woman left the field early to collect firewood (which she might carry home on her back) and fetch water from a stream or well. (If she was lucky, she had children to help her with water-toting, one of the worst forms of domestic drudgery; they would follow along behind her, carrying piggins, pails, or cups according to their size.) The noontime meal often consisted of food left over from breakfast, supplemented (if they were fortunate) by turnip or collard greens from the family garden during the months of summer and early fall. The additional time required to fish, hunt for wild game, and pick berries, and the money needed to purchase additional supplies, meant that many sharecropping families subsisted on a substandard, protein-poor diet of "meat, meal, and molasses," especially in the winter and spring. The decline in black fertility rates during the late nineteenth century and the strikingly high child mortality rates during the same period were probably due at least in part to the poor health of rural women and their families.

In the afternoon, work in the fields resumed. Once again, "the house was left out of order [as it was] in the morning, the cooking things scattered about the hearth just as they were used, and the few dishes on the old table . . . unwashed too." Indeed, travelers and social workers often remarked on the dirty dishes and unmade beds that were the hallmark of a sharecropper's cabin. Sympathetic observers realized that women who spent "twelve hours of the day in the field" could hardly hope to complete certain "homemaking" chores. The routine of meal preparation was repeated in the evening. After she collected firewood, brought up the water, and milked the cow, a wife began to prepare the final meal of the day. Once the family had finished eating, she might light a pine knot—"No lamps or oil are used unless some one is sick"—but usually family activity ceased around sunset. After a long day of physical labor, "nature overcomes the strongest and sleep is sought by all of the family"—for some, on mattresses stuffed with corn shucks and pine needles and pillows full of chicken feathers.

Few rural women enjoyed respite from the inexorable demands of day-to-day household tasks or the annual cycle of cotton cultivation. Nursing a newborn child and cooking the family's meals; digging, hoeing, and chopping in the fields—these chores dictated the daily and seasonal rhythms of a black wife's life. But they represented only the barest outline of her domestic obligations. On rainy days, or by the light of a nighttime fire, she sewed quilts and mended clothes. "I worked many hours after they was in bed," recalled one mother of nine; "Plenty of times I've been to bed at three and four o'clock and get up at five the first one in the morning." During the day she had to carve out time to grind corn for meal, bathe the children, weed the garden, gather eggs, and do the laundry. Periodically she devoted an entire day to making soap out of ashes and lard or helping with the hog butchering.

At this point, it is important to note that, unlike their slave grandmothers, most sharecropping women did not have the necessary equipment to spin cotton into thread and weave thread into cloth; the expense and bulk of spinning wheels and looms precluded household self-sufficiency in the area of textile production. Ironically, then, although the rural black family lived surrounded by raw cotton, its clothing had to be purchased from a local white merchant. A woman's freedom from the seemingly endless chores of spinning and weaving required a family's increased dependence on credit controlled by whites.

Her involvement with very poor women in the Alabama backcountry at the turn of the century convinced social worker Georgia Washington that "the mother has to hustle all through the winter, in order to get anything" for the family. The "wife and children are worked very hard every year" to pay for the bare necessities, but where "the family is large they are only half fed and clothed. . . ." As a result, most wives attempted to supplement the family income in a variety of ways, few of which earned them more than a few extra cents at a time. Some picked and sold berries or peanuts, while others marketed vegetables, eggs, and butter from the family's garden, chickens, and cow. A "midder" (midwife) found that her services were frequently in demand. Part-time laundresses took in washing and worked at home with the assistance of their older children.

Although modest in terms of financial return, these activities were significant because they yielded small amounts of cash for families that had to rely chiefly on credit. Furthermore, they allowed mothers to earn money and simultaneously care for their small children, and provided them with an opportunity to engage in commercial exchange on a limited basis and in the process gain a measure of self-esteem through the use of shrewd trading skills. This form of work contrasted with their husbands' responsibilities for crop production, which included not only field labor but also monthly and annual dealings with white landowner-merchants. Thus men's income-producing activities took place in the larger economic sphere of a regional cotton market, while women worked exclusively within the household and a localized foodstuff and domestic-service economy.

Husbands preferred that their wives not work directly for whites, and, if they had to, that they labor in their own homes (as laundresses, for example) rather than in a white woman's kitchen. Still, out of economic necessity, a mother's money-making efforts could periodically compel her to leave her house. Although relatively few Cotton Belt women worked regularly as servants for whites (4.1 percent in 1880; 9 percent in 1900), some performed day service during the slack season. In addition, if a black household was relatively large and productive (that is, if it included a sufficient number of "hands" to support itself), a woman might hire herself out to a local planter for at least part of the year. In 1910, 27 percent of all black female agricultural laborers earned wages this way. One Alabama mother managed to combine childcare with wage earning; she took her stepson along when she "went

and chopped cotton for white folks." He later recalled, "My stepmother wanted my company; but she also wanted to see me eat two good meals" provided each day by the landowner. As three-quarter hands, women could make about 35 cents per day for "full hours in the field."

Children often helped in and around the house; they supplied additional (though somewhat unpredictable) labor and supposedly stayed within their mother's sight and earshot in the process. Youngsters of five or six also worked in the fields, dropping seeds or toting water. As mentioned earlier, white planters often shaped a family's priorities when it came to the use of children as workers; as a general rule, landowners believed that "the raising of children must not interfere with the raising of cotton," and they advanced food to a household in proportion to its "working hands" and not its actual members. W. E. B. DuBois, in his 1899 study, "The Negro in the Black Belt," found sharecroppers' children to be "poorly dressed, sickly, and cross," an indication that poor nutrition combined with hard work took their toll at an early age. Parents at times hired out children to white employers in order to lessen the crowding at home and bring in extra money.

The sexual division of labor between boys and girls became more explicit as they grew older. For example, some families put all their children to work in the fields with the exception of the oldest daughter. Most girls served domestic apprenticeships under their mothers, but at the same time they learned to hoe and pick in the cotton fields and, in some cases, to chop wood and plow (these latter two were usually masculine tasks). In 1900 over half of all Cotton Belt households reported that at least one daughter aged sixteen or less was working as a field laborer. Still, girls probably worked in the fields less often, and in proportionately smaller numbers, than boys, and their parents seemed more willing to allow them to acquire an education; school attendance rates among black females remained higher than those among males throughout the period 1880 to 1915, producing an early form of the "farmer's daughter effect." In the fifteen-to-twenty-year age bracket, only seven black males attended school for every ten females. By 1910 literacy rates among young people revealed that girls had surpassed boys in literacy, although the situation was reversed among elderly men and women.

The financial imperatives of sharecropping life produced rates of prolonged dependency for both sexes compared to those of rural wage-earning economies. Black youths who worked on the sugar plantations of Louisiana often grew resentful of having to turn over their wages to their parents, and struck out on their own when they reached the age of fourteen or fifteen. As a result, it was economically feasible for "both boys and girls [to] mate early, take houses, and set up for themselves." On the other hand, sharecroppers' sons could draw upon little in the way of cash resources if they wanted to marry, forcing them "to wait for the home attractions." Men in the Cotton Belt married around age twenty-five, women at age twenty, reflecting, once again, the lessened demands made upon daughters as field workers.

The demographic and economic characteristics of rural black families demonstrate the continuous and pervasive effects of poverty. From 1880 to 1910 the fertility of black women declined by about one-third, due to disease and poor nutrition among females all over the South and their particularly unhealthful living conditions in urban areas. The life expectancy of black men and women at birth was only thirty-three years. If a woman survived until age twenty, she could expect to see one out of three of her children die before its tenth birthday and to die herself (around the age of fifty-four) before the youngest left home. Those women who outlived their husbands faced the exceedingly difficult task of trying to support a farm family on their own. Even women accustomed to plowing with a team of oxen and knowledgeable about the intricacies

of cotton cultivation could find the process of bargaining with a white man for seed, supplies, and a sufficient amount of land to be an insurmountable barrier. Many widows relied on the assistance of an older son or other male relative, consolidated their own household with that of neighbors or kin, or moved to the city in search of paid work.

Women headed about 11 percent of all rural black southern households at any one time between 1880 and 1900, but not all of those who managed a farm or supervised the field work of their children were single mothers or widows. Some sharecropping fathers regularly left home to work elsewhere, resulting in a distinction between the "real" (that is, blood) family and the "economic" (cohabitating) household. In the Cotton Belt, men might leave their wives and children to till their land while they hired themselves out to a nearby planter. (In 1910 one-half of all southern black men employed in agriculture earned wages on either a year-round or temporary basis.) This pattern was especially common in areas characterized by noncotton local economies that provided alternative sources of employment for men.

For example, on the South Carolina coast, some black men toiled as day laborers in the rice industry, while others left their farms for Savannah or Charleston in order to earn extra money (usually only a few dollars each week) as stevedores or cotton-gin workers. Phosphate mining in the same area enabled husbands, fathers, and older sons to work together as "dredge han's" and to escape the tedium of rural life. A poor harvest or a natural disaster (like the great hurricane of 1896) affecting the Sea Islands prompted a general exodus of male household members old enough to work for wages; some went north, while most settled for indefinite periods of time in other parts of the South. Sugar plantations (in Louisiana), sawmills and coal mines (in Tennessee), lumbering and turpentine camps (along the Florida and Alabama coast), brickyards, and railroad construction projects provided income for men who sought to work for cash rather than "credit." While the "real" family never changed, then, the "economic" household responded to seasonal opportunities and to its own specific economic needs.

As older children began to leave a mature family, the economic gains achieved at the height of its productivity gradually slipped away. These established households sometimes took in boarders or relatives to offset the loss of departed offspring. There seemed to be no single pattern of either work or dependency among the rural elderly. For instance, DuBois noted of Black Belt communities in general, "Away down at the edge of the woods will live some grizzle-haired black man, digging wearily in the earth for his last crust; or a swarthy fat auntie, supported in comfort by an absent daughter, or an old couple living half by charity and half by odd jobs."

Widows throughout the South represented extremes of hardship and well-being. An elderly woman living alone sometimes took in a young "mudderless" or "drift" (orphan) for mutual companionship and support. Like Aunt Adelaide, who "received less and less when she needed more and more" once her children left home, some of these women lamented their loss of self-sufficiency: "I ben strong ooman," said Adelaide, "I wuk fo' meself wid me han'. I ben ma[r]sh-cuttin' ooman. I go in de ma[r]sh and cut and carry fo' myself." At the other end of the spectrum was the widow Mrs. Henry; she supported herself by farming and "peddling cakes" until her health failed—or rather, faltered. After that she made a comfortable living selling sweet potatoes, poultry, hogs, and vegetables with the aid of two other women and a child.

Regardless of their physical circumstances, these women formed a bridge of "bent backs and laboring muscles" between "the old African and slavery days, and the sixty difficult years of freedom" for their grandchildren and all younger people in the community. Although men headed individual households, it was not unusual to find an elderly woman presiding over a group of people who in turn cared for her. In Charlotte, North Carolina, the former slave Granny Ann lived alone but "everybody respected" her and "they never would let her cook for herself." She served as spiritual advisor to the neighborhood. To cite another case, according to the 1900 census, Winnie Moore, aged eighty and mother of ten children, lived alone in Perry County, Alabama, with no visible means of support. But at least five nearby households included Moores. Among them was that of John (aged thirty-four) and his wife Sarah (thirty) who had a daughter of twelve named Winnie. Together grandmother and granddaughter Winnie reached from slavery into the twentieth century, and in their lives comingled the anguish of bondage and the ambiguity of freedom.

Despite the variations in these commercial economies, certain patterns of family organization remained characteristic of blacks in the rural South throughout the period from 1880 to 1915. For most households, a single, sudden misfortune—a flood, a summer drought, high prices for fertilizer, the death of a mule or cow—could upset the delicate balance between subsistence and starvation. Husbands and wives, sons and daughters, friends and kinfolk coordinated their labor and shifted their place of residence in order to stave off disaster—a process that was never-ending. Yet even the poorest families sought to preserve a division of labor between the sexes so that fathers assumed primary responsibility for the financial affairs of the household and mothers oversaw domestic chores first and labored as field hands or wage earners when necessary.

WOMEN'S WORK AND ASPIRATIONS

To outsiders, rural life, set within a larger framework of southern economic backwardness, seemed bleak indeed. DuBois himself asserted that the rural black person's "outlook in the majority of cases is hopeless." Perhaps on the surface the struggle for a living was waged "out of the grim necessity . . . without query or protest," as he suggested. But below that surface ran a deep current of restlessness among even the least fortunate. In St. Meigs, Alabama, Georgia Washington worked with farm wives who "looked pretty rough on the outside." She soon discovered that these mothers were "dissatisfied themselves and anxious to change things at home and do better, but had no idea how or where to begin." They especially wanted the time and resources "to mend or clean up the children before sending them to school in the morning." According to Washington, their "dissatisfaction" was a hopeful sign, proof that they had not succumbed to a paralyzing fatalism.

Two developments in late-nineteenth-century southern society—increasing literacy rates and a general urban in-migration among southern blacks—suggest that at least some families managed to wrench themselves from the past and look to the future. Neither books nor a home in the city would guarantee freedom, but they did afford coming generations a way of life that differed in important respects from the neoslavery of the rural South. Because black girls attended school in greater numbers than boys, and because southern towns had disproportionately large black female populations, it is important to examine the relevance of these developments in regard to Afro-American women and their aspirations for their daughters and sons.

It was not uncommon for sharecroppers' children who acquired some schooling later to credit their mothers with providing them with the opportunity to learn. Speaking from experience, William Pickens declared, "Many an educated Negro owes his enlightenment to the toil and sweat of a mother." The saying "chickens for shoes" referred to women's practice of using the money they earned selling eggs and chickens to buy shoes for their children so that they could attend school in the winter. Rossa B. Cooley pointed out that some black mothers were particularly concerned about rescuing

their daughters from a fate they themselves had endured. For example, born and raised in slavery, the Sea Island woman Chloe had "one idea" for her daughter Clarissa and that was "an education that meant going to school and away from all the drudgery, the chance to wear pretty clothes any day in the week, and as her utmost goal, the Latin and algebra offered by the early Negro schools in their zeal to prove the capacity of liberated blacks." Female college graduates who responded to a survey conducted by Atlanta University researchers in 1900 frequently mentioned the sacrifices of their mothers, who, like Job, were "patience personified."

Frances Harper, a black writer and lecturer, suggested that black mothers "are the levers which move in education. The men talk about it . . . but the women work most for it." She recounted examples of mothers who toiled day and night in the fields and over the washtub in order to send their children to school. One mother "urged her husband to go in debt 500 dollars" for their seven children's education. This emphasis on women's support for schooling raises the question of whether or not mothers and fathers differed in their perception of education and its desirability for their own offspring.

Although girls engaged in some types of field and domestic labor at an early age, we have seen that parents excused them more often and for longer periods of time (compared to their brothers) to attend the neighborhood school. For instance, the George C. Burleson family listed in the 1900 federal manuscript census for Pike County, Alabama, included four children. Ida May, the oldest (aged sixteen), had attended school for six of the previous twelve months. Her younger brother, Clifford (aged eleven) had worked as a farm laborer all year and had not gone to school at all. In 1910 the Bureau of the Census remarked upon higher female literacy rates among the younger generation by observing, "Negro girls and younger women have received at least such elementary school training as is represented by the ability to write, more generally than have Negro boys and men."

If literate persons prized their own skills highly, they might have felt more strongly about enabling their children to learn to read and write. Apparently, in some rural families the different experiences and immediate concerns of fathers compared to mothers prompted conflicting attitudes toward schooling. Perhaps the experiences of Martin V. Washington were not so unusual. Born in 1878 in South Carolina, Washington grew up in a household composed of his parents and ten siblings. His mother had received a grammar-school education, but his father had never gone to school. "Because of the lack of his education," explained Washington, "my father was not anxious for his children to attend school; he preferred to have them work on the farm." On the other hand, his mother, "who knew the value of an education," tried to ensure that all of her children acquired some schooling.

For blacks in the rural South, even a smattering of education could provoke discontent and thereby disrupt family and community life. Martin Washington's father might have feared that his children would move away; Martin himself eventually emigrated to New York City. Nate Shaw put the matter succinctly: "As a whole, if children got book learnin enough they'd jump off of this country; they don't want to plow, don't want no part of no sort of field work." He believed that the "biggest majority" of literate blacks sooner or later moved to town to find a "public job." If education was a means of personal advancement, then it could splinter families, as young people, eager to flee from the routine of rural life, abandoned the farms of their parents.

The Pickens family of South Carolina moved from the country to the village of Pendleton in the late 1880s. The various factors that shaped their decision revealed how considerations related to both work and schooling attracted people to the towns. (The 1880s represented the peak period of black urban in-migration between 1865 and 1915.) Mrs. Pickens had a great desire "to school the children," but they could hardly attend classes on a regular basis as long as the family's white landlord "would not tolerate a tenant who put his children to school in the farming season." Working together, the Pickenses just barely made ends meet in any case; cotton prices had fallen to the point where a hand earned only 35 or 40 cents a day for picking one hundred pounds.

In Pendleton, the children could attend a better school for longer stretches at a time. Their father relinquished the plow in order to become a "man of all work," and their mother found a job as a cook in a hotel. She preferred this type of employment over field work because it allowed her "somewhat better opportunities" to care for her small children (she probably took them to work with her). William Pickens believed that town life afforded a measure of financial independence for the family, compared to his experiences on a tenant farm where "my father worked while another man reckoned." The young man himself went on to become a scholar and an official of the early National Association for the Advancement of Colored People (NAACP).

By 1910 about 18 percent of the southern black population lived in towns of 2,500 inhabitants or more (an increase of 11 percent over 1860). Since emancipation, small but steadily increasing numbers of former slaves had made their way cityward. As wives, widows, and daughters, black women participated in this gradual migration in disproportionately large numbers. Some women accompanied their husbands to town so that the family as a whole could benefit from the wider variety of jobs available to blacks. Unmarried women—including daughters eager to break away from the "dreary drudgery" of the sharecropper's farm and widows desperate to feed and clothe their children—found an "unlimited field" of jobs, but only in the areas of domestic service and laundering. As a result, all of the major southern cities had an imbalanced sex ratio in favor of women throughout the late nineteenth century. The selection process at work in this population movement, like any other, indicates that black women possessed a spirit of "upward ambition and aspiration" at least equal to that of their menfolk.

Throughout this period, then, some black women demonstrated a restlessness of mind as well as body. In their willingness to move from cabin to cabin and from country to town, they belied the familiar charge that women were more "conservative" than men, less quick to take chances or to abandon the familiar. Perhaps even more dramatic were mothers' attempts to school their children, for in the process they risked losing them. Nate Shaw never went to school because, he thought, "my daddy was scared I'd leave him, so he held me down." Shaw's father had his own priorities, and at least he never had to share the pain felt by a Sea Island mother who read in a note from her self-exiled son, "It pays a man to leave home sometimes, my mother, and he will see more and learn more."

BLACK AND WHITE CULTURE AND MEN AND WOMEN IN THE RURAL SOUTH

Late-nineteenth-century middle-class white women derived their status from that of their husbands. Unproductive in the context of a money-oriented, industrializing economy, and formally unable to take part in the nation's political process, they enjoyed financial security only insofar as their spouses were steady and reliable providers. In contrast, black working women in the South had a more equal relationship with their husbands in the sense that the two partners were not separated by extremes of economic power or political rights; black men and women lacked both. Oppression shaped these unions in another way. The overlapping of economic and domestic functions combined with the pressures imposed by a surrounding, hostile white society meant that black working women were not so dramatically dependent upon their husbands as were middle-class white

wives. Within black families and communities, then, public–private, male–female distinctions were less tightly drawn than among middle-class whites. Together, black women and men participated in a rural folk culture based upon group cooperation rather than male competition and the accumulation of goods. The ways in which this culture both resembled and diverged from that of poor whites in the South helps to illuminate the interaction between class and racial factors in shaping the roles of women.

Referring to the world view of Alabama sharecropper Hayes Shaw, Theodore Rosengarten (the biographer-interviewer of Shaw's son Nate) observed that "righteousness consisted in not having so much that it hurt to lose it." Nate himself remembered that his father as a young man had passed up promising opportunities to buy land because "he was blindfolded; he didn't look to the future." Ruled by "them old slavery thoughts," Hayes Shaw knew that

whenever the colored man prospered too fast in this country under the old rulins, they worked every figure to cut you down, cut your britches off you. So, it . . . weren't no use in climbin too fast; weren't no use in climbin slow, neither, if they was goin to take everything you worked for when you got too high.

Rural black communities that abided by this philosophy sought to achieve self-determination within a limited sphere of action. In this way they insulated themselves from whites and from the disappointment that often accompanied individual self-seeking. They lived like Nate's brother Peter; he "made up his mind that he weren't going to have anything and after that, why nothin could hurt him."

Rural folk relied on one another to help celebrate the wedding of a young couple, rejoice in a preacher's fervent exhortation, mark the annual closing of the local school, minister to the ill, and bury the dead. Women participated in all these rites and communal events. In addition, they had their own gender-based activities, as well as societies that contributed to the general good of the community. On the Sea Islands, young women would "often take Saturday afternoon as a time for cleaning the yard or the parlor, for ironing their clothes, or for preparing their hair." (Their brothers gathered at a favorite meeting place or organized a "cornfield baseball game.") Quilting brought young and old women together for a daylong festival of sewing, chatting, and feasting. Supported by the modest dues of their members, female voluntary beneficial societies met vital social-welfare needs that individual families could not always afford; these groups helped their members to pay for life insurance, medical care, and burial services. Even the poorest women managed to contribute a few pennies a month and to attend weekly meetings. In turn-of-the-century Alabama, "The woman who is not a member of one of these is pitied and considered rather out of date."

The impulse for mutual solace and support among rural Afro-Americans culminated in their religious institutions and worship services. At monthly meetings women and men met to reaffirm their unique spiritual heritage, to seek comfort, and to comfort one another. Black women found a "psychological center" in religious belief, and the church provided strength for those overcome by the day-to-day business of living. For many weary sharecroppers' wives and mothers, worship services allowed for physical and spiritual release and offered a means of transcending earthly cares in the company of one's friends and family. Faith created "a private world inside the self, sustained by religious sentiment and religious symbolism . . . fashioned to contain the world without." "Spiritual mothers" served as the "main pillars" of Methodist and Baptist churches, but they also exercised religious leadership outside formal institutional boundaries; elderly women in particular commanded respect as the standard-bearers of tradition and as the younger generation's link with its ancestors.

Of course, life in "places behind God's back" was shaped as much by racial prejudice as by black solidarity, and the "ethos of mutuality" that pervaded rural communities did not preclude physical violence or overt conflict between individuals. At times a Saturday night "frolic" ended in a bloody confrontation between two men who sought courage from a whiskey bottle and self-esteem through hand-to-hand conflict. Similarly, oppression could bind a family tightly together, but it could also heighten tensions among people who had few outlets for their rage and frustration. Patterns of domestic conflict reflected both historical injustices and daily family pressures. These forces affected black women and men in different ways.

On a superficial level, the roots of domestic violence are not difficult to recognize or understand. Cramped living quarters and unexpected setbacks provoked the most even-tempered of household heads. Like their slave parents, mothers and fathers often used harsh disciplinary techniques on children, not only to prepare them for life in a white-dominated world where all blacks had to act cautiously, but also to exert rigid control over this one vital facet of domestic life. If whites attempted to cut "the britches off" black fathers and husbands, then these men would try to assert their authority over their households with even greater determination. At times that determination was manifested in violence and brutality.

Hayes Shaw epitomized the sharecropping father who lorded over his wives (he married three times) and children. More than once the Shaw children watched helplessly as their father beat their mother, and they too were "whipped . . . up scandalous" for the slightest infraction. Hayes divided his time between his "outside woman"—an unmarried laundress in the neighborhood—and his "regular" family, and he made no effort to conceal the fact. The Shaw women-folk were hired out or sent to the fields like children, without daring to protest, while Hayes spent his days in a characteristically masculine fashion—alone, away from the house, hunting. According to Nate Shaw, his "daddy'd have his gun on his shoulder and be off on Sitimachas Creek swamps, huntin," after commanding his wife to "Take that plow! Hoe!" The son remembered with bitterness years later that his stepmother (who had borne his father thirteen children) "put part of a day's work in the field" before she died one night.

Hayes Shaw was undoubtedly an extreme example of a domestic tyrant, but he and other husbands like him inspired white and black women community leaders, educators, and social workers to formulate a critique of Afro-American family life in the late nineteenth century. Sensitive to the economic problems confronted by black marriage partners, these observers charged that black men enjoyed certain male prerogatives without the corresponding striving and ambition that those prerogatives were meant to reward. Juxtaposed with this "irresponsible" man was his wife—no doubt a "real drudge," but certainly "the greatest sufferer from the stress and strain attendant upon the economic conditions" faced by all Afro-Americans. The chief problem seemed to stem from the fact that black women played a prominent role in supporting the family in addition to performing their domestic responsibilities. In the eyes of their critics, black men as a group were not particularly concerned about "getting ahead" in the world and thus fell short of their wives' spirit of industry and self-sacrifice.

White teacher–social workers like Rossa Cooley and Georgia Washington and black writers and educators like Anna J. Cooper, Katherine Davis Tillman, Frances Harper, and Fannie Barrier Williams focused on the domestic achievements of poor women and with varying degrees of subtlety condemned their "worthless" husbands. Their critique of black womanhood marked the emergence of the "black matriarchy thesis," for they suggested that the main problem in Afro-American family life was an "irresponsible" father who took advantage of his "faithful, hardworking

women-folks." By the mid-twentieth century sociologists had shifted public attention to the "irresponsible" father's *absence*; the relatively large number of single, working mothers in the nation's urban ghettos seemed to lend additional credence to an argument that originally purported to deal with the problems of rural women. Thus the image of the strong, overburdened black mother persisted through the years, and it was usually accompanied by the implicit assumption that women wielded authority over men and children in Afro-American families.

Yet Hayes Shaw's household was never a "matriarchy." Recent historians who have labeled the postemancipation rural black family "patriarchal" hardly help to clarify the issue. The difficulty in conceptualizing black male–female roles derives from the fact that most observers (whether writing in the nineteenth or twentieth century) have used as their basis for comparison the white middle-class model of family life. Black men headed the vast majority of southern rural families, and they self-consciously ruled their wives and children; hence the use of the term patriarchy to describe family relationships. But these households deviated from the traditional sexual division of labor in the sense that wives worked to supplement the family income, and fathers often lacked the incentive to try to earn money so that they could purchase property or goods and thus advance the family's status. These men worked hard—they had to, in order to survive the ruthlessly exploitative sharecropping system—but most realized that even harder work would not necessarily enable them to escape poverty. Those who confronted this dilemma hardly deserved the epithet "worthless manhood." Still, for the two sexes, relative equality of economic function did not imply equality of domestic authority.

Although a husband and wife each made an essential contribution to the welfare of the household, they were compensated in different ways for their labor. This reward differential reflected their contrasting household responsibilities and produced contrasting attitudes toward work and its personal and social value. As a participant in a staple-crop economy, a black father assumed responsibility for a crop that would be exchanged in the marketplace at the end of the year. He supposedly toiled for future compensation in the form of cash. However, not only did his physical exertion gain him little in the way of immediate reward, in fact he tilled the ground only to repay one debt and to ensure that he would have another in the coming year. Under such conditions, most men took pride in their farming abilities, but worked no more strenuously than was absolutely necessary to satisfy white creditors and keep their own families alive in the process.

Their wives, on the other hand, remained relatively insulated from the inevitable frustrations linked to a future-oriented, market economy. For example, women daily performed discreet tasks that yielded tangible results upon completion. Meal preparation, laundering, egg gathering—these chores had finite boundaries in the course of a day. Childcare was a special case, but it had its own special joys. It was an ongoing responsibility that began when a woman had her first baby and ended only years later when her youngest child left home. On a more mundane level, childcare was a constant preoccupation of mothers during their waking hours, and infants' needs often invaded their sleep. Yet a woman's exclusive authority in this area of domestic life earned her emotional gratification. Her husband hardly derived a similar sense of gratification from his responsibility for the cotton crop; he "earned" only what a white man was willing to pay him. Hence the distinction between work patterns simplistically labeled by some contemporary writers as male "laziness" and female "self-sacrifice" actually represented a complex phenomenon shaped by the different demands made upon black men and women and the degree of personal satisfaction resulting from the fulfillment of those demands.

Despite the transition in labor organization from slavery to sharecropping, the work of black women in the rural South continued to respond to the same human and seasonal rhythms over the generations. By the early twentieth century, they still structured their labor around household chores and childcare, field and wage work, and community welfare activities. Moreover, emancipation hardly lessened the demands made upon females of all ages; young girls worked alongside their mothers, and elderly women had to provide for themselves and their families as long as they were physically able. Although the specific tasks performed by women reflected constantly changing priorities (determined by the cotton-growing cycle and the size and maturity of individual households), the need for a woman to labor rarely abated in the course of a day, a year, or her lifetime.

In its functional response to unique historical circumstances, the rural black household necessarily differed from the late-nineteenth-century middle-class ideal, which assumed that men would engage in individual self-aggrandizement. Furthermore, according to this ideal, women were to remain isolated at home, only indirectly sharing in the larger social values of wealth and power accumulation. In contrast, rural black women labored in harmony with the priorities of cooperation and sharing established by their own communities, even as their husbands were prevented from participating in the cash economy in a way that would answer to white-defined notions of masculinity.

Despite the hard, never-ending work performed by rural women—who, ironically, were labeled part of a "lazy" culture by contemporaries and recent historians alike—they could not entirely compensate for the loss of both a husband (through death or another form of permanent separation) and older sons or male relatives who established households on their own. The sharecropping family strove to maintain a delicate balance between its labor resources and its economic needs, and men, as both negotiators in the public sphere and as field workers, were crucial to that balance. Therefore, during the latter part of the nineteenth century, when the natural selection process endemic to commercial crop agriculture weeded out "unfit" households, it forced single mothers, widows, and unmarried daughters to look cityward. Many of them would discover that while the southern countryside continued to mirror the slave past, in the towns that past was refracted into new shapes and images.

GLOSSARY

W. E. B. DuBois (1868–1963): African American civil-rights leader and author. One of the first exponents of full and immediate racial equality, he cofounded the National Association for the Advancement of Colored People in 1910, edited the NAACP magazine, *The Crisis*, until 1932, and late in life promoted worldwide black liberation and Pan-Africanism.

New South: The ideal of industrial development in the southern states following the Civil War.

Millenarian: Relating to the doctrine of the millennium.

IMPLICATIONS

Jones' essay discusses the lives of African American women in the turn-of-the-century South. In what ways do you think the experiences of African American women were different from those of African American men? Do you think the lack of employment opportunities was the sole cause of these differences?

PAST TRACES

One of the most consequential responses to the economic changes and population growth of the late nineteenth and early twentieth centuries was the rise of a conservation movement that sought to preserve at least part of America's natural landscape. More than any other public figure, John Muir became the national symbol of this movement and the best-known spokesman for the preservation of America's wilderness. This essay is introduced by one of Muir's most influential essays, an account of his ascent of Mount Ritter in 1872.

John Muir, Mount Ritter (1911)

At a distance of less than 3,000 feet below the summit of Mount Ritter you may find tributaries of the San Joaquin and Owen's Rivers, bursting forth from the ice and snow of the glaciers that load its flanks; while a little to the north of here are found the highest affluents of the Tuolumne and Merced. Thus, the fountains of four of the principal rivers of California are within a radius of four or five miles.

Lakes are seen gleaming in all sorts of places round, or oval, or square, like very mirrors; others narrow and sinuous, drawn close around the peaks like silver zones, the highest reflecting only rocks, snow, and the sky. But neither these nor the glaciers, nor the bits of brown meadow and moorland that occur here and there, are large enough to make any marked impression upon the mighty wilderness of mountains. The eye, rejoicing in its freedom, roves about the vast expanse, yet returns again and again to the fountain-peaks. Perhaps some one of the multitude, excites special attention some gigantic castle with turret and battlement, or some Gothic cathedral more abundantly spired than Milan's. But, generally, when looking for the first time from an all-embracing standpoint like this, the inexperienced observer is oppressed by the incomprehensible grandeur, variety, and abundance of the mountains rising shoulder to shoulder beyond the reach of vision; and it is only after they have been studied one by one, long and lovingly, that their far-reaching harmonies become manifest. Then, penetrate the wilderness where you may, the main telling features, to which all the surrounding topography is subordinate, are quickly perceived, and the most complicated clusters of peaks stand revealed harmoniously correlated and fashioned like works of art eloquent monuments of the ancient ice-rivers that brought them into relief from the general mass of the range. The can~ons, too, some of them a mile deep, mazing wildly through the mighty host of mountains, however lawless and ungovernable at first sight they appear, are at length recognized as the necessary effects of causes which followed each other in harmonious sequence Nature's poems carved on tables of stone the simplest and most emphatic of her glacial compositions.

Could we have been here to observe during the glacial period, we should have overlooked a wrinkled ocean of ice as continuous as that now covering the landscapes of Greenland; filling every valley and canon with only the tops of the fountain-peaks rising darkly above the rock-encumbered ice-waves like islets in a stormy sea those islets the only hints of the glorious landscapes now smiling in the sun. Standing here in the deep, brooding silence all the wilderness seems motionless, as if the work of creation were done. But in the midst of this outer steadfastness we know there is incessant motion and change. Ever and anon, avalanches are falling from yonder peaks. These cliff-bound glaciers, seemingly wedged and immovable, are flowing like water and grinding the rocks beneath them. The lakes are lapping their granite shores and wearing them away, and every one of these rills and young rivers is fretting the air into music, and carrying the mountains to the plains. Here are the roots of all the life of the valleys, and here more simply than elsewhere is the eternal flux of Nature manifested. Ice changing to water, lakes to meadows, and mountains to plains. And while we thus contemplate Nature's methods of landscape creation, and, reading the records she has carved on the rocks, reconstruct, however imperfectly, the landscapes of the past, we also learn that as these we now behold have succeeded those of the pre-glacial age, so they in turn are with-ering and vanishing to be succeeded by others yet unborn.

But in the midst of these fine lessons and landscapes, I had to remember that the sun was wheeling far to the west, while a new way down the mountain had to be discovered to some point on the timber-line where I could have a fire; for I had not even burdened myself with a coat. I first scanned the western spurs, hoping some way might appear through which I might reach the northern glacier, and cross its snout; or pass around the lake into which it flows, and thus strike my morning track. This route was soon sufficiently unfolded to show that, if practicable at all, it would require so much time that reaching camp that night would be out of the question. I therefore scrambled back eastward, descending the southern slopes obliquely at the same time. Here the crags seemed less formidable, and the head of a glacier that flows north-east came in sight, which I determined to follow as far as possible, hoping thus to make my way to the foot of the peak on the east side, and thence across the intervening can~ons and ridges to camp.

The inclination of the glacier is quite moderate at the head, and, as the sun had softened the ne, I made safe and rapid progress, running and sliding, and keeping up a sharp outlook for crevasses. About half a mile from the head, there is an ice cascade, where the glacier pours over a sharp declivity and is shattered into massive blocks separated by deep, blue fissures. To thread my way through the slippery mazes of this crevassed portion seemed impossible, and I endeavored to avoid it by climbing off to the shoulder of the mountain. But the slopes rapidly steepened and at length fell away in sheer precipices, compelling a return to the ice. Fortunately, the day had been warm enough to loosen the ice-crystals so as to admit of hollows being dug in the rotten portions of the blocks, thus enabling me to pick my way with far less difficulty than I had anticipated. Continuing down over the snout, and along the left lateral moraine, was only a confident saunter, showing that the ascent of the mountain by way of this glacier is easy, provided one is armed with an axe, to cut steps here and there.

The lower end of the glacier was beautifully waved and barred by the outcropping edges of the bedded ice-layers which represent the annual snow-falls, and to some extent the irregularities of structure caused by the weathering of the walls of crevasses, and by separate snowfalls which have been followed by rain, hail, thawing and freezing, etc. Small ribs were gliding and swirling over the melting surface with a smooth, oily appearance, in channels of pure ice their quick, compliant movements contrasting most impressively with the rigid, invisible flow of the glacier itself, on whose back they all were riding.

Night drew near before I reached the eastern base of the mountain, and my camp lay many a rugged mile to the north; but ultimate success was assured. It was now only a matter of endurance and ordinary mountain-craft. The sunset was, if possible, yet more beautiful than that of the day before. The Mono landscape seemed to be fairly saturated with warm, purple light. The peaks marshaled along the summit were in shadow, but through every notch and pass streamed vivid sunfire, soothing and irradiating their rough, black

angles, while companies of small luminous clouds hovered above them like very angels of light. Darkness came on, but I found my way by the trends of the can~ons and the peaks projected against the sky. All excitement died with the light, and then I was weary. But the joyful sound of the waterfall across the lake was heard at last, and soon the stars were seen reflected in the lake itself, Taking my bearings from these, I discovered the little Pine thicket in which my nest was, and then I had a rest such as only a tired mountaineer may enjoy. After lying loose and lost for a while, I made a sunrise fire, went down to the lake, dashed water on my head, and dipped a cupful for tea. The revival brought about by bread and tea was as complete as the exhaustion from excessive enjoyment and toil. Then I crept beneath the pine-tassels to bed. The wind was frosty and the fire burned low, but my sleep was none the less sound, and the evening constellations had swept far to the west before I awoke.

After thawing and resting in the morning sunshine, I sauntered home— that is, back to the Tuolumne camp— bearing away toward a cluster of peaks that hold the fountain snows of one of the north tributaries of Rush Creek. Here I discovered a group of beautiful glacier lakes, nestled together in a grand amphitheater. Toward evening, I crossed the divide separating the Mono waters from those of the Tuolumne, and entered the glacier-basin that now holds the fountain-snows of the stream that forms the upper Tuolumne cascades. This stream I traced down through its many dells and gorges, meadows and bogs, reaching the brink of the main Tuolumne at dusk.

8

John Muir: The Mysteries of Mountains

Peter Wild

The final phase of America's westward expansion involved the exploration and settlement of the far western frontier. From the end of the Civil War through the early twentieth century, hundreds of thousands of native-born and immigrant Americans flooded into the region between the Rocky Mountains and the Pacific Coast to begin new lives as farmers and small-town businesspeople. But unlike America's earlier frontiers, the Far West brought more than farmers and shopkeepers. The region's dense forests and rich mineral deposits also attracted eastern lumber and mining companies intent on exploiting these lucrative natural resources. By the turn of the century, years of unrestricted logging, hydraulic mining, and careless dam-building threatened to destroy the natural beauty of America's last frontier.

This heedless exploitation of the wilderness of the Far West did not go unchallenged, however. Beginning in the 1880s, scientists and government officials joined together in a national conservation movement that sought to preserve the country's wilderness areas for the enjoyment and education of future generations of Americans. If any one man symbolized the conservationist impulse, it was the Scottish immigrant John Muir. Explorer, nature writer, and general spokesman for wilderness America, Muir played a pivotal role in popularizing the cause of conservation in America. In this biographical essay, Peter Wild traces Muir's love of nature to the restrictions of his early life and follows his efforts to preserve America's wilderness as a counterweight to modern industrial society.

I must explain why it is that at night, in my own
house,
Even when no one's asleep, I feel I must whisper.
Thoreau and Wordsworth would call it an act of
devotion . . .
                                        —*Reed Whitemore*

At sunset in the Sierras some hikers chant John Muir's words: "I am always glad to touch the living rock again and dip my head in high mountain air." To them John Muir is a hero, the high priest of those who escape to the wilderness.

And well he might be. By tradition Americans long for the freedom of wilderness, a wilderness fast disappearing. Muir said that all he needed to flee was to "throw some tea and bread in an old sack and jump over the back fence." How can the schedule-bound and traffic-weary commuter not envy the man who, as Yosemite's cliffs collapsed around him, rushed into the night shouting, "A noble earthquake, a noble earthquake!" At times he seems one of the daring Americans who, we like to imagine, led us West through our short history. We prefer our heroes dressed in a simple guise, but with a vigor and joie de vivre just beyond our ken.

The danger is that Muir tends to become lost in his mythology, some of it his own making. A closer look shows him a complex man, like others capable of gloom and hesitation. After years of private struggle and doubt, he beat his conflicting practical and mystical bents into an unusually consistent and powerful personality. Yet the most dramatic events of his life are indeed telling, though often not fully appreciated.

One of the most famous of these, a catastrophe that ended in a spiritual change, occurred in 1867. While he adjusted a new belt in an Indianapolis carriage factory, a file flew from his hand, blinding his right eye. Soon after, the other eye went dark as though in sympathetic reaction. For weeks he lay in agony: "My days were terrible beyond what I can tell, and my nights were if possible more terrible. Frightful dreams exhausted and terrified me." Muir was twenty-nine, an age of trial and decision for many prophets.

Up to this time, chances for a lucrative but unsatisfying career as an inventor contended with his love of extended wanderings through the woods. In his blindness he saw an answer: if his eyes healed he would give up tinkering with man's inventions and devote his life to "the study of the inventions of God." As he tossed in his room, slowly his sight returned. Significantly, he described his deliverance in religious terms: "Now had I arisen from the grave. The cup is removed, and I am alive!" From then on he would consistently equate God with light.

Likeable and talented, Muir was asked by his employers Osgood & Smith to stay on. However, a promotion to foreman, a raise, shorter hours, and a future partnership couldn't sway him. Lifting his pack containing a change of underwear and a few favorite books, he was off. His goal was to walk the thousand miles across the South—no mean feat in the bandit-ridden forests after the Civil War—to the tip of Florida, and from there to hitch a ride by boat to the Amazon. In the words of his biographer, Linnie Wolfe, he was resolved to become "one of God's fools." Yet as dramatic as the file incident might appear, the resulting conversion was neither simple nor complete. The five-month trip provided him with the time and space to mull over conflicts that had troubled him since childhood.

John Muir was born in Dunbar, Scotland, in 1838. Over the years his father's zealousness crossed the blurred line into a religious fanaticism the merchant brought with him when he settled his family in America. Daniel Muir sat in his homestead reading the Bible while his sons labored in the Wisconsin fields. When they returned weary at the end of the day, he beat them for sins they might have committed. To him books, paintings—even an adequate diet—smacked of the Devil. Precocious John, however, discovered that he could do with only a few hours sleep; in the darkness of early morning he'd secretly crawl down into the cellar to read and to whittle a variety of curious clocks.

Though Daniel scowled when he found out about the inventions, neighbors urged his son to exhibit them at the State Agricultural Fair. At the age of twenty-two, suffering his father's parting anger, John shouldered his pack stuffed with strange devices and headed for the state capital. There in the Temple of Art, Madison's citizens marveled at the youth from the backwoods, whose early-rising machine whirred and creaked to propel the reluctant sleeper out of bed.

But Muir found more than local fame in Madison. Like many an aspiring American youth, he strolled with opening eyes among the buildings of the nearby university, envious of the students who had stepped into a larger world of intellectual opportunity. Sometime later he enrolled with money earned from odd jobs, to spend two and a half pleasant years at the University of Wisconsin. There, after glimpsing the cosmos through his courses, he amused the other students with the devices that clicked and wheezed through their bizarre paces in his room at North Hall.

Restlessness overtook him in the spring of 1863, and he wandered through Canada, then back again into the Midwest. He was by now in his mid-twenties, a late bloomer tinged with guilt that he hadn't done more with his life. Far from being simply an enjoyable interim, however, the time spent in Madison would change and serve him more profoundly than he realized. In the frontier's atmosphere of intellectual democracy, Muir had made friends. His professors ignored the long hair and careless dress of the country boy and offered him confidence in his eccentric development. Dr. Ezra Carr and his wife Jeanne had graciously opened their Madison home and their private library to Muir. On the scientific side, Professor Carr instilled his students with Louis Agassiz's theory that a great Ice Age had carved out much of the northern hemisphere's topography. This grounding in science would result in

Muir's first public controversy and his fame in California's Sierras. As for philosophy, both Carr and his wife were self-appointed missionaries of Ralph Waldo Emerson's transcendental ideas. They believed that through the oneness of nature a person could arrive intuitively at spiritual truth, if not ecstasy. It was just what young Muir needed to assuage his guilt and to justify wandering as a spiritual adventure.

And so with his boyhood and Madison as backgrounds, the dropout sat writing in his notebook among the palmettos and sand dunes of Florida's west coast, recording his thoughts and working his philosophical and personal conflicts into a unified view, the basis for future publications. He saw nature as a whole, a unity in flux. Man should stand in nature's temple, witnessing the eternal "morning of creation" occurring all about him. Emerson would have applauded the imagery, yet Muir went beyond the Concord philosopher. Unlike the flights of the cerebral Emerson, Muir's arose from perceptions grounded in science and elemental experiences in nature. Whether collecting specimens or hanging perilously by his fingertips from some yet unclimbed peak, he recognized that "a heart like our own must be beating in every crystal and cell" of the surrounding wilderness. Muir's ability to survive, botanize, and philosophize in the wilds was a rare power.

As his thinking developed, he realized—as Emerson did not—that if nature is a holy place, then civilization, with its sheep, axes, and dynamite, is the infidel, the wrecker in the temple. As Thomas Lyon has pointed out, the view represents a reversal of Muir's boyhood Calvinism. God, not the Devil, is to be found in the wilderness. Nature, not man, is the center of a timeless universe. With this in mind, Muir set his spiritual sights south on the Amazon basin; there he could glory in a nature steaming and writhing in the speeded-up processes of the jungle. But the semitropical winds already had blown him ill. Wracked by malaria, he turned back at Havana, Cuba, in hopes that the Sierra cold would purge his blood. The retreat made all the difference to a beginning conservation movement that as yet had no heroes.

In the early spring of 1868, the former inventor stepped off the boat in San Francisco. All around him that bustling city of commerce—a commerce based largely on resources hauled out of the interior—displayed "the gobble gobble school of economics." In a typical Muir scene, he told of stopping a carpenter to ask the fastest way out of town. Puzzled, the workman inquired where he wanted to go. Muir replied, "Anywhere that is wild." About the time that John Wesley Powell was bounding through the unknown Grand Canyon in his little boat, Muir was beginning a decade of Sierra exploration.

At first he supported himself by coming down out of the mountains to work on sheep ranches. The job disgusted him, and he branded the bleating, overgrazing creatures, degenerate cousins of the noble bighorns living high in his range of light, "hooved locusts." Eventually he chose Yosemite as a home base. Though accessible only by foot or horse, the striking canyon scenery attracted the more rugged variety of tourist. Muir took a job operating the sawmill for one of the two expanding hotels—with the stipulation that he would work only on wind-downed logs. On the sunny side of the valley, the sawyer built a little cabin for himself, complete with a wild fern growing inside and a brook running through it. Except for intermittent concessions to working for a few supplies, he was at peace, free to wander and enjoy the unexplored peaks.

Despite his pleasure in solitude, it should not be supposed that Muir was a cranky malcontent. Though he could chide people with his Scottish humor, he enjoyed company; if he had any social fault beyond his slipshod dress, it was his garrulousness. When in the mood around a camp fire, Muir could hold forth on the glories of the surroundings long after foot-weary companions wished they were in their sleeping bags. Even before he was stirring up the public in print, with the help of friends he had become something of a celebrity, something of the "John of the Mountains" figure that persists to this day. Professor and Mrs. Carr of Madison days had moved to the University of California. They sent a stream of vacationing writers and scientists—many of them eminent personages from the East— knocking on the Hutchings Hotel door, asking to be shown Yosemite's wonders by the only authority on them, ragtag John Muir. He more than satisfied tourist expectations of a romantic character of the Wild West.

As he befriended these Eastern visitors, the amateur naturalist made connections that would serve him in future conservation battles. He guided scientific expeditions and showed off the valley to his aging Concord guru. Emerson added the young transcendentalist to his list of "My Men," but he seemed a little taken aback by all the wilderness, so much more wild than his modest Massachusetts woods. Whether intentionally or not, Muir charmed Viscountess Thérèse Yelverton, victim of a scandalous English divorce tangle, who viewed him as a transcendental noble savage. She wanted him to run away with her to Hong Kong, but to his credit he gently turned her aside. However, she continued the romance on a unilateral basis, writing the novel *Zanita*, which featured John Muir as its Pre-Raphaelite hero.

More importantly, in later years he camped out with President Theodore Roosevelt, who happened to be scanning the nation for places to preserve. In his boyish enthusiasm, TR declared that he had a "bully" time with Muir—a man who if pressed would admit that in attempting to scale Mount Whitney he had danced the Highland fling all night to keep from freezing in the −22° cold. Yet California, the bellwether of America, was fast filling with settlers and developers. John Muir's rugged peace could not last long. In one of several striking shifts in his life, he exchanged it for a public career as a writer and for a reputation that holds to this day as the nation's foremost protector of wilderness.

As a late bloomer, John Muir wrote his first article at the age of thirty-four, his first book at fifty-six. Drawing heavily from the journals kept throughout his adult life, he tended to poeticize the facts. Then, too, his mysticism slowed him down; he found his adventures so spiritually satisfying that writing about them gave only a secondary thrill. "Ink cannot tell the glow that lights me at this moment in turning to the mountains," he explained. On the other hand, his beliefs eventually compelled him to write in defense of nature; and, when the writing fire burned in him, he was far more than the reluctant author. A scientific wrangle provided the first spark.

California's State Geologist, Josiah D. Whitney, applied the popular cataclysmic theory of geology to Yosemite. Basically, Whitney maintained that in a dramatic shift of the earth's crust the floor had suddenly fallen out of the valley, creating the present gorge. Schooled in Agassiz's contrary glacial theory and believing in the slow processes of nature espoused by Emerson, Muir viewed Whitney's pronouncement as an affront. By the early 1870's proprietary feelings about the Sierras ran deep in Muir. He, after all, knew his "range of light" far better than any geologist, regardless of his lack of degrees and professional standing. Glaciers grinding over eons had carved out Yosemite, not a super earthquake. As it turned out, Muir happened to be right, though there was at least as much emotion as science on both sides of the debate.

Urged by visiting scientists supporting his minority opinion, he sent off "Yosemite Glaciers." When the New York *Tribune* not only published the article but paid him for the effort, it set the practical side of his Scottish mind to whirling. At the time, journalism offered far more lucrative returns than it does today; writing might be an alternative to his periodic bondage at the sawmill—as well as a vehicle for rebuffing exploiters. Boosted by influential contacts, his articles, both celebrating his country and warning the public of its imminent demise, won the praise and concern of readers of the *Overland Monthly*, *Harper's*, and the *National Geographic*. Unlike many of the nature writers of the time, Muir grounded his rhapsody in the details of personal experience. He took readers with him from one detailed Sierra adventure to the next. Here he is edging along a cliff face to get a grand view of plunging Yosemite Creek:

> . . . the slope beside it looked dangerously smooth and steep, and the swift roaring flood beneath, overhead, and beside me was very nerve-trying. I therefore concluded not to venture farther, but did nevertheless. Tufts of artemisia were growing in clefts of the rock near by, and I filled my mouth with the bitter leaves, hoping they might help to prevent giddiness. Then, with a caution not known in ordinary circumstances, I crept down safely to the little edge, got my heels well planted on it, then shuffled in a horizontal direction twenty or thirty feet until close to the outplunging current, which, by the time it had descended thus far, was already white. Here I obtained a perfectly free view down into the heart of the snowy, chanting throng of comet-like streamers, into which the body of the fall soon separates.

It is perhaps a bit difficult for an age sated with television spectacles to appreciate the impact of his revelations, based on the union of the physical and spiritual. Upon considering a new Muir manuscript, one editor declared that he almost felt as if he had found religion. On the mystical side, the poetry of Muir's words had the ecstatic ring of a man who was "on the side of the angels and Thoreau," as Herbert Smith describes him. Muir was having the best of two worlds: new economic freedom allowed him to garner material for magazines while he enjoyed trips to Utah, Nevada, and Alaska.

Yet there was a hitch; at the age of forty, "John of the Mountains" longed for a home life. Again his friends came into play, this time in matchmaking. Jeanne Carr introduced Muir to Louie Wanda Strentzel, eligible daughter of a wealthy medical doctor exiled from Poland. The match was not as unlikely as it first sounds. Despite his wanderings, Muir could carry himself like a gentleman; by this time he was a writer of some note; he knew the value of money and had $1,000 in the bank. It took patience and subtle urgings on the part of Mrs. Carr, but in the middle of April, 1880, John Muir married Louie Strentzel. The groom's literary abilities lapsed into cliché, however, when he expressed his genuine domestic joy: "I am now the happiest man in the world!"

For a wedding present, Dr. Strentzel gave his new son-in-law an orchard and a house in Martinez, across the bay from San Francisco. Perhaps middle-aged Muir needed a rest from freezing on mountaintops and eating monk's fare from a bread bag. Whatever the case, his old farming instinct asserted itself. With the exception of significant trips to Alaska, in the next few years he stayed fairly close to home, laboring in the vineyards that provided the modest fortune that would support his final and most important years of activism. To his credit, though Muir showed astute business sense, he also was generous with his money, supporting relatives, giving heavily to charity. "We all loved him," said a friend, "for his thoughtfulness for others." And Muir loved the banter and refuge of a comfortable household, one much different from that of his severe childhood.

John Muir's grapevines prospered, but his health and writing, cut off from the strength of the Sierras, suffered. In a way that might not be fashionable today, his wife rearranged her life to deal with the problem. Louie insisted that he spend July through October, the slack season for orchardmen in Contra Costa County, trying to regain his vital contact with the mountains. Though she loved music, when he was laboring in his study, she kept her piano closed. Editors hadn't forgotten Muir; joined by his wife, they connived to get him out into the wilderness and his pen working again.

In time they succeeded in rebaptizing Muir with his old power—redoubled when Robert Underwood Johnson of *Century Magazine* took him on a camping trip to see what unre-

strained sheep and lumbermen had done to his beloved Yosemite. The plots of his friends worked just in time; the 1880's and 1890's marked the first cohesion and substantial victories of the early conservation movement. Pen in hand and backed by Johnson, the aging mountain man stood at its forefront. In 1890 the Eastern press reprinted his articles "Treasures of the Yosemite" and "Features of the Proposed Yosemite National Park." Telegrams and letters flooded Congressmen's offices. Saving Muir's old stamping grounds became a cause célèbre of national proportions. Congress reacted to the outcry for government preservation—a novel idea. Forced by popular pressure to ignore commercial interests opposing the plan, it created Yosemite National Park and provided a cavalry detachment to patrol the area. Muir and Johnson took advantage of the public's ire at its loss of scenic places and of its hope for saving what remained of them. Through writing and lobbying, in the same year they compelled a publicity-conscious Congress to add Sequoia and General Grant to the growing list of National Parks.

Things were going well for conservation. Supported by a core group of activists, including the young forester Gifford Pinchot in the East, the Enabling Act of 1891 allowed timberlands to be set aside by executive order. Before he left office, President Harrison created the forerunners of the National Forests by designating 13,000,000 acres of public land as Forest Reserves. Through these years, editor Johnson continued to be the man behind the somewhat shy John Muir. Individual concerns, however deep, could be effective in the political maelstrom only through united effort, Johnson urged. In 1892 Muir gathered a number of prominent Californians into a San Francisco law office to incorporate the Sierra Club, an organization Muir led until his death. One of the earliest citizen groups of its kind, the Club continues in the tradition of its founder to "explore, enjoy, and preserve" the country's resources. To support the movement, Muir was writing, writing—*The Mountains of California*

(1894), *Our National Parks* (1901), *My First Summer in the Sierra* (1911)—for a public that looked to the written word as a guide for its judgments.

Yet in the seesaw of politics, for a time it looked as if the new Forest Reserve system—if not the new National Parks—might be lost. Those whose livelihoods depended on exploiting the natural heritage were quick to call in political debts and mount an effective counterattack. By then, however, other magazines followed the example of *Century* with strong stands for conservation. And from John Muir's pen came prose with a stentorian thunder that echoed the fire and brimstone of his childhood. Readers opening the August, 1897, issue of the *Atlantic Monthly* found both their religion and patriotism at the stake:

> The forests of America, however slighted by man, must have been a great delight to God; for they were the best he ever planted. The whole continent was a garden, and from the beginning it seemed to be favored above all the other wild parks and gardens of the globe . . . Everywhere, everywhere over all the blessed continent, there were beauty, and melody, and kindly, wholesome, foodful abundance.

Muir knew his rhetoric. After presenting an historical survey of America's forests, comparing their abuse with the stewardship of Germany, France, and Switzerland, he concluded with a poetic appeal for firm government action:

> Any fool can destroy trees. They cannot run away; and if they could, they would still be destroyed,—chased and hunted down as long as fun or a dollar could be got out of their bark hides. . . . Through all the wonderful, eventful centuries since Christ's time—and long before that—God has cared for these trees, saved them from drought, disease, avalanches, and a thou-

sand straining, leveling tempests and floods; but he cannot save them from fools,—only Uncle Sam can do that.

Only ignorance and greed could challenge Muir's plea. There were successes—passage of the Lacey Antiquities Act of 1906, for example. Its provisions allowed creation of National Monuments by Presidential decree. Because of Muir's urging, Roosevelt set aside Petrified Forest and parts of the Grand Canyon. And Muir, at the age of seventy-four, would fulfill his youthful urge to explore the Amazon. But in the last years John Muir fought his most significant and agonizing battle—and lost.

In 1913, after years of bitter feuding, Congress voted to dam the Hetch Hetchy Valley, fifteen miles northwest of Yosemite, in order to provide water and power for San Francisco. Like so many plans touted by politicians as cure-alls, Hetch Hetchy proved a miserable, unnecessary boondoggle, a windfall for a few, with the public paying the bills. It hurt Muir that his friend and ally of the past, Forest Service Chief Gifford Pinchot—his eye always on use rather than preservation—joined its loudest promoters. Worse still, the Hetch Hetchy project violated the purpose of a National Park. Muir knew that it was a commercial wedge into an ideal, a wedge that has since been sunk into other parks. In Wolfe's words, Muir "was a prophet of the shape of things to come."

Yet to a reform-minded nation, the lost Hetch Hetchy Valley, whose beauty had once rivaled Yosemite's, became a symbol, part of John Muir's legacy. Stung by its mistake, Congress three years later passed a comprehensive National Parks bill. In 1914 "John of the Mountains" died, but he had shown the way to Aldo Leopold, Enos Mills, and Stephen Mather—and to thousands of others.

GLOSSARY

Ralph Waldo Emerson (1803–1882): One of America's most renowned writers and a central figure of American transcendentalism. His poems, orations, and especially his essays are regarded as landmarks in the development of American thought and literary expression.

IMPLICATIONS

Muir's writings and the environmental movement he symbolized had wide resonance in American society. Why do you think so many Americans were concerned about the American environment? Which groups would you expect to be most receptive to Muir's ideas?

PAST TRACES

Progressivism was one of the great reform movements in American history, yet historians have never fully agreed about the nature of the movement. Who was a Progressive and who was not? What was the true nature of the diverse Progressive movement? This essay begins with a central contemporary statement of Progressive aims, Herbert Croly's linkage of democracy and social reform.

Herbert Croly, Progressive Democracy (1914)

[W]hile fully admitting that the transition may not be as abrupt as it seems, we have apparently been witnessing during the past year or two the end of one epoch and the beginning of another. A movement of public opinion, which believes itself to be and calls itself essentially progressive, has become the dominant formative influence in American political life.

The best evidence of the power of progressivism is the effect which its advent has had upon the prestige and the fortunes of political leaders of both parties. For the first time attractions and repulsions born of the progressive idea, are determining lines of political association. Until recently a man who wished actively and effectively to participate in political life had to be either a Democrat or a Republican; but now, although Republicanism and Democracy are still powerful political forces, the standing of a politician is determined quite as much by his relation to the progressive movement. The line of cleavage between progressives and non-progressives is fully as important as that between Democrats and Republicans. Political leaders, who have deserved well of their own party but who have offended the progressives, are retiring or are being retired from public life. Precisely what the outcome will be, no one can predict with any confidence; but one result seems tolerably certain. If the classification of the great majority of American voters into Democrats and Republicans is to endure, the significance of both Democracy and Republicanism is bound to be profoundly modified by the new loyalties and the new enmities created by the aggressive progressive intruder. . . .

[T]he complexion, and to a certain extent even the features, of the American political countenance have profoundly altered. Political leaders still pride themselves upon their conservatism, but candid conservatives, in case they come from any other part of the country but the South, often pay for their candor by their early retirement. Conservatism has come to imply reaction. Its substantial utility is almost as much undervalued as that of radicalism formerly was. The whole group of prevailing political values has changed. Proposals for the regulation of public utility companies, which would then have been condemned as examples of administrative autocracy, are now accepted without serious public controversy. Plans of social legislation, which formerly would have been considered culpably "paternal," and, if passed at the solicitation of the labor unions, would have been declared unconstitutional by the courts, are now considered to be a normal and necessary exercise of the police power. Proposed alterations in our political mechanism, which would then have been appraised as utterly extravagant and extremely dangerous, are now being placed on the headlines of political programs and are being incorporated in state constitutions. In certain important respects the radicals of 1904 do not differ in their practical proposals from the conservatives of 1914. . . .

Thus by almost imperceptible degrees reform became insurgent and insurgency progressive. For the first time in four generations American conservatism was confronted by a pervasive progressivism, which began by being dangerously indignant and ended by being far more dangerously inquisitive. Just resentment is useful and indispensable while it lasts; but it cannot last long. If it is to persist, it must be transformed into a thoroughgoing curiosity which will not rest until it has discovered what the abuses mean, how they best can be remedied, and how intimately they are associated with temples and doctrines of the traditional political creed. The conservatives themselves have provoked this curiosity, and they must abide by its results.

Just here lies the difference between modern progressivism and the old reform. The former is coming to be remorselessly inquisitive and unscrupulously thorough. The latter never knew any need of being either inquisitive or thorough. The early political reformers confined their attention to local or to special abuses. Civil service reform furnishes a good example of their methods and their purposes. The spoils system was a very grave evil, which was a fair object of assault; but it could not be successfully attacked and really uprooted merely by placing subordinate public officials under the protection of civil service laws and boards. Such laws and boards might do something to prevent politicians from appropriating the minor offices; but as long as the major offices were the gifts of the political machines, and as long as no attempt was made to perfect expert administrative organization as a necessary instrument of democracy, the agitation for civil service reform remained fundamentally sterile. It was sterile, because it was negative and timid, and because its supporters were content with their early successes and did not grow with the growing needs of their own agitation. In an analogous way the movement towards municipal reform attained a sufficient following in certain places to be embarrassing to local political bosses; but as long as it was a nonpartisan movement for "good government" its successes were fugitive and sterile. It did not become really effective until it became frankly partisan, and associated good municipal government with all sorts of changes in economic and political organization which might well be obnoxious to many excellent citizens. In these and other cases the early political reformers were not sufficiently thorough. They failed to carry their analysis of the prevailing evils far or deep enough, and in their choice of remedies they never got beyond the illusions that moral exhortation, legal prohibitions and independent voting constituted a sufficient cure for American political abuses. . . .

All this disconnected political and economic agitation had, however, a value of which the agitators themselves were not wholly conscious. Not only was the attitude of national self-satisfaction being broken down in spots, but the ineffectiveness of these local, spasmodic and restricted agitations had its effect on public opinion and prepared the way for a synthesis of the various phases of reform. When the wave of political "muck-raking" broke over the country, it provided a common bond, which tied reformers together. This bond consisted at first of the indignation which was aroused by the process of exposure; but it did not remain for long merely a feeling. As soon as public opinion began to realize that business exploitation had been allied with political corruption, and that the reformers were confronted, not by disconnected abuses, but by a perverted system, the inevitable and salutary inference began to be drawn. Just as business exploitation was allied with political corruption, so business reorganization must be allied with political reorganization. The old system must be confronted and superseded by a new system—the result of an alert social intelligence as well as an aroused individual conscience.

9

"Modernism Gone Mad": Sex Education Comes to Chicago, 1913

Jeffrey P. Moran

The early twentieth century witnessed the rise of the modern social sciences in America. Beginning as academic disciplines late in the nineteenth century, by 1900 the fields of sociology, anthropology, history, political science, and psychology had produced thousands of university-trained graduates who worked in public and private bureaucracies throughout the country. These professionals differed widely in their areas of expertise, but they shared a common identity as "experts," that is, men and women whose social scientific knowledge gave them privileged insights into the workings of American society. Drawn inevitably by training and occupation into the turbulent social transformations of early twentieth-century America, these experts viewed the many problems of their society as, at base, problems of education and knowledge. For them, church, family, and community—the institutions charged with regulating society in previous centuries—had become inadequate and outmoded. In the eyes of these experts, the myriad social problems that moralists had long blamed on vice, moral turpitude, and human depravity could now be seen as having specific social and economic causes and equally specific solutions. Acting as functionaries and policy-makers in public and private agencies, these experts set about remaking American society from the ground up.

But, as Jeffrey P. Moran demonstrates in this essay, social regulation was never a one-way street. In following the early career of sex education in the Chicago public schools, he shows that the application of social scientific knowledge by middle-class experts was not always received with gratitude by its working-class (and sometimes even its middle-class) recipients. In Chicago, the professionals' modern campaign of

" 'Modernism Gone Mad': Sex Education Comes to Chicago, 1913." *Journal of American History*, 83:2 (1996), pp. 481–513. Reprinted by permission.

"sex hygiene," designed to retard the growth of nonmarital pregnancy and venereal disease, ran up against a populace for whom the "old-fashioned" institutions of church, family, and community remained the proper regulators of youthful sexuality. As the ensuing struggle over sex education reveals, there were many important aspects of American life that professional social scientists did not yet fully understand.

....

"Certainly it is important for the growing child to know his own body as it is to know arithmetic," said Ella Flagg Young, Chicago's superintendent of schools, in 1913. At the turn of the century, American educators were increasingly concerned about their students' health: at conferences and in educational periodicals, they discussed the hygiene of classroom design, the hygiene of seating, the hygiene of recess and fresh air—even the hygiene of mathematics. For all this solicitude for the body, however, Young and her allies were coming to realize that the Chicago schools utterly failed to convey certain essential anatomical knowledge. "So far as any information the Illinois school physiologies contain, is concerned," the superintendent explained, "people have no sex organs."

Indeed, the Chicago public high schools, since their founding in 1856, had generally omitted sexual topics without anyone taking notice, let alone complaining. But that was about to change, not only in Chicago but throughout the nation. As urban reformers grew increasingly concerned about sexual vice, prostitution, and venereal disease in the first two decades of the twentieth century, they began to suspect that these carnal errors were the direct result of the public's massive sexual ignorance. If scholastic silence about sex did not safeguard innocence so much as it invited error, argued reformers, then the schools' reticence about sex was illogical and even dangerous. As an educational innovator and a longtime ally of Chicago's Progressive reformers, Young was eager to enlist the public schools in the campaign against vice. In June 1913, Young therefore rose before the Chicago

School Management Committee, a subcommittee of the Chicago Board of Education, and recommended that it institute for all students in the Chicago public secondary schools a series of lectures on what was coming to be known as "sex hygiene."

Young's was the first attempt in American history to implement sex education in a city-wide system of public schools, but the program's significance radiated beyond the confines of educational history. The Chicago movement for sex hygiene grew out of the Progressive reformers' peculiar analysis of urban decay, and it exemplified their novel tendency to seek to ground social order less in traditional agents of moral authority, such as the church or the family, and more in bureaucracy, expertise, and scientific ways of knowing. That analysis and the responses to it would have far-reaching implications for social reform throughout the twentieth century.

Supporters of the "social hygiene" movement (as the Progressive crusade against prostitution and venereal disease came to be known) were deeply threatened by evidence that individuals and institutions were failing to rebuff the modern city's temptations, but they were confident that they, as an enlightened elite, had the ability to stop the decay. Eschewing the outmoded approaches of religious exhortation and external coercion, many reformers turned to sex education as a modern weapon for attacking the sexual vice and misery that seemed so characteristic of the new urban order. In contrast to the supposedly disintegrating moral agents of church, community, and home, public education in the early decades of the twentieth century was institutionally cohesive and increasingly self-assured. Sex education comported closely with the educated middle-class reformers' world view, for it promised to roll back the new culture's challenges to sexual respectability while it replaced the old enforcers of respectability with institutions more congenial to the reformers' embrace of science and bureaucratic rationality. The "Chicago experiment," Ella Young's sex education program, was the most intimate expression of the broader tendency of public schools and other bureaucratic agencies to extend their influence over functions once reserved for the church and the home.

But a significant number of Chicagoans resisted this intimate intrusion. This article, therefore, is about more than elite interpretations of social disorder and its solutions. As much as the Chicago experiment demonstrated the rise of the expert, it also underscored the popular opposition to this attempted ascendancy. Historians who have examined other, comparable aspects of the cultural trend away from communal sanctions and toward the rule of experts have typically confined their explorations to the elite level of experts and their ideas, leaving untouched the difficult question of popular reception. In particular, historians have avoided the story of popular antagonism toward bureaucracy, scientific naturalism, and expertise, but events in Chicago would demonstrate that dissenters from these aspects of modernity were significant and, for a time, more powerful than the experts themselves. Opponents recognized that sex education was part of a fundamental break with the social order of the past, but, rather than cheer the arrival of the expert and of scientific ways of knowing, they decried the Progressives' modernizing pretensions. Thus, not only did Young's attempt to implement sex education expose the social aspirations of the national social hygiene movement and Progressive reform in general, but its controversial denouement also made clear that replacing the old institutions would not be easy or inevitable.

CHICAGO AND SOCIAL HYGIENE

Young's proposal for sex education was the sign of a society in rapid transition. "Five years ago such a notion would hardly have been understood," commented a sympathetic *Chicago Record-Herald* editorialist, "today it is regarded as natural and commendable." The sex education plan was indeed novel: Although a handful of individual teachers and principals throughout the country were quietly teaching some of the facts about sex and reproduction, nothing like a systematic program of sex education had ever been attempted in a large American city. But at least now it was conceivable, if not as universally commended as the editorialist hoped. Clearly, the context for education and sex had changed, and changed greatly, in the half decade or so before 1913. The Chicago experiment was the culmination of national trends in medicine, morality, and reform, trends that displayed themselves with particular force in Chicago.

Sex education grew directly out of the social hygiene movement, which was gaining in influence by adding a medical rationale and a professional approach to older evangelical Protestant movements against prostitution. Beginning in the late nineteenth century, such evangelical groups as the Woman's Christian Temperance Union, the American Purity Alliance, "moral education societies," and "vigilance" groups agitating for legal suppression of vice had attempted scattered crusades against prostitution and social immorality. These organizations had some successes in beating back attempts to legalize prostitution outright, as in St. Louis during the 1870s, but their involvement was sporadic and their effectiveness against prostitution was dissipated by the inclusion of temperance and child welfare on their agendas. A more powerful national crusade against the "social evil" developed with the entry of physicians devoted to the newly professionalized field of public health and its potential for ending the scourges of syphilis and gonorrhea. For decades, physicians had been convinced that most venereal disease cases could be traced back to prostitutes and their customers, but doctors had done little to eradicate the diseases beyond individually treating their own patients. In 1904, however, a pious and charismatic New York dermatologist named Prince A. Morrow launched a fundamental challenge to the therapeutic apathy surrounding venereal disease with the publication of *Social Diseases and Marriage*. In this major work and in dozens of speeches delivered throughout the country, Morrow explained that syphilis and gonorrhea were far more destructive than physicians had thought, and that these diseases struck not only the prostitute and her customer but also "respectable married women who had been infected by their husbands" and such unhappy couples' children. To eradicate venereal contagion, Morrow urged physicians to draw upon their professional respectability and influence to commence their own crusade against prostitution. He hoped that medical imperatives, statistics, and steady public pressure would carry forth what evangelical fervor alone had failed to accomplish.

Tension existed between the imperatives of morality and those of health, but Morrow's antagonism toward prostitution and immorality created sufficient agreement for moralists and medical personnel to cooperate in the social hygiene movement. "Public hygiene is to develop proper health conditions," he insisted, "and in its highest expression is inseparable from public morality." For physicians in the social hygiene movement, as for their allies in the purity and vigilance societies, "public morality" tended to embody a middle-class, Victorian conception of sexual respectability. All demanded female abstinence outside of marriage, and social hygienists also echoed the purity crusaders' indictment of certain expressions of *male* sexuality—particularly the idea that unmarried young men were physiologically compelled to release their excess sexual energies with prostitutes or other willing partners. Feminist antiprostitution crusaders may

have originated the attack on this biological justification for prostitution, but Morrow did not hesitate to echo their criticism.

The vigilance movement and Morrow's crusade soon found energetic allies among Chicago's physicians and Progressive reformers. Organized in 1906, the Chicago Society for Social Hygiene quickly became one of the most active social hygiene groups in the country, issuing numerous pamphlets and holding lectures at the Young Men's Christian Association (YMCA) and local colleges on the dangers of vice for young people. The Chicago society's vigor was not happenstance. No other city seemed to possess such a powerful infrastructure for reform, for Chicago was home to Hull House, the University of Chicago, and a variety of women's clubs active in municipal and social improvement. Jane Addams herself was a charter member of the American Vigilance Association's executive board, along with other prominent Chicagoans such as John G. Shedd and Julius Rosenwald, and the University of Chicago furnished many founding members for the city's social hygiene society.

No other city seemed to need the social hygiene movement quite so much. "They tell me you are wicked and I believe them," wrote Carl Sandburg in the poem "Chicago," "for I have seen your painted women under the gas lamps luring the farm boys." Just how many "painted women" were out after dark became clear in 1911, when a municipal investigative unit, the Vice Commission of Chicago, reported on the prevalence—perhaps "ubiquity" is more accurate—of prostitution in the city.

What the Vice Commission uncovered was shocking. Many Chicagoans, like Sandburg, already knew of red-light districts such as the blocks by the levee, where previous mayors had attempted to confine the hitherto scattered prostitution economy, but few observers were prepared for the magnitude of the vice there. "There are not far from 5,000 [women]," the commission reported, "who devote their time wholly to the business of prostitution." By this admittedly "ultra conservative estimate," one Chicago woman in every two hundred was involved in prostitution, and this army of women delivered to themselves and to the "lords of the levee"—the procurers and tavern and hotel owners who controlled the district—profits of fifteen or sixteen million dollars annually. With a great fondness for statistical precision, the commission's principal investigator, George J. Kneeland, further estimated that these earnings derived from 5,540,700 "assignations" per year. Again, this was a conservative estimate, for it excluded women whom the commission tellingly labeled "clandestine prostitutes (or more correctly the immoral girls or women, married or otherwise)," although these formed "a large class in Chicago." The necessity for reform cried out from Kneeland's cold figures. Aside from the moral decay prostitution represented, the sheer volume of vice in Chicago threatened to engulf the citizenry in an epidemic of venereal disease.

Kneeland's findings were sensational, but the Vice Commission's indictments—indeed, Morrow's movement and the whole antiprostitution crusade—drew additional power from their resonance with preexisting condemnations of urban perils. Evil in itself, prostitution also embodied for middle-class Protestant reformers the modern city's union of individual moral breakdown and large-scale social and economic exploitation. Modern urban life threatened not only sexual respectability but also the larger code of civilized morality and its emphasis upon piety, community, and absolute standards of right and wrong.

Although historians have made much of Progressives' desires to control the "lower orders" of society, social hygienists were less concerned about immigrants and the lower classes than about the moral fiber of their own "people," the native-born middle class. In the reformers' view, the poor had perhaps always behaved badly, but when white middle-class young people began to visit dance halls and prostitutes, that was cause for alarm. Chicago's

red-light districts beckoned not only Sandburg's farm boys, but also, complained a youth worker, men and boys from "some of the best homes in the suburbs." "It was a common experience to find from two to three thousand men and boys in that district in a single hour," Herbert Gates, a volunteer social worker, reported around 1909, "and they were by no means all of them from the lower class." A similar concern over the spread of venereal disease and licentiousness to the "better classes" lay behind the popularity of Eugène Brieux's drama *Damaged Goods*, whose run on Broadway and at Chicago's Blackstone Theater in 1913 was subsidized by antiprostitution and social hygiene societies. In both cities, theatergoers crowded in to hear Brieux's high-minded "Doctor" roundly criticize the sexual morals of his well-to-do Parisian patients. Prince Morrow had recognized from the beginning of his crusade that syphilis and gonorrhea showed no respect for class lines, and dismay over the moral decline of the middle class animated his followers and allies. In Chicago, reformers feared that the siren song of urban vice called out to the native born as well as to the Pole and the Italian.

Reformers feared the inability of society to suppress not only the commercialized prostitution of red-light districts but also what the Vice Commission labeled "clandestine prostitution," that is, promiscuous female behavior. Indeed, in the less regulated atmosphere of the city, moralists despaired of controlling even open challenges to sexual conventions. The summer of 1913 witnessed not only the Chicago superintendent's proposal for sex hygiene education, but also the "slit skirt" fashion controversies, the progress of which the *Chicago Record-Herald* dutifully recorded over several months. Moralists sniffed sexual danger in other unlikely places. Late in 1913 Chicago aldermen held a mass meeting at Victoria Hall on whether to ban the "tango dance" as "indecent, immoral, suggestive, repulsive." A near riot occurred when young tango enthusiasts showed up in force to jeer and taunt their equally numerous opponents, until one of the aldermen, fearing an outbreak of violence over this controversial issue, abruptly adjourned the proceedings. Well before the more publicized sexual challenges of the 1920s, the urban environment seemed to be breeding what one historian has labeled a "revolution in manners and morals."

Social hygienists and their allies were not simple anti-sex zealots, concerned solely with the individual moral failings that prostitution embodied. Rather, they analyzed prostitution in its relation to the many malfunctions of modern city life. The Vice Commission of Chicago, for example, devoted one chapter of its report, *The Social Evil in Chicago*, to the ubiquitous graft that flowed from the prostitution racket, for the money that rented the prostitute's body tainted everyone from the brothel owner and the local police officer to the judge handling a case and the politician protecting the business. Prostitution undermined justice and the law. More broadly, the spectacle of open prostitution buttressed attempts by such reformers as Jane Addams to condemn the urban industrial system as inhumane and unjust. In a series of articles based on the Vice Commission of Chicago's report, which she then turned into *A New Conscience and an Ancient Evil*, Addams proclaimed that prostitution was the consequence of a misdirected modern society, built on extremes of wealth and poverty, in which some women could survive only by adopting a life of sin. Prostitution was indeed a major moral error, but laissez-faire capitalism had inevitably fostered that error.

The social evil, claimed reformers, grew out of a combination of human frailty and inescapable urban conditions. "The very fact that the existence of the social evil is semi-legal in large cities," wrote Addams, "is an admission that our individual morality is so uncertain that it breaks down when social control is withdrawn and the opportunity for secrecy is offered." In the anonymity of the city, it seemed, many people were for the first

time free from the communal restraints of religious strictures, an intimate family life, and public opinion—all presumably operating with far more force in the country than in the city, in the past than in the present. Social hygienists interpreted the exploitative businessman and the thriving prostitute as symptoms of the modern city's broader impact upon the moral order of the church, family, and community.

Laments about the decline of these ordering institutions suffused social hygiene rhetoric. "The need of our work would be far less," noted the psychologist G. Stanley Hall in an address to a New York social hygiene society, "if religion had not lapsed to a subordinate place in the life of the average youth." George A. Coe, a prominent liberal theologian at Northwestern University, echoed Hall in his conviction that social upheaval in the cities was exposing children to unprecedented temptations while the churches could no longer present clear religious lessons through the schools, and families and Sunday Schools appeared incapable of picking up the slack. Indeed, just when the forces of modernity seemed to be weakening religious ties, the pressures of modern city life seemed to threaten the family's ability to pass on a fund of moral knowledge. Besides the prevalence of sexual vice, the exploding divorce rate seemed clear evidence that the urban family was in disarray. As one of Coe's allies maintained nostalgically, the urban "home" was no longer a spacious, economically integrated farmhouse, but was now "too often only a four-roomed flat in which the children hardly ever see their father." Thus urban children lacked both the ennobling rural contact with nature and the enlightening influence of working alongside their parents at the plow or churn. Some Progressive reformers also suggested that the new society was simply leaving parents behind—especially sexually—because average parents did not possess scientific information about sexual hygiene and other critical aspects of modern living and suffered from overly traditional and ineffectual attitudes.

"Parenthood," asserted Dr. Helen Putnam, an early convert to the social hygiene cause, "rarely confers the ability to train twentieth-century citizens." She observed that "a very large part of recent legislative and social endeavor concerning ignorance and idleness, vice, intemperance, and child labor" had been summoned into existence precisely because of "parental incapacity." If parents had done their part in raising children whose hygiene and morality were sound, the "social evil" could never have taken root. Finally, the parents' ineffectiveness was related to the loss of communal social control in the city. In contrast to rural areas, Chicago was so populous that a man could patronize a prostitute without fear of retribution, secure in his anonymity, and a woman living on her own could "fall" into an immoral life or consciously choose that path with none to stop her. Neither the strictures of the church nor the internal moral voice of the parents nor the censure of the community seemed equal to the forces of modern city living.

Thus, urban reformers conceived of prostitution and venereal diseases not solely as medical problems or personal moral failings but also as barometers of social disorganization. Both the social hygiene crusade and the Vice Commission's report gained influence as they mobilized this broader fear. To the Chicago reformers, the medical, moral, and social concerns seemed all of a piece. The message was clear. Chicago was reaching new depths of degradation, and all the old institutions of moral order seemed helpless to lift the city back to the plane of righteousness. Was Chicago ready for new solutions? Great changes had indeed occurred in the five years before Ella Flagg Young's proposal for sex hygiene.

SOCIAL HYGIENE TURNS TO THE PUBLIC SCHOOLS

"Until the hearts of men are changed," asserted the Vice Commission, "we can hope for no absolute annihilation of the Social Evil." Faced with evidence of pervasive vice in Chicago, social hygienists did not propose to regulate its exchanges or ameliorate its effects, but rather proclaimed their ambition to exterminate it completely. Despite the Vice Commission's allusion to religious conversion—to change in the "hearts of men"—social hygienists and their allies based their solution to vice on bringing sex into the realm of rational, scientific knowledge. Religion and community sanctions had already proved incapable of enforcing morality in the city, so the Chicago reformers concentrated on more reliable modern institutions. The coercive mechanisms of medicine and of the law promised to have some effect on venereal disease and prostitution, but to change the hearts of men (and women) social hygienists turned deliberately toward the transformative power of mass education and, eventually, the public schools.

To effect a true change of heart, reformers agreed that they must direct their energies toward a younger audience. "You cannot teach a drunkard abstinence after he has become a drunkard," noted a physician during a debate over social hygiene education, "you must teach him before he has become an inveterate drunkard. If you want young men to be chaste, you must teach them about sex matters before they ever had any such connections." "In all things for the reform of the world and for betterment," agreed a midwestern public health official, "we must commence with the child. There seems to be no good results attending reform work with adults." Rather than coercing adherence to their moral standards or exhorting adults who had already been corrupted, social hygienists hoped to educate malleable youths toward a change of heart, for conversion was more thoroughgoing than coercion could ever be. Internal moral regulation, and not external repression, was the ultimate goal, if only reformers could reach their audience in good time.

Sex education could help people attain the ideal of carnal restraint, in Morrow's influential and perhaps overly optimistic opinion, because sexual vice was the product of ignorance rather than innate viciousness. Social hygienists and purity crusaders agreed that prostitution was based upon a fallacious belief in male "sexual necessity," the folk wisdom that young men suffered from the periodic buildup of spermatic pressure in their testes and that their continued health depended upon releasing the pressure. Such scientific nonsense, insisted reformers, induced young men to seek release with prostitutes and other women, all the while ignoring their own "safety-valve" for excess spermatic pressure—the nocturnal emission. Reformers complained that young women, too, believed in the male's "sexual necessity" and thus tolerated the double standard of morality. Equally damaging to sexual health was the widespread ignorance about connections between venereal disease and prostitution, for what but ignorance would allow young men to expose themselves to the prostitute's contagion? Young men "should be warned of the pitfalls and dangers which beset the pathways of dissipation," wrote Morrow, "they should be instructed in the knowledge that venereal diseases are the almost invariable concomitant of licentious living." Believing in the power of rational understanding and a wholesome fear of disease, social hygienists felt that an individual who comprehended the true functions of the sexual organs and the dangers of venereal disease would no longer be in thrall to lust.

The path to sexual reform was easy to see but difficult to travel. All that was necessary to achieve a "single standard" of sexual behavior, Morrow suggested, was for young men and women to understand the morality and healthfulness of sexual continence, but such understanding was in short supply in the first decades of this century. Although they decried the prevalence of obscenity and "low talk," reformers complained that a "conspiracy of silence" existed to prevent the dissemination of *responsible* sexual information. In popular

Lockean psychology, which considered children to be *tabulae rasae*, silence about sexual matters was a logical strategy to prevent the child's blank slate from being defaced with vulgar and obscene messages. Antiobscenity crusaders such as Anthony Comstock were typical in equating ignorance with innocence and knowledge, therefore, with corruption. "The subject of sex and sexual functions," noted Winfield S. Hall, a professor of physiology at the Northwestern University Medical School, in 1908, "has long been associated with prevarication, secrecy, and other mental attitudes . . . prejudicial to the proper moral development of the child. It would be impossible to find any other subject regarding which children are so uniformly lied to." As heirs to decades of medical, legal, and religious discourse about sexuality, reformers certainly exaggerated the strength of the "conspiracy of silence," but formal sex education in the schools was indeed nowhere to be found.

The official silence, however, did not preserve young people's purity. The alarming prevalence of prostitution and venereal disease was the simplest and clearest proof that silence did not protect innocence. Some argued that such effects meant society needed more silence about sex, not less, but social hygienists asserted that innocence as popularly understood was impossible. In a fundamental shift away from the Victorian idealization of youthful purity, reformers began to awaken to a more modern, biological view of youthful sexuality. Sigmund Freud's opinions about the sexual nature of children were barely known outside a smallish circle of psychiatrists and intellectuals, but the argument of Clark University psychologist G. Stanley Hall, a social hygienist—that sexual impulses were crucial in child development—was having an enormous impact on teachers and psychologists. Following Hall, a substantial number of educated persons, especially those involved with education, broke away from the sentimental ideal of purity as the "natural" state of youth.

Reformers recognized further that certain social forces were already "educating" young people's biological impulses. Although they denied that sexual impulses entered the child only from the outside, social hygienists did not absolve the urban environment of responsibility for misleading youth. The commercialized forces of sex, in particular—prostitutes, dance hall operators, distributors of obscene literature—all tried to make a profit by inciting the youth's innate sexual impulses. Confined to red-light districts, these businesses had become in effect a densely packet advertisement for vice. The high visibility of brothels, streetwalkers, and pornography was sufficiently demoralizing, but young people were also subject to the fallacious sexual advice given by their more "sophisticated" peers. The conspiracy of silence did not prevent sex education of a degraded sort.

To social hygienists who observed the urban environment and followed Hall's work, the choice was therefore, not between knowledge and innocence, but between corrupt knowledge and a scientific knowledge that could preserve the essence, if not the traditional form, of innocence. "I do not know of a single scientific fact that will harm the child," maintained R. E. Blount, a biology teacher in Chicago, in a characteristic defense of science's purifying powers. "The scientific way of looking at sex cannot possibly harm a child." Even as Morrow's followers continued to support laws banning prurient literature, they fought to allow freer scientific and moral discussions of sex. To eradicate the ignorance that led to prostitution and venereal disease, they hoped to substitute the doctor and the teacher's expert knowledge for the degraded information of the street.

Recognizing the importance of educating youth to a path of virtue, the Vice Commission of Chicago, the local social hygiene society, and the Chicago Woman's Club recommended that the Chicago Board of Education experiment with teaching social hygiene to older pupils in the public schools. The Chicago Woman's Club had begun the teaching on its own to parents and teachers, but ultimately Chicago reformers agreed with national social hygiene sentiment that the key to their struggle was the public school, for as other institutions of communal life seemed to be declining, the public schools were exploding in attendance and influence. Attendance at the Chicago public high schools had skyrocketed from a daily average of 1,043 during 1880–1881 to 25,322 in 1914–1915, and several times that number attended grammar school under the compulsory education laws. The prospect of such a large captive audience was no doubt attractive to reformers, and the schools presented other favorable features. By the late nineteenth century, speakers to the National Education Association (NEA) were dilating comfortably upon the school's new mission to educate children for "complete living"—that is, for healthy living—and for morality. Like the campaigns for temperance education in the 1880s, sex education could fit into this broader vision of public education as a transmitter of hygienic and ethical values.

ELLA FLAGG YOUNG'S PROGRAM

Large social forces pressured reformers toward sex education, but social forces are always channeled—in the sense also of being directed or diverted—through individual actors. As a guiding spirit in the expansion of the Chicago public schools, Young was a particularly receptive audience for the agitation against venereal disease and prostitution.

At first glance, Superintendent Young seemed an unlikely sex crusader: Sixty-eight years old in 1913, she appeared in her wire spectacles and high, starched collar to be "austere and even cold"—the model of a prim nineteenth-century schoolteacher. She was born and reared in Buffalo, New York, the sheltered, precocious daughter of devout but liberal Presbyterians of Scottish descent. From the beginning, Ella Flagg impressed all as smart and forceful, but the nineteenth century held few career opportunities for women uninterested in child rearing and domestic toil. Flagg therefore turned to teaching in the public primary schools, interrupting her career only briefly for marriage in 1868 to a much older man, a merchant named William Young. He promptly left the childless bride behind in Chicago to seek his health in the West, where he died alone in 1873. An intensely private and driven woman, Ella Flagg Young never remarried, though in her later years she shared her home with an aide, Laura Brayton. Young's personal life offered few clues to her interest in sex hygiene.

In her public existence, Young was always at the forefront of reform, from education to suffrage to teacher unionization. She fit well into that firmament of Chicago female reformers that included Jane Addams, Ellen Henrotin of the Chicago Woman's Club, and numerous social investigators associated with the University of Chicago. Young's appointment as the first female superintendent of a major school system was only the latest chapter of a long career in progressive education for Chicago. In her years as teacher and administrator, Young pioneered field trips, teachers' councils, vocational education, and Montessori instruction for young pupils. Chief among the school's purposes, in Young's mind, was training the rising generation in ethics. Foreshadowing her affinity with the social hygiene movement, Young in 1902 had published *Ethics in the School*, in which she advocated that schools undertake moral training based upon knowledge and intellect rather than coercion. Young's *Ethics* bore the marks of her long association with John Dewey, for she had made her presence felt in his afternoon seminars on "logic, ethics, metaphysics, and Hegel's philosophy," at the University of Chicago from 1895 to 1899. More a peer of Dewey's than a student—he always considered her "the wisest person in school matters"—Young helped supervise Dewey's laboratory school when she joined the university's education faculty and pursued her doctorate at the turn of the century. In 1909, when the school board made Young superintendent, its business-oriented

members were hoping only to mollify the city's teachers, but they also found themselves with a leader who was far more qualified than any of her predecessors.

Although Young had not previously shown much interest in sexual issues, she had built her career on the Progressive conviction that the public schools existed to pass on to each generation the knowledge and skills necessary for modern living. Indeed, far from being fixed in the past, Young herself grew more flexible and liberal over time. She did not, however, forget her sheltered upbringing in Buffalo nor lose faith in her parents' Presbyterian morality. Childless and sexually inexperienced, Young could nevertheless discern the threat that urban Chicago posed to young people. "In all the years of service in schools," wrote her contemporary biographer, "she recognized the dangers to children of the excitements of modern city life which she saw in the light of her own more primitive, quiet, sympathetic world of home."

In this spirit, Young insisted shortly after she became superintendent in 1909 that the school board appoint a Committee on Sex Hygiene as the first step toward instituting a full sex education program. The committee was no minor operation. Its leader was Dean Walter Sumner, of the Episcopal Church and the Vice Commission of Chicago. Sumner approached the delicate task of sex education cautiously: at his committee's recommendation, the school board first continued the Chicago Woman's Club experiment by offering trial lectures in sex hygiene to groups of *parents* before it considered conveying sex information to their children. Sumner's experience with those lectures, however, reinforced the conviction he shared with social hygienists that efforts must begin with the child, for the small number of parents who attended (classes averaged only sixty each) was utterly incommensurate with the reformers' ambitious goals. In response to this failure, Young and Sumner prevailed upon Jacob Loeb, a conservative real estate developer and trustee of the school management committee, to propose that the Chicago public high schools inaugurate a sex hygiene course.

Young explained the need for sex education in the language of progressive education. "The child is told in school that if he doesn't keep his skin clean, his system will fill up with poison, that if he abuses his stomach, he'll suffer with indigestion, if he gathers the contagion of tuberculosis, he'll die of consumption, but never a word of sex organs and the terrible cost of abuses." Young expected that a course on sex hygiene would prove "highly beneficial, and not alone in its effects on the health of the pupils but in its ethical effects." Her intellectual commitments had prepared Young to add sex education in the public schools to the vigorous Chicago crusades against venereal disease, prostitution, and urban immorality. Convinced but unenthusiastic, Loeb recommended that responsibility for formulating and implementing the course should lie with the innovative superintendent.

At the end of June 1913, Young proposed a course of three lectures to be given by outside physicians at each of Chicago's twenty-one high schools. The first talk would outline some fundamental biological and physiological facts—a necessary first step when physiology textbooks of the day displayed human torsos but trailed off discreetly somewhere below the waist. In the following lectures, the physician would explain "personal sexual hygiene" and "problems of sex instincts," before concluding with "a few of the hygienic and social facts regarding venereal disease." Young recognized that under 20 percent of eligible young people stayed in the educational system long enough to attend high school, so she also recommended that specialists in "personal purity" give one less detailed talk to students in middle school and in the upper elementary grades. In keeping with the developing common wisdom of the sex education movement, male physicians would speak to the boys, female physicians to the girls, and parents, if they desired, could pull their children out of the lectures.

Despite the program's novelty, Young and her allies acted on the most sexually conservative motives. They intended these sex hygiene lectures, not to arouse the students' interest, but to satisfy and thereby suppress their curiosity about carnal matters. Young was finally prepared to invite sexual knowledge into the public schools, but it would have to enter quietly. Far from embracing sexual libel and openness, Ella Flagg Young and Prince Morrow sought merely to enforce an older sexual ideal by new means. Characteristically Progressive, they hoped that medical and educational expertise could conserve what was essential and fundamental in the past.

DISSENT

Unfortunately for Young's proposal, a substantial body of Chicagoans disagreed strenuously with her claims that expert knowledge was critical to conserve society's moral code. Rather than embrace the social hygiene program's essential traditionalism, Chicago's Catholic weekly, the *New World*, denounced the sex hygiene lectures as "modern fadism—modern and mischievous, too.... We believe this to be a very dangerous—a very bad step, one that is almost certain to be most injurious to public morals." The opposition thus underlined how far the reformers' new faith in rational knowledge and state power had carried them from traditional moral concerns. Despite the reformers' ethical intentions, when they questioned the inherited image of the innocent child, when they attempted to usurp parental authority, and when they arrogated to themselves the proper functions of religion, it seemed they had gone too far. Just how far became clear in the hail of editorial and ministerial denunciations that broke loose upon the board of education.

Opponents of sex education were fundamentally convinced that the radical means of open sexual discussion could only undermine the traditional end of sexual virtue. "Smut smutches," commented one acerbic editorialist,

and he denied that "smut" was any less dangerous in the classroom than it was in "the cheap
theatre, in the department store . . . or on the
street." In the opponents' opinion, children
were indeed *tabulae rasae*, and sex information
would mar their minds just as surely as exposure to tuberculosis would destroy their bodies.
Similar arguments against the external contagion of sexual knowledge had for decades buttressed the "conspiracy of silence" and related
censorship crusades. Such a tradition did not
crumble at the first signs of threat. At the same
time as Young proposed her lectures, Gov. E. F.
Dunne of Illinois vetoed sex instruction even
for undergraduates at the University of Illinois,
in fear that it "may create, and probably will
create, in their young minds a prurient curiosity which will induce, rather than suppress,
immorality and unchastity." A similar course
for high school students seemed unlikely to
meet universal approval. If instruction in sex
hygiene aroused a curiosity that had not previously existed, asked opponents, then how was
it protecting the innocent youth? "Safety,"
remonstrated a Jesuit educator, "lies in divert-
ing the attention from sex details." Opponents
thus rejected the supporters' belief in the efficacy of scientific knowledge.

Young and her allies compounded their
offense of corrupting the child by attempting
to interfere with parental prerogatives. Viewing
the Chicago controversy from afar, one intem-
perate Boston mother threatened to "horse-
whip" any educator who needed a lesson in
"respecting the rights of parents to bring up
their little ones in innocence of the terrible evils
of life." The "rights of parents" to teach or not
to teach their children as they saw fit was one
of the opponents' most potent arguments, for it
spoke to fears that were larger than the struggle
over sex education. Opponents were disturbed
in general by what the educator Charles Keene,
addressing the NEA, called "the downward
tendency of the home for throwing off its
duties and the equally downward tendency of
outside agencies to take from the home its privileges." By "outside agencies," the educator

intended precisely those creations in which
Progressive social reformers took such pride:
social settlements, the courts, social work,
the schools. Nothing seemed to exemplify the
"downward tendency" better than the schools'
taking over the intimate family function of
teaching sex behavior.

Such fears of corruption and lost authority
were prevalent throughout the country, but in
Chicago the opposition to sex education was
intensified by the influence of the Catholic
Church. For years, Catholics in Chicago—especially immigrant Catholics—had felt themselves to be disproportionately the targets
of Progressive "reforms," so they were from
the beginning suspicious of any purportedly
"moral" project emanating from Chicago's
reforming elite. Decrying "the recent, reiterated
and spasmodic attempts made in this city
towards improving our public morals," the
Chicago Citizen, an "Irish National Secular
Paper" heavily imbued with Catholic doctrine,
cast ridicule upon "the idea of a number of
practical politicians, merchant adventurers,
and meddlesome, childless women preaching
morals." Catholic editorialists saw sex education as one of a long series of ill-considered
social policies that included divorce, socialism,
and other attempts to interfere with the "natural" order of human relationships. "Today it
is eugenics," complained one writer.
"Tomorrow it will be sex hygiene."

Worse, Catholics recognized that the vice
crusades, of which the movement for sex education formed part, were suffused with an air
of militant Protestant reform: not only was the
antiprostitution movement led by Protestant
ministers, but its parades and rallies were
always conspicuously studded with prohibi-
tionists and sabbatarians. Little in their experience had prepared Chicago Catholics to
welcome either the antivice movement or sex
education.

The Catholic press interpreted sex education
as a representative of the modern tendency
away from the spiritual interpretation of life
and toward a mechanistic or naturalistic one.

The *Citizen* had long complained of the pernicious influence of Darwinism and decried in particular the sociologists' reliance on Darwinian notions in their prescriptions for government and human conduct. Their "crude and extravagant notions," an editorialist maintained, would "degrade man to the level of an irresponsible piece of cosmic machinery." Eugenics and sex education seemed particular offenders in this degradation. Rather than reduce children to the level of their biological and mental impulses, pleaded the *Citizen*, "Suffer them to regard themselves as something higher than mere animals." Such a regard not only ennobled children but also laid the only solid foundation for morality. "Good morals," concluded the *Citizen* in its clearest statement of the Catholic position, "is the efflorescence of religion."

Although the public schools claimed to teach what Felix Adler, founder of the quasi-religious Ethical Culture movement, referred to as a "common fund of moral truth" in an increasingly pluralistic society, Catholic writers warned that the separation of church and state allowed the schools to teach only a "low naturalism" with minimal ethical effect. The *New World* asked:

> What evidence, and what assurance are we to have that the new pedagogy is not going to be the last word in breaking down every vestige of supernatural restraint? For what motive or sanction can the teacher of sex hygiene give for his teachings? What can he teach, other than hygiene is good as the ten commandments, and that disinfectants are an excellent substitute for the moral code?

Thus Catholic opponents disaggregated the sex educators' easy equation of health knowledge and virtue. In the Catholic position (as laid out in 1583, during the Counter Reformation, by Silvio Cardinal Antoniano) only moral education, suffused with a faith in the supernatural, could teach morality. Lacking connection with such faith, "intellectualist or naturalist" sex education could not avoid disaster. Even if the

sex educators' motives were entirely pure—and the *New World* did not concede this point—their methods led ineluctably to degradation and further vice.

Even as they condemned the innovation, Catholic commentators thought sex hygiene might make Catholic education attractive in comparison. The *New World* leavened its attacks on sex hygiene with an eager anticipation that the program would drive more families to the parochial schools that advertised in the Catholic weekly's pages. Here children could learn morality while preserving their innocence, for the Catholic schools taught ethics, not through scientific acquisition, but by "distracting the mind from sexual matters" and prescribing religious sanctions. Further, the Catholic schools rejected what the *Citizen* called "all the sciences, fads and furbellows," including Darwinism and sociology, that were so important to "progressive" educators in the public schools. Sex education had made the dangerous tendencies of these educational novelties all too clear.

Invoking such arguments, priests and ministers in many of the city's pulpits decried Ella Flagg Young's immoral innovation, while their parishioners flooded the president of the board of education, Peter Reinberg, a Catholic florist, with hundreds of protest letters, many of them bearing a suspicious resemblance to one another. The *Chicago Citizen* and the *New World* both kept up a drumbeat of protest and ridicule. Under the weight of such protests, the board of education as a whole met on June 25, 1913, and overrode its school management committee's decision to support sex hygiene. The board rescinded as well ten thousand dollars the finance committee had earmarked for the program. The opponents appeared triumphant.

REGROUPING AND DEFEAT

With the forces of Chicago's Progressive elite arrayed behind her, Young fought back. Once again the school board suffered under an avalanche of mail, but these letters bore the signatures of Jane Addams and other prominent Chicagoans, such as A. W. Harris, the president of Northwestern University, Clara F. Seippel, the assistant city physician, and friendly ministers such as Sumner and the Reverend J. P. Brushingham, an organizer of the Municipal Voters' League of Chicago and pastor of the First Methodist Episcopal Church. All demanded that the board heed Young's demands. Further, Chicago's teachers had always been staunch supporters of "their" superintendent. Such entreaties were hard to ignore. On July 9, the chastened school management committee again met to discuss Young's proposal. After Jacob Loeb changed the name of the course from "sex hygiene education" to the less vivid "personal purity" talks—a change the *New World* decried as a dishonest "sterilization"—the board of education passed the new curriculum by a vote of eleven to two. Two Catholic board members, Mrs. John MacMahon and Thomas Kelly, voted nay (opponent Harry A. Lipsky, a Prussian Jew, was absent), but the other Catholics on the board—President Reinberg, Michael Collins, and Julius Smletanka—joined the majority in the affirmative. "They must be prepared to share the blame," warned the *New World*, but such threats did not immediately drown out the victory for Young and the social hygienists.

As students filed back to high school that fall, the "personal purity" talks went forward successfully. By Thanksgiving, at least twenty thousand pupils had attended the lectures on physiology, moral hygiene, and venereal disease. As planned, a male physician addressed the boys on the fundamentals of male anatomy before pushing ahead to explode the common sexual fallacies that supposedly underlay the popularity of prostitution, such as the doctrine of sexual necessity. Lectures stressed the fundamental healthfulness of continence, cleanliness, and clean thoughts. Finally, the visiting physicians forcefully outlined the social and physical devastation that "inevitably" accompanied

prostitution or virtually any promiscuity. A female physician lectured in rather less detail to groups of high school girls. Lecturers broke the conspiracy of silence delicately.

Young Chicagoans received the talks with only minor complaints. A pair of physicians who went into several schools circulated a questionnaire among students after the talks. In one school, they found that over 90 percent of the girls favored introducing the topic regularly into the curriculum, though the girls preferred it be taught by a familiar teacher, for they were too shy to ask their questions of a stranger. Students also expressed "an almost universal demand for more plain facts," but they were not satisfied with merely biological teaching. "There was also a strong demand," noted one physician, "for advice regarding the attitude of one sex toward another." And though parents were perhaps less enthusiastic for further innovations, they withdrew fewer than 8 percent of the high school students from the lectures.

Despite these encouraging signs, the Chicago experiment in sex education did not last past the 1913–1914 school year. Although urban fears and the social hygiene movement had certainly prepared the ground for sex education, the controversial program had passed almost solely on Young's personal prestige, and that was a finite resource. From the first, a board of education member had advised Young that if she continued to advocate sex hygiene, she would arouse still-dormant board opposition to all of her proposals. After the proposal for "personal purity" talks passed, conservative board members stepped into the open to end Young's autonomy in disciplining teachers and choosing school materials. Their attacks led Young to resign in protest late in July 1913, and though Mayor Carter Harrison wisely decided not to accept his celebrated superintendent's resignation, Young's ability to support sex hygiene, Montessori training, domestic science, and vocational education was undercut.

Much emboldened by the sex hygiene dispute, Young's opponents on the board of education attempted to remove her in December 1913 when she adopted a spelling textbook printed with non-union labor. Chicago Typographical Union no. 16 did not confine its criticism of the superintendent to her choice of textbooks but also submitted resolutions against the teaching of "sex hygiene" as an "unwarranted interference with the rights and prerogatives of the parents." Young again rebuffed the "hecklers," as she called her enemies on the board, but these battles took their toll on the educator. In November the United States attorney had ruled that circulars containing excerpts from the physicians' talks were obscene and therefore, by the "Comstock Act," excluded from the mails. Given the continued opposition to the teaching of sex hygiene, as well as a general reaction against her "progressive" methods, Young was unable to prevent the curriculum from sliding into disuse after its first year. Young held on to her superintendency, but a new mayor soon strengthened the conservative side of the school board, and in 1915 the board conclusively forced the superintendent's resignation over her refusal to enforce the "Loeb Rule" prohibiting teachers from participating in union activities. The Chicago experiment, which had aroused such high feelings on both sides, was by then only a fading memory.

THE CHICAGO EXPERIMENT AS CULTURAL BATTLE

The lessons of Chicago radiated beyond the confines of the social hygiene movement. Although the social hygienists, like many other Progressive reformers, were attempting to replace traditional institutions with "modern" methods of social ordering, the resistance they met in Chicago suggests that this transition was neither easy nor complete. Historians specializing in the managerial synthesis and other interpretations of the modernizing impulse need to take into account actual historical confrontations before they proclaim the managerial elite's victory over a manipulable polity. Rather

than signaling the birth of expert hegemony, the Chicago experiment illuminates the origins of a cultural divide over questions of state action and scientific authority that would persist throughout the century. Supporters and opponents of sex education agreed that the code of civilized morality was under siege in the city. But while social hygienists turned toward professional medicine and public education for reform, they faced numbers of people who did not agree that the old religious and communal sanctions needed replacing. In the long run, victory went to the educated elite, at least according to historians who have concentrated on the scientists and other experts with whom they have so much in common, but the Chicago experiment suggests that the outcome was marked less by resolution than by mutual retreat.

The prevalence of Protestant reformers on one side and Catholic opponents on the other underlines the importance of faith and morality in this cultural split, though it would be wrong to interpret these antagonists as more than representative types for conflicting views on modernity. Their dispute did not reproduce either the religious antagonism of the mid-nineteenth century or later divisions over sex education. Indeed, the middle-class, Protestant Progressives who supported sex education did so, not because they were preoccupied with controlling Catholics and immigrants, but because they worried about moral decline among their own "people." Sex educators and other prominent Progressives, including Morrow, Young, and Addams, tended to come from mainstream Protestant or from Jewish backgrounds, at a time when these religious establishments seemed to be holding less sway over their constituents in an increasingly secular and pluralistic American society. Thus Progressives were acutely aware of the erosion of religious sanctions for behavior, either in their own lives, as they left religious fervor behind for professional careers in medicine, science, or education, or in the lives of the people surrounding them, as they ignored religion altogether or imbibed a diluted and increasingly irrelevant pastoral message. The native-born, middle-class youths who patronized the levee district every night certainly seemed to have left behind the Protestant moral code that was once the signature of their class.

Rather than shore up a religious establishment whose efficacy they doubted and to which they no longer felt a deep commitment, middle-class Progressives sought a new foundation for morality. But they did not discard the moralistic inclinations that had formerly seemed inextricable from Protestant reform. "As transcendental sanctions are losing their power," wrote G. Stanley Hall in 1918, while war in Europe further battered the inner ramparts of civilized morality, "we must build up on a natural basis a new prophylaxis and be able to show that anything is right or wrong according as it is physiologically *and socially* right or wrong." Right and wrong still existed for Hall—in fact, the new right and wrong differed from the old religious virtues and sins not at all—but he and many Protestant Progressives were convinced that morality must now be grounded in the natural, not the supernatural. Young accordingly proposed ethical and hygienic education in the public schools as a necessary step toward virtuous self-control. Over the next several decades, the educated elite's continuing embrace of secular science met with extensive approval among those middle-class Americans who shared the elite's disenchantment with religion and community and who came to accept public institutions and academic research as sufficient replacements.

The character of secularizing urban Protestantism and, in some cases, Judaism became clearer in contrast to early-twentieth-century Catholicism. Catholic commentators insisted that modern fads such as sex education indicated that mainstream culture was diverging dangerously from traditional concerns. "Never since paganism died out in its fastnesses," lamented the *Chicago Citizen*, "were men of the old principles so far separated from the world about them." As members of an expanding faith that rested squarely on those "old principles," Catholics who opposed sex education could rely upon "transcendental sanctions" to safeguard chastity with a sense of security that many mainstream Protestants no longer shared. "In the public schools," explained the Catholic *New World*, "the pupils have been educated as pagans, in the parochial as Christians. Now the proposal is to remedy the situation in the public schools by teaching sex hygiene." "The parochial schools," confident in their own path according to the editorialist, "will keep on teaching morality."

The Catholic opposition to sex education in Chicago in 1913 thus exemplified what was to become a tenacious resistance against the Progressive contention that "modern" methods were necessary to conserve or replace traditional morals. In this case, the resistance was led by Catholics, but the configuration of their dissent would appear later in the rhetoric of Fundamentalist Protestantism and militant anticommunism. If responsibility for moral decline in the cities lay anywhere, suggested opponents, then it lay with social reformers, with the meddling authorities and irreligious scientists who interfered with the integrity of the family and undermined public faith in the supernatural. Nor did opponents acquiesce in physicians' arrogation of moral authority in society. Many Americans in later years might defer to the physician in most of his pronouncements about venereal disease, but they remained adamant that the morality of sexual behavior logically lay outside the doctor's purview. Opponents of sex education and other reforms agreed with supporters that the social order was threatened by bureaucratization, secularization, and rationalization, but opponents did not agree that the solution to disorder was therefore more bureaucracy, less religion, and more scientific knowledge. Particularly where "scientific" sex education conflicted with the inherited sentimental image of the innocent child, social hygienists ran up against the limits of tolerance for their advanced methods.

They did not, however, surrender their larger project. As evidenced by the move toward "integrated" sex education, sex educators, in response to failure in Chicago, simply decided that the public was no longer to be trusted with important reform decisions, especially where the reform involved questions of scientific or medical expertise. Indeed, the desire to regularize the reform impulse and lessen social hygiene's reliance upon public fervor had from the beginning motivated Prince Morrow's attempts to implement sex education in the public schools. The public's "irrationality" in the face of enlightened reform was a central factor in the increasing emphasis upon expert authority at the expense of democratic involvement, not just in the social hygiene movement, but throughout the ranks of educated reformers. Walter Lippmann's post–Great War embrace of scientific rule was only a highly intellectualized version of the turn sex educators and many Progressive reformers had already made in the face of public disappointment.

At the same time, the substantial body of conservative opponents seemed to fade out of sight, for reformers did not attempt to engage them in any meaningful way. Nor did opponents attempt to engage the elite modernizers in a sustained intellectual exchange. The conservatives, however, never really disappeared, as demonstrated by recurrent paroxysms of conflict such as the 1925 trial of John Scopes for teaching about Darwinian evolution or the Right's discovery of "social issues" after the defeat of Barry Goldwater in the 1964 presidential election. They simply opted out of many aspects of twentieth-century institutional life except when they grew overconfident of their own strength or when forced into open opposition.

The historical course of the social hygiene movement exemplifies this mutual retreat. Deflated by defeat in its first major initiative, the movement for sex education after Chicago became less a sustained public dialogue about the role of youth, sexuality, and education in society than a quiet conversation among experts punctuated by spasms of public controversy. In tracing varieties of response to what I refer to as the loss of society's ordering institutions and what Philip Rieff has called "deconversion" from the West's "unitary system of common belief," historians would do well not only to portray the "deconverted" but also to recognize the ideology and the stubborn persistence of the "still-converted."

GLOSSARY

Progressive Reform: A loose-knit group of reformers at the turn of the twentieth century who promoted progress toward better social conditions by employing new policies, ideas, and methods.

Women's Christian Temperance Union: An organization founded in 1874 dedicated to ending the traffic in liquor.

Young Men's Christian Association: An organization founded in London in 1844 dedicated to the spiritual and social well-being and the physical and intellectual development of young men.

Anthony Comstock (1844–1915): Organizer and secretary of the New York Society for the Suppression of Vice, notorious for his moral crusades against literature and artwork that he considered obscene.

IMPLICATIONS

Like many present-day historians, Moran is concerned with the intersection of the private and public realms. Why do you think Progressive reformers viewed sex education as a powerful means of reforming society and creating "public morality"? What do you see as the fundamental conflict between Progressive reformers and the working-class people they sought to reform?

PAST TRACES

When it was first introduced on a mass scale, radio was like no other previous media phenomenon. Treating radio personalities and announcers as guests in their homes, many Americans responded to radio broadcasts with the same sense of intimacy they normally reserved for family members and residents of their local towns. But the purpose behind radio broadcasts wasn't so much to entertain listeners as to sell products. This essay begins with two examples of contemporary radio advertising. Like radio itself, these advertisements appealed to people's deepest social and psychological needs.

Advertisements (1925, 1927)

Advertisement for Berkey & Gay Furniture Company (1925)

Do they know Your son at MALUCIO's?

There's a hole in the door at Malucio's. Ring the bell and a pair of eyes will look coldly out at you. If you are known you will get in. Malucio has to be careful.

There have been riotous nights at Malucio's. Tragic nights, too. But somehow the fat little man has managed to avoid the law.

Almost every town has its Malucio's. Some, brightly disguised as cabarets—others, mere back street filling stations for pocket flasks.

But every Malucio will tell you the same thing. His best customers are not the ne'er-do-wells of other years. They are the young people—frequently, the best young people of the town.

Malucio has put one over on the American home. Ultimately he will be driven out. Until then THE HOME MUST BID MORE INTELLIGENTLY FOR MALUCIO'S BUSINESS.

There are many reasons why it is profitable and wise to furnish the home attractively, but one of these, and not the least, is—Malucio's.

The younger generation is sensitive to beauty, princely proud, and will not entertain in homes of which it is secretly ashamed.

But make your rooms attractive, appeal to the vaulting pride of youth, and you may worry that much less about Malucio's—and the other modern frivolities that his name symbolizes.

A guest room smartly and tastefully furnished—a refined and attractive dining room—will more than hold their own against the tinsel cheapness of Malucio's.

Nor is good furniture any longer a luxury for the favored few. THE PRESCOTT suite shown above, for instance, is a moderately priced pattern, conforming in every detail to the finest Berkey & Gay standards.

In style, in the selection of rare and beautiful woods, and in the rich texture of the finish and hand decorating, it reveals the skill of craftsmen long expert in the art of quality furniture making. The PRESCOTT is typical of values now on display at the store of your local Berkey & Gay dealer. Depend on his showing you furniture in which you may take deep pride—beautiful, well built, luxuriously finished, and moderately priced.

There is a Berkey & Gay pattern suited to every home—an infinite variety of styles at prices ranging all the way from $350 to $6,000.

Advertisement for Eveready Flashlight and Battery (1927)

The Song that STOPPED!

A child of five skipped down the garden path and laughed because the sky was blue. "Jane," called her mother from the kitchen window, "come here and help me bake your birthday cake." Little feet sped. "Don't fall," her mother warned.

Jane stood in the kitchen door and wrinkled her nose in joy. Her gingham dress was luminous against the sun. What a child! Dr. and Mrs. Wentworth cherished Jane.

"Go down to the cellar and get mother some preserver . . . the kind you like."

"The preserves are in the cellar," she chanted, making a progress twice around the kitchen. "Heigh-ho a-derry-o, the preserves are . . ." her voice grew fainter as she danced off. ". . . in the . . ."

The thread of song snapped. A soft *thud-thud*. Fear fluttered Mrs. Wentworth's heart. She rushed to the cellar door.

"Mother!" . . . a child screaming in pain. Mrs. Wentworth saw a little morsel of girlhood lying in a heap of gingham and yellow hair at the bottom of the dark stairs.

The sky is still blue. But there will be no birthday party tomorrow. An ambulance clanged up to Dr. Wentworth's house today. Jane's leg is broken.

If a flashlight had been hanging on a hook at the head of the cellar stairs, this little tragedy would have been averted. If Jane had been taught to use a flashlight as carefully as her father, Dr. Wentworth, had taught her to use a tooth-brush, a life need not have been endangered.

An Eveready Flashlight is always a convenience and often a life-saver. Keep one about the house, in the car; and take one with you wherever you go. Keep it supplied with fresh Eveready Batteries— the longest-lasting flashlight batteries made. Eveready Flashlights, $1.00 up.

NATIONAL CARBON CO., INC. EVEREADY FLASHLIGHTS & BATTERIES

A THOUSAND THINGS MAY HAPPEN IN THE DARK

10

Messenger of the New Age: Station KGIR in Butte
Mary Murphy

Before 1920, newspapers and magazines defined the limits of mass media in the United States. Until the end of World War I, Americans had learned about national and international events, sports contests, and the offerings of the new consumer culture by reading the columns of their local newspapers, by perusing the pages of such magazines as *Saturday Evening Post* and *Harper's Weekly*, or by browsing through nationally circulated catalogs such as those distributed by Sears, Roebuck, and Montgomery Ward. This all changed during the 1920s, however, as radio stations proliferated throughout the nation. First thought of as a public medium of education and moral uplift, by the end of the decade radio took on a new aspect as local stations and national networks began accepting commercial advertisements as a regular part of their programming. For the first time, Americans—even those living in the remotest parts of the country—could listen to "live" news coverage and participate in a national culture of consumption focused on the sale of an ever-increasing variety of goods.

In this essay, Mary Murphy uses the letters written by listeners to Station KGIR in Butte, Montana, to explore the impact that radio had on the lives of ordinary people. These letters, the equivalent to "letters to the editor" written to local newspapers, provide a rare opportunity to get inside the thoughts of people for whom sources are usually all but unobtainable.

As these letters reveal, KGIR listeners, like Americans everywhere, enthusiastically welcomed the new medium into their homes. On remote ranches and in small towns, families gathered around the radio to listen to news, sports, and especially the comedy and drama programs broadcast by the national networks. Even the Great Depression

"Messenger of the New Age: Station KGIR in Butte." *Montana: The Magazine of Western History*, 39 (Autumn, 1989), pp. 52–63. Reprinted by permission of the publisher.

failed to curtail the appeal of commercial radio in Butte, as radio helped to lift the spirits of local listeners and made people realize that they weren't alone in dealing with economic distress. During the 1930s, Murphy argues, radio became a companion for millions of Americans and created a national mass culture that altered the nation in fundamental ways.

....

Was dead from the waist both ways till I tuned in on KGIR but now hot dog I could climb a cactus bush sixty eight feet high with a panther under both arms trim my toe nails with a forty-five when I reached the summit slide back to earth without a scratch hot dawg whoopee cmon have one with us fellas wine for the ladies n everything.

With that classic western accolade greeting its inaugural program, radio station KGIR arrived in Butte, Montana, on February 1, 1929, just ahead of the Great Depression. It performed a dual, sometimes contradictory function during that economic crisis. In a time of almost universal belt-tightening, the allure of the radio impelled people to buy receivers on credit, and commercial programming bombarded listeners with advertisements designed to increase their desire for consumer goods. But the radio also provided a source of comfort, news, and entertainment for the unemployed and underemployed who could no longer afford movies, vacations, restaurant meals, and other pleasures of the consumer society. A radio was a substitute for many of the leisure activities that people gave up during those hard years, but it also prepared them to indulge freely in consumerism once good times returned. Through network programming, KGIR introduced Butte listeners to a developing national culture, while also giving considerable air time to local performers and shows. In this way, Butte's first commercial radio station created an amalgam of news and entertainment that celebrated local talent and served community groups, while exposing its audience to programs of national popularity and significance.

KGIR was Edmund B. Craney's brainchild. Until it began broadcasting, the only radio signals emanating from Butte were those of amateur operators. Arriving in Butte in 1927, Craney saw a potential market and applied for a commercial broadcast license. With wide-ranging and farsighted interests, Craney was the first station owner in Montana to affiliate with a national network, the National Broadcasting Company, in 1931. KGIR also became the flagship of a statewide network of radio stations known as the Z-Bar. In accordance with his own personal philosophy, Craney attempted through radio to instill in citizens of the Big Sky a sense of themselves as Montanans, rather than as isolated residents of an archipelago of small towns and cities.

Radio was the medium of communication of the 1920s and 1930s. The nation's first radio station, KDKA, Pittsburgh, broadcast the results of the Harding–Cox presidential election in 1920 and began regularly scheduled programs in 1921. Early radio fans were attracted not so much by regular transmissions or even the content of programs, but by the romance of distance. Radio telescoped the vast expanses of the West, bringing to rural dwellers the sounds of the city, facilitating communication between towns and outlying ranches, easing the loneliness of isolated lives. Edward P. Morgan, an Idahoan who became a broadcast commentator in Washington, D.C., dated the start of his love affair with radio to his father's purchase of a DeForest set in the mid-1920s. "My night sounds had been the sharp haunting bark of coyotes," Morgan remembered, "but now the boundaries of my world suddenly dilated far beyond the sagebrush hills of Idaho, and through the hissing swish of static, like a bell pealing in a snowstorm, came the sweet, wavering voices of KHJ, Los Angeles, KDKA, Pittsburgh, and, one enchanted evening, Havana, Cuba."

While entrancing, the signals from distant stations were irregular and spurred some Montanans to build local stations. Without the resources common in metropolitan areas, commercial radio in the state developed slowly and sporadically. Between 1922, when KDYS, Montana's first commercial station, debuted in Great Falls, and 1929, when KGIR went on the air in Butte, small stations opened in Havre, Missoula, Vida, Kalispell, and Billings. Programs depended on local talent and leaned heavily toward stock and grain market reports, coverage of school sports, updates on the weather, and direct messages to farm and ranch families.

Throughout the 1920s, commercial radio was distinctly non-commercial. Advertising agencies, sponsors, radio manufacturers, and broadcasters viewed the new medium as an educational tool, an avenue of cultural uplift. Sponsors limited their advertising to modest announcements of who was paying for the program at its beginning and end, or they attached brand names to orchestras and performers, such as the A & P Gypsies, the Lucky Strike Orchestra, and the Best Food Boys. Owen D. Young, chairman of General Electric and RCA, announced in 1926 that he considered the companies' new subsidiary, NBC, to be "semi-philanthropic."

By 1929, advertisers' insistence on sponsorship had faded. The advertising industry had mushroomed during the 1920s; its successful cultivation of a consumer society fed its continued growth. Agencies realized that the intimacy of radio offered an unprecedented opportunity to personalize advertising, and they discovered that listeners did not mind commercials. Listeners often heard the ads as part of the entertainment, and pollsters had found that what radio fans wanted was entertainment. Advertisers began to design commercials as

part of the show and to listen to radio station managers who advised: "Ditch Dvorak. They want 'Turkey in the Straw.'"

Radio in Butte bypassed the semiphilanthropic days of the 1920s. When the Symons Company of Spokane announced its intention to start up KGIR, the *Montana Free Press* reported that the station would be "frankly a commercial proposition." Ed Craney, KGIR's manager, had been involved in the radio business for seven years when he came to Butte. Already an amateur operator when he graduated from high school in Spokane in 1922, Craney got a job running a radio parts store owned by lawyer Thomas W. Symons, Jr. As in many small metropolitan areas, the absence of good radio signals in Spokane made it difficult to sell receiving sets, so Craney and Symons started their own radio station to boost equipment sales. KFDC, Spokane went on the air in October 1922, one of the more than fourteen hundred stations that received licenses from the Department of Commerce in 1922–1923. Business picked up, and the two men expanded their sales to western Montana. It was during the course of his sales trips that Craney pinpointed Butte, "a real rip-roaring town," as a plum site for a new station.

Craney received a license for KGIR in 1928 and began construction on the station late that year. He built studios in the third floor of Shiner's furniture store in uptown Butte and, to make sure the transmitter's antenna was fully supported, rigged it from Shiner's roof across the street to the roof of the opposite building. Radio fans avidly followed Craney's progress and geared up for the initial broadcast, scheduled for January 31. Shiner's offered a special price on "Freshman" radios, and the *Butte Daily Post* promised a free crystal set to any boy or girl who enrolled three new subscribers to the paper. Craney later claimed that radio dealers told him they sold three thousand crystal sets during the first week of broadcasting.

On the night of January 31, Butte listeners tuned in to a recording of the "Star Spangled

Banner" and the dedication of the station by the Catholic bishop, a Methodist minister, and a rabbi. Then followed twelve hours of musical selections and orations performed by men, women, and children from the Butte area, directed by three prominent Butte music teachers. Hundreds of letters and telegrams sent to the station the next day testified to listeners' delight.

About a month after KGIR's debut, Craney arranged to broadcast Herbert Hoover's inauguration. It was KGIR's first hookup with NBC and more than any other event illustrated the radio fever that gripped Butte. Days before the broadcast, a festive spirit infused the city, as radio owners planned "inauguration breakfasts" so that friends and relatives could gather to eat and drink and listen to Hoover's swearing-in. On inauguration day, crowds massed outside the stores of radio dealers who had hung loudspeakers on their buildings. The Butte Radio Club and the Montana Stock and Bond Company hosted open houses for listeners. Restaurants and department stores aired the broadcast for diners and shoppers. Public and Catholic high school students listened in their auditoriums. Two thousand seventh and eighth graders heard the program over a loudspeaker installed in the Broadway Theater and cheered as the bands passed the reviewing stand in Washington, D.C. The following day, the *Montana Standard*, which had absorbed most of the cost of the program, reported: "The inauguration was made actual, vital—something a great deal more than a remote happening . . . it was as if the listener here were standing among the throngs on the capital lawn. . . ."

The inauguration broadcast stimulated radio sales in Butte. Orton Brothers music store, which had lamented that "the only difficulty in recent months has been to obtain a sufficient number of sets to supply the demands of our customers," announced the imminent arrival of a major shipment of new radios. One trainload of four thousand Majestic receivers, the "biggest single shipment of radio receivers

ever routed to the northwest," arrived at the Butte depot on March 23. Butte business directories had listed no radio dealers during the 1920s; by 1930 there were five, and by 1934 seven were serving the city's fans. People added radios to the list of durable goods, such as automobiles and furniture, that they purchased on installment plans. They accepted indebtedness for the delights provided by the radio and the ability of KGIR to link Butte to a larger world in ways more intimate and immediate than newspapers, traveling theater, or even the movies.

Between 1929 and 1931, before KGIR affiliated with NBC and began receiving nationally syndicated programs, the station explored the potential of broadcasting from Butte. Management created fanciful promotions to multiply advertising revenues, engaged local talent who performed in the station's studios, supplementing the phonograph records and occasional transcriptions that formed the bulk of programming, increased coverage of local events, and groped toward a determination of listeners' pleasures. Craney's unfamiliarity with Butte led to some gaffs that other staff members caught. A few months after its debut, for example, the station began a request hour. One night when Craney was running the program, his salesman Leo McMullen came in and asked what he was doing. Craney replied, "We're having request hour." "Request hour, hell," replied McMullen, "you're advertising every whore in Butte." "Gladys at 2 Upper Terrace" and "Dorothy at 8 Lower Terrace" had quickly discovered the commercial benefits of local broadcasting.

Most broadcasts, however, were aboveboard. Local celebrities like Howard Melaney, the "singing fireman" of the Northern Pacific Railway, joined a roster of performances by the Camp Fire Girls, the Rocky Mountain Garden Club, and other civic groups. In May 1929, KGIR observed National Music Week with a special choral broadcast of eighty-five Butte mothers and daughters. Craney solicited local groups to put on their own shows. The Marian

White Arts and Crafts Club proudly noted that "our radio station" wanted programs from the club's various departments and promptly responded with short talks three times a week. In the fall of 1929, KGIR broadcast the Rotana Club's Montana Products Dinner from the Masonic Temple, a gala evening celebrating Montana-grown products, speeches, and music.

Beginning in 1929 Craney had appealed to NBC for "programs of national importance" and sought affiliate status with the network. He described the isolation of many Montana listeners who "can receive no other station than KGIR and many of them depend on our station for the newspaper can reach them only from 24 to 72 hours late." NBC was concentrated in the East. At the time of Craney's request it had extended its service to only a few cities west of the Mississippi and feared the unprofitability of a hook-up in a small market like Montana. Craney persuaded Senator Burton K. Wheeler to intercede; and NBC, hoping to please an increasingly powerful politician, partially accommodated Craney. On November 28, 1931, KGIR affiliated with NBC, although the network supplied only an incomplete roster of programs to the station.

Despite the new shows available through NBC, Craney continued to solicit local talent sponsored by local advertisers and to balance commercial broadcasting with community service. One of the most successful programs of the 1930s was the amateur hour sponsored by Symons Department Store. Ray Schilling, advertising manager for the store, decided to test the powers of radio, and Symons scheduled a sale and advertised only on KGIR; nothing appeared in the newspapers. The response was overwhelming, and Schilling was converted. He and his brother then developed Butte's own amateur hour—a fad that was sweeping the radio world during the mid-1930s. Art Chappelle played his accordion on the amateur hour; and shortly thereafter Craney approached Art's father, the owner of Chappelle's Cleaning Works, to sponsor a fif-

teen-minute program of Art's accordion music. Art, who during high school had a band called the Whirlwinds and still moonlighted as a musician in addition to driving his father's delivery truck, was happy to oblige. Three times a week he stopped his truck at the KGIR studio, brought in his accordion, and played a selection of polkas and waltzes. Often he performed melodies popular with Butte's ethnic communities—an entire selection of Italian music, or Irish, Polish, or Finnish songs. Art played requests, signed an occasional autograph, and was delighted when he dropped off someone's dry cleaning and they said, "I just heard you on the radio!"

While hundreds of Butte residents performed on KGIR, thousands participated in station-sponsored contests or wrote unsolicited letters. In 1930, Craney began conducting listeners' surveys to determine the average number of hours each radio receiver was turned on each day (in 1930, ten hours; in 1937, nine and a half); how many hours it was tuned to KGIR (in 1930, seven hours; in 1937, eight and a half); what the favorite programs were and why; and what suggestions for new programs and new sponsors listeners might have. The responses that have been preserved reveal a wealth of detail about the likes and dislikes of Butte's radio audience and the role that radio played in the lives of KGIR listeners during the darkest days of the Great Depression. For instance, Craney determined that jazz and old-time string-band melodies were Butte's favorite kind of music and that comedy programs eased the worries of economic hard times.

Through the polls and the success of a few new programs, broadcasters and advertisers across the country discovered that during the Depression audiences wanted lighter fare than classical music and Department of Agriculture reports. The tremendous popularity of "Amos 'n' Andy" demonstrated the potential audience for comedy programs. Advertising agencies, who were producing most shows by the 1930s, experimented with transposing to radio many of the genres already present in popular literature—western, detective stories, serialized melodramas—as well as developing new formats like amateur hours and quiz shows.

Soap operas, churned out in assembly-line style, dominated air time between ten o'clock in the morning and five o'clock at night. Criticized by some for encouraging neuroses in housewives, "washboard weepers" also had their defenders in those who interpreted them as morality plays, easily digested lessons in good and evil. A national study discovered that despite the far-fetched story lines, women found the serials useful sources of information regarding interpersonal relationships. Listeners drew from the dramas some "dos and don'ts" of child-rearing, dating, and marriage. They saw in the characters reflections of people in their own families, or they put themselves in analogous situations and hoped to pattern their behavior to attain similarly successful outcomes. One young woman who followed a soap opera argument between a jealous boy and his girlfriend, observed: "that is just like my boyfriend . . . listening to the stories like that makes me know how other girls act and listening to the way the girl argued I know how to tell my boyfriend where he can get off at." A Butte woman wrote KGIR that her favorite program was the serial "One Man's Family," because "I have a younger brother like Jack and I have grown to understand his ways listening to Jack and Claudia talk." Another testified about the same program: "it is a thirty-minute picture of American life that might as well have been taken in Butte."

Historians of radio have noted how directly and personally Americans responded to the new medium. Listeners welcomed broadcasters into their family circle; and through their letters to stations, fans created a democratic dialogue of praise, criticism, and suggestion in which they conveyed a sense of themselves as direct participants in the broadcast experience. Stations and the networks encouraged fans to correspond with them. During the early 1930s, more than two-thirds of all NBC programs explicitly requested audiences to write in, and the volume of mail was phenomenal. In 1926, NBC received 383,000 communications; in 1929, one million; and in 1931, seven million. CBS claimed that it received over twelve million pieces of mail in 1931.

Much of the mail to stations during the 1930s was in response to free offers of prizes in exchange for a cereal box top or some other evidence of the purchase of a sponsor's product. Pictures of Little Orphan Annie, magnet rings, slide whistles, and Tom Mix decoder rings kept the mail bags of America full during the Depression. During the 1937 Christmas season, KGIR offered a free prize for every letter to Santa Claus it received. For a seasonal program, selected letters were read on the air, interspersed with chatter between Santa and his helpers. After two such shows, the station had received three thousand letters and exhausted its grab bag. Hoping to slow the flow of mail, it asked that future letters include a sales receipt from a station advertiser. Three thousand more letters poured in. Broadcasters' invitations to the radio audience encouraged a letter-writing habit that ranged from participating in contests to conveying intimate thoughts and opinions to the President of the United States. Ed Craney confirmed that at times the largest volume of mail received by KGIR was in response to a program sponsored by the Farmers' Union, which discussed New Deal legislation and urged people to write to President Roosevelt.

During the mid-1930s, KGIR kept a tally of the mail it received: 5,770 in 1934 and 23,065 in 1938. Butte women outnumbered men two to one as correspondents, paralleling national trends in which women outdistanced men who wrote radio fan mail. National studies also determined that lower income people and those with little education wrote the most letters to radio stations, radio stars, and advertisers. The small number of letters to KGIR that were saved, 165 of them from 1933 and 1935, tends to support that claim. Nevertheless, Butte was a working-class community, and it is natural that the majority of letters to KGIR would have come from working-class households. Of the 15,322 men employed in Butte in 1930, 62 percent of them were engaged either in mining or manufacturing, in contrast to the 10 percent employed as professionals or in clerical positions. Of those whose occupations could be determined, miners compromised 31 percent of the adult males who wrote letters preserved in KGIR's files. Of the remaining adult male writers, only one was a management position. A few women married to professionals, managers, and business owners also sent their opinions to the station. Eighty percent of the adult women writers, however, were wedded to working-class men or were themselves wage-earners.

National studies estimated that the majority of letter-writers wrote to stations in response to contests. But KGIR correspondents sent as many unsolicited letters and replies to surveys that did not promise any material reward as they did to prize offers. During nine months in 1934, the station received 2,121 survey responses, compared to 2,071 responses to offers. In 1935, the number of letters seeing prizes was only 76 more than the 6,253 other letters received. Clearly, KGIR listeners believed that it was not only appropriate, but perhaps also necessary, to share their opinions with station management.

Gratuitous advice, pungent criticism, and heartfelt best wishes accompanied both thoughtful and absurd suggestions. Some wrote to say that KGIR was the "only half-way decent program on the air," others to warn that it was playing too much jazz and should "crowd the trash off the air." George Hardesty, a carpenter, conveyed most eloquently the fondness that many listeners felt for their radios and for KGIR. Writing in 1933, Hardesty described his radio as a powerful spur to the imagination and spoke of the relief it delivered during the psychologically bleak days of the 1930s:

There was a time when I saw a Movie twice a week, but not in these slim times. And with my radio, I really can't say that I mind so much. Any evening there are shows come to me over KGIR, but Wednesday evening when Sherlock Holmes unravels his mysteries, I am positive I don't miss my shows. I can see the two old gentlemen, as if they were in my room, poreing over their G. Washington Coffee [the show's sponsor]. Certainly I am entirely unaware of a depression when one of these life and death mysteries is on, and honestly, anything that can make me do that is worth a lot. Thats one of the reasons I like it, perhaps the main one.

All over the country radio fans attested to the cheering effects of comedy and drama programs during the Depression, and the Butte audience was no exception. The character that elicited far and away the most responses from KGIR listeners was Ed Wynn's "Fire Chief," sponsored by Texaco. Fans wrote: "He will cure the worst case of the Blues and even make you forget the Depression"; "Ed sure keeps the radio audience in an uproar from start to finish, which is just what is needed by all of us during these trying times . . .", "It is humorous and produces a '*good laugh*' which I consider necessary to offset the serious problems of this strenuous life of ours." Wynn's show provoked some poignant compositions on the part of fans. Young Harry Lonner sent in this dispatch:

A dance orchestra is on the air. Dad is reading the newspaper. Ma is busy with some sewing or other household task. Sis and I are doing schoolwork. Suddenly, comes the shrill scream of a siren! The clang of bells! Ed Wynn is on the air! Dad lets the newspaper drop in his lap, Ma comes into the parlor and sits close to the radio; and Sis and I stop our schoolwork. . . . Dad, Sis and I grin and chuckle after every joke, but Ma laughs till her sides ache. This is the one big reason why I like the Texaco Program. For fifteen minutes Dad forgets about his job, Ma quits worrying about how she is going to pay the bills, and I am happy to see them happy. Old Man Depression is forgotten and Happiness is King.

Time and again writers expressed gratitude that they had been able to buy their radios during good times, because now they were their only source of pleasure and news. Using empathy and imagination, radio listeners transported themselves, however briefly, from their surroundings. Listening to the travails of Little Orphan Annie made "our troubles so small compared to our more unfortunate fellow beings." The radio compensated those not able to travel during the vacation season—even though unemployment guaranteed "most of us are having quite a long vacation"—by taking them to the Mountains of the Moon, the jungles of Malaya and Africa. And the radio was democratic. As Ted Wilson, a clerk at Southside Hardware, remarked: "it is a A one entertainment equally alluring for the rich or poor."

By the 1930s, radio had become part of many people's daily lives, a companion that did more than lift the blues of the Depression. Mrs. George McCoy wrote KGIR that the comedy of an early morning show, "The Gazooks," along with three cups of coffee "make it possible to face the horrors of the new day with a smile." Mrs. Nellie Sacry chronicled a day "beginning with the Gazooks—who help us get up better natured for you can't be grumpy when someone makes you laugh." Her eight-year-old son waited at the door with his coat on to dash out to school as soon as "Cecil and Sally" was over, and the family's day continued through the "Music Box" at dinner time. Mrs. George Hardesty praised the sweet music that calmed her frayed nerves after a day of housework and made her "a better me, to meet my husband and family."

Radio fans took programs far more seriously and invested them with more importance than advertising men or writers ever imagined. They accepted radio almost uncritically, as a wise seer who provided advice, pleasure, and testimonials for reliable products. Listeners wrote amazingly innocent and intimate letters to fictional characters and national corporations. Mrs. J. W. Larson, a miner's wife, lauded a children's program sponsored by General Mills:

Personally, Skippy's program has helped me a great deal. My little girl is four years old, she can't tell time yet, but she never lets me forget Skippy. Skippy has taught her to brush her own hair and not to forget to clean her theeth [sic] and fingernails. Before Skippy was on the air I couldn't get her to eat any cereal, but now I have no trouble. She don't get Wheaties very often now, as her father isn't working. But she eats her oatmeal every morning. She had Wheaties every morning when her Dad was working.

Craney's calls during the 1930s for new programs and sponsors elicited a wide variety of suggestions and documented the energy and thought that many listeners put into "their station." More than one person thought a show relating tales of Butte and Montana history would be entertaining. Mrs. T. H. Wilkinson suggested having pioneers relate their experiences of settling the area or perhaps retelling some tales of hunting and fishing. "After all," she concluded, "Butte is a good old town and just full of good stories to tell." H. C. Howard proposed a different way of exploring Montana, a series of "short enthusiastic talks" recounting the "delights of motoring in Montana and describing each week some historical or scenic spot that is little known in the state and describing how it is reached, the condition of the roads to this spot and various points of interest along the route." The show would be accompanied by popular music and paid for by service stations, hotels, auto camps, or businesses patronized by tourists.

Housewives recommended programs that would interest them during the day: a morning exercise routine, advice to young housekeepers on arranging furniture, reports on new clothing styles, a menu contest of meals "that the average housewife could afford to serve." From Mrs. Adah Daugherty, wife of a salesman, came a letter that could have gotten her a job in any advertising agency:

There are things dear to the heart of every woman, and dearest of these things is her personal appearance. If she could go to the radio and tune in on a beauty talk that would deal with any phase of a woman's face, hair, figure, hands, and feet, I dare say that only the door bell could draw her away. These things she might be able to get in the advertisements in the current magazines, or an occasional article, but the busy woman has very little time for reading. There is a psychological difference between reading the printed word, and hearing the same spoken. The latter catches the instant attention and is retained longer. With this given by some firm or firms in Butte, and the talk read by a woman, it would prove most effective.

Mrs. Daugherty continued with a discussion of possible sponsors and a reflection on the future of advertising: "Radio is the new means of advertising, and is here to stay. More and more firms are going to adopt clever methods of advertising, and owing to the depression, more vigorous methods." She acknowledged that the intrinsic worth of the product was immaterial and that by appealing to women's vanity a manufacturer could successfully peddle anything. "Woman is eternally looking for the foundation of youth . . . she will be a susceptible listener to a program on beauty talks, and the firm to which she is listening will be the one to gain." And in words reminiscent of the personal testimony advertisements that were popular in magazines of the time, she concluded: "I am a woman. I know."

Mrs. Daugherty was unusual in analyzing the advertising industry's relationship to radio with such perspicacity. The overwhelming majority of listeners who wrote the station and mentioned sponsors conveyed a simple gratitude that corporations were providing them with so many hours of delight. Some avowed they enjoyed the advertising as much as the programming. Mrs. Henry Webking claimed that "the K.G.I.R. announcer tells us so much about the firm and its products during the course of the program, and in so few well chosen words, that we really enjoy the advertising and absorb it as much as we do the request numbers." Fans appeared to feel that the least they could do to demonstrate their appreciation was to buy the sponsor's product.

Margaret Carolus, who enjoyed the Jack Benny program paid for by Jello, found the advertising so compelling "that it has encouraged me to eat and like Jello—though I had never cared for it before." Clarence Roper testified that smoking Edgeworth tobacco gave him as much of a thrill as the music on the Edgeworth program. Ruth O'Brien begged KGIR to "keep Orphan Annie on the radio for a little ten-year-old like me" and promised, "I'll drink lots and lots of Ovaltine."

Such promises and testimonials are weighty evidence of the power that advertisers exerted on the radio audience. Craney's device for generating new ideas may have provided the kernels for only a few marketable programs, but it reaped a harvest of radio fans participating actively in their own seduction by consumer culture. The lure of winning a prize coaxed them into experimenting with the language of sales, extolling the virtues of any and all products. The impetus of a contest may have led listeners to embellish their appreciation of certain products, but the internal structure of their letters, the way in which they linked product use to their daily lives, and the effort by which men, women, and children sat down to write lengthy missives—often much longer than that required or desired by contest rules—testify to the earnestness with which most correspondents wrote.

When Helen and Robert Lynd observed the popularity of radio in Middletown in the early 1920s, they also hypothesized that radio, along with national advertising and syndicated newspapers, would act to standardize much of Middletown's culture. Writer Dorothy Johnson certainly found that to be the case in Montana:

Everybody, all over, could listen to the same demagogues, howl at the same comedians, make a fad of the new slang. Everybody with a radio . . . suddenly was sophisticated, part of the great outside world. . . . Listeners became addicts, so accustomed to having sounds of any old kind coming into the house that they were nervous when it was quiet. . . . For better or worse, the quiet, the isolation, the parochialism was gone.

KGIR brought those forces of homogenization to Butte. Yet, throughout the 1930s, the station continued to air programs that spotlighted local talent, that extolled the unique virtues of the Montana landscape, that caused listeners to feel an allegiance to their local station—not only gratitude to national sponsors. As much as fans appreciated syndicated shows, they loved listening to themselves and their neighbors more. Jim Harmon declared that "the very stuff of radio was imagination," and KGIR permitted citizens to let their imaginations run riot. Symons's amateur hour nourished the dreams of local performers. Neighbors guessed at the hidden messages conveyed by songs on the request hour. Families gathered around the radio to listen to their sons and daughters sing, play in jazz bands, and recite poetry. Members of Butte's different ethnic communities waited for special holiday programs that featured their musical heritage. Private delights, broadcast over the air, assumed a cloak of public importance.

The effect that radio had on listeners is evident in the long and pleasurable memories that people associate with KGIR. Mona Daly "vividly" recalled in 1988 the afternoon in the 1930s on which her voice teacher at the Webster school chose her and a classmate to go to the KGIR studio and sing a duet of "Juanita"—"a definite thrill." Fifty years after he first heard the melodies, Jacob Jovick could name eighty-one songs that KGIR played on the request hour and thirty-one different programs that he listened to and apologize because "there were others I don't recall."

Ed Craney, his small staff, and the KGIR audience composed a score that harmonized strains of local, regional, and national culture. Craney had hoped that radio would make Montanans "realize that there was more in Montana than the little town that they lived in." To gain that end, he invited Montanans' participation in his enterprise. Miss May Gates of Opportunity was one of twenty-four would-be news editors who volunteered their services to pass on the tidings of their communities to the KGIR audience. KGIR's listeners thus had access not only to national news, New York opera, and southern string-band music, but also to "all the news and gossip that is told each evening at the Opportunity store"—and in stores in Butte, Melrose, Rocker, Deer Lodge, Twin Bridges, and a handful of other communities in KGIR's broadcast radius. KGIR introduced its audience to nationally standardized programs that some analysts feared would erase the cultural diversity of America. The station's commitment to airing the voices of its own region, however, guaranteed a medley of cultural expression. Listeners greeted radio's first decade in Butte with uncritical pleasure. KGIR became a source of delight, education, and emotional relief to thousands weathering the Great Depression, and May Gates spoke for many when she exclaimed, "What a wonderful invention the radio has been."

GLOSSARY

Antonin Dvôrák (1841–1904): Czech composer best known for his Symphony in E Minor, from *The New World*, written while he was in the United States.

Little Orphan Annie: Popular comic strip character.

Tom Mix (1880–1940): Film actor noted for his performances in silent Westerns.

Middletown: An early sociological study of an American community during the 1920s.

IMPLICATIONS

In this essay, Murphy reveals the multiple impacts that radio had on the lives of ordinary people in Butte, Montana. Why do you think ordinary Americans responded so personally to early radio broadcasts and advertising?

PAST TRACES

Since the Panic of 1819, Americans have learned to adjust to the upswings and downturns of the nation's economy. Enjoying the fruits of ample employment in good times and tightening their belts in bad, ordinary Americans have long drawn upon personal and family resources in weathering the cycles of American industrial life.

Yet nothing prepared the American people for the experience of the Great Depression of the 1930s. Beginning with the stock market crash of October 1929, Americans absorbed one economic blow after another until, by 1933, a quarter of the nation's workforce was unemployed. In the end, few families escaped the impact of the declining incomes and diminished expectations of the Depression era.

In this document, taken from the pages of the popular-radical magazine, *The Masses*, Meridel LeSueur takes us into the world of the unemployed. Focusing on people searching for work at a local employment bureau in Minneapolis, LeSueur documents the anxiety, frustration, and despair felt by millions of Americans in an era when there were few social programs—unemployment insurance, Medicare, or family income support—to aid those in need.

As you read this article, you may want to ask yourself to what degree the author's own views shaped the story she wrote. LeSueur's sympathies clearly lay with the plight of the unemployed; she went on to join the Communist party and to write about the labor movement and national politics for the remainder of her career. In what ways do you think LeSueur's personal history influenced the subjects she chose to write about and what she had to say? Could her account of the unemployed be objective despite her personal sympathies and point of view?

Meridel LeSueur, Despair of Unemployed Women

I am sitting in the city free employment bureau. It's the women's section. We have been sitting here now for four hours. We sit here every day, waiting for a job. There are no jobs. Most of us have had no breakfast. Some have had scant rations for over a year. Hunger makes a human being lapse into a state of lethargy, especially city hunger. Is there any place else in the world where a human being is supposed to go hungry amidst plenty without an outcry, without protest, where only the boldest steal or kill for bread, and the timid crawl the streets, hunger like the beak of a terrible bird at the vitals?

We sit looking at the floor. No one dares think of the coming winter. There are only a few more days of summer. Everyone is anxious to get work to lay up something for that long siege of bitter cold. But there is no work. Sitting in the room we all know it. That is why we don't talk much. We look at the floor dreading to see that knowledge in each other's eyes. There is a kind of humiliation in it. We look away from each other. We look at the floor. It's too terrible to see this animal terror in each other's eyes.

So we sit hour after hour, day after day, waiting for a job to come in. There are many women for a single job. A thin sharp woman sits inside a wire cage looking at a book. For four hours we have watched her looking at that book. She has a hard little eye. In the small bare room there are half a dozen women sitting on the benches waiting. Many come and go. Our faces are all familiar to each other, for we wait here every day.

This is a domestic employment bureau. Most of the women who come here are middle-aged, some have families, some have raised their families and are now alone, some have men who are out of work. Hard times and the man leaves to hunt for work. He doesn't find it. He drifts on. The woman probably doesn't hear from him for a long time. She expects it. She isn't surprised. She struggles alone to feed the many mouths. Sometimes she gets help from the charities. If she's clever she can get herself a good living from the charities, if she's naturally a lick spittle, naturally a little docile and cunning. If she's proud then she starves silently, leaving her children to find work, coming home after a day's searching to wrestle with her house, her children.

Some such story is written on the faces of all these women. There are young girls too, fresh from the country. Some are made brazen too soon by the city. There is a great exodus of girls from the farms into the city now. Thousands of farms have been vacated completely in Minnesota. The girls are trying to get work. The prettier ones can get jobs in the stores when there are any, or waiting on tables, but these jobs are only for the attractive and the adroit. The others, the real peasants, have a more difficult time.

Bernice sits next to me. She is a Polish woman of thirty-five. She has been working in people's kitchens for fifteen years or more. She is large, her great body in mounds, her face brightly scrubbed. She has a peasant mind and finds it hard even yet to understand the maze of the city where trickery is worth more than brawn. Her blue eyes are not clever but slow and trusting. She suffers from loneliness and lack of talk. When you speak to her, her face lifts and brightens as if you had spoken through a great darkness, and she talks magically of little things as if the weather were magic, or tells some crazy tale of her adventures on the city streets, embellishing them in bright colors until they hang heavy and thick like embroidery. She loves the city anyhow. It's exciting to her, like a bazaar. She loves to go shopping and get a bargain, hunting out the places where stale bread and cakes can be had for a few cents. She likes walking the streets looking for men to take her to a picture show. Sometimes she goes to five picture shows in one day, or she sits through one the entire day until she knows all the dialog by heart.

She came to the city a young girl from a Wisconsin farm. The first thing that happened to her, a charlatan dentist took out all her good shining teeth and the fifty dollars she had saved working in a canning factory. After that she met men in the park who told her how to look out for herself, corrupting her peasant mind, teaching her to mistrust everyone. Sometimes now she forgets to mistrust everyone and gets taken in. They taught her to get what she could for nothing, to count her change, to go back if she found herself cheated, to demand her rights.

She lives alone in little rooms. She bought seven dollars' worth of second-hand furniture eight years ago. She rents a room for perhaps three dollars a month in an attic, sometimes in a cold house. Once the house where she stayed was condemned and everyone else moved out and she lived there all winter alone on the top floor. She spent only twenty-five dollars all winter.

She wants to get married but she sees what happens to her married friends, left with children to support, worn out before their time. So she stays single. She is virtuous. She is slightly deaf from hanging out clothes in winter. She had done people's washings and cooking for fifteen years and in that time saved thirty dollars. Now she hasn't worked steady for a year and she has spent the thirty dollars. She had dreamed of having a little house or a houseboat perhaps with a spot of ground for a few chickens. This dream she will never realize.

She has lost all her furniture now along with the dream. A married friend whose husband is gone gives her a bed for which she pays by doing a great deal of work for the woman. She comes here every day now sitting bewildered, her pudgy hands folded in her lap. She is hungry. Her great flesh has begun to hang in folds. She has been living on crackers. Sometimes a box of crackers lasts a week. She has a friend who's a baker and he sometimes steals the stale loaves and brings them to her.

It's one of the great mysteries of the city where women go when they are out of work and hungry. There are not many women in the bread line. There are no flop houses for women as there are for men, where a bed can be had for a quarter or less. You don't see women lying on the floor at the mission in the free flops. They obviously don't sleep in the jungle or under newspapers in the park. There is no law I suppose against their being in these places but the fact is they rarely are.

Yet there must be as many women out of jobs in cities and suffering extreme poverty as there are men. What happens to them? Where do they go? Try to get into the Y.W. without any money or looking down at heel. Charities take care of very few and only those that are called "deserving." The lone girl is under suspicion by the virgin women who dispense charity.

I've lived in cities for many months broke, without help, too timid to get in bread lines. I've known many women to live like this until they simply faint on the street from privations, without saying a word to anyone. A woman will shut herself up in a room until it is taken away from her, and eat a cracker a day and be as quiet as a mouse so there are no social statistics concerning her.

I don't know why it is, but a woman will do this unless she has dependents, will go for weeks verging on starvation, crawling in some hole, going through the streets ashamed, sitting in libraries, parks, going for days without speaking to a living soul like some exiled beast, keeping the runs mended in her stockings, shut up in terror in her own misery, until she becomes too super-sensitive and timid to even ask for a job.

Bernice says even strange men she has met in the park have sometimes, that is in better days, given her a loan to pay her room rent. She has always paid them back.

In the afternoon the young girls, to forget the hunger and the deathly torture and fear of being jobless, try to pick up a man to take them to a ten-cent show. They never go to more expensive ones, but they can always find a man willing to spend a dime to have the company of a girl for the afternoon.

Sometimes a girl facing the night without shelter will approach a man for lodging. A woman always asks a man for help. Rarely another woman. I have known girls to sleep in men's rooms for the night on a pallet without molestation and be given breakfast in the morning.

It's no wonder these young girls refuse to marry, refuse to rear children. They are like certain savage tribes, who, when they have been conquered, refuse to breed.

Not one of them but looks forward to starvation for the coming winter. We are in a jungle and know it. We are beaten, entrapped. There is no way out. Even if there were a job, even if that thin acrid woman came and gave everyone in the room a job for a few days, a few hours, at thirty cents an hour, this would all be repeated tomorrow, the next day and the next.

Not one of these women but knows that despite years of labor there is only starvation, humiliation in front of them.

Mrs. Grey, sitting across from me, is a living spokesman for the futility of labor. She is a warning. Her hands are scarred with labor. Her body is a great puckered scar. She has given birth to six children, buried three, supported them all alive and dead, bearing them, burying them, feeding them. Bred in hunger they have been spare, susceptible to disease. For seven years she tried to save her boy's arm from amputation, diseased from tuberculosis of the bone. It is almost too suffocating to think of that long close horror of years of child-bearing, child-feeding, rearing, with the bare suffering of providing a meal and shelter.

Now she is fifty. Her children, economically insecure, are drifters. She never hears of them. She doesn't know if they are alive. She doesn't know if she is alive. Such subtleties of suffering are not for her. For her the brutality of hunger and cold. Not until these are done away with can those subtle feelings that make a human being be indulged.

She is lucky to have five dollars ahead of her. That is her security. She has a tumor that she will die of. She is thin as a worn dime with her tumor sticking out of her side. She is brittle and bitter. Her face is not the face of a human being. She has borne more than it is possible for a human being to bear. She is reduced to the least possible denominator of human feelings.

It is terrible to see her little bloodshot eyes like a beaten hound's, fearful in terror.

We cannot meet her eyes. When she looks at any of us we look away. She is like a woman drowning and we turn away. We must ignore those eyes that are surely the eyes of a person drowning, doomed. She doesn't cry out. She goes down decently. And we all look away.

The young ones know though. I don't want to marry. I don't want any children. So they all say. No children. No marriage. They arm themselves alone, keep up alone. The man is helpless now. He cannot provide. If he propagates he cannot take care of his young. The means are not in his hands. So they live alone. Get what fun they can. The life risk is too horrible now. Defeat is too clearly written on it.

So we sit in this room like cattle, waiting for a nonexistent job, willing to work to the farthest atom of energy, unable to work, unable to get food and lodging, unable to bear children—here we must sit in this shame looking at the floor, worse than beasts at a slaughter.

It is appalling to think that these women sitting so listless in the room may work as hard as it is possible for a human being to work, may labor night and day, like Mrs. Grey wash streetcars from midnight to dawn and offices in the early evening, scrub for fourteen and fifteen hours a day, sleep only five hours or so, do this their whole lives, and never earn one day of security, having always before them the pit of the future. The endless labor, the bending back, the water-soaked hands, earning never more than a week's wages, never having in their hands more life than that.

It's not the suffering of birth, death, love that the young reject, but the suffering of endless labor without dream, eating the spare bread in bitterness, being a slave without the security of a slave.

—*Source*: Meridel LeSueur, "Women on the Breadlines," *New Masses*, January 1932.

11

What the Depression Did to People
Edward R. Ellis

The American economy has a long history of cyclical recessions and depressions dating back to the eighteenth century. But none of the depressions could compare in severity or longevity to that which struck Americans between 1929 and 1941. Following a decade of unprecedented prosperity, which saw the rapid expansion of consumer goods production and the introduction of consumer credit to pay for these goods, the Great Depression took Americans by surprise. What had gone wrong?

Modern historians and economists now view the Depression as the consequence of underconsumption—that is, the overproduction of goods for sale and the lack of buyers with sufficient wages to purchase them. But to the unemployed workers, the dispossessed farmers, and their families, the Depression—whatever its cause—was the most disastrous event of their lives. By 1931, over eleven million workers, nearly a third of the labor force, were unemployed, and the average farm income had declined to 60 percent of 1929 levels. In this essay, Edward R. Ellis provides a wide panorama of life during the Depression, surveying its effects on the rich as well as the poor. He finds that the Great Depression scarred the lives of all people, regardless of social class, and shaped the outlook of everyone who lived through it.

The Depression smashed into the nation with such fury that men groped for superlatives to express its impact and meaning.

Edmund Wilson compared it to an earthquake. It was "like the explosion of a bomb dropped in the midst of society," according to the Social Science Research Council Committee on Studies in Social Aspects of the Depression.

Alfred E. Smith said the Depression was equivalent to war, while Supreme Court Justice Louis D. Brandeis and Bernard Baruch declared that it was worse than war. Philip La Follette, the governor of Wisconsin, said: "We are in the midst of the greatest domestic crisis since the Civil War." Governor Roosevelt agreed in these words: "Not since the dark days of the Sixties have the people of this state and nation faced problems as grave, situations as difficult, suffering as severe." A jobless textile worker told Louis Adamic: "I wish there would be war again." In a war against a foreign enemy all Americans might at least have felt united by a common purpose, and production would have boomed.

Poor and rich alike felt anxious and helpless. Steel magnate Charles M. Schwab, despite his millions and the security of his Manhattan palace, freely confessed: "I'm afraid. Every man is afraid." J. David Stern, a wealthy newspaper publisher, became so terrified that he later wrote in his autobiography: "I sat in my back office, trying to figure out what to do. To be explicit, I sat in my private bathroom. My bowels were loose from fear." Calvin Coolidge dolorously told a friend: "I can see nothing to give ground for hope."

Herbert C. Pell, a rich man with a country estate near Governor Roosevelt's, said the country was doomed unless it could free itself from the rich, who have "shown no realization that what you call free enterprise means anything but greed." Marriner Eccles, a banker and economist who had *NOT* lost his fortune, wrote that "I awoke to find myself at the bottom of a pit without any known means of scaling its sheer sides." According to Dwight W. Morrow, a Morgan associate, diplomat and

Senator: "Most of my friends think the world is coming to an end—that is, the world as we know it." Reinhold Niebuhr, the learned and liberal clergyman, said that rich "men and women speculated in drawing-rooms on the best kind of poison as a means to oblivion from the horrors of revolution."

In Youngstown, Ohio, a friend of Mayor Joseph L. Heffernan stood beside the mayor's desk and said: "My wife is frantic. After working at the steel mill for twenty-five years I've lost my job and I'm too old to get other work. If you can't do something for me, I'm going to kill myself." Governor Gifford Pinchot of Pennsylvania got a letter from a jobless man who said: "I cannot stand it any longer." Gan Kolski, an unemployed Polish artist from Greenwich Village, leaped to his death from the George Washington Bridge, leaving this note: "To All: If you cannot hear the cry of starving millions, listen to the dead, brothers. Your economic system is dead."

An architect, Hugh Ferriss, stood on the parapet of a tall building in Manhattan and thought to himself that the nearby skyscrapers seemed like monuments to the rugged individualism of the past. Thomas Wolfe wrote: "I believe that we are lost here in America, but I believe we shall be found." Democratic Senator Thomas Gore of Oklahoma called the Depression an economic disease. Henry Ford, on the other hand, said the Depression was "a wholesome thing in general."

Obviously, the essence of a depression is widespread unemployment. In one of the most fatuous remarks on record, Calvin Coolidge said: "The final solution of unemployment is work." He might have added that water is wet. Senator Robert Wagner of New York called unemployment inexcusable.

A decade before the Crash the British statesman David Lloyd George had said: "Unemployment, with its injustice for the man who seeks and thirsts for employment, who begs for labour and cannot get it, and who is punished for failure he is not responsible for by the starvation of his children—that torture is something that private enterprise ought to remedy for its own sake." Winston Churchill now used the same key word, "torture," in a similar comment: "This problem of unemployment is the most torturing that can be presented to a civilized society."

Before Roosevelt became President and named Frances Perkins his secretary of labor, she was so pessimistic that she said publicly it might take a quarter century to solve the unemployment problem. A Pennsylvania commission studied 31,159 workless men and then reported that the typical unemployed man was thirty-six years old, native-born, physically fit and with a good previous work record. This finding contradicted Henry Ford's belief that the unemployed did not want to work.

However, the Pennsylvania study was *not* typical of the unemployed across the entire nation. Negroes and aliens were the last hired and the first fired. Young men and women were graduated from high schools and colleges into a world without jobs. Mississippi's demagogic governor and sometime Senator, Theodore G. Bilbo, vowed the unemployment problem could be solved by shipping 12,000,000 American blacks to Africa. The United Spanish War Veterans, for their part, urged the deportation of 10,000,000 aliens—or nearly 6,000,000 more than the actual number of aliens in the United States. Some noncitizens, unable to find work here, voluntarily returned to their homelands. With the deepening of the Depression, immigration dropped until something strange happened in the year 1932: More than three times as many persons left this country as entered it. No longer was America the Promised Land.

The Depression changed people's values and thus changed society.

The Chamber of Commerce syndrome of the Twenties became a mockery in the Thirties. Business leaders lost their prestige, for now it had become apparent to all Americans that these big shots did not know what they were talking about when they said again and again and again that everything would be all right if it were just left to them. Worship of big business was succeeded by greater concern for human values. The optimism of the speculative decade was replaced by the pessimism of the hungry decade, by anguished interest in the problem of having enough food on the table.

People eager to make a big killing in the stock market had paid scant attention to politics, but now they wondered about their elected representatives and the kind of political system that could permit such a catastrophe to happen. Indifference gave way to political and social consciousness. Dorothy Parker, the sophisticate and wit, cried: "There is no longer I. There is WE. The day of the individual is dead." Quentin N. Burdick, who became a Senator from North Dakota, said long after the Depression: "I guess I acquired a social conscience during those bad days, and ever since I've had the desire to work toward bettering the living conditions of the people." Sylvia Porter, who developed into a financial columnist, said that while at Hunter College she switched from English to economics because of "an overwhelming curiosity to know why everything was crashing around me and why people were losing their jobs."

People lost their houses and apartments.

Franklin D. Roosevelt said: "One of the major disasters of the continued depression was the loss of hundreds of thousands of homes each year from foreclosure. The annual average loss of urban homes by foreclosure in the United States in normal times was 78,000. By 1932 this had increased to 273,000. By the middle of 1933, foreclosures had advanced to more than 1,000 a day."

In New York City, which had more apartments than private houses, there were almost 200,000 evictions in the year 1931. During the first three weeks of the following year there were more than 60,000 other evictions. One judge handled, or tried to handle, 425 eviction cases in a single day! On February 2, 1932, the *New York Times* described the eviction of three families in the Bronx:

166 A Modernizing People

Probably because of the cold, the crowd numbered only about 1,000, although in unruliness it equalled the throng of 4,000 that stormed the police in the first disorder of a similar nature on January 22. On Thursday a dozen more families are to be evicted unless they pay back rents.

Inspector Joseph Leonary deployed a force of fifty detectives and mounted and foot patrolmen through the street as Marshall Louis Novick led ten furniture movers in to the building. Their appearance was the signal for a great clamor. Women shrieked from the windows, the different sections of the crowd hissed and booed and shouted invectives. Fighting began simultaneously in the house and in the street. The marshal's men were rushed on the stairs and only got to work after the policemen had driven the tenants back into their apartments.

In that part of New York City known as Sunnyside, Queens, many homeowners were unable to meet mortgage payments and were soon ordered to vacate. Eviction notices were met with collective action, the residents barricading their doors with sandbags and barbed wire, flinging pepper and flour at sheriffs who tried to force their way inside. However, it was a losing battle; more than 60 percent of Sunnyside's householders lost their homes through foreclosure.

Harlem Negroes invented a new way to get enough money to pay their rent. This, as it came to be called, was the house-rent party. A family would announce that on Saturday night or Thursday night they would welcome anyone and everyone to their home for an evening of fun. Sometimes they would print and distribute cards such as this: "There'll be plenty of pig feet / And lots of gin; / Jus' ring the bell / An' come on in." Saturday night, of course, is the usual time for partying, while Thursday was chosen because this was the only free night for sleep-in black domestics who worked for white people. Admission to a house-rent party cost 15 cents, but more money could be spent inside. A festive mood was established by placing a red bulb in a light socket, by serving food consisting of chitterlings and pigs' feet and by setting out a jug of corn liquor. These parties

often went on until daybreak, and the next day the landlord got his rent. The innovation spread to black ghettos in other big cities across the land, and some white people began imitating the Negroes.

In Chicago a crowd of Negroes gathered in front of the door of a tenement house to prevent the landlord's agent from evicting a neighborhood family, and they continued to stand there hour after hour, singing hymns. A Chicago municipal employee named James D. O'Reilly saw his home auctioned off because he had failed to pay $34 in city taxes at the very time the city owed him $850 in unpaid salary.

A social worker described one pathetic event: "Mrs. Green left her five small children alone one morning while she went to have her grocery order filled. While she was away the constable arrived and padlocked her house with the children inside. When she came back she heard the six-weeks-old-baby crying. She did not dare to touch the padlock for fear of being arrested, but she found a window open and climbed in and nursed the baby and then climbed out and appealed to the police to let her children out."

In widespread areas of Philadelphia no rent was paid at all. In this City of Brotherly Love evictions were exceedingly common—as many as 1,300 a month. Children, who saw their parents' distress, made a game of evictions. In a day-care center they piled all the doll furniture in first one corner and then another. One tot explained to a teacher: "We ain't got no money for the rent, so we's moved into a new house. Then we got the constable on us, so we's moving again."

In millions of apartments, tension mounted and tempers flared toward the end of each month, when the rent was due. Robert Bendiner, in his book *Just Around the Corner*, wrote about conditions in New York City:

Evictions and frequent moves to take advantage of the apartment market were as common in middle-income Washington Heights as in the poor areas of town, and apartment hopping became rather a way of life. My own family moved six times in seven years. . . . Crises occurred monthly, and several times we were saved from eviction by pawning leftover valuables or by my mother's rich talent for cajoling landlords. On one more than routinely desperate occasion she resorted to the extreme device of having one of us enlarge a hole in the bathroom ceiling and then irately demanding repairs before another dollar of rent should be forthcoming.

In moving from one place to another, some families left their furniture behind because it had been bought on the installment plan and they were unable to meet further payments. Time-payment furniture firms owned warehouses that became crammed with tables and chairs and other items reclaimed from families without money. Whenever a marshal, sheriff or constable evicted a family from a house or apartment, the landlord would simply dump the furniture on the sidewalk. If the installment company failed to pick it up, each article would soon be carried away by needy neighbors.

What happened to people after they were dispossessed? Many doubled up with relatives—or even tripled up, until ten or twelve people were crammed into three or four rooms. Human beings are like porcupines: they like to huddle close enough to feel one another's warmth, but they dislike getting so close that the quills begin pricking. Now, in teeming proximity to one another, the quills pricked and relatives quarreled bitterly.

The Depression strained the family structure and sometimes shattered it. Well-integrated families closed ranks in the face of this common danger and became ever more monolithic. Loosely knit families, on the other hand, fell apart when the pressures on them became too great.

After a man lost his job, he would trudge from factory to factory, office to office, seeking other employment, but after weeks of repeated rejections he would lose heart, mutely denounce himself as a poor provider, shed his self-respect and stay at home. Here he found himself unwelcome and underfoot, the target of puzzled glances from his children and hostile looks from his wife. In the early part of the Depression some women simply could not understand that jobs were unavailable; instead, they felt there was something wrong with their men. In Philadelphia one unemployed man begged a social worker: "Have you anybody you can send around to tell my wife you have no job to give me? She thinks I don't want to work."

The idle man found himself a displaced person in the household, which is woman's domain, and in nameless guilt he crept about uneasily, always finding himself in the way. He got on his wife's nerves and she on his, until tension broke in endless wrangles. If the man tried to help by washing dishes and making beds, he lost status in the eyes of the rest of the family.

The Depression castrated some men by dethroning them from their position as the breadwinner and the head of the family. Ashamed, confused and resentful, they became sexually impotent. In Western culture a man tends to think of himself in terms of the work he does, this self-identity being what Jung calls his persona. Man does. Woman is. To rob a man of his work was to rob him of his idea of himself, leaving him empty and without much reason for living. The displacement of the man as the head of the family and the way some women moved in to fill this vacuum were described sensitively by John Steinbeck in his novel *The Grapes of Wrath*. This great book tells the story of the flight of the Joad family from the dust bowl of Oklahoma to the green valleys of California:

> "We got nothin' now," Pa said. "Comin' a long time—no work, no crops. What we gonna do then? How we gonna git stuff to eat? . . . Git so I hate to think. Go diggin' back to a ol' time to keep from thinkin'. Seems like our life's over an' done."
>
> "No, it ain't," Ma smiled. "It ain't, Pa. An' that's one more thing a woman knows. I noticed that. Man, he lives in jerks—baby born an' a man

dies, an' that's a jerk—gets a farm an' loses his farm, an' that's a jerk. Woman, it's all one flow, like a stream, little eddies, little waterfalls, but the river, it goes right on. Woman looks at it like that. We ain't gonna die out. People is goin' on—changin' a little maybe, but goin' right on."

Some adolescent girls felt their fathers' agony and tried to comfort them with lavish expressions of love, much to the embarrassment of the man and the uneasiness of his wife. This did emotional damage to father, mother and the young girl, whose fixation on her father retarded her normal interest in boys her own age.

Strife between parents, together with the realization that it cost money to marry and have babies, resulted in a decision by many young people to postpone their weddings. One young man joined the Communist Party and swore he never would marry or have children under "the present system." Unable to repress their human needs, however, young men and women made love secretly and guiltily, regarding pregnancy as a disaster. Despite an increase in the sale of contraceptives, the abortion rate rose, and so did venereal disease. The birthrate dropped.

It has been estimated that the Depression postponed 800,000 marriages that would have occurred sooner if it had not been for hard times. Margaret Mead, the noted anthropologist, argued that there was nothing wrong about letting girls support their lovers so they could marry sooner. Surprisingly, there even was a decline in marriages among members of the *Social Register*. Liberals and feminists pointed out that half of all births were in families on relief or with incomes of less than $1,000 a year; they strongly advocated birth control. Who could afford babies when a sixty-one-piece layette cost all of $7.70? Gasps of horror arose when it was reported in Illinois that a sixteenth child had been born to a family on relief.

Housewives suffered as acutely as their husbands. Many had to send their kids to live with relatives or friends. Others took part-time jobs, while a few wives actually became temporary whores to earn enough money to keep the family going. Lacking money for streetcars and buses, without the means to buy clothes to keep them looking attractive, they remained cooped up in their homes until their nerves screamed and they had nervous breakdowns.

All too often their men simply deserted them. A California woman said: "My husband went north about three months ago to try his luck. The first month he wrote pretty regularly. . . . For five weeks we have had no word from him. . . . Don't know where he is or what he is up to."

A young man who lived in the French Quarter of New Orleans was solicited by five prostitutes during a ten-block stroll, each woman asking only 50 cents. In Houston a relief worker, curious about how the people were getting along, was approached by one girl after another. For the benefit of an insistent streetwalker, the man turned his pockets inside out to prove that he had no money. Looking at him ruefully, she said: "It doesn't cost much—only a dime!"

The close relationship between poverty and morals shocked Franklin D. Roosevelt, who told reporters about an investigator who went to southeastern Kentucky: "She got into one of those mining towns," Roosevelt said, "and started to walk up the alley. There was a group of miners sitting in front of the shacks, and they pulled down their caps over their faces. As soon as she caught sight of that she walked up and said, 'What are you pulling your caps down for?' They said, 'Oh, it is all right.' 'Why pull your caps down?' They said, 'It is sort of a custom because so many of the women have not got enough clothes to cover them.' "

The Depression made changes in the country's physical appearance.

Fewer pedestrians were to be seen on the streets since many men did not go to work and women shopped less frequently; for lack of warm clothing and fuel, many people stayed in bed most of the day during winter. The air became cleaner over industrial cities, for there was less smoke from factory chimneys. The downtown business districts of most cities had long rows of empty shops and offices. Trains were shorter, and only rarely did one see a Pullman car. However, gas stations multiplied because millions of Americans drove their battered family cars here and there in endless quest of work. In conflicting attempts to solve their problems, farmers moved into town while city folks moved into the country to build their own houses and grow their own food. More and more blacks were seen in northern cities as desperate Negroes fled from the hopeless South. Telephones were taken out of homes, and mail deliveries were lighter. Houses and stores, parks and fences sagged and lapsed into unpainted, flaked ugliness for want of money to make repairs.

In his novel called *You Can't Go Home Again*, Thomas Wolfe described a comfort station in front of New York City Hall:

... One descended to this place down a steep flight of stairs from the street, and on bitter nights he would find the place crowded with homeless men who had sought refuge there. Some were those shambling hulks that one sees everywhere, in Paris as well as in New York. ... But most of them were just flotsam of the general ruin of the time—honest, decent, middle-aged men with faces seamed by toil and want, and young men, many of them mere boys in their teens, with thick, unkempt hair. These were the wanderers from town to town, the riders of freight trains, the thumbers of rides on highways, the uprooted, unwanted male population of America. They drifted across the land and gathered in the big cities when winter came, hungry, defeated, empty, hopeless, restless, driven by they knew not what, always on the move, looking everywhere for work, for the bare crumbs to support their miserable lives, and finding neither work nor crumbs. Here in New York, to this obscene meeting place, these derelicts came, drawn into a common stew of rest and warmth and a little surcease from their desperation.

Heywood Broun devoted a column to a description of a slum in San Antonio, Texas:

... The Church of Guadalupe stands upon the fringe of what had been described to me as the most fearsome slum in all America. It covers four square miles. At first I thought that the extreme description might have been dictated by local pride. It was my notion to protest and say, "Why, we in New York City know worse than that." But after we had gone up the third back alley I had to confess defeat gracefully.

You can see shacks as bad as these in several States, but I do not know of any place where they have been so ingeniously huddled together. This is flat, sprawling country, and there is much of it, and so it seems devilish that one crazy combination of old lumber and stray tin should be set as a flap upon the side of another equally discreditable. I did not quite comprehend the character of the alley until I discovered that what I took to be a toolhouse was a residence for a family of eleven people.

And these are not squatter dwellings. People pay rent for them, just as if a few rickety boards and a leaky roof constituted a house. They even have evictions and go through the solemn and obscene farce of removing a bed and a frying pan as indication that the landlord's two-dollars-and-a-half rent has not been forthcoming. ...

Back at the Church of Guadalupe, the priest said, "I have other letters from those who fight federal housing because they like their rents." He tossed over an anonymous message, which read, "I could start a story that there is a priest who writes love letters to young girls and gives jewels to women of his congregation."

"Doesn't this worry you?" one of us asked.

"No," said the priest. "Last month we buried thirty-nine persons, mostly children, from this little church alone.

"I am worried," he said, "about people starving to death.

Louis Adamic and his wife were living with her mother in New York City in January, 1932. Born in Yugoslavia, now a naturalized American, he was a writer, a tall young man with a look of eager curiosity in his eyes. One cold morning at seven forty-five the doorbell rang, and Adamic, thinking it was the postman, opened the front door. In his book called *My America*, he told what happened next.

There stood a girl of ten and a boy of eight. They had schoolbooks in their arms, and their clothing was patched and clean, but hardly warm enough for winter weather. In a voice strangely old for her age, the girl said: "Excuse me, mister, but we have no eats in our house and my mother she said I should take my brother before we go to school and ring a doorbell in some house"—she swallowed heavily and took a deep breath—"and ask you to give us . . . something . . . to eat."

"Come in," Adamic said. A strange sensation swept over him. He had heard that kids were ringing doorbells and asking for food in the Bronx, in Harlem and in Brooklyn, but he had not really believed it.

His wife and her mother gave the children some food. The girl ate slowly. Her brother bolted his portion, quickly and greedily.

"He ate a banana yesterday afternoon," said his sister, "but it wasn't ripe enough or something, and it made him sick and he didn't eat anything since. He's always like this when he's hungry and we gotta ring doorbells."

"Do you often ring doorbells?"

"When we have no eats at home."

"What made you ring our bell?"

"I don't know," the girl answered. "I just did."

Her name was Mary, and her brother's name was Jimmie. They lived in a poor neighborhood five blocks away.

Mary said: "We used to live on the fourth floor upstairs and we had three rooms and a kitchen and bath, but now we have only one room downstairs. In back."

"Why did you move downstairs?"

The boy winced.

"My father," said the girl. "He lost his job when the panic came. That was two years ago. I was eight and Jimmie was six. My father he tried to get work, but he couldn't, the depression was so bad. But he called it the panic."

Adamic and the two women were astonished at her vocabulary: "panic" . . . "depression."

"What kind of work did your father do?"

"Painter and paperhanger. Before things got so bad, he always had jobs when his work was in season, and he was good to us—my mother says so, too. Then, after he couldn't get any more jobs, he got mean and he yelled at my mother. He couldn't sleep nights and he walked up and down and talked, and sometimes he hollered and we couldn't sleep, either."

"Was he a union man?"

"No, he didn't belong to no union."

"What did your father holler about?"

"He called my mother bad names."

At this point in the conversation, Adamic wrote, the little girl hesitated, and her brother winced again. Then she continued: "Uh . . . he was angry because my mother, before she married him, she was in love with another man and almost married him. But my mother says it wasn't my father's fault he acted mean like he did. He was mean because he had no job and we had no money."

"Where's your father now?"

"We don't know. He went away four months ago, right after Labor Day, and he never came back, so we had to move downstairs. The landlord didn't want to throw us out, so he told my mother to move in downstairs."

Between sips of milk the girl said her mother did household work whenever she could find a job, but earned very little money this way. A charity organization had been giving her $2.85 a week, but lately it had stopped. Mary did not know why. Her mother had applied for home relief, but had not yet received anything from that source.

The boy stopped eating, turned to his sister and muttered: "You talk too much! I told you not to talk!"

The girl fell silent.

Adamic said: "It's really our fault, Jimmie. We're asking too many questions."

The little boy glared and said: "Yeah!"

In Detroit someone gave another little girl a nickel, which seemed like such a fortune to her that she agonized three full days about how best to spend it.

In Erie, Pennsylvania, a seven-year-old boy named Tom received a tiny yellow chick as an Easter present. Using some old chicken wire, he built a coop for his pet beneath the back step to the house and fed and tended it carefully. His father was an unemployed molder, and the family often ate nothing but beans. Time passed. Now the little chick had grown into a full-sized chicken. One day Tom's father announced that the boy's pet would have to be killed and served for Sunday dinner, since everyone was hungry. Tom screamed in horrified protest but was unable to prevent his father from taking his chicken into the backyard and chopping off its head. Later that day the family sat around the table feasting on fowl, while the boy hunched in his chair, sobbing.

In 1933 the Children's Bureau reported that one out of every five children in the nation was not getting enough of the right things to eat. A teacher in a coal-mining town asked a little girl in her classroom whether she was ill. The child said: "No. I'm all right. I'm just hungry." The teacher urged her to go home and eat something. The girl said: "I can't. This is my sister's day to eat." In the House of Representatives, during a debate about appropriations for Indians living on reservations, a Congressman said that eleven cents a day was enough to feed an Indian child. A Senate subcommittee learned that the president of a textile firm had told his workers they should be able to live on six cents a day.

AFL President William Green said: "I warn the people who are exploiting the workers that they can only drive them so far before they will turn on them and destroy them. They are taking no account of the history of nations in which governments have been overturned. Revolutions grow out of the depths of hunger."

Sidney Hillman, president of the Amalgamated Clothing Workers of America, appeared at a Senate hearing in 1932 and was told that it was not yet time to give federal relief. Angrily, he cried: "I would ask by what standards are we to gauge that time! Must we have hundreds of thousands of people actually dead and dying from starvation? Must we have bread riots? What is necessary to convince them that there is a need for federal and speedy relief?"

The Communists took up the slogan: "Starve or fight!"

At the University of Pennsylvania a prim audience was shocked to hear Daniel Willard, president of the B & O Railroad, say: "While I do not like to say so, I would be less than candid if I did not say that in such circumstances I would steal before I would starve."

Obviously, less fortunate Americans agreed. Petty thievery soared. Children hung around grocery stores begging for food. Customers emerging from groceries had bundles snatched from their arms by hungry kids, who ran home with the food or ducked into alleys to gobble it as fast as they could. Small retail stores had their windows smashed and their display goods stolen. Grown men, in groups of two or three, walked into chain store markets, ordered all the food they could carry and then quietly walked out without paying for it. Chain store managers did not always report these incidents to the police for fear that publicity would encourage this sort of intimidation. For the same reason the newspapers engaged in a conspiracy of silence.

People of means thought up ways to protect themselves from panhandlers and from begging letters. Boston's mayor, James M. Curley, had a male secretary named Stan Wilcox, who was adept at brushing off approaches. Whenever a beggar asked if he had a quarter, Wilcox would reply: "Heavens, no! I wouldn't dream of taking a drink at this hour!" Alfred E. Smith received the following letter from Milwaukee: "This is unusual, but I am in need. Would you send me $2,500, as this is the amount I am in need of. I will give you as collateral my word of honor that I will repay you if possible. If not, let the good Lord repay you and he will also pay better interest."

Governor Gifford Pinchot of Pennsylvania flatly declared that starvation was widespread. Among the many pathetic letters he received was this one: "There are nine of us in the family. My father is out of work for a couple of months and we haven't got a thing eat [sic] in the house. Mother is getting $12 a month of the county. If mother don't get more help we will have to starve to death. I am a little girl 10 years old. I go to school every day. My other sister hain't got any shoes or clothes to wear to go to school. My mother goes in her bare feet and she crys every night that we don't have the help. I guess that is all, hoping to hear from you."

John Steinbeck has told how he survived the early part of the Depression before he became a famous author. "I had two assets," he wrote. "My father owned a tiny three-room cottage in Pacific Grove in California, and he let me live in it without rent. That was the first safety. Pacific Grove is on the ocean. That was the second. People in inland cities or in the closed and shuttered industrial cemeteries had greater problems than I. Given the sea, a man must be very stupid to starve. That great reservoir is always available. I took a large part of my protein food from the ocean.

"Firewood to keep warm floated on the beach daily, needing only handsaw and ax. A small garden of black soil came with the cottage. In northern California you can raise vegetables of some kind all year long. I never peeled a potato without planting the skins. Kale, lettuce, chard, turnips, carrots and onions rotated in the little garden. In the tide pools of the bay, mussels were available and crabs and abalones and that shiny kelp called sea lettuce. With a line and pole, blue cod, rock cod, perch, sea trout, sculpin could be caught."

The sale of flower seeds shot up as Americans, tired of the ugliness of their lives, turned to the beauty of homegrown flowers. As might have been expected, there was widespread cultivation of vegetable gardens. Many did this on their own, while others received official encouragement. Big railroads rented garden plots for their workers. The United States Steel Corporation used social workers and faculty members of Indiana University to develop an extensive garden project for its workers in Gary, Indiana. In New York State, in the summer of 1933, jobless men and women were tending 65,000 gardens. The city of Detroit provided tools and seed for "thrift gardens" on empty lots, an idea which Mayor Frank Murphy said he had borrowed from Hazen S. Pingree. During the Panic of 1893 Pingree had been the mayor of Detroit, and confronted with a city of jobless men, he provided them with gardens to cultivate— "Pingree's Potato Patches," receiving national attention.

Now, in the present emergency, Henry Ford ordered all his workmen to dig in vegetable gardens or be fired. Out of his imperious command there developed what the Scripps-Howard Washington *News* called 50,000 "shotgun gardens." Rough-grained Harry Bennett, chief of Ford's private police, supervised this vast project and kept a filing system on all Ford employees. If a man had no garden in his own backyard or on some neighborhood lot, he was assigned a patch of earth somewhere on Ford's 4,000 acres of farmland around Dearborn, Michigan. Each workman had to pay fifty cents to have his strip plowed.

More than one-third of the men employed in Ford's Dearborn plant lived 10 to 20 miles away, and some protested that since they did not own a car they would have to spend an extra two hours daily just traveling to and from their allotted patches. A Bennett henchman would snarl: "Why don't-cha buy a car? You're makin' 'em, ain't-cha?" Bone-weary workmen who simply couldn't muster the energy to toil on their garden plots soon were brought into line by Bennett's personal deputy, Norman Selby, the former boxer "Kid McCoy."

There was nothing surprising about the fact that men would risk injury or death by falling off a horse to earn an extra $3 a day. People felt that if they could just live through the Depression, they could *endure* anything else life had to offer. To *endure* was the main thing. Many took pay cuts without a murmur. A young man just out of college with a Bachelor of Journalism degree accepted a job on a newspaper at exactly *nothing* per week; a month later he was grateful to be put on the payroll at $15. Graduate engineers worked as office boys. College graduates of various kinds ran elevators in department stores. Unemployed architects turned out jigsaw puzzles. One jobless draftsman, Alfred Butts, used his spare time to invent the game of Scrabble.

Young men who might have grown into greatness chose, instead, to seek the security of civil service jobs, becoming policemen, firemen, garbage collectors. Fewer sailors deserted from the Navy. Enlistments rose in all branches of the nation's military establishment. When Congress voted a 10 percent pay cut for all federal employees, President Hoover secretly asked the Senate to make an exception for soldiers and sailors, because he did not wish to rely on disgruntled troops in case of internal trouble.

Women and children toiled for almost nothing in the sweatshops of New York City, welfare workers reporting these grim examples:

- A woman crocheted hats for 40 cents a dozen and was able to make only two dozen per week.
- An apron girl, paid $2\frac{1}{2}$ cents per apron, earned 20 cents a day.
- A slipper liner was paid 21 cents for every seventy-two pairs of slippers she lined, and if she turned out one slipper every forty-five seconds she could earn $1.05 in a nine-hour day.
- A girl got half a cent for each pair of pants she threaded and sponged, making $2.78 a week.

Connecticut's state commissioner of labor said that some sweatshops in that state paid girls between 60 cents and $1.10 for a fifty-five-hour week. In Pennsylvania men working in sawmills were paid 5 cents an hour, men in tile and brick manufacturing got 6 cents per hour, while construction workers earned $7\frac{1}{2}$ cents an hour. In Detroit the Briggs Manufacturing Company paid men 10 cents and women 4 cents an hour, causing auto workers to chant: "If poison doesn't work, try Briggs!" Also in Detroit, the Hudson Motor Car Company called back a small-parts assembler and then kept her waiting three days for a half hour of work, forcing her to spend 60 cents in carfare to earn 28 cents.

Two Marine fishermen put out to sea at four o'clock one morning and did not return to port until five o'clock that afternoon. During this long day of toil they caught 200 pounds of hake and 80 pounds of haddock. They burned up eight gallons of gas at 19 cents a gallon and used 100 pounds of bait costing two cents a pound. For their catch they were paid one cent a pound for the hake and four cents a pound for the haddock. Thus they earned less than two cents an hour for their day's work.

Meantime, Henry Ford was declaring: "Many families were not so badly off as they thought; they needed guidance in the management of their resources and opportunities." Ford needed no guidance. He managed to transfer $41\frac{1}{2}$ percent of stock in the Ford Motor Company to his son, Edsel, without paying a cent in inheritance or estate taxes.

Ford, who liked to boast that he always had to work, declared in 1930 that "the very poor are recruited almost solely from the people who refuse to think and therefore refuse to work diligently." Roger W. Babson, the statistician, pontificated two years later: "Better business will come when the unemployed change their attitude toward life." Most rich men were quick to moralize.

The concept of hard work was central to capitalism and the Protestant ethic. Americans had been raised on a diet of aphorisms praising work and self-reliance. Benjamin Franklin said: "God helps them that help themselves." The Bible insisted: "In the sweat of thy face shalt thou eat bread." Thomas Carlyle said: "All work, even cotton-spinning, is noble; work alone is noble." Elizabeth Barrett Browning wrote: "Whoever fears God, fears to sit at ease." It was either Bishop Richard Cumberland or George Whitefield (no one is sure) who first said: "Better to wear out than to rust out." Most Americans agreed, but now in these Depression times men did sit at home and rust, through no fault of their own, losing the fine edge of their skills.

Idle, dispirited, hungry, defeated, withdrawn, brooding—people began to feel that somehow they were to blame for everything, that somehow, somewhere, they had failed. Maybe the Depression was punishment for their sins. After all, Protestant Episcopal Bishop John P. Tyler attributed it to the lack of religion. Perhaps Christians, if they wished to be good Christians, should bow to fate by accepting Christ's words that "to everyone that hath shall be given; and from him that hath not, even that which he hath shall be taken from him." But some found it difficult to find comfort in a sermon preached by the Reverend William S. Blackshear, an Episcopalian clergyman, in the bleak year of 1932. Blackshear said in part: "Christ was happy to be at the banquets of the rich. It was at such a place that the woman broke the vial of costly ointment and anointed His feet. There were those who cried out for the improvident and rebuked the woman, saying that this should have been converted into cash and given to the poor. It was then that Christ spoke on the economic plan, 'The poor ye have always with you.'"

This kind of sermon, representing conservative Protestantism, offended liberal clergymen. Forced by the Depression to rethink their values, they began searching for a new theology. Some began with the premise that if the church were to serve any purpose or perform realistically, it had to divorce itself from economic and political values. This developing viewpoint was expressed with crystal clarity by H. Richard Niebuhr, a pastor and a brother of Reinhold Niebuhr. He wrote:

The church is in bondage to capitalism. Capitalism in its contemporary form is more than a system of ownership and distribution of economic goods. It is a faith and a way of life. It is faith in wealth as a source of all life's blessings and as the savior of man from his deepest misery. It is the doctrine that man's most important activity is the production of economic goods and that all other things are dependent upon this. On the basis of this initial idolatry it develops a morality in which economic worth becomes the standard by which to measure all other values and the economic virtues take precedence over courage, temperance, wisdom and justice, over charity, humility and fidelity. Hence nature, love, life, truth, beauty and justice are exploited or made the servants of the high economic good. Everything, including the lives of workers, is made a utility, is desecrated and ultimately destroyed. . . .

Other dissenters noted the supremacy of capitalism over every other value in the fact that church property was exempt from taxation. State constitutions and special statutes declared that no real estate taxes could be levied on church-owned properties, such as the church building itself, parochial schools, parsonages, the parish house and cemeteries. Why? A Missouri Supreme Court decision said that "no argument is necessary to show that church purposes are public purposes."

But was this really true? The United States of America was a Christian nation nominally, but not legally. No single religion, sect or church was recognized as the established church. Although the phrase "separation of church and state" does not appear in the Constitution of the United States or in that of any state but Utah, the idea for which it stands is found in the constitutional provisions against religious tests and in the words of the First Amendment: "Congress shall make no law respecting an establishment of religion. . . ."

During the Depression some liberal Christians, agnostics, atheists and others fretted about the special status given churches and church property. A few scholars recalled that President Ulysses S. Grant had said: "I would suggest the taxation of all property equally, whether church or corporation, exempting only the last resting place of the dead, and possibly, with proper restrictions, church edifices." Dissenters objected on principle to the exemption of church property, regarded this as an indirect subsidy by the state to religion and pointed out that personal taxes might be less if churches bore their share of the tax burden.

They got nowhere. At the core of capitalism was the belief that God looked with favor on the rich. This idea had been expressed as long ago as 1732 by one of J. P. Morgan's ancestors, the Reverend Joseph Morgan, who sermonized: "Each man coveting to make himself rich, carries on the Publick Good: Thus God in His Wisdom and Mercy turns our wickedness to Publick Benefit. . . . A rich Man is a great friend of the Publick, while he aims at nothing but serving himself. God will have us live by helping one another; and since Love will not do it, Covetousness shall."

J. P. Morgan himself flatly told a Senate committee: "If you destroy the leisure class you destroy civilization." When reporters pressed for a definition of the leisure class, Morgan said it included all who could afford a maid. In 1931, according to *Fortune* magazine, there still were 1,000,000 families with servants. One wealthy family announced that it had solved its Depression problem by discharging fifteen of its twenty servants—although the family members showed no curiosity or concern about the fate of the unemployed fifteen.

John Jacob Astor came of age in 1933 and thereupon inherited about $4 million. Nonetheless, he dabbled at a job in a downtown Manhattan brokerage house. Before long he quit with the explanation: "I didn't finish until five o'clock and by the time I got uptown it was six. And then I had to get up early the next morning." At a later date Astor was employed briefly by a shipping firm, and when he quit this second job, he commented: "I have discovered that work interferes with leisure."

He was a representative of that leisure class which Morgan felt must be maintained to save civilization.

When Dwight Morrow was running for governor of New Jersey, he said: "There is something about too much prosperity that ruins the fiber of the people. The men and women that built this country, that founded it, were people that were reared in adversity." Morrow made this statement and died before Adolf Hitler declared: "It was poverty that made me strong." Joseph P. Kennedy, a busy member of the leisure class, felt that the rich had to make some sacrifices. Writing about the Depression, Kennedy said: "I am not ashamed to record that in those days I felt and said I would be willing to part with half of what I had if I could be sure of keeping, under law and order, the other half."

One member of the enormously wealthy Du Pont family seems to have been out of touch with reality. An advertising agency wanted his company to sponsor a Sunday afternoon radio program, but this Du Pont rejected the idea, saying: "At three o'clock on Sunday afternoons everybody is playing polo."

Everybody except the millions of Americans gobbling the last morsel of food from their plates in the fear that it might be their last meal—a habit that persisted in some people down through the next three decades. As Sinclair Lewis commented in his novel *It Can't Happen Here*, people were so confused, insecure and frustrated that they hardly could do anything more permanent than shaving or eating breakfast. They were tortured with feelings of inadequacy and guilt.

A young Alabama schoolteacher with eight years of tenure was fired after the Wall Street Crash. Eager to work, willing to take any job however low in the social scale, she became a maid in a private home. However, upon learning that she would be expected to work seven days a week, getting room and board but no wages, she quit. Then she took a job in a convalescent home which paid her room and board and $3 a week, but soon the home closed for lack of funds. The gentle school-teacher completely lost faith in herself, confessing to a caseworker: "If, with all the advantages I've had, I can't make a living, then I'm just no good, I guess!"

Forty experienced secretaries found work after being unemployed a year, but the first few days on the job they were unable to take dictation from their bosses without weeping from sheer nervousness. After seeking employment for a long time, a man finally landed a job and became so overwrought with joy that he died of excitement. A corporation executive was given the nasty chore of firing several hundred men. A kind and compassionate person, he insisted on talking to each of them personally and asking what plans each had for the future. In a few months the executive's hair had turned gray.

The Depression began to erode freedom.

Some Americans, a little more secure than others, asked harsh questions. How about fingerprinting everyone on relief? Was it proper for a man on relief to own a car—even if he needed it to try to find work? Wasn't it wrong to sell liquor to the head of a family on relief? Did anyone owning a life insurance policy deserve relief? Should reliefers be allowed to vote? Did they deserve citizenship?

In New Orleans a federal judge denied citizenship to four qualified persons because they were on relief and therefore, in the judge's words, "unable financially to contribute to the support of the government." In California another judge withheld citizenship from Jacob Hullen; in response to the judge's questions Hullen had said he believed in municipal or federal ownership of public utilities.

In New York City, one cold and rainy day, the police arrested 38 men who had taken shelter in the Pennsylvania Railroad's ferry terminal on Cortlandt Street. All were marched to the nearest police station. Fifteen of them, able to prove that they had a few nickels and dimes in their pockets, were released. The other 23 men, who did not have a cent on them, were led before a magistrate, who sentenced them to jail for vagrancy. Newspaper stories about this obvious injustice raised such a hullabaloo, however, that the 23 prisoners soon were freed.

Robert Morss Lovett, a professor of English literature at the University of Chicago, wrote in his autobiography:

> An example of the injustice meted out to foreign-born workers involved a Yugoslav named Perkovitch. When conditions were at their worst in 1932–33 the unemployed on the West Side [of Chicago] were in the habit of crossing the city to the South Side where food was sometimes available from bakeries, disposing of yesterday's bake, and where, at least, the garbage was more lavish.
>
> One morning these itinerants were picked up by the police and held at the station house on the absurd pretext that a revolution was planned. Perkovitch told me that he and about one hundred others were kept in the basement all day without food. Once a lieutenant with a bodyguard of patrolmen raged through the room, striking and kicking the men in an ecstasy of sadism. At six the prisoners were released with no charges.

Paul D. Peacher, the town marshal of Jonesboro, Arkansas, arrested a group of Negro men without cause and forced them to work on his farm. A federal grand jury indicted him under Title 18 of the Anti-Slavery Act of 1866 for "causing Negroes to be held as slaves" on a cotton plantation. This was the first case ever tried under the slavery statute. A county grand jury absolved Peacher, but the federal Department of Justice would not drop the case. Now the marshal was forced to stand trial—this time before a *federal* jury. Taking the witness chair in his own behalf, he denied that he had done anything wrong. However, the jury disagreed with him and found him guilty. Peacher was sentenced to two years in prison and fined $3,500. He appealed, lost his appeal, paid the fine and accepted a two-year probationary sentence.

Someone asked Eugene Talmadge, the governor of Georgia, what he would do about the millions of unemployed Americans. Talmadge snarled: "Let'em starve!" It made him happy when the city fathers of Atlanta put unwanted nonresidents in chain gangs. When some textile workers went on strike in Georgia the governor had barbed-wire concentration camps built and threw pickets into them. Frank Hague, the mayor and ruthless boss of Jersey City, called for the erection in Alaska of a concentration camp for native "Reds."

Wise and temperate men worried about the growing loss of liberty in America, the land of the free and the home of the brave. George Boas, a professor of philosophy, sadly said: "It is taken for granted that democracy is bad and that it is dying." Will Durant, busy writing his many-volumed *Story of Civilization*, asked rhetorically: "Why is it that Democracy has fallen so rapidly from the high prestige which it had at the Armistice?"

GLOSSARY

Social Register: A directory listing persons of social prominence in a community.

Pullman Car: A railroad sleeping car.

Children's Bureau: An agency of the Labor Department that dealt with issues involving children, especially early nurture, poverty, and child labor.

American Federation of Labor: The nation's central trade union organization from the 1890s to the present.

John Steinbeck (1902–1968): Writer whose works are marked by a compassionate understanding of the world's disinherited. His best-known novel, *The Grapes of Wrath*, treats the plight of 1930s Dust Bowl farmers turned migrant laborers.

Reinhold Niebuhr (1892–1971): Theologian who wrote primarily about morality and Christianity's refusal to confront social problems.

IMPLICATIONS

The Depression disrupted the personal and public fabric of American life in a variety of ways. What do you see as the most important changes that the Depression brought to American life? What creative adaptations did Americans make to the new circumstances of their lives?

PAST TRACES

The 1940s witnessed not only the entry of the United States into World War II, but also the maturity of the civil rights movement in African American communities. This essay begins with a speech by A. Philip Randolph, one of the nation's foremost African American leaders, urging African American men and women to serve in the still-segregated armed forces. But, while he called for wartime service, he also served notice that the price of African American participation in the war effort would be an end to segregation and discrimination.

A. Philip Randolph, "Why Should We March?" (1942)

Though I have found no Negroes who want to see the United Nations lose this war, I have found many who, before the war ends, want to see the stuffing knocked out of white supremacy and of empire over subject peoples. American Negroes, involved as we are in the general issues of the conflict, are confronted not with a choice but with the challenge both to win democracy for ourselves at home and to help win the war for democracy the world over.

There is no escape from the horns of this dilemma. There ought not to be escape. For if the war for democracy is not won abroad, the fight for democracy cannot be won at home. If this war cannot be won for the white peoples, it will not be won for the darker races.

Conversely, if freedom and equality are not vouchsafed the peoples of color, the war for democracy will not be won. Unless this double-barreled thesis is accepted and applied, the darker races will never wholeheartedly fight for the victory of the United Nations. That is why those familiar with the thinking of the American Negro have sensed his lack of enthusiasm, whether among the educated or uneducated, rich or poor, professional or nonprofessional, religious or secular, rural or urban, north, south, east or west.

That is why questions are being raised by Negroes in church, labor union and fraternal society; in poolroom, barbershop, schoolroom, hospital, hair-dressing parlor; on college campus, railroad, and bus. One can hear such questions asked as these: What have Negroes to fight for? What's the difference between Hitler and that "cracker" Talmadge of Georgia? Why has a man got to be Jim Crowed to die for democracy? If you haven't got democracy yourself, how can you carry it to somebody else?

What are the reasons for this state of mind? The answer is: discrimination, segregation, Jim Crow. Witness the navy, the army, the air corps; and also government services at Washington. In many parts of the South, Negroes in Uncle Sam's uniform are being put upon, mobbed, sometimes even shot down by civilian and military police, and on occasion lynched. Vested political interests in race prejudice are so deeply entrenched that to them winning the war against Hitler is secondary to preventing Negroes from winning democracy for themselves. This is worth many divisions to Hitler and Hirohito. While labor, business, and farm are subjected to ceilings and doors and not allowed to carry on as usual, these interests trade in the dangerous business of race hate as usual.

When the defense program began and billions of the taxpayers' money were appropriated for guns, ships, tanks and bombs, Negroes presented themselves for work only to be given the cold shoulder. North as well as South, and despite their qualifications, Negroes were denied skilled employment. Not until their wrath and indignation took the form of a proposed protest march on Washington, scheduled for July 1, 1941, did things begin to move in the form of defense jobs for Negroes. The march was postponed by the timely issuance (June 25, 1941) of the famous Executive Order No. 8802 by President Roosevelt.But this order and the President's Committee on Fair Employment Practice, established thereunder, have as yet only scratched the surface by way of eliminating discriminations on account of race or color in war industry. Both management and labor unions in too many places and in too many ways are still drawing the color line.

It is to meet this situation squarely with direct action that the March on Washington Movement launched its present program of protest mass meetings. Twenty thousand were in attendance at Madison Square Garden, June 16; sixteen thousand in the Coliseum in Chicago, June 26; nine thousand in the City Auditorium of St. Louis, August 14. Meetings of such magnitude were unprecedented among Negroes. The vast throngs were drawn from all walks and levels of Negro life—businessmen, teachers, laundry workers, Pullman porters, waiters, and red caps; preachers, crapshooters, and social workers; jitterbugs and Ph.D.'s. They came and sat in silence, thinking, applauding only when they considered the truth was told, when they felt strongly that something was going to be done about it.

The March on Washington Movement is essentially a movement of the people. It is all Negro and pro-Negro, but not for that reason anti-white or anti-Semitic, or anti-Catholic, or anti-foreign, or anti-labor. Its major weapon is the non-violent demonstration of Negro mass power. Negro leadership has united back of its drive for jobs and justice. "Whether Negroes should march on Washington, and if so, when?" will be the focus of a forthcoming national conference. For the plan of a protest march has not been abandoned. Its purpose would be to demonstrate that American Negroes are in deadly earnest, and all out for their full rights. No power on earth can cause them today to abandon their fight to wipe out every vestige of second class citizenship and the dual standards that plague them.

A community is democratic only when the humblest and weakest person can enjoy the highest civil, economic, and social rights that the biggest and most powerful possess. To trample on these rights of both Negroes and poor whites is such a commonplace in the South that it takes readily to anti-social, anti-labor, anti-Semitic and anti-Catholic propaganda. It was because of laxness in enforcing the Weimar constitution in republican Germany that Nazism made headway. Oppression of the Negroes in the United States, like suppression of the Jews in Germany, may open the way for a fascist dictatorship.

By fighting for their rights now, American Megroes are helping to make America a moral and spiritual arsenal of democracy. Their fight against the poll tax, against lynch law, segregation, and Jim Crow, their fight for economic, political, and social equality, thus becomes part of the global war for freedom.

12

The Politics of Sacrifice on the American Home Front in World War II
Mark H. Leff

In 1941, the United States embarked on its largest military struggle since the Civil War. By the end of World War II, sixteen million men and women had served in the armed forces and 405,000 had given their lives in defeating the Axis powers. On the home front, Americans donated blood; recycled paper and scrap metal; planted "victory gardens" to help feed the nation; limited their purchases through rationing; and invested their savings in government "Liberty Bonds." Reinforced by government propaganda that emphasized the need for national sacrifice, Americans at home were urged to feel a sense of shared sacrifice and commitment with the men and women who risked their lives serving in the European and Pacific theaters.

In most wars, however, the initial *rage militaire* is not universal and wears thin as the military struggle lengthens. In this essay, Mark H. Leff challenges what he calls "the mystique of home front sacrifice" by focusing on two case studies: President Franklin Delano Roosevelt's unsuccessful attempt to limit wage and salary increases during the war and the advertising industry's more successful effort to profit from the production of wartime propaganda. Looking at the political meaning of sacrifice during World War II and focusing on the ways in which wartime cooperation was achieved, he finds that the theme of sacrifice had distinctly political overtones. Who sacrificed and how much, and whether sacrifices were equally borne by all segments of society, became questions argued out and resolved by the political process. Americans on the home front made many personal sacrifices, to be sure, but Leff demonstrates that there were limits to what could be achieved even in wartime and that the entire idea of sacrifice, meant to bind the country together, could generate controversy and division.

"The Politics of Sacrifice on the American Home Front in World War II." *Journal of American History,* 77 (1991), pp. 1296–1318. Copyright © 1991 by the Organization of American Historians. Reprinted by permission of the *Journal of American History.*

War is hell. But for millions of Americans on the booming home front, World War II was also a hell of a war. Both then and today, the mystique of home front sacrifice suffused visions of that wartime experience. The politics set in motion by a peculiar blend of profits and patriotism, of sacrifice amid unprecedented prosperity, gave a distinctive cast to American wartime life.

In subsequent American civic mythology, the public-spirited wartime community of World War II holds a cherished place. It is nostalgically recalled as *our* "finest hour," when Americans freely sacrificed selfish desires, did without, went all out, and "pulled together" in common purpose and spirit with "only one thing on their minds—winning the war." The allure of this golden age of home front sacrifice is not merely retrospective. During World War II, Americans gloried in the feeling that they were participating in a noble and successful cause by making "sacrifices." In common parlance sacrifice did not require the suffering of terrible loss. It instead comprehended a range of activities—running the gamut from donating waste paper to donating lives—in which narrow, immediate self-interest was subordinated to the needs of the war effort.

Despite, or even because of, its variegated usage, *sacrifice* decisively shaped the discourse of wartime politics. But polychromatic concepts can raise unsettling questions. Most Americans conceded that they had not made any "*real* sacrifices," a freighted expression largely reserved for our boys at the front. While it was more apparent in the war years than it is in retrospect that not everyone was going all out, the consecration of sacrifice inspired declarations of willingness to shoulder new burdens. Admittedly no specific additional sacrifice jumped readily to mind, but Americans in public opinion polls pledged their support—at least in principle—to an imposing list of wartime activities and restrictions, including wage and price freezes, no-strike pledges, rationing, and higher taxes. Amid these affirmations of unstinting patriotism, one contemporary commentator on wartime morale explained that the war had "subordinated or shelved" the precious "aims and values of individual citizens and special groups," as Americans "generally respond whole-heartedly to a major demand made of them when its essential necessity to the winning of the war is made clear."

The mystique of unconditional sacrifice, forged in the war itself and celebrated in collective memory, has not fared well as an interpretive guide to wartime politics and mobilization. Even at the time, staffers of American mobilization agencies commonly despaired of the difficulties of transforming "willingness into action" and cracking "the shell of public apathy," given "desultory, half-hearted" citizen involvement and "reluctance to forego the ordinary pleasures and comforts of 'life as usual.'" Americans, they noted, were often able to compartmentalize their advocacy of the principle of sacrifice, to excuse failures of civic responsibility by claiming that their sacrifices would not really have helped the war anyway, that someone else was receiving favored treatment, or that some blockheaded bureaucrat was bungling the whole thing. In the quest for alibis, standards of proof could be conveniently low. "Each of us," a top mobilization official conceded, "is likely to be slightly more eager to hold down the other fellow's prices, wages or profits, and to raise the other fellow's taxes. . . . Each of us will be looking for the moat in the other fellow's eye." President Franklin D. Roosevelt himself, despite warnings from pollsters that his "scolding approach" toward the shortcomings of American sacrifice might only impede cooperation, voiced his disgust at "the whining demands of selfish pressure groups who seek to feather their nests while young Americans are dying."

As recent historians who expand upon this indictment remind us, what Americans called sacrifice often involved limits on substantial gains rather than the horrific deprivations and destruction suffered by the citizens of other belligerents. Such reassessments can lead to a Manichaean dialogue as to whether Americans on the home front in World War II were saints or sinners—a singularly unpromising question in which assessments of virtue depend on the assessors' original inclinations and selectively applied standards. More productive challenges await: not to gauge the extent of American cooperation in the war effort, but to examine how that cooperation was achieved, to clarify the principles by which policy makers decided that certain groups would have to give up something or forgo gains for the good of the whole, and to understand how the ubiquitous ethos of wartime sacrifice set the terms of wartime political discourse, shaping the public actions and manipulatory strategies of potentially affected groups.

What were the boundaries of sacrifice in a global war that disrupted customary patterns of limited government? What could be required and of whom? Sacrifice was clearly a subject for negotiation across a broad range of issues encompassing both public and private choices. In public forums—in the speeches and press conferences of political leaders, in the public opinion polls commissioned by government departments, in the internal correspondence of mobilization officials—concern centered on what might be termed the calculus of political obligation. This article examines the public choices made there, the politics.

The wartime recasting of political obligation touched many facets of American political life, but this article focuses on two case studies. The first treats a celebrated but surprisingly insubstantial and ultimately abortive effort: Franklin Roosevelt's executive order capping all wartime salaries. This startling assault on the ethos of boundless individual achievement demonstrates both the apparently open-ended possibility for renegotiating symbolic values (was the ethic of sacrifice powerful enough to neutralize the American Dream?) and, in its quick and crushing repeal by Congress, the actual limits to the wartime revaluation of values. Interwoven in the seeming challenge to traditional marketplace values was a politics in which the level of comparative sacrifice—the degree of sacrifice relative to other groups—became a standard of justice.

The second case study offers a marked contrast: the successful merchandising of sacrifice through the formation of the War Advertising Council to coordinate a vast private advertising campaign supporting wartime programs and propaganda themes. The unique and consequential American arrangement whereby privately donated advertising carried the brunt of the domestic propaganda effort not only shows the adaptability of the imagery of sacrifice; it also raises provocative questions about the interplay of political forces in the United States that allowed certain groups to domesticate and delimit the meaning of sacrifice—to define it in terms that reinforced the validity of their own political interests and claims. What ultimately stands out in the calculus of home front obligation in World War II is a political process in which claimed sacrifices and contributions could be parlayed into political advantage or into efforts to shift war burdens to others. That process, which I have labeled the politics of sacrifice, established a dynamic that mobilizers and interest groups alike took into account.

Though sounding radical by current standards, President Roosevelt's salary limitation proposal emerged in stages throughout 1942, rather prosaically, as part of a coordinated effort to control inflationary pressures. In April FDR announced that price stabilization could only be effective if pursued on all fronts; thus he supplemented proposals for across-the-board price ceilings, wage controls, and rationing with a proposed 100 percent "super-tax" that would draw off any "excess" income over $25,000 ($50,000 for families) once the federal income tax had been paid. This income limitation proposal garnered popular approval as "a symbol of the idea of equality of sacrifice," but editorialists soon buried it as a "Rooseveltian pleasantry." Just as deadly was the congressional response: utter dismissal—one contemporary comparison was to "a burp in church, something to be overlooked and forgotten as quickly as possible." But in October Roosevelt used a broadly phrased authorization for price stabilization that he had just forced through Congress as the pretext for an executive order clamping an after-tax limit of $25,000 (equivalent to $200,000 in 1990 dollars) on all salaries. The order did not apply to total incomes or profits, partly because no interpretation of existing law sanctioned such use of independent executive action.

From today's vantage point, one can easily predict the ferocious response from some quarters to this apparently daring initiative. Labeling it a product of communistic philosophy and class hatred, attackers called it an un-American assault on free enterprise that threatened the production necessary for an effective war effort. When the 1942 elections the next month buoyed the congressional conservative bloc with substantial Republican gains, the salary ceiling was doomed, despite FDR's efforts to save it. In March 1943 most House Democrats joined the Republicans to repeal it by attaching a rider to a veto-proof debt limit bill; the bill then passed the Senate by a 74-to-3 vote. Less than six months after FDR released his executive order and before it had really gone into effect, salary limitation had been beaten back.

Why did the administration open itself to damagingly reproachful defenses of private property and free enterprise? Did the logic of sacrifice extend so quickly to the core of capitalism? A number of less extreme answers come to mind. Scape-goating campaigns against the abuses of "economic royalists" had long been a staple of Rooseveltian politics. In part, they can be traced to the president's patrician distaste for ostentatious wealth. Before the war, lessons embedded in the political culture about profiteering "merchants of death"—the unresolved public resentment over issues of sacrifice in World War I—spurred Roosevelt to proclaim that the "burdens of possible war" should be equalized to prevent "war millionaires" from enriching themselves from the sufferings of others. Once World War II began, Roosevelt's acute awareness of the privileged position of the United States also made him

indignant at what he saw as selfish bickering and maneuvering for partisan or monetary gain at home. His sense of equitable and active war participation as a paramount moral obligation also shaped such politically divergent Rooseveltian lost causes as his national war service "labor draft" proposal and his veto of a loophole-ridden tax bill as "not for the needy but for the greedy."

The salary limitation proposal had one other attraction: its potential victims were few and far between. The proposed ceiling applied to *after*-tax salaries. Given unprecedentedly high wartime tax rates, a salary earner needed to receive at least $67,200 (well over half a million in 1990 dollars) to fall under its provisions—a fate confined to roughly one in fifty thousand Americans. It is no wonder that one congressman was unsure if the salary order applied to any of his constituents. Roosevelt must have been aware of the advantages of his order's delimited impact in narrowing the potential base of opposition and in sidestepping any truly systemic challenge to economics as usual. In 1941, when batting around the idea of applying a $99\frac{1}{2}$ percent tax rate to income above $100,000, he jokingly dismissed doubts by asking, "Why not? None of us is ever going to make $100,000 a year. How many people report on that much income?"

So why bother? The salary order would have had no significant direct effect either in slowing inflation or in narrowing the budget deficit. The key lies in the order's symbolic value, in the messages it was intended to send, particularly to the labor movement. As Nelson Lichtenstein reports in *Labor's War at Home*, leaders of the Congress of Industrial Organizations (CIO) and CIO-affiliated United Automobile Workers (UAW) in 1942 urged a $25,000 income limit. In March 1942 CIO leaders capitulated to corporate and government demands to extend factory schedules and thus speed production by relinquishing a major union objective and achievement: "premium pay" for weekend and holiday work. To forestall a revolt and to show that its weekend pay concession should not be read as a sign that it had gone soft, the UAW executive board simultaneously publicized a broad "Victory through Equality of Sacrifice Program" that included a call for a $25,000 limit on incomes. The logic was clear: By prescribing "what other groups in the nation should give up to correspond to labor's sacrifice," UAW leaders sought to anticipate and quiet rank-and-file resentment about shouldering a disproportionate share of the war's burdens.

As early as 1940, "labor trouble" was very much on the president's mind. It is "a damn sight simpler," he explained, "for all of us to appeal to [worker] patriotism if we say we are using exactly the same principle for the owners of industry as we are with the workers in industry." In a closed-door meeting with his Business Advisory Council, Roosevelt urged a measure of restraint: "I can hold labor to the present level if I can say to them, 'You [industry] won't profiteer.'" The Treasury Department highlighted the strategy, noting that "if we are to expect all classes of society, including laborers and farmers, to accept the sacrifices of the emergency period and not to press for every possible dollar of advantage, they must be convinced that sacrifices are being distributed according to ability and that no one is making unreasonably large profits."

In a wartime economy, other groups besides labor manifested this mind-set. If the anti-inflation effort was to succeed, everyone had to shoulder new burdens: price ceilings for farmers, frustrating shortages and rationing for newly flush consumers, ballooning tax bills for the millions of Americans of average income previously exempt from income tax. Getting each group to accept its burden was no easy trick; Roosevelt's budget director despaired of what he termed "you-go-first" arguments in which "each group tries to shift the sacrifices to others." Roosevelt himself openly recognized the politics of sacrifice. In a fireside chat he

explained that some were perfectly willing to endorse his entire anti-inflation package "except the one point which steps on their individual toes," while others "seem very willing to approve self-denial—on the part of their neighbors." The Roosevelt administration thus sought some sensational demonstration to show each group that it did not face economically painful restrictions alone. A proposed ceiling on incomes was an attractive vehicle for this drama: The absolute limit demonstrated the urgency of the situation, but the targeting of a relatively small number of rich salaried corporate executives (rather than, say, profits) personalized the demanded sacrifices without really threatening production. It was, as the president of the National Farmers' Union reminded Roosevelt, "most important as a symbol and token."

Many union leaders embraced the salary limitation effort as a way to take full advantage of the politics of comparative sacrifice. They challenged employers to "match us in corresponding sacrifices," explaining that workers were "sore" not "because they are being asked to sacrifice" but "because they are being asked to tighten their belts when other people are outgrowing theirs because they are too damned small to go around their fat bellies." The articles and cartoons in union newspapers and pamphlets were no less hard-hitting. "What sacrifices are these fat cats making?" the *American Federationist* asked. "Will someone tell us, please?" One much-reprinted CIO cartoon depicted a "War Sacrifice Blood Bank." Two donors—"labor" and "farmer"—were laid out on hospital beds with their arms hooked up to a container labeled "war sacrifice." In the foreground were two typical capitalist caricatures, complete with top hats and bulging vests upon which were emblazoned "corporate profits" and "big incomes." As they casually waved off the idea of donating their blood, a no-nonsense Dr. FDR, with tubing in hand, pointed insistently to the empty beds. The cartoon was entitled "Labor Should Help Put These Fellows to Bed."

On this battleground of corporate salaries and profits, defenders of business were at a clear psychological disadvantage. Some gave it their best shot, however. The *New York World-Telegram* pulled its readers' heartstrings by reporting that a utility holding company magnate and his wife "closed four of their five homes, put eight cars in storage, reduced the number of their household servants from twenty-five to ten, and shut off all except two floors of the thirty-room pink colonial brick mansion at 1130 Fifth Avenue where they now live." "Millionaires," it concluded, "are on the skids." The *Wall Street Journal* ran an eight-part series called "The New Poor" about the prospective plight of illustrious corporate executives under salary limitation. The forecast included dwindling country club memberships, imperiled vacation homes, and the forced dismissal of faithful servants. Other newspapers interviewed prominent society women about the prospective damage to their clothing budgets.

Such articles were deliciously easy to parody (the National Farmers' Union sponsored a satirical essay contest on "How to Live on $25,000 a Year") and only played to the strength of salary limitation supporters. The issue itself, after all, was fundamentally symbolic; not only was the ceiling pegged at a stratospheric level but the salary order also specifically exempted investment income, the most important source of great wealth. Yet, to win cooperation with mobilization efforts, precisely measured equivalency—real "equality of sacrifice"—was scarcely the point. Merely targeting luxurious "excess income" promised to soothe resentments over new burdens and perceived inequalities.

The second case study, the formation of the War Advertising Council, illuminates and verifies this transition. Under the tutelage of this private organization, corporate executive targets of the call to sacrifice broadcast that call. Defensive recitations of "the truth about advertising" and attacks on the New Deal gave way to the merchandising of the industry's con-tributions to the war effort. This new politics of sacrifice, adopted with uncanny precision at the moment of Pearl Harbor, proved a brilliant strategic political shift, as advertisers seized the rhetoric and imagery of sacrifice to validate prewar goals of self-defense and expansion.

On the face of it, the saga of the War Advertising Council seems quite straightforward. According to a radio propaganda show sponsored by Wrigley's chewing gum in November 1945, it was a standard story of selfless sacrifice in which businessmen wholeheartedly lent their skills and high reputation to the war:

Narrator: There was advertising . . . winning a big place for itself in our national life . . . and there was American business . . . just as anxious as you were to use all its resources, all its knowledge and experience, to help win the war. . . .

Businessman: Then, our place in the effort is clear. We, who have by our advertising earned the confidence of the public, can use that advertising as a vehicle for the messages of the government to the people.

Voices: Right. Thats the way to do it . . .

Businessman: . . . Now—let's prove we are worthy of the faith and trust given us. I say—ask the government to tell us *what* is needed—and *we'll* take the information to the public—*in our own way!*

Narrator: That's the way it happened,—that's how the War Advertising Council came into being.

Truth has never been the essence of the propagandist's skill. In fact, in 1941 Madison Avenue was running scared. Mobilization demands were increasingly allowing manufacturers to sell effortlessly whatever they produced, removing the main rationale for big advertising budgets. Advertising representatives were also painfully aware that their reputation had taken a beating in the depression decade. They found it very easy to spook themselves by compiling long lists of "anti-advertising New Dealers" who had attacked "the accuracy and truth of advertising," branded it an economic waste, or warned of its contribution to inflation. A "pessimistic miasma" descended on much of Madison Avenue at the prospect of such figures making do-or-die decisions on the fate of the advertising industry. As the "growing alarm" indicated, the war itself posed special threats that advertising was "going to be throttled." Foremost among advertisers' concerns was the question of whether the government would consider advertising a legitimate business expense for the purpose of corporate taxes and war contracts.

On the eve of Pearl Harbor, advertising trade journals overflowed with evidence of a siege mentality. One warned that "advertising is threatened today as it has never been threatened before." Another concluded that "all of American industry is in a mental state like anticipating a trip to the dentist." Sounding the alarm on the "imminence of the danger to all," the president of the Association of National Advertisers called on the industry to create "a united front." Rallying to the call that "the common cause . . . is survival" (the pervasive martial imagery is all the more striking since the issue was not the nation's survival, but the industry's), the nation's two main advertising associations summoned a joint meeting of 630 advertising, industry, and national media executives for November 1941. In that meeting one speaker after another stridently denounced the unfair and uninformed attacks on the industry. An influential group of "moderate" voices at this meeting talked of advertising's potential social contributions in wartime. Those moderates brought in government speakers who took the edge off the meeting's belligerent mood by announcing their desire to work with advertisers in furthering the war effort. Yet even the

moderates compared advertisers to "His Majesty's Loyal Opposition" and urged a commitment to winning "the war of business" by defending free enterprise and preparing "the Case for Advertising."

The result of the conference was thus mixed. A consensus supported the need for advertisers to present a common front and to defend the advertising industry and the virtues of free enterprise. Yet some advertising executives feared that "a concerted campaign to preach the gospel of advertising at this juncture would fall on deaf or unfriendly ears" and advised that one essential part of the case for advertising was to "actively cooperate in solving national problems." In the immediate aftermath of the conference, its key organizers began to plan a new "governing group of the new Advertising Council or whatever it is to be called" to make that case.

Then came Pearl Harbor. From a strategic point of view, it was a godsend, a ticket to respectability for a battered industry. As one advertising executive later recalled, "we were losing" but "we were saved by the bell." "Now advertising has a chance to redeem itself . . . to prove it has a right to exist," a leading advertising journal rejoiced. The war provided "the greatest, the most golden, the most challenging opportunity ever to face American advertising," adman Walter Weir proclaimed. "If we make advertising fight today, we'll never again have to defend its place in our economy." Government mobilization officials encouraged advertisers' urge to serve, portraying it as a patriotic duty (though Donald Nelson, the "production czar," rather menacingly added in an off-the-record meeting that advertisers might ultimately need to choose between closing down—in which case "your future chances of coming back are something less than doubtful"—or converting to war-related advertising, which would preserve skills and facilities for postwar survival).

Thus the advertising industry formed what became the War Advertising Council, a private organization—currently called the

Ad Council—that has dominated American "public service" advertising ever since. Composed of volunteer representatives from major advertising agencies, large corporate advertisers, and the media, the War Advertising Council worked with such government agencies as the Office of War Information to plot out public information campaigns. By the war's end, it had supervised well over a hundred campaigns, using donated space to push war bonds, blood drives, food conservation, labor recruitment, and other mobilization demands deemed worthy of advertising support—with a value in space and personnel estimated (by the advertisers themselves, admittedly no strangers to exaggeration) at over a billion dollars.

One would be ill advised to dismiss those donations as mere artifice and calculation. In urging advertisers to sponsor public service messages under the company name or to inject official war messages into their product pitches, the War Advertising Council drew upon strong strains of patriotism. Win-the-war appeals anchored the council's efforts to gain industry cooperation.

Patriotic exhortation was of course paired with reminders that "public service advertising is shrewd business," since hook-ins to the war enhanced the ad and the firm's reputation. Shrewdness here was all-important; clients with no consumer goods to sell or no need to use advertising to sell their goods faced the "evaporation" of buyer and dealer loyalty. Advertising strategies shifted accordingly. One disarming solicitation for advertising explained, "Advertisers have but one thought in mind: post war 'prestige.' Not just 'prestige,'—but 'dollars and cents prestige,' the kind that will reflect itself in actual sales in the future." But how to maintain brand visibility without clashing with the wartime ethic of sacrifice and without creating unfulfillable product demands? Combining the company name with public service messages offered an answer, providing "momentum" to secure future sales and influence.

In the advertising industry, as in other sectors of American life, patriotism and public relations, sacrifice and self-interest intertwined. As one board member of the War Advertising Council put it, "Not for one minute is it necessary to say to an advertiser that he should try to win the war with his copy for the sake of winning the war." Instead, the advertiser was urged "that he can best serve his own selfish interests" by sensitivity to public demands, including the demand for information on how to contribute to the war. The War Advertising Council, its leaders repeatedly boasted, had combined "sensible idealism with the profit motive" in a show of social responsibility "which brings rich returns to those who act on it." That promise was an enduring part of the ethos of the Ad Council. As its president explained in 1947, "True, you are casting your bread upon the waters—but it will return to you well buttered."

With advertisers' show of sacrifice, the feared government barriers to the growth of the advertising industry crumbled. Soon advertisers could display an honor roll of glowing commendations, emanating from Franklin Roosevelt on down, of the inspiring example advertisers had set in their support of the war effort. In May 1942 the Treasury Department, reliant on the War Advertising Council and private donations to promote its war bond campaigns, granted Madison Avenue what one trade journal later called "advertising's Magna Charta under the tax laws." This ruling's generous interpretation of necessary and legitimate business expenses allowed full deduction of advertising costs from taxable incomes, even when firms had next to nothing to sell to ordinary consumers. With high excess-profits tax rates, that meant that the government was footing more than 80 percent of some companies' advertising bills. Especially at these cut rates, goodwill advertising directed toward post-war sales, the continued allegiance of distributors, employee productivity, or political aims became a highly attractive investment.

Thus the predicted wartime freefall in advertising budgets never took place. Even in the face of vanished consumer markets and supply shortages, expenditures on advertising—especially advertising in nationwide media—rose substantially, much to the relief of the industry itself. Favorable government decisions allowing certain advertising expenses to be factored into war contract prices and protecting advertised brands by including advertising in regulators' calculation of maximum allowable prices only bolstered the industry's assurance that the once-feared government was "friendly," "cooperative," and "helpful." "The important thing," admen exulted, "is that people *do* give us credit for doing the job." The council predicted all along that its show of sacrifice would reverse the antiprofiteering and antiadvertising attitudes that the industry had faced before Pearl Harbor, and the war indeed sharply raised the prestige of advertisers in particular and business in general.

The mystique of home front sacrifice did indeed permeate American life and politics in World War II. But changes in the vocabulary of political obligation did not imply automatic or open-ended commitment to the exercise of civic responsibility. The central role of sacrifice in wartime political discourse might have threatened "free enterprise" values, as the push for "equality of sacrifice" through income limitation seemed to suggest. But in the struggle over the meaning of sacrifice, at least as judged from the foregoing case studies, ascendant political forces were positioned to curb its subversive potential and channel it in more established political directions, so that much of the political topography could survive in recognizable form. Sacrifice proved symbolically malleable. It could justify mobilization programs or policy positions, revitalize deep-rooted political and economic values, mask privileged status or shield it from political challenge, or project war aims that helped reshape the contours of American political culture. The long-term consequences of this manipulation of symbolic content were not negligible; the privatizing of the wartime propaganda apparatus and war aims through the advertising industry, for example, resonated in the postwar consumer culture long after the war's end.

GLOSSARY

Manichaeism:	A dualistic philosophy that divides the world between good and evil.
Congress of Industrial Organizations:	National labor union THAT focused on organizing entire industries during the 1930s and 1940s; merged with the American Federation of Labor in 1955.
Pearl Harbor:	The Japanese attack on the U.S. fleet at Pearl Harbor, Hawaii, in 1941, which brought the United States into World War II.
Magna Charta:	Originally, the charter of English political and civil liberties granted by King John at Runnymede in June 1215; more generally, a document or piece of legislation that serves as a guarantee of basic rights.

IMPLICATIONS

Most governments attempt to mobilize their populations during wartime by appealing to patriotism and a sense of common sacrifice among all members of society. Here Leff investigates the politics of "common sacrifice" in World War II America. Why do you think it was necessary for the government to create a myth of mutual sacrifice during the war? Do you think Americans would have sacrificed equally without government intervention?

PART THREE

A Resilient People

The post–World War II generation lived through a unique era in the nation's history. Driven by the world's strongest economy, protected by the world's preeminent military establishment, and enjoying unprecedented personal prosperity at home, ordinary people and national leaders alike looked forward to living in what one observer dubbed the "American Century." In the end, however, that century would last a mere 20 years. By 1967, the costs of the Vietnam War pushed the nation's economy into an inflationary spiral; during the 1970s, foreign products made serious inroads into American markets; and in 1974, the Vietnam War ended in American withdrawal and defeat. Pressed economically and with national pride diminished by failure in Vietnam, the United States witnessed a resurgence of conservatism that threatened the existence of the liberal welfare state.

By the late 1940s, the American people found themselves fighting a "Cold War" against international communism, with an enormous impact on the nation's social and political life. In "Rebels Without a Cause," Nils Kristian Bogen analyzes the impact of the Cold War on the youth culture of the postwar era. He argues that the anti-Communist crusade of Senator Joseph McCarthy served to dampen the reformist impulses of postwar youth and, in the process, created an alienated but materialistic youth culture in the 1950s.

The postwar era marked a critical turning point in the lives of American women. Beginning in the 1950s, growing numbers of married women entered the workforce both to supplement family income and to seek a sense of personal fulfillment. By the 1960s, a resurgent and powerful feminist movement advanced women's claims for equality in all aspects of society with unprecedented success. In "Reconstructing Motherhood," Lynn Y. Weiner measures the changes in women's roles in the postwar era by following the changing fortunes of the La Leche League—an organization that promoted the breastfeeding of infants and the enhancement of women's traditional domestic roles. She finds that attitudes easily accepted during the 1950s gradually became less and less accepted in the following eventful decades.

The unprecedented prosperity of the immediate postwar decades created a virtual revolution in consumer goods and in the consumption patterns of ordinary Americans. One result was the creation of what Kenneth T. Jackson calls a "Drive-In Culture," based on a precipitous rise in automobile ownership during the postwar years. By the 1960s, motels and drive-in restaurants, movies, banks, and even churches were a regular part of everyday life in the United States.

The collapse of postwar prosperity beginning in the late 1960s and early 1970s cast a lengthening shadow over the lives of ordinary Americans. As wages failed to keep pace with inflation, growing numbers of married women with preschool-aged children were forced into the labor market simply to maintain the postwar standard of living. The political fallout of economic decline was immediate and long-lived. In "The Overthrow of LBJ," Allen J. Matusow argues that the combination of a faltering economy and the failure of the United States to achieve a decisive victory in Vietnam brought down one of the most powerful political leaders of the postwar era.

One of the truly momentous developments of the postwar era occurred in the realm of race relations. As record numbers of African Americans moved from the South during World War II and gained better-paying jobs in defense industries and greater power and acceptance in northern and western cities, they began to demand an end to discrimination and segregation throughout the nation. The Civil Rights and Voting Rights acts of 1964 and 1965 capped a decades-long struggle by African Americans to end discrimination and achieve equal opportunity in American society. In "After Civil Rights: The African American Working and Middle Classes," Robin D. G. Kelley explores the impact of the civil rights revolution on African Americans in the decade following the passage of the Civil Rights Acts. He finds that a nationwide economic downturn during the 1970s crippled attempts by the black working class to achieve equality in the workplace while, at the same time, some black professionals and entrepreneurs prospered because of the removal of formal racial barriers. This divergence, he notes, would continue to shape African American life through the remainder of the twentieth and into the twenty-first century.

As the economy began to recover in the late 1980s and boomed during the 1990s, Americans went on a national spending spree. Moving from modest homes to "McMansions," leasing expensive and prestigious cars and SUVs, investing in the stock market via then Internet, millions of Americans redefined the middle-class standard of living. In "The Insidious Cycle of Work and Spend," Juliet B. Schor evaluates the consequences of this new lifestyle. She finds that the middle-class emulation of wealthy lifestyles has come at the price of unremitting work, little leisure, and a frantic pace of life.

PAST TRACES

The 1950s is usually thought of as a decade of gray conformity, personal repression, and political conservatism. Yet from this seemingly uncreative period emerged a number of powerful reform movements among America's youth. This essay begins with an early document of the student movement, the Port Huron Statement of the Students for a Democratic Society. In it, the SDS articulates a view of American life very different from their own experiences growing up during the 1950s.

Students for a Democratic Society, The Port Huron Statement (1962)

We are the people of this generation, bred in at least modest comfort, housed now in the universities, looking uncomfortably to the world we inherit.

When we were kids the United States was the wealthiest and strongest country in the world; the only one with the atom bomb, the least scarred by modern war, an initiator of the United Nations that we thought would distribute Western influence throughout the world. Freedom and equality for each individual, government of, by, and for the people—these American values we found good, principles by which we could live as men. Many of us began maturing in complacency.

As we grew, however, our comfort was penetrated by events too troubling to dismiss. First, the permeating and victimizing fact of human degradation, symbolized by the Southern struggle against racial bigotry, compelled most of us from silence to activism. Second, the enclosing fact of the Cold War, symbolized by the presence of the Bomb, brought awareness that we ourselves, and our friends, and millions of abstract "others" we knew more directly because of our common peril, might die at any time. We might deliberately ignore, or avoid or fail to feel all other human problems, but not these two, for these were too immediate and crushing in their impact, too challenging in the demand that we as individuals take the responsibility for encounter and resolution.

13

Rebels without a Cause: Towards an Understanding of Anxious Youth in Postwar America

Nils Kristian Bogen

Almost every aspect of life in post–World War II America was touched by the geopolitical and ideological contest between the United States and the Soviet Union. Beginning during World War II, the Cold War entered the public domain with Winston Churchill's "Iron Curtain" speech of 1946. That speech, which warned Americans of the imminent threat that Soviet Communism posed to the "free world," joined with Harry Truman's Cold War policies to create an atmosphere of tension and misunderstanding in Russian-American relations lasting until the present day.

It was from this atmosphere of profound distrust between the Soviet Union and the United States that the phenomenon known as "McCarthyism" rose to dominate American media, popular culture, and politics in the 1950s. McCarthy, a little-known senator from Wisconsin until his anti-Communist campaign placed him in the public spotlight, used the power of congressional inquiry to intimidate and harass political enemies and liberal intellectuals alike. Employing deceit, innuendo, falsification, and badgering, McCarthy fueled a climate of fear and paranoia throughout the country that made all but the most innocuous forms of collective activity appear potentially subversive and unpatriotic.

In this essay, Nils Kristian Bogen explores the impact of the Cold War and McCarthyism on the American youth culture of the 1950s. Bogen finds that unlike their predecessors of the 1930s, who looked beyond the hardships of the Depression to the prospect of community involvement and the defeat of fascism, post–World War II American youths were caught in a web of anxiety about their place in the postwar

"Rebels without a Cause: Towards an Understanding of Anxious Youth in Postwar America." *Studies in Popular Culture*, XI:2 (1989), pp. 1–19. Reprinted by permission of *Studies in Popular Culture*.

world and forced by the pressures of McCarthyism to retreat from potentially "subversive" public activities. Other writers have attributed the "conformity" of the postwar years to a mass desire to attain material prosperity. But Bogen argues that the anxiety brought about by the Cold War and McCarthyism were the true sources of the apolitical and consumption-oriented youth culture of the 1950s.

....

"We are people of this generation, bred in at least modest comfort, housed now in universities, looking uncomfortably to the world we inherit." These are the opening lines of *The Port Huron Statement*, authored by 59 young radicals at the Students for a Democratic Society's national convention in Port Huron, Michigan, June 11–15, 1962. The document was not only to become a manifesto for the New Left in the early sixties and thereby founding the basis for much of the mass student protest in the decade to come. Equally important, *The Port Huron Statement* also suggests a way to understand post–World War II youth culture in the late forties and fifties. In spite of widespread material comfort in the post-war era, the authors argue, society was penetrated by events "too troubling to dismiss." The image of American virtue seemed to them to tarnish, and "when the hypocrisy of American ideals was discovered, . . . [they] began to sense that what [they] had originally seen as the American Golden Age was actually the decline of an era." Looking back on the 1950s as an age of anxiety, the authors of *The Port Huron Statement* concluded that:

America is without community impulse, . . . The apathy here is first, *subjective* [sic]—the felt powerlessness of ordinary people, the resignation before the enormity of events. But subjective apathy is encouraged by the *objective* [sic] American situation—the actual structural separation of people from power. The very isolation of the individual—from power and community and ability to aspire—means the rise of a democracy without publics.

The intensely felt anxiety and powerlessness, however, contradicts our understanding of the era. The authors of *The Port Huron Statement* obviously had in mind the interaction between culture and politics in the 1950s, a period in which the most powerful political movement was the rise of McCarthyism and anti-communism. Yet, while many historians of the era diligently record and deplore the excesses of McCarthy, they also assume that it had little effect on the lives of ordinary people.

Given this historical understanding of the period, there is no way we can comprehend *The Port Huron Statement*. Indeed, what seems to be the dominant popular perception of the 1950s is of it largely as being a safe and fun era. Assuming that the anxieties were basically an intellectual concern, no one has closely investigated what the implications of a cold war climate in American society were to youth. One reason why historians do not fully give us a satisfactory understanding of youth is the *way* youth has been studied. What is called for is a more thorough look at the specific social and political setting of youth culture, providing an in-depth study of how these relations change over time. This study is a modest beginning towards that goal. It explores the institutional changes that took place in youth culture from the 1930s to the 1950s at two Minnesota high schools and at the University of Minnesota. This is not a random selection. Whereas most previous studies on youth have been based on primary sources such as student newspapers and yearbooks, this article's findings are based on a major social science study on student interests and degree of public involvement which was undertaken by the University of Minnesota in the early 1930s and again in the late 1940s.

The latter study took special care to include the same areas of inquiry that also were investigated in 1933. When the two were compared, the 1948 study concluded that there was a "general decrease in participation in both on- and off-campus activities. . . ." Although there was an increased amount of time and money spent on social activities oriented towards leisure in 1948 as compared to 1933, "many students were dissatisfied with the social life they had at the university." It is important to be aware that the study defined "social activity" as being "dating, dancing, and card playing." What we witness is that students were drawn towards a more privatized life. Thus as early as 1948 students began to withdraw from social life. The investigators also found that the students in 1948 were less happy about this aspect of life than the students of 1933 had been. Furthermore, the researchers seemed to look back on the 30s with a sort of nostalgia, suggesting that social life was more rewarding in the past. This essay will show that the findings of these two studies on student life are so different because of the political context of the time. In the depression years, the politics of reform engaged young people in a commitment to change their society through communal and public institutions at the high school and college level. But in the postwar period the politics of McCarthyism and the Cold War served to undercut the public life of students, leaving them with a sense of a privatized but alienated affluence.

In order to understand the changes in the experiences of adolescents that took place after World War II in Minnesota as well as the nation as a whole, we need to recognize the social basis for this culture. Historians have always recognized certain institutional forces at work in this process. The American commitment to education is one such key pillar, and the way schools interpret the society in which their students live is important for young people's understanding of it. Education in the U.S.A. has been viewed as a fundamental part of the democratization process and indeed as part of democracy itself.

After World War II education as a social basis for youth was also intimately linked with the rise of an unprecedented affluence. For the first time in history a whole generation had access to material prosperity. In spite of an uneven redistribution of this wealth, millions of Americans were far better off than they had ever before been and, although a considerable number of university students in the 1950s came from this upper income group, higher education was now also something that extended to lower-income groups.

This commitment to education and, eventually, the promise of an affluent society enabled more and more children to escape from the workforce. Not until the 1920s, as Paula Fass has shown in her extensive study of that era, do we see in schools and colleges a separate youth culture. Films, books, periodicals, radio, and, eventually, television were instrumental in that process. By the 1950s, adolescents were an important new consumer group representing a tremendous economic potential to the corporate industry. By 1959 it was estimated that American youth had somewhere between $9.5 and $11 billion to spend annually. A look at the time clearly shows these forces at work. Middle-class children participated in the "freewheelin' and easygoing" lifestyle of the fifties apparently without giving it any second thoughts at all. Seemingly, they had the leisure, the money, and a market more than ready to serve them.

Far from all aspects of this different youth culture were well received by the peers. The outflow of a series of sometimes bizarre activities in the 1950s, the so-called fads, serves as a good example. On May 19, 1952, the *Minnesota Daily* reported about the University of Minnesota's first panty raid in which a thousand sweatshirt clad male students raided the co-ed dormitories and sorority houses. University officials were deeply shocked and disturbed by the event and immediately ex-

196 A Resilient People

pelled several of those thought to have been the leaders and put others on probation. Hostile reactions to incidents such as this one appeared even in the *Minnesota Daily*'s Monday magazine, the *Ivory Tower*. Under the title "The New Morality of the 'Cool Generation,'" one commentator delivered a frontal attack on teenagers' behavior, morals, and attitudes, qualities which he claimed had deteriorated rapidly during recent years. And he concluded: "That something has happened there can be no doubt. What it is hard to say. Maybe it is the times, the uncertainty."

In response to accusations such as this one, one student confessed that he had "seldom met any of Mr. Reeder's Cool Generation who was not a scared kid underneath his coolness." Another claimed that it appeared as if the students were exhibiting "the signs of the times; too much money, too much leisure, too much emphasis on 'growing up,' too much fear of the future." At the same time an editor of a high school newspaper urged his fellow students "to rebuild the moral standards [they had] lost!" Selfishness, irresponsibility, and loss of concern for their fellow men he stated as reasons for this loss. A Minneapolis high school principal began his address to the graduating class of 1951 in this way: "Today we face an age as drastic, as perilous and uncertain as any age this country of ours has faced since its founding. Our civilization, our democratic way of life is being threatened." A writer in a 1952 Minnesota high school yearbook was worried about the onset of the Atomic Age. The ending of the book provides a good example as it leaves off in the following philosophic mood: "What does the Atomic Age have in store for me? . . . Receiving this 1952 *Tiger* makes me wonder what our life's calling will be in this Era of the Atom." That this fear was something widespread is supported by the fact that as early as March 1946, 33% of those questioned in a public opinion poll nurtured fear of a possible "war with Russia, civil war [or] world war."

To adult observers of the time, this anxiety was a fundamentally new quality in youth culture, something radically different from the past. Constantly they asked what had happened. That it was something of great concern to students and university administration is shown by the fact that the administration at the University of Minnesota in 1948 undertook a major investigation of the student body to find out the interests and activities among the students and their participation in public life!

The report's main conclusion was that the students' interests and activities in the 1950s were very diverse, but there was a general decrease in participation in on-campus organized activities. What is also very clear is that the study shows that there was a sharp decline in public activity from 1933 to 1948, e.g., lecture attendance, participation in theater and concert activities, numerous civic organizations, and politics in general. Paralleling this decline was the increase in more privatized activities such as dating, dancing, and radio listening. In fact the 1948 study, when assessing the distribution of student activities, stated that "there is a very sharp decline in frequency beyond one activity, . . . the typical student does not participate in organized activities to any appreciable extent." Neither did it seem as if the students desired any further participation. "Apparently," the study assumed, "most of the students who were polled did not desire further participation in off-campus activities. Only 8 per cent of the men and 3 per cent of the women in the sample gave responses indicating a desire to join such organizations." The diversity of participation in organized campus activities showed a similar trend. As the study observed, "even the most popular, organized activity was participated in by fewer than one third of the total group." In leisure-time activities oriented towards public life the trend was also "toward a lower percentage of participation in [most] activities." Accompanying this decrease was a greater intensity of participation in those leisure activities students did participate in, a trend that seems to strengthen the tendency towards a more privatized form of activity among students in the late 1940s.

Somehow this finding seems quite startling. How could youth culture in the heart of the depression seem to provide a richer and more meaningful existence for young people than in the midst of affluence? This may at first glance seem strange when we know that the gross national product dropped from $104.4 billion in 1929 to $56.0 billion in 1933. During that same period of time personal income fell from $85.9 billion to $47.0 billion. In order to comprehend this apparent change, we need to investigate how youth related to social institutions in the pre–World War II culture. The 1933 study undertaken by the administration at the University of Minnesota does acknowledge that "the situation described probably represented the worst period of the depression from the standpoint of college students." Consequently many students experienced a shortage of means to participate as actively as they would have wished. The study observes, however, that "only two per cent stated that their non-participation was because of lack of interest in social activities." This finding is at variance with the tendency found in the 1948 study that in postwar society, students were basically dissatisfied with the quality of social life and tended to withdraw from it. In the 1930s, however,

> students [would] avail themselves of cultural opportunities if they [were] accessible and inexpensive. Excellent concerts [had] recently been offered on the campus at nominal prices and the free University gallery [had] been established. Each of these the students [had] attended in large numbers.

As Dean Williamson, the investigator in charge of the 1933 study, summed up when comparing the participation in group activities: "The general trend may be summarized in these terms: the 1933 students were more active than were the 1948 group."

Certainly one reason why students could look optimistically on the times was the fact

that funding for education was not dramatically affected by the economic downturn. As D. Tyack and E. Hansot point out in an article on public schooling in the 1930s, it "remained remarkably stable in funding and continued its long-term trend of institutional expansion." Contrary to all other public institutions, education in the 1930s continued almost without interruption its general 20th century trend of expansion, and if we look at the numbers of high school graduates, we see a steady increase throughout the thirties. We also see in the 1930s a more vibrant communal and social life among students. Commenting on the magnitude of clubs and organizations, the Assistant Principal at a Minnesota high school says in a 1930 yearbook: "Through the sponsorship of the social life of the school, each student is given an opportunity to enjoy and cultivate the social graces necessary to the 'worthy use of leisure.'" That same yearbook is a remarkable example of the gay and happy tone that had been so characteristic of the previous decade of prosperity: Pictures, fancy collages, and "jazzy" letters are merged to produce an optimistic entity. This positive air endured for a few more years, during which students had both the time and energy to put a lot of work into their yearbooks.

Tensions between youth and adults, as in the 20s and 50s, did of course exist. Moviegoing may serve as one such example of what could cause controversy in high schools. Amidst this timeless generational conflict, however, students seemed surprisingly estranged from the fact that America was in the midst of a depression. At high schools remarkable efforts were put into all kinds of extracurricular activities such as theater plays, Homecoming, Ice Carnivals, and Senior and Junior proms. One high school principal optimistically claimed in 1931 that "the future is before us" and "soon it will be sunlight." This "new freedom" is reflected on college campuses and in popular culture. One example was the increase in what by the 1960s Americans would call "lifestyle" ads in college newspapers during this period of time. In the *Minnesota Daily*, this could be seen in the sharp increase in use of ads on clothes, cigarettes, and leisure activities, and that weekly columns, such as *Minnesota Daily*'s "The Clothes Line" (on women's clothes), started to appear.

The media also played an important role in young people's lives as well as in their parents'. High school students formed radio clubs. The ad space spent on "radio shows" in college newspapers was formidable; one typical example would be Robert Burns' Panatela Program on WCCO radio station titled: "For Young Men . . . and Men with Young Ideas." Similarly, if we threw a glance at a copy of the *Minnesota Daily* one day, we might see the "Socially Speaking" column announcing that "pledging . . . Open Houses . . . and Romances Animate Social Life."

Yet, unlike the 1950s, this youth culture coexisted with the political and civic realities of the time. By the mid-thirties a distinct politicization was taking place, and it did not only focus on the problems caused by the Depression. Although the importance of a good education in order to "succeed" in a society suffering from a shortage of jobs and stiff competition was stressed, there is also a concern towards the larger questions of keeping peace in the world and what role America should play in that process. The new European situation that was emerging in the mid-thirties raised a serious concern among many American students. In October 1930 the *Minnesota Daily* briefly mentioned that "[a] Fascist leader had written a book called *My Fight* in which he foresees his Fatherland playing the part of world conqueror." The newspaper offered strong criticism of the ideas expressed in the book. However, not until the mid-thirties did the issue again resurface. In late 1934 the same newspaper reported that an antifascist rally had been held at the University of Minnesota. Indeed, from that time on anti-war protest seemed to have been a concern among students. In early 1935 more than 100 colleges throughout the country voted on a

set of identical questions concerning war and peace and what stand America should take in relation to the increasing threat of war in Europe.

Another significant example of students' involvement in Minnesota in the mid-thirties was whether or not to take the Oxford pledge. It was hoped then that the number taking the pledge would disclose how much support the pacifist idea had among college youth. Yet this was not just rhetoric. In fact, it linked students to the larger public world of politics carried by adults. The peace "strikes," a characteristic of the politicized campus in the 30s, are a good example. April 27, 1938, was proclaimed official "Student Peace Day" by Minnesota Governor Elmer A. Benson, and the campus newspaper reported that more than 40 organizations on campus would back that year's strike against governments of the world making plans for war. The increased interest for world affairs among students can also be seen by the fact that the university newspaper initiated a large front page column titled "Late News Flashes," which contained news from the international scene. This also was something that extended to high schools. As one commentator put it, youth programs in the thirties, such as the Civilian Conservation Corps (CCC) and National Youth Administration (NYA):

> provided opportunities toward which young people could direct their energies and make some contribution to society. The mid-thirties saw college and high school kids . . . demand control over school activities. They joined organizations to protest war, poverty, and school policy. On April 13, 1934, twenty-five thousand participated in a national student strike against war. Two years later, three hundred and fifty thousand college students followed suit and joined a walkout.

Editorials in high school papers commented on the threat of war in Europe and one newspaper saw the American society endangered by the same fascism and totalitarianism that threatened Europe. The editor urged American youth to distance themselves from those already under "the Fascist, Nazi, and Communistic symbols."

After the U.S.A. entered World War II, the political activity intensified. In 1943 a Minneapolis high school named their yearbook of that year *World Democracy* and dedicated it to the "People's March of the United Nations and to South High School's contribution to the War Effort." The whole book reflected a serious devotion on the students' behalf to make their contribution to the war effort. All clubs and organizations at the school centered their activities around the war. One could find headings such as: "Blue Triangle Organization Centers All Activities Around War, School Projects" and "Christian Fellowship Club Offers Daily Prayer for Success of the United Nations." The presentation of faculty members was headed "Officers—'On the March'" and the graduate students were listed as "Soldiers—'On the March.'"

At this point it is also possible to get perspective on the two studies of student attitudes. The 1933 study and our findings in student newspapers and yearbooks of the 1930s and early 1940s show us that students were involved in and concerned with what was going on in the world and their own lives and showed a willingness to try to do something about it. They lived in a world filled with just as much danger and anxiety as anything to be found in the 1950s. Yet, as the study of students in the 1950s showed, after the war students no longer were in control of their own lives, and their energies and anxieties were merely free-floating without focus or intent.

In 1953 the *Minnesota Daily* editor rhetorically asked: "Why have we been classified as the 'silent generation'?" In his answer, the editor pointed out that "our beliefs and principles are only notions—habits that we have been told are good. And we are silent because the foundations for our beliefs are shoddy and we haven't learned or don't take the time to dig any deeper." He calls for the educational institutions to assume responsibility when he says

that it is "time our educators took this talk about the 'silent generation' to heart, especially at the high school and junior college level. Our first job is to learn to think and reason intelligently for ourselves."

Similarly, in an article submitted to the *Minnesota Daily* the same year, the author expressed his concern about the collapse of idealism when he claimed that the students were left in an intellectual void which lacked "an anchor of concrete values," and that students tried to fill this void with a middle-of-the-road decency. And he went on to state what we have been taught to see as only an intellectual concern of the 1950s when he remarks that students:

face the world more realistically and less hopefully than their predecessors. . . . Students know the truth of the cliché that there will come a time when the world will be theirs to cope with. They know this, but, *unlike younger generations before them*, they are not particularly anxious for that time to come [emphasis added]. They have no panaceas up their sleeve, which might explain why "they are nowhere near the rostrum." The mood is one of quiet pessimism, tempered perhaps, by a faith in their capacity to fill the void. . . . Meanwhile, [the student] attempts to live out his college days as if nothing is wrong out there. He dates, crams before tests, chews gum, smokes (too much, probably), drinks a bit, boos the referee and awaits his degree—and he listens in relative silence, while an older, careworn and draft-proof generation continues to speculate on what the young folks are coming to.

What was it that caused this change? It was a question asked by investigators in school administrations at the time, but they had no explanation for this; they only observed the change taking place. However, when one looks at student newspapers, one explanation for the difference between the two eras lies in the realm of politics, namely the impact of McCarthyism. On numerous occasions, college newspapers warned students against dangerous ideas, the willingness to scrap freedoms when they apply to "undesirable" minorities, and the willingness to insist that students be "forced" at college level into an "acceptable" mode. In early April 1953 the *Minnesota Daily* ran a student poll about communist activities on campus. As many as 91.4 per cent of the student body reported that they did not know of any communist activities at the University of Minnesota and looked upon such accusations as unfounded. Yet in the same year E. G. Williamson published his study, the *Minnesota Daily* reported that "Redscare" was infiltrating campus, and numerous organizations, which in one way or another represented minorities or opinions that were not "mainstream," faded away out of fear of being persecuted. People were afraid to be seen in the wrong company.

The students' concern was real. A look into the directories of student organizations during these years shows that the *Minnesota Daily*'s suspicions were correct. In 1949–50 fourteen organizations were listed under "Political and Social Action" organizations, and all were active. In 1951 two pacifist and peace clubs, "Student Fellowship of Reconciliation" and "United World Federalist," disappeared. The year after they were followed by the "Marxian Socialist Club." In 1953 NAACP and the "League for Democratic Socialism" faded away. In 1954 two student government organizations, "All-Campus Party" and "All-Residence Party," vanished together with "Young Progressives of America." What is significant here is that not only did the redscare appear to strip the campus of organizations with socialist or communist sympathies, it also forced many middle-of-the-road organizations off the university. Few others than mainstream clubs such as the "University Republican Club" and "Young Democratic Farmer Labor Club" survived the McCarthy era. The 1953–54 directory listed as many as seventeen organizations, but reported six to be "not active." For the next academic year, 1954–55, the number had decreased to ten. These findings suggest that McCarthyism had far-reaching effects for college students. Not only did it discourage

public activity of students there, but it heightened the drive towards seeking fulfillment in the private realm.

Given this climate, many college students also observed that they were not allowed to participate in the decisionmaking of the university. There are strong indications that students in the 1930s to a much greater extent had participated in the formulation of university policies. A leaflet prepared by The University of Minnesota News Service in the mid-thirties pointed out that "students participate in forming and carrying out campus policies" and it specifically mentioned the *All-University Council* whose purpose was "to supervise and coordinate all student activities; to stimulate intelligent thinking upon college problems; to encourage closer cooperation between students and university authorities, and to represent the entire student body in matters affecting students' interest." The lack of such opportunities in the postwar era seemed to be the essence of the critique of the university role in the 1950s raised by then Assistant Professor Mulford Q. Sibley at the Dept. of Pol. Science. He said, in 1959, that he did not believe the university's role as "in loco parentis" had been healthy. The paternalistic tradition of university should be broken down and the students given more responsibility through student government. The Big Brother tactics would only create apathy and conformity.

In the wake of young people's experience after World War II, it should be clear that what the authors of *The Port Huron Statement* saw in 1962 was not something that occurred in a vacuum. In the mid-thirties, large numbers of young people had felt responsibility when fascism was on the rise in the world and actively engaged to fight it. In spite of the hardships of the 1930s, American society at the time provided the young with a communal spirit and a sense of involvement. By the 1950s, in a society haunted by the Cold War, this ability seemed to have disappeared as authorities discouraged any community involvement and youth culture took a much more privatized form. The combined effect of these events created a backdrop for the student anxiety as witnessed in the 1950s. With this in mind the larger question that the Port Huron radicals asked should by now make more sense: "Some would have us believe that Americans feel contentment amidst prosperity—but might it not better be called a glaze above deeply felt anxieties about their role in the new world?" Thus, the information revealed in this article should also help us reach a new understanding of *The Port Huron Statement* itself. It is hard to make sense of this manifesto's ideas and its impact on the New Left and the broader spectrum of the sixties' culture without understanding its true origins in the previous decade.

Indeed, the 1950s was not, as many have assumed, an era of "golden youth." Contrary to what historians of the postwar era as well as specialists concerning themselves with youth culture have so far assumed, alienation was something that extended far beyond a limited group of people such as artists, beats, or intellectuals. As we have seen from these two major social science studies at the University of Minnesota, college life after the war did not represent a return to the happy, involved life of the 1920s and 30s. On the contrary, as this study suggests, young people were part of a generation cut off from its roots of public life as witnessed in the prewar youth culture and suffered from an alienation that differed sharply from the 1930s. Instead, a consumer culture had taken its place that, until the early sixties, prevented the fears and anxieties of youth from surfacing in social movements dedicated to political and social change.

GLOSSARY

McCarthyism: Named after Senator Joseph McCarthy, the practice of publicizing accusations of political disloyalty or subversion with insufficient regard to evidence in order to suppress opposition.

My Fight: Reference to Adolf Hitler's *Mein Kampf*.

"**In loco parentis**":   The doctrine that an institution stands in the same place as a parent.

IMPLICATIONS

In this essay, Bogen concludes that the consumer culture of the 1950s redirected the energies of postwar youth away from social causes and turned them toward private concerns. Why do you think consumption was so much more attractive to young people than participation in social movements?

PAST TRACES

After drawing thousands of women into wartime industries during the 1940s, postwar American culture highlighted domesticity—the return of women to the home and the rearing of children. This reading is introduced by an account of domestic life in the mid-1950s. Drawn from a popular women's magazine, the article reveals both the promises and limitations of postwar domesticity.

Ladies Home Journal, The Young Mothers of the 1950s (1956)

Mrs. Gould: As editors and parents we are extremely interested in this whole problem. The welfare of our society depends upon the type of children you young mothers and others like you are able to bring up. Anything that affects the welfare of young families is most crucial, and I do feel that the young mother, any young mother in our day, should get far more general recognition and attention than she does—not so much for her own sake as for society as a whole, or just out of sheer common sense.

Miss Hickey: And understanding. I think there is a lack of understanding, too. Since it would take all day to tell what a busy woman does all day . . . how about your high points?

Mrs. Petry: I would say in the morning—breakfast and wash time. I put the breakfast out, leave the children to eat it and run into the bathroom—that is where the washer is—and fill it up. I come back into the kitchen and shove a little in tne baby's mouth and try to keep the others eating. Then I go back in the bathroom and put the clothes in the wringer and start the rinse water. That is

about the end of the half-hour there. I continue then to finish the wash, and either put them out or let them see one program they like on television, and then I go out and hang the wash up.

Miss Hickey: You put that outside?

Mrs. Petry: Yes. Then I eat.

Mrs. Gould: Can you sit down and eat in peace? Are the children outdoors at that time or watching television?

Mrs. Petry: They are supposed to be outside, but they are usually running in and out. Somebody forgot something he should have eaten, or wants more milk, or a toy or something. Finally I lock the screen door. I always read something while I'm eating—two meals a day I read. When my husband isn't there, and if I am alone, or maybe just one child at the table, I read something quick. But I time it. I take no more than half an hour for eating and reading.

Miss Hickey: You work on schedule quite a bit. Why do you do that?

Mrs. Petry: Because I am very forgetful. I have an orange crayon and I write "defrost" on the refrigerator every now and then, or I forget to defrost it. If I think of something while I am washing,

I write it on the mirror with an eyebrow pencil. It must sound silly, but that is the only way I can remember everything I have to do. . . .

Miss Hickey: Mrs. Ehrhardt, your quietest half-hour?

Mrs. Ehrhardt: I would say . . . that when I go out to take the wash in. There is something about getting outdoors—and I don't get out too often, except to hang out the wash and to bring it in. I really enjoy doing it. If it is a nice day, I stand outside and fold it outdoors. I think that is my quietest hour.

Miss Hickey: How often do you and your husband go out together in the evening?

Mrs. Ehrhardt: Not often. An occasional movie, which might be every couple of months or so, on an anniversary. This year is the first year we celebrated on the day we were married. We were married in June. We always celebrated it, but it might be in July or August.

It depends on our babysitter. If you cannot get anyone, you just cannot go out. I am not living near my family and I won't leave the children with teenagers. I would be afraid it might be a little hectic, and a young girl might not know what to do. So we don't get out very often. . . .

Miss Hickey: Let us hear about Mrs. Petry's recreation.

Mrs. Petry: Oh, I went to work in a department store that opened in Levittown. I begged and begged my husband to let me work, and finally he said I could go once or twice a week. I lasted for three weeks, or should I say he lasted for three weeks.

Mrs. Gould: You mean you worked in the daytime?

Mrs. Petry: Three evenings, from six until nine, and on Saturday.

Mrs. Gould: And your husband took care of the children during that time?

Mrs. Petry: Yes, but the third week, he couldn't stand it anymore, Saturday and all. In fact, I think he had to work that Saturday, so I asked if I could just come in to the store during the week. My husband was hoping they would fire me, but they didn't. But I could see that it wasn't really fair to him, because I was going out for my own pleasure.

Mrs. Gould: In other words, your working was your recreation.

Mrs. Petry: Yes, and I enjoyed it very much.

Miss Hickey: Why did you feel you wanted to do this?

Mrs. Petry: To see some people and talk to people, just to see what is going on in the world. . . .

Miss Hickey: How about your shopping experiences?

Mrs. McKenzie: Well, I don't go in the evening, because I cannot depend on Ed being home; and when he is there, he likes to have me there too. I don't know. Usually all three of the children go shopping with me. At one time I carried two and dragged the other one along behind me in the cart with the groceries. It is fun to take them all. Once a man stopped me and said, "Lady, did you know your son is eating hamburger?" He had eaten a half-pound of raw hamburger. When corn on the cob was so expensive, my oldest one begged me to buy corn on the cob, so I splurged and bought three ears for thirty-nine cents. When I got to the check-out counter, I discovered he had eaten all three, so he had to pay for the cobs.

Miss Hickey: You go once a week?

Mrs. McKenzie: Once a week or every ten days now, depending on how often I have the use of the car. That day we usually go to the park, too. . . .

Miss Hickey: Tell us about your most recent crisis.

Mrs. McKenzie: I had given a birthday party for fifteen children in my little living room, which is seven by eleven. The next morning my son, whose birthday it had been, broke out with the measles, so I had exposed fifteen children to measles, and I was the most unpopular mother in the neighborhood.

He was quite sick, and it snowed that day. Ed took Lucy sleigh riding. Both of them fell off the sled and she broke both the bones in her arm.

Mrs. Gould: Did she then get the measles?

Mrs. McKenzie: She did, and so did the baby. . . . My main problem was being in quarantine for a month. During this time that all three had measles and Lucy had broken her arm, we got a notice from the school that her tuberculin test was positive—and that meant that one of the adults living in our home had active tuberculosis. It horrified me. I kept thinking, "Here I sit killing my three children with tuberculosis." But we had to wait until they were over their contagion period before we could all go in and get x-rayed.

Miss Hickey: And the test was not correct?

Mrs. McKenzie: She had had childhood tuberculosis, but it was well healed and she was all right. About eight of ten have had childhood tuberculosis and no one knows it.

Mrs. Gould: It is quite common, but it is frightening when it occurs to you.

Were your children quite sick with measles?

Mrs. McKenzie: Terribly ill.

Mrs. Gould: They had high temperatures?

Mrs. McKenzie: My children are a great deal like my father. Anything they do, they do to extreme. They are violently ill, or they are as robust as can be. There is no in-between. . . .

Dr. Montagu: There is one very large question I would like to ask. What in your lives, as they are at present, would you most like to see changed or modified?

Mrs. Ehrhardt: Well, I would like to be sure my husband's position would not require him to be transferred so often. I would like to stay in place long enough to take a few roots in the community. It would also be nice to have someone help with the housework, but I don't think I would like to have anyone live in. The houses nowadays are too small. I think you would bump into each other. Of course, I have never had any one in, so I cannot honestly give an opinion.

Mrs. Townsend: At the present time, I don't think there is anything that I would like to change in the household. We happen to be very close, and we are all very happy. I will admit that there are times when I am a little overtired, and I might be a little more than annoyed with the children, but actually it doesn't last too long. We do have a problem where we live now. There aren't any younger children for my children to play with. Therefore, they are underneath my heels just constantly, and I am not able to take the older children out the way I would like to, because of the two babies.

Miss Hickey: You have been in how many communities?

Mrs. Townsend: I have lived in Louisiana, California, New York, and for a short period in Columbia, South Carolina. . . .

Miss Hickey: Mrs. Petry, what would you change?

Mrs. Petry: I would like more time to enjoy my children. I do take time, but if I do take as much time as I like, the work piles up. When I go back to work I feel crabby, and I don't know whether I'm mad at the children, or mad at the work or just mad at everybody sometimes.

I would also like to have a little more rest and a little more time to spend in relaxation with my husband. We never get to go out together, and the only time we have much of a conversation is just before we go to bed. And I would like to have a girl come and do my ironing.

I am happy there where we live because this is the first time we have stayed anywhere for any length of time. It will be two years in August, and it is the first home we have really had. That is why my husband left the Navy. I nearly had a nervous collapse, because it seemed I couldn't stand another minute not having him home and helping, or not helping, but just being there.

14

Reconstructing Motherhood: The La Leche League in Postwar America

Lynn Y. Weiner

The post–World War II era witnessed some of the greatest changes in women's roles in all of American history. Before the war, fewer than 7 percent of married women worked for wages and most of them labored in traditionally female, low-paid occupations such as domestics, secretaries, and unskilled factory operatives. The Second World War changed this pattern dramatically, bringing many married women into the workplace for the first time. Serving as replacement workers for men in the Armed Forces, fully three of every four wartime women workers were married, the majority with children. Then, with the end of the war in 1945, married women were again expected to withdraw from the workplace and again take up their "proper" place in the home, caring for their husbands and nurturing what would come to be called the "baby boom" generation.

Yet although the media, government agencies, and general social norms all proclaimed that women's place was in the home, beginning in the 1950s and in increasing numbers ever since, married women left their homes to enter, or reenter, the workplace. Already in 1950, 21 percent of married women worked (often after their youngest child was in school) and by 1970 that proportion had risen to 40 percent. 1980 marked an important watershed in postwar American life; for in that year a majority of married women—even those with young children—were active participants in the paid workforce. From 1980 onward, the dual wage-earning household increasingly became the norm.

As increasing numbers of married and divorced women worked in order to offset declining family purchasing power (see reading 18), they increasingly turned to public and private child-care agencies to care for their children. As Lynn Y. Weiner notes in

Lynn Y. Weiner, "Reconstructing Motherhood: The La Leche League in Postwar America." *Journal of American History* 80:4 (1994), pp. 1357–1381. Reprinted by permission.

her study of the La Leche League, not all Americans were comfortable with the rapid increase in the number of working mothers. Created as an organization to promote the breastfeeding of infants and the emotional bonding of children to their mothers, the La Leche League reflected traditional social norms, assuming that new mothers would stay at home with their infants. As Weiner's essay reveals, the League's attempt to deal with the reality of working mothers epitomized the tensions that developed in postwar society between those who believed that the mother–infant bond required stay-at-home mothers and those who believed that working mothers and successful child rearing were fully compatible. Equally important, the League's position also reflected divisions within the emerging postwar feminist movement. Some feminists supported the League, Weiner shows, because they viewed motherhood as a uniquely female source of power; others disagreed, arguing that power came only from the ability to pursue an independent career. Although the La Leche League ultimately answered the challenge of working mothers by maintaining its traditionalist position, the debate over work and motherhood continues to this day.

....

For almost four decades, the La Leche League—a voluntary association of women—has championed its cause of "good mothering through breastfeeding" in the United States and around the world. Although the league has been largely overlooked in scholarly discussions of women in the postwar era, it represents an important piece in the puzzle of twentieth-century social history. The league's publication, *The Womanly Art of Breastfeeding*, has sold some two million copies since 1958, and millions of women have attended league support groups, read league literature, or otherwise encountered league ideology. By the mid-1980s, the league claimed over four thousand support groups in forty-eight countries, and in the United States it had a reputation among many women as the primary source of expertise on motherhood—a position earlier held by the United States Children's Bureau.

The La Leche League was organized during a turbulent period when the social roles of American women as mothers and as workers were contested in both ideology and practice. Nineteenth-century middle-class cultural definitions had promoted "the intense, essentially private nature of the mother-child bond and the primary responsibility of mothers for the well-being of their children." In the mid-twentieth century, those definitions were challenged by developments in fertility patterns, new scientific childbirth and infant-feeding techniques, feminism, and the rapid growth of the female labor force. Science had entered the nursery, which growing numbers of women would soon leave behind.

The La Leche League arose to defend traditional domesticity against the assaults of modern industrial life and to dignify the physical, biological side of motherhood in ways that proved to have surprising appeal to many Americans. Whereas the nineteenth-century version of middle-class "true womanhood" emphasized moral purity and piety in a secular and industrializing age, the league, in the scientific twentieth century, emphasized naturalism. Mother and baby were not so much icons of purity as symbols of nature and simplicity. But they were not just symbols. The founders of the league had a social outlook that can be called maternalist; that is, they implied that an empowered motherhood defined by "female" qualities would improve society. Their faith in this maternalist prescription enabled La Leche League women to focus their efforts. From the mid-1950s to the present, the La Leche League has pursued a steadfast mission: to "bring mother and baby together again" through the "womanly art of breastfeeding."

That mission attracted a variety of supporters. To those suspicious of the intrusion of experts into family life, the league presented a social role for mothers that restored a sense of autonomy to the private domestic realm. Health benefits to mother and child from breastfeeding, childbirth as a natural process, trust in one's own instincts—these notions found favor among women who questioned "scientific motherhood," an ideology initially developed during the late nineteenth and early twentieth centuries that promoted the authority of experts in the realm of child rearing. By the 1950s, "scientific motherhood" dominated mainstream approaches to family life. In addition, the social movements of the 1960s and 1970s welcomed the "natural" methods of the league and its challenge to the patriarchy of the medical establishment.

The league grew rapidly, especially in the 1960s and 1970s. From one meeting of twelve friends in the fall of 1956, the number of league groups multiplied to 43 in 1961, 430 in 1966, 1,260 in 1971, and to about 3,000 in 1976. By 1981, some 17,000 women had been trained as league leaders. While it is difficult to ascribe credit for the rise in breastfeeding in the United States from the mid-1950s through the mid-1980s, the incidence of breastfeeding by new mothers grew from about 20 to about 60 percent.

If some women saw the league's vision of motherhood as empowering and progressive, there was a catch. To meet league standards of on-demand breastfeeding, mother and infant must remain together This was not too difficult in the 1950s, when fewer than one in five married mothers of young children under the age of six worked outside the home, but by 1980, that number had risen to almost one in two. As maternal employment norms changed, a posture critical of working mothers made the La Leche League seem increasingly conservative. Like maternalist ideologies of past centuries, La Leche League motherhood gave public purpose

to the private activities of domestic life; like advocates of those past ideologies, too, the league urged that women subsume their individualism for the greater good of the family and society. This essay will introduce the history of the league and explore the paradox embedded in the league's maternalist ideology—the way in which it simultaneously promoted women's autonomy and restricted women's roles.

At a picnic in the Chicago suburb of Elmhurst, Illinois, during the summer of 1956, two mothers—Mary White and Marian Tompson—sat under a tree nursing their babies. As other women approached them and admired what seemed a difficult and unusual task in an era when bottle-feeding was the norm, these mothers determined to help others learn the "womanly art" of breastfeeding. With five friends they formed the La Leche League, to give "mother to mother" help to women who wanted to nurse their infants. The "founding mothers" at first struggled to find a suitable name, for in those days, according to founder Edwina Froehlich, "you didn't mention 'breast' in print unless you were talking about Jean Harlow." The solution of "La Leche League" was offered by Mary White's husband, obstetrician Gregory White, who often gave his pregnant patients medals from a shrine in St. Augustine, Florida, dedicated to a Spanish madonna, Nuestra Señora de La Leche y Buen Parto, or, loosely translated, "Our Lady of Happy Delivery and Plentiful Milk."

The seven founders of the league were Roman Catholic, white, middle-class women who had become acquainted in two ways: through activism in the Christian Family Movement (CFM), an ecumenical Christian organization, and through a common interest in natural childbirth and breastfeeding. Like many white Americans in that era, all but one of the founders grew up in cities, but by the mid-1950s all but one lived in the suburbs. Three of the seven founders had college degrees; the husbands of most worked in professional occupations. Several of the founders were patients of Gregory White, who in his obstetrical practice favored natural childbirth procedures.

The first La Leche group meeting was held in Franklin Park, Illinois, on an October evening in 1956. That night, the seven founders and five of their pregnant friends discussed a *Reader's Digest* article advocating breastfeeding. Soon, with thirty and forty women crowding into living rooms, the meetings had grown so large that new groups formed to accommodate the demand. League founders quickly developed a series of five rotating sessions on pregnancy, birth, infant feeding, nutrition, and child rearing. Women gathered in members' houses and studied the material that eventually became the basis for *The Womanly Art of Breastfeeding*, first published in 1958. One meeting was held every three weeks, so that over the course of four months a participant attended all five; men were often invited to an additional "For Fathers Only" meeting as well. These small group sessions were facilitated at first by the founders and later by "league leaders," women who had successfully breastfed their babies at least a year and shared the league's maternalist philosophy. The groups provided information and emotional support for women wanting to breastfeed. Founder Mary Ann Cahill suggested, "we were considered . . . extremely radical . . . and this is why the [groups] were so important, because they gave you contact with other women who were also kind of thinking crazy."

The creation of small all-female groups of peers seems to have been an important source of the league's strength. The groups may have helped to break down the isolation of mothering in nuclear families—a growing problem during the era of rapid suburbanization and geographic mobility. In moving to the new postwar suburbs, many women moved farther away from relatives who in earlier times might have provided information and support for the task of mothering. One grandmother wrote the league, for example, that her daughter had

moved away to a new city and felt lonely "until she discovered the existence of La Leche League there." Like the earlier CFM groups, the breastfeeding groups enabled women to practice collectively what might have been difficult for them to achieve on their own. And like the later consciousness-raising groups of the women's liberation movement, the breastfeeding support groups made common the problems of individual women and nurtured their sense of belonging to a special subculture. One league member, Mary Jane Brizzolara, recalled attending a meeting in 1957 and finding "instant rapport" with every woman in the room." In those days, any woman who wanted to have her baby naturally and breastfeed it thought she was the only person in the world who wanted those things," she said, "but to go to that first meeting and discover a whole room full of women who had the same feelings and the same values—it was great."

The woman-to-woman approach of the groups was also evident in the league's hot-line telephone service and its publications. The league from the start received letters and telephone calls from women seeking advice about specific breastfeeding problems. The founders answered these queries "at home surrounded by . . . babies and children," and it was in response to the "never-ending stream of mail and the frantic phone calls" that the first version of *The Womanly Art of Breastfeeding* was put together, in loose-leaf folders sold as a "Course By Mail." The league newsletter first appeared in May of 1958 and was meant "to keep mothers in touch and give them somebody else to relate to or identify with . . . because at that time few mothers had anyone in their circle of friends who was breastfeeding," recalled founder Marian Tompson. The newsletter featured communications, poetry, photographs, and articles by league members. By 1960, four years after the founding of the organization, its headquarters averaged three hundred telephone calls and four hundred letters monthly. One member explained the reason she turned to the league for information."My doctor has never had a baby. My doctor has never nursed a baby . . . Sally Jones . . . has nursed three babies. Darlene Smith has nursed four. . . . So this is why I called them instead of my doctor." According to the league, breastfeeding was not a medical issue but rather a "womanly art," and "it's up to women who have learned it to pass it on." Emphasizing the experience and wisdom of mothers rather than the expertise of doctors, the league by the mid-1950s anticipated later feminist calls for a women's health movement by questioning the medicalization of birth and infant care and challenging the influence of "experts" on changing definitions of motherhood.

As membership in the league grew, it attracted a wider range of supporters who did not share the Catholic roots of the founders. Photographs and letters in league publications identified women who were African-American, Asian, and Hispanic as well as white, Jewish as well as Christian. In its writings the league itself maintained a nonsectarian posture. But women of color appear to have been in the minority of the membership. A 1970 survey by the psychologist Alice Kahn Ladas indicated that the majority of active league members were white, middle-class, native-born women, with those identifying themselves as either Catholic or of "no religious identity" present in larger numbers than in the general population. As membership grew, governance of league affairs broadened. While the founding mothers controlled both office hiring practices and the executive board that made policy directions well into the 1980s, local regional chapters (known as sections) were organized by the early 1960s. The first national league convention in 1964 drew some 425 mothers and 100 babies to the Knickerbocker Hotel in Chicago, after which coordinators were appointed on the national and state levels. By 1964, too, the league had become international, with 6 groups in other countries as well as 115 in the United States. Fifteen years later there were La Leche

League groups in 42 countries around the world.

Although the league's founders had not initially planned for any kind of growth or set up a formal organizational structure beyond that of a local "club for nursing mothers," the league did grow, in part because of its complicated interactions with larger social trends. Though founded by women enmeshed in a distinctive Catholic subculture, the league clearly spoke to the enthusiasm felt by many Americans in the 1950s for nuclear family life. That the league emerged when it did was not surprising. The "baby boom" peaked in the mid-1950s in the United States as fertility rates, which had been steadily declining for nearly two centuries, sharply rose, as did the rate of marriage. Women coming of age during the 1950s gave birth to an average of 3.2 children, compared to an average of 2.4 children for women reaching adulthood during the 1930s. The founders of the league had many more children than was common even for the baby boom. The seven La Leche League founders claimed a total of fifty-three offspring (an average of more than 7 per mother); their families ranged from 3 to 11 children. While all seven founders were Roman Catholic, they have suggested it was not religious impulse but rather the desire to deal with the reality of households full of infants that motivated the league's beginning. Motherhood was clearly of central concern to these women who chose to shape a public meaning for their private lives.

The increased birth rate of the 1950s was accompanied by a pronatalist ideology, defined by the historian Elaine Tyler May as the "belief in the positive value of having several children." Many Americans in the postwar years believed that personal happiness for both men and women was to be found in an intensive family life focused on children, and that full-time motherhood was the ultimate fulfillment of femininity. The league gave formal expression to these pronatalist ideals, asserting that motherhood was "natural" and beneficial to women, children, and the social order.

The popularity of the league also reflected unease with approaches to motherhood and family life common among physicians and other experts in the 1950s. The kind of motherhood experts advocated was anything but "natural"—instead it was "scientific." Professional advice was to replace maternal instinct, and so childrearing manuals, mothers' clubs, and physicians' counsel brought "modern" ideas about motherhood into the home. Earlier maternalist women's groups, such as the National Congress of Mothers, had argued that motherhood was so important to society that women must be trained to "be the best mothers possible for the good of the race." A School of Mothercraft, for example, was established in New York in 1911 to train mothers in the "intelligent and efficient" art of child care. By the 1930s, the authority of professionals on the subject of motherhood was institutionalized in the disciplines of social work, child guidance, preschool education, and, above all, medicine. Scientific motherhood came to favor the bottle over breastfeeding, medicated hospital birth over natural home birth, and rigidly scheduled days and nights over a more fluid approach to time. Motherhood, in short, was to be controlled by experts rather than directed by instinct. Rationality and order, then important in such other arenas of industrial American culture as business, home economics, and education, informed proper mothering as well. Standards of efficiency, time, and measurement were to control a baby's day as well as a factory's routine.

Bottle-feeding was the preferred way to nourish a baby in 1956. The incidence of breastfeeding at one week of age had fallen to about 18 percent, a decline from about 38 percent in 1948 and from over 80 percent before 1920. Bottle-feeding first became popular in the United States in the late nineteenth century in part because of concerns about high infant mortality rates among the urban poor. Middle-

class women soon adopted the new infant feeding method because of a desire to be fashionable and scientific. The historian Rima Apple suggests that the introduction of infant formula and the rise of pediatrics as a medical field led to the development of a mutually advantageous relationship between infant food companies and physicians. Taking another perspective, the historian Harvey Levenstein has argued that the male physicians who were replacing midwives by the turn of the century, "perhaps afflicted by . . . prudishness . . . tended to shy away from urging breastfeeding by mothers."

In the mid-twentieth century, bottle-feeding was a complicated and time-consuming affair. Mothers followed elaborate methods for preparing formula using evaporated, powdered, or whole milk, carefully calculated total milk volume spread over a certain number of bottles per day, and conscientiously sterilized bottles, rubber nipples, and bottle caps. Babies were often weighed before and after feedings. Advice books insisted that mothers consult their doctors about techniques and schedules; doctors were to "prescribe" breastfeeding or bottle-feeding and to mandate all aspects of mothering. Dr. Benjamin Spock, for example, in the 1946 edition of *The Pocket Book of Baby and Child Care*, offered advice on schedules "only for those parents who are unable to consult a doctor regularly" and suggested that ideally "your doctor will prescribe the baby's schedule on the basis of his needs, and you should consult him about any changes." A 1953 publication circulated by the Beech Nut Company, *Happy Mealtime for Babies*, stated

> Before we go any further, let's emphasize one important point: your doctor knows your baby— and he knows you. How your particular baby should be cared for, *whether he's sick or well*, is a matter that should be decided by your doctor— not by the neighbors, relatives or books.

The Federal Children's Bureau, in the 1940 edition of its popular booklet *Infant Care*, offered a detailed daily schedule for infants, which could "be varied according to the directions of the physician."

Childbirth, like infant feeding, was defined as "scientific" in the 1950s. Advocates of scientific motherhood had by the 1920s and 1930s labeled childbirth a medical problem rather than a natural function, in part as a response to high infant and maternal mortality rates. As childbirth became medicalized, control of the birthing process fell away from women and their midwives and into the hands of physicians. By the mid-1950s, 95 percent of all births in the United States took place in hospitals—compared to about 50 percent in 1940 and fewer than 5 percent in 1900—and a high proportion of those births involved the use of pain-killing drugs, forceps, and other medical interventions. This medicalization of childbirth, begun earlier in the century in an attempt to secure safety and comfort for woman, now was seen by some as unpleasant, alienating, and manipulative. Further, medicated childbirth affected infant feeding because a mother who was drugged could not nurse her baby. And delivery in a hospital affected feeding because without flexible nursery policies, the baby could be brought to the mother only at certain times of the day, leading to tightly scheduled feedings.

Scientific motherhood was not uncontested. There was a "motherhood reform" community made up of people—health care providers as well as mothers and fathers—interested in returning mothering from the artificial or scientific to the "natural" sphere. By the mid-1950s there were throughout North America and Europe critics representing a variety of social perspectives who challenged invasive childbirth methods, artificial infant-feeding techniques, and rigid child-rearing practices. Some, for example, the British natural childbirth educator Grantly Dick Read, believed that motherhood embodied "essential femininity" and that childbirth was "woman's supreme triumph." Others presented arguments for women-centered childbirth or more general critiques of

modern industrial life. La Leche League founders communicated with many of these varied reformers, including the advocates of family-centered maternity care who in 1960 formed the International Childbirth Education Association. League founders read about natural childbirth, nutrition, and child-rearing techniques in *Child-Family Digest*, published in the United States, and in the *Natural Childbirth Trust Newsletter* from Great Britain. They corresponded with Read about his manual *Childbirth without Fear*, and in 1957 they sponsored him as their first guest speaker. In short, they began to communicate, founder Froehlich recalled, with a growing network of "people who had this healthy thinking about the body."

Much attention focused on how to feed infants—on schedules or on demand, by the bottle or at the breast. Breastfeeding support groups were active in California during the 1940s. In 1942, medical workers in Detroit, including psychiatrists, pediatricians, obstetricians, and allied professionals, founded the Cornelian Corner to advocate breastfeeding and relaxed approaches to child-rearing practices such as toilet training. The Cornelians were named for the legendary Roman matron Cornelia, who said of her children, "these are my jewels," and also for the corner of the family kitchen toward which she turned while nursing. According to one observer, the Cornelians "say that in many ways we have forgotten that a baby is a baby. Rather he has been thought of as a piece of physiological machinery to be handled by standardized methods."

Pioneering public health physician Alice Hamilton was an early critic of the trend toward bottle-feeding. She wrote the Children's Bureau in 1949 that "for years . . . I watched this increasing opposition on the part of physicians and nurses toward breastfeeding." Young mothers, she suggested, "nowadays are under the impression that suckling a baby is an unusual activity, granted only to the specially gifted," and she urged Katherine Bain, director of the bureau's Division of Research in Child Development, to publicize findings supporting the importance of breastfeeding. Bain responded, "As I go around the country it appears to me that more physicians are becoming interested in breastfeeding and that some mothers themselves are pressing for it. I hope that I am right."

La Leche League leaders built strong ties with others in the international motherhood reform community of the postwar years, but they were especially influenced by two Chicago-area physicians critical of scientific motherhood: Gregory White, the husband of league founder Mary White, and White's former teacher, Herbert Ratner, a Chicago-area health commissioner. During the early 1950s, these doctors encouraged their patients to attempt home birth, natural childbirth, and breastfeeding, and they urged their patients to talk with each other about natural mothering techniques. Founder Mary Ann Cahill recalled how White recognized the importance "of mother-to-mother help in breastfeeding" and "recognized that one woman needed another" for advice and support. Several of the league's founders were patients of White and Ratner, who, with a medical advisory board, provided La Leche League with "credibility and acceptability in the scientific community." This was especially important during the early years of the organization, when some considered mothers talking about infant feeding to be, according to founder Froehlich, "interfering with medicine."

Doctors Ratner and White urged league founders to broaden their interests from breastfeeding to the more general issue of mothering. Like many in the motherhood reform community, these men held an essentialist view of women that presupposed a natural and biologically based social role. To Ratner, breastfeeding symbolized woman's place in the social order. At the first league convention in 1964, his keynote address focused on the "art of mothering." He believed Americans had abandoned a family ideology that nurtured women and chil-

dren. "Motherhood," he stated, "is an opportunity for growth. Three children nurture motherhood more than one. Each mothering experience enriches." He also suggested that women who bottle-fed their babies could too easily separate from them and "become vulnerable to other persuasions," and that a decision to bottle-feed "may be a sign of emotional difficulties in the mother." White also saw breastfeeding as a key to good motherhood. The mother who bottle-feeds, he stated, does not have high levels of prolactin, the hormone that contributes to milk production, and therefore she does not have the same physical feelings toward her baby."She's handicapped," he said, "she may turn out to be a pretty good mother. But she could have been a lot better mother if she had breastfed." By 1958, league founders had begun to shape a maternalist philosophy centered on "good mothering through breastfeeding" that reflected this essentialist model of womanhood.

At the heart of the La Leche League's philosophy was the notion that the needs of the infant—as interpreted by the mother rather than a doctor—should determine the practice and pace of mothering. League founder Cahill said that "one of our mottos was 'give the baby back to the mother, that's who it belongs to.'" The basic need of the infant was for mother's milk and for mother herself. Therefore breastfeeding and bottle-feeding were not two equally acceptable options for mothers, as the Children's Bureau and Dr. Spock had advised. In the words of a league publication, breastfeeding was a moral imperative, no less than "God's plan for mothers and babies."

Breastfeeding, as defined by the league, offered important advantages for the baby, the mother, and the social order. The first and most important beneficiary of breastfeeding was the child. According to the league, breast milk was the best infant food, fitted to the human digestive system; its use would lead to infant health, a gain in natural immunities, and the avoidance of allergies. A baby would also learn love and trust so that he or she might "go out and make a better world." The league advocated prolonged breastfeeding because its founders believed that the emotional and physical health of an infant was strengthened by allowing the child, rather than a doctor's chart, to determine the duration of breastfeeding and the initiation of weaning. The idea that the child, her needs interpreted by the mother, should set the schedule for feedings and later for weaning distinguished the league from physicians who favored a breastfeeding regimen regulated by external norms of time. Many medical authorities approved nursing for a short period from a few days to nine months, and they usually mandated feeding on a strict schedule of every three or four hours. For example, Frederic H. Bartlett wrote in the 1943 edition of his best-selling guide *Infants and Children*, "If you have plenty of milk you should nurse . . . perhaps not longer than 7 months," and he recommended a regular feeding schedule of the "usual" hours of 6 A.M., 10 A.M., 2 P.M., 6 P.M., 10 P.M., and 2 A.M. But the league urged instead that mothers nurse their babies on demand for at least a year, and preferably longer."Let him nurse until he wants to stop," the league advised. "Your baby may need the special kind of mothering he gets from breastfeeding for a longer time than someone else's baby." Techniques for, and defense of, breastfeeding older toddlers have long been a common and controversial theme in league literature.

Second, the league promoted breastfeeding as beneficial to the mother. Breastfeeding would get women back into shape after pregnancy, help prevent breast cancer, and provide a natural form of birth control. Perhaps most important, breastfeeding would facilitate a woman's realization of her full potential as a person. In the first league statement of policy, circulated in 1964, the leaders suggested:

> a mother who chooses to mother through breastfeeding, finds it an excellent way to grow in mothering as her baby grows in years. And since the woman who grows in mothering thereby grows as a human being, any other role she may

fill in her lifetime will be enriched and deepened by the insights and humanity she will bring to it from her experience as a mother.

The basic requirement for successful child rearing was a full-time, attentive mother who understood and accepted her "special vocation in life." As a corollary, league writers urged women to avoid such "mother substitutes" as pacifiers, high chairs, baby carriages, playpens, and, of course, bottles.

Finally, not only babies and women but also society would benefit from breastfeeding, because good mothering would foster trust and security in children who would become, as league founder Betty Wagner said, "secure, well-adjusted adults, healthy adults, who will make this world a better place to live." In this sense the La Leche League echoed earlier ideals of motherhood that directed women's energies into domestic activities and claimed a higher civic purpose in the raising of children. League leaders believed that breastfeeding "is the ideal way to initiate good parent-child relationships and to strengthen the family and hence the whole fabric of our society." League leaders also believed that their movement would promote social cohesion in another way. By emphasizing the common bond of gender, league leaders, like earlier maternalists, minimized class and racial distinctions between women. According to founder Marian Tompson, women who differed in other ways could meet on the "common ground" of breastfeeding.

The league took the act of breastfeeding and transformed it to symbolize an entire agenda for motherhood. For nearly four decades, league founders consistently argued that breastfed babies required a different type of mothering than did bottle-fed babies. "If you were breastfeeding in the way we were suggesting . . . on demand," said founder Wagner, "then your baby expected a lot more and you were responding differently to this baby, and so we had to bring in the mothering." "Good mothering through breastfeeding" meant communicating with the baby, providing full-time love and care, and "accepting that his wants and needs are the same." The mother, closely attentive to her child, should turn to natural instinct rather than to charts, books, or schedules.

La Leche League leaders sometimes struck others as radical. Indeed, some of them welcomed the description. "Everything we did was radical," Cahill said, from supporting breast-feeding to advocating the later introduction of solid foods to "listening to the baby." They certainly offered a program radical in its challenge to basic assumptions of mid-twentieth-century American culture, whether patriarchal or feminist. In a society much taken with efficiency, the clock, and precision, league attitudes to time and nature can be described as preindustrial. The league encouraged women to let their babies, instead of the clock and the calendar, set the time for eating and the time for weaning, to orient themselves to a variable natural time pattern rather than a fixed schedule based on external authority. A 1962 poem in the newsletter was typical in its approach to time and nature:

Observe her, her child at her breast.
Pause from the day's whirling activity
and consider her meaningful passiveness . . .
Look closer.
Discern her faith, somewhat unique in
a mechanized world.
Faith in the quiet order of nature,
in the complete and unstinting productivity
of her healthy young body.
Faith in herself, in her womanliness.

This faith in "God's plan" focused on interpersonal relationships and "meaningful passiveness," rather than schedules and other externally mandated norms of behavior. The league urged women to "refuse to accept the attempted mechanization of human beings or to abandon their true, womanly role."

The league also questioned the pervasive glorification of individual achievement in American society. It is not surprising that the league showed more sympathy with mothers driven to work outside the home by financial need than with those who prized the possibility of achievement offered by a public career. In the league outlook, achievement in this sense meant less than did connection with people. Not only the league but many Americans assumed that women were by nature more attuned to people than were men. One author widely cited by league members, Arlene Rossen Cardozo, argued in her 1976 book, *Woman at Home*, that a "male model" of achievement and success had misled feminists, who "fled home in imitation of Man. And the man of the day was the Hollow Man, the Computerized Man" who placed a success ethic higher than human relationships. In this cherishing of personalism and emphasis on the claims of others, league advocates echoed earlier maternalist ideologies and appealed to many American women in the twentieth century. The essentialism of the league, moreover, prefigured aspects of a later strain of radical feminism that was committed to preserving and celebrating gender differences.

Radical or conservative, the league's philosophy raised questions about American mores. The La Leche League's emphasis on intensive mothering led its leaders to criticize the consumerist "happy housewife" image of the 1950s that was first labeled in Betty Friedan's 1963 best seller, *The Feminine Mystique*. The happy housewife was concerned with appearances, of herself and of her house, and was above all a consumer of material goods. She was *not* first and foremost a mother. League leaders criticized this prescriptive image, urging mothers to attend to their children first. The league ran counter to American norms by implying that it was more important to build intense affectional ties between family members than to acquire and maintain the material trappings of a middle-class family. "What's important in your life," founder Mary White told a league convention in 1966, "is the people and not the things. And . . . especially while you have babies and small ones around, the most important people are your children." Time spent on housework, league leaders argued, was better spent with the family. Founder Cahill believed that to deemphasize housework was liberating. She said, "It was not unusual in those days for a mother to put the little one in the crib to entertain herself or to cry while mother spiffed up the house. You weren't to have dirty dishes in the sink, or unmade beds." Another founder, Viola Lennon, agreed that in the 1950s, "The rules were very severe . . . I think we were greatly responsible for changing the emphasis, that you were home to take care of the baby (instead of the house)."

If the league's maternalism codified a social role for women within a family defined less by consumerism than by personalism, it also prescribed a domestic role for men. The league argued that a father should, by supporting and encouraging the mother, enable her to nurture the baby more completely. Fathers should focus on family life rather than on professional success alone, spend more time with their children "because the joys of parenthood are meant to be shared," and participate fully in domestic tasks because the "authoritative, masculine man knows his dignity and stature are not in jeopardy when he performs a kitchen chore." The league newsletter on occasion published a June "Father's Day" issue that addressed such topics as how to offer support to a breast-feeding wife, and *The Womanly Art of Breastfeeding* discussed fatherhood in each edition. Just as the league helped shape a dimension of pronatalist womanhood, in its attention to fathers it helped shape notions of manhood in postwar American society.

Some women and men rejected the philosophy of the league because they disliked its moral fervor, complaining that the league used scare tactics and dogmatism to inflict feelings of guilt on women who failed to breastfeed or breastfed only a short time. Others argued that children who were breastfed too long might become infantilized and have difficulty separating from their mothers, who were overeager to

conform to maternalist ideology. League policy makers, recognizing that reputation, warned leaders to avoid overzealousness. "League mothers need to be . . . noncritical with their non-breastfeeding friends, instead of militant and crusading about the subject," the newsletter editor cautioned in 1972. "Because we know we're onto a good thing, we sometimes put people off. . . . We need to relax and appreciate other people . . . even when we don't agree with some of their ideas." Lennon suggested that the league's reputation for fanaticism came "out of the fact that when you're walking up hill, as the road gets steeper, you might . . . have leaders [who were militant]. I don't think as an organization, top level, we were militant, but . . . some of our leaders once in a while would . . . take a very aggressive stand." At a 1968 convention, a panel titled "Can breastfeeding be carried too far?" discussed the public relations problem caused by the "holier than thou" attitude of some group leaders who were "more League than League" in their insistence on prolonged breastfeeding and full-time motherhood. The working or bottle-feeding mother, league leaders suggested, was not "beyond the pale"; league mothers should not criticize or pass judgment, but neither should they "carry acceptance to the point of imitation." More important was the effort to bring information on mothering through breastfeeding to all women, even to those who disagreed with league ideology. "Our goal," according to the league leaders' handbook, "is to avoid diluting the philosophy while helping a mother grow toward it—without antagonizing the other along the way."

During the late 1960s and after, falling fertility rates, the rise of feminism, and an increase in maternal employment inspired a lively debate among league members about the meaning of motherhood in American society. While the basic message—that the ideal role for women was full-time motherhood focused on the natural needs of the baby—remained constant, the public reception of that message changed. The league initially challenged scientific motherhood and promised to empower women by helping them reclaim the arts of childbirth and infant feeding from the domain of experts. Now, the league was vocally challenging employed motherhood. To the league, both practices—health professionals intervening in the realm of motherhood and women working outside the home—represented a falling away from nature in a scientific age. In both cases, the prescription for social health was a return to "natural" behavior by women, where mother and child would form a "nursing couple" better to reflect traditionalist values. Thus an ideology of maternalism that in the mid-1950s sounded radical and empowering thirty years later impressed some as "extremely conservative." Tompson, one of the founders, wrote in 1970 that breastfeeding *was* conservative because it "ranks in status with traditional values of God, motherhood, and love of country."

The social context surrounding the league shifted dramatically from the time of its founding in 1956 through the 1980s. Fertility rates fell from a high in 1957 of 123 per thousand women between the ages of 15 and 44, to 96.6 in 1965, and to 66.7 in 1975. At the same time, economic pressures and opportunities for women outside the home increased. Maternal employment began a steady climb. In 1950, fewer than 12 percent of mothers with children under the age of six worked outside the home; by 1960, this had climbed to 19 percent, and by 1970, to 30 percent. By 1980, nearly 50 percent of mothers with children under six were in the labor force. These figures increasingly included the mothers of very young children. In 1978, the United States Census Bureau for the first time counted mothers of infants under the age of one year who were at work. That year, a startling 30 percent of mothers of infants were working, at least part time; 41 percent of all mothers with children under the age of two were employed. This "normalization" of maternal employment, combined with the growth of the feminist movement in the late 1960s and 1970s, put the league into sharpen-

ing conflict with women's lives and attitudes. The premise that a woman contributed to the world mainly by what she did within the home became anachronistic as family norms shifted to include maternal employment and less time-intensive child rearing. In response, league leaders and members increasingly addressed the issues of feminism and working mothers.

And yet the league flourished during these challenging years of social change. During the decade of the 1970s, the number of active La Leche League groups more than tripled, growing from 1,260 in 1971 to 4,327 ten years later. There were certainly many women claiming no allegiance to any philosophy other than traditional domesticity, and the league gave them a voice. But, in addition, the commonality between league practice and that of feminists and the counterculture may have overridden the ideological differences between them. League practice dovetailed, for example, with the "return to nature" ethos of the counterculture. Founder Lennon recalled that "by the time the '60s rolled around, people were beginning to accept certain things that were in 1956 really way out." League founders believed that the "hippie movement" aided in the popularization of the league "because they embraced all this natural stuff" and because their rebellion against the establishment included the medical establishment. Of the counterculture, founder Mary Ann Cahill said, "We were there, ready and in place when the big push came from those people flocking to the La Leche League . . . they had the idealism, but we had it all in place . . . they were looking for literature and information which they were able to find from us."

The alliance of the counterculture with the league and, indeed, a general broadening of the league's constituency through the 1970s were not without tension. Many of the new members attempted to bring to the league agenda such issues as advocacy of natural foods, environmental politics, civil rights, home schooling, and family planning; others wanted the group to take a stand on abortion. But the league cautioned against "mixing causes," arguing in its 1973 "Statement of Policy" that, whatever the merit of other concerns, the message about mothering through breastfeeding must not be diluted. "People who support good mothering," the league stated, "may reject the League if it seems to be part of another movement." Where other historical maternalist movements had encompassed a broader range of reforms, the league's belief in the importance of breastfeeding as a key to good mothering pushed it to cast as wide a net as possible over the varied female population of the late-twentieth-century United Sates; advocacy of any other controversial cause might take away resources from the promotion of breastfeeding or, worse, might turn some potential breastfeeding mother away. With the practice of breastfeeding by a wider variety of women came some interesting nuance, such as the popularization of the electrical breast pump or the sight of a working mother nursing her baby at work. In both cases, the spread of breastfeeding, although initially motivated by an interest in tradition and naturalism, ironically helped blur longstanding demarcations between home and work, and between nature and science.

Another source of league growth was its increasing acceptance in the medical community. At first physicians who favored scientific motherhood considered the league marginal, believing that "breastfeeding fell into the medical domain, and that one nursing mother was not qualified to advise another." Gradually, however, the league gained respectability. Although the founders believed that "most of the questions and problems a nursing mother may encounter are not medical," they stressed that they did not "intend to invade the jurisdiction of the physician." From the beginning they consulted with physicians. They formed a "medical advisory board" for editorial approval of materials and advice on specific medical problems. By 1960, a physician in North Carolina cited the league's work favorably, saying that it advocated "a revival of the

age-old conviction that nature is more reliable than science, that mother-love is more effective than aseptic precautions." In 1968 the *Journal of Pediatrics* published "A Salute to La Leche League International," cautioning the league against dogmatism but wishing them "continuing success." Physicians spoke to mothers at league conventions. Informal programs for physicians that were started in the late 1950s evolved into a Physician's Breastfeeding Seminar in 1973, which the American Medical Association and other medical groups recognized for continuing education credit. Local league groups facilitated hospital prenatal programs and initiated Information Service Centers to distribute breastfeeding information to mothers and health care professionals; by 1978 there were seventy centers, twenty of them in the United States. The league succeeded in winning public and professional support for its belief that the feeding of well babies was not a medical problem. More problematic was the reception of its maternalistic philosophy.

The founders of La Leche League have described themselves as early feminists, for they believed women should reclaim control of their bodies through natural childbirth and breastfeeding. An editorial in the league newsletter in 1966 stated that "feminism was with us long before Betty Friedan." In the early 1960s, league founders discussed Friedan's pioneering book, *The Feminine Mystique*; they remember agreeing with some of her views while rejecting her "negative analysis of motherhood." If they did not accept the feminist critique of gender roles, they too thought that women should not be subservient to men in the domain of mothering. In the 1963 edition of *The Womanly Art of Breastfeeding*, the authors wrote, "Breastfeeding is part of a womanly heritage, and it would naturally follow, in fact it seems almost inevitable, that mothers should initiate the revival in breastfeeding." Cahill recalled that when she was pregnant with her fourth child in 1955 she was looking "for ways to have a more natural delivery and then to breastfeed . . . because I wanted to be in control. I wanted to have some say in this. I did not want somebody to just knock me out and say, 'leave it to us, we'll take care of everything and you'll have the baby.' "

Elements of the maternalist ideology of the La Leche League had a natural appeal for some late-twentieth-century feminists. Although many of the women who launched the women's liberation movement of the 1960s and 1970s attacked motherhood as a patriarchal construct reproducing traditional relationships within the family, others argued for a feminist version of maternalism. Both league maternalism and feminism questioned the control of childbirth and child rearing by the medical establishment, and both promoted a collective female consciousness reinforced by small group meetings. The league shared the feminist conviction stated by the philosopher Joyce Trebilcot in 1984 that "mothering must now be defined and controlled by women."

Feminists liked the league's emphasis on reclaiming the arts of breastfeeding and natural childbirth, but with some qualification. For example, the Boston Women's Health Book Collective, in the first edition of the widely read health manual, *Our Bodies, Our Selves*, recommended *The Womanly Art of Breastfeeding*, "if you can get past the sickening stuff about [how] a woman's role is to bear and raise kids." Five years later, the collective, perhaps recognizing more common ground, wrote that *The Womanly Art of Breastfeeding* "will give you facts and confidence . . . but its philosophy is different from ours. We do not believe that breastfeeding has to dominate your life." The collective suggested, however, that the "women's health movement" could bring together "different groups of women." A medical sociologist stated in 1975 that breastfeeding was a feminist issue, asking, "Where and by whom are the definitions of woman's body made? Who will control how she uses it?" Feminists applauded the league's involvement in legal cases involving women's right to breastfeed in public and at the workplace; the

league also provided information for lawsuits and criminal charges concerning breastfeeding and maternity leave extensions, jury duty, women prisoners, child neglect, and child custody.

By the late 1960s, league publications directly addressed feminism. Founder Mary White told the second international league convention in 1966 that most league women had wanted to "*be* somebody and get married too." And once women "accept—not just accept, but embrace wholeheartedly, the idea that mothering is a rewarding job, a job filled with all sorts of satisfactions, then we'll be able to see and enjoy all the benefits it has to offer." League members found satisfaction in embracing this active definition of motherhood. Beginning in the early 1970s, letters and articles in league publications debated the problem of woman's proper place. How should mothering be defined? What was a feminist? Could you be a feminist and a full-time mother? Readers thought so, the founding mothers thought so, and if their definition of feminism was dismissed by some, it nonetheless reflected the thinking of a significant number of American women. According to a 1972 survey, league members saw their organization as "traditionalistic in its advocacy of the family role of wife and mother [but] . . . liberating because it teaches members actively to define and achieve satisfying goals within this role." Members placed "their confidence in themselves and their sisters rather than passively following the advice of licensed professionals." Breastfeeding provided a link to other mothers and was therefore a sign of "womanly power."

Many women writing to the league newsletter appropriated the language of feminism to argue that maternalism was liberating. In 1971, a league member from Ohio wrote, "I've been reading and hearing a lot about Women's Liberation and I think I would like to be liberated too! I want to be free to have my babies with dignity and joy. . . . I want to be free to nurse my baby on the delivery table. . . . I want to be free to, of all things, feed my baby when he is hungry. . . . Yes, I want to be liberated! I want to be free! I want to be free to be a woman!" A Chicago woman wrote that "the thrust of the Woman's Movement is toward each person being able to do what suits her best (and the League way of mothering suits me)." A league leader from Minnesota wrote the next year that the league reassured women that "mothering is a valid vocation" and "indeed, a 'liberating career.' "

If league supporters often appropriated the language of feminism, most rejected feminist philosophy, especially the idea that women could work for wages and mother at the same time; they reacted to growing public acceptance of women workers with a strong reaffirmation of housewifery and motherhood. A woman's self-esteem and sense of worth, league representatives suggested, could be found at home as well as at work. The newsletter in the 1970s and 1980s printed reams of articles and correspondence about mothers who had planned to work or were working while their children were young but later decided to stay at home. In a typical letter of this kind, published in 1972, a woman who had planned to work after the birth of her child decided she could not leave her baby; she proclaimed, "The only stimulation I felt I needed was the stimulation of my baby nursing at my breast." Another writer suggested that sometimes women could combine family and career, if work was flexible enough, but if a woman *had* to work "one simply has to make the best of a bad situation." There is a decidedly defensive cast to many of these articles, as there is in publications promoted by the league "for the woman who chooses to stay at home to raise her family, and for whom forming close human relationships is the first priority." By the mid-1970s, even as membership continued to rise, the league seemed aware that the full-time mother devoted to the care of others, once in the mainstream, was now threatened by social change.

League leaders strongly criticized the materialism and consumerism that, they believed,

pushed women into the labor force. Many articles and letters from readers offered concrete ways in which families could survive on lower incomes by budgeting, bartering, and lowering living standards. But others recognized the economic need pulling many women into the work force and proposed maternalist public policies, such as mothers' pensions, to support women at home. In 1979, for example, founder Marian Tompson told a league conference that:

> In our society where two income families are close to becoming an economic necessity, traditional mothering is being systematically stamped out. What we desperately need are policies that will allow women the choice of staying home to care for their babies without having to opt for poverty. Breastfeeding, once considered a medical problem, now becomes a political issue.

The league's service to working mothers was not consistent. Some La Leche League groups excluded working mothers, but others welcomed them. A 1984 survey found several groups in California, Connecticut, Florida, New Mexico, and New York that accepted or were oriented toward working mothers. The league has for over a decade been involved in peer-counseling programs for poor inner-city women, most of whom have to work for wages. League leaders estimated that by the 1980s, when membership began to slide after some twenty-five years of growth, up to half of the women attending meetings were employed outside the home. But if the league has in practice in some times and places been supportive and nonjudgmental about working mothers, ideologically it consistently valued full-time mothering for families. To be accredited as a group leader through the early 1980s, a woman "had to be pretty much at home" rather than at work.

League founder Mary White expressed the organization's general attitude toward working mothers when she stated at a league conference in 1981 that "any weakening in the link between the mother and her baby endangers the future health and security of the child." She added:

> We in La Leche have just as great an obligation to help [working mothers]...breastfeed their babies as we have any mother who comes to us for help...but, knowing what we know about mothering...shouldn't we want to do more? I think we must show all mothers how important full-time mothering is to their babies, to themselves, and to their whole families. How the needs of their babies are not only for mother's milk, or mother's breast, but for all of her.

Each successive edition of *The Womanly Art of Breastfeeding* offered more acknowledgment of working mothers. The most recent (1991) edition contains a chapter on breastfeeding tips for working mothers, followed by a chapter titled "Making a Choice" that urges mothers to consider staying at home while their children are young. The league's philosophy, then, while acknowledging the tremendous changes in women's lives, has remained steadfast in its vision of breastfeeding and full-time parenting of young children as the essence of "good mothering."

League maternalism, based on the notion of difference rather than equality between men and women, represented an important voice in the chorus of postwar interpretations of gender in the United States. The league embraced a biosocial understanding of women by defining female success and achievement through motherhood rather than through economics or politics. Because of the league's maternalism, which both asserted women's authority over the practice of motherhood and emphasized the importance of full-time motherhood, the group's history presents an interesting paradox. On the one hand, by the mid-1950s the league anticipated a strand of the feminist movement that was concerned with women's control over health care issues centered on childbirth and child rearing. On the other hand, by the early 1970s the league also challenged the emerging feminist ideology by questioning the consequences for children of the movement of women away from the home and into the workplace. In both cases, the league decried aspects of modern life that seemed to distance women from essentially natural behavior. The La Leche League reconstructed mothering in a way that was both liberating and constricting and so ironically offered both prologue and counterpoint to the emerging movement for women's liberation.

GLOSSARY

Children's Bureau: An agency of the Labor Department that dealt with issues involving children, especially early nurture, poverty, and child labor.

IMPLICATIONS

Weiner's essay raises the important issue of authority in postwar America. As she shows, the La Leche League directly challenged the advice of Dr. Benjamin Spock, the nation's foremost authority on children's health care. Do you think this challenge to one of the cornerstones of postwar domestic authority was idiosyncratic or part of a larger questioning of authority in the postwar world? How does the experience of those in the La Leche League compare to the experiences of young people discussed by Bogen in the previous essay?

PAST TRACES

One of the most significant pieces of legislation of the postwar era was the passage of the G. I. Bill. Providing subsidized education and guaranteed mortgages to returning soldiers and their families, the G. I. Bill contributed greatly to the postwar economic boom that made the United States the envy of the world. One of the results of government-guaranteed mortgages was the development of large-scale housing tracts, such as that in Levittown, Pennsylvania. This essay is introduced by the Levittown covenants—the rules homeowners agreed to follow. Drawing from a wide range of classes, the covenants enforce a firmly middle-class standard of community life in Levittown.

Restrictions of Levittown (late 1940s)

Every good community has restrictions that will insure its continued maintenance. As a result property values increase and greater enjoyment results to all homeowners. Here is a summary of those at Levittown. If you read them carefully you will see that they have but one purpose in mind: that you and your neighbors benefit from them.

1. You can add another carport or garage or room—IF it is similar in architecture, color and material to the dwelling—IF it doesn't project in front of the original house at all, or *more than 15 feet* in back of it—and IF at all times there still remain at least 20 feet of open yard in the rear and 7 feet on each side. (On corner lots, *each* side of the house facing a street is considered a front. If your house fronts on 2 streets you must leave at least 6 feet of open yard at one interior side and 15 feet at the other; if you bought one of the rare corners fronting on 3 streets, you must leave at least 6 feet of open yard at the remaining interior side).

2. You may display a residence sign but don't make it more than one square foot in size.

3. You may keep a couple of household pets (dogs or cats, etc.) but no commercial breeding or maintaining is allowed.

4. If you are a physician or a dentist or other similar professional person, you may have your office in your home *BUT no business of any kind is permitted*—the *residential* sections of Levittown must remain residential.

5. When you put your garbage out for collection make sure it is in a *tightly closed* metal container. Don't strew rubbish or garbage around your property.

6. You may plant a shrub or other *growing* fence *BUT* keep it no

higher than 3 feet. If you have a young child or a pet and want to pen them in, try a good thorny barberry or similar hedge fence of that height—it should do the job perfectly. NO FABRICATED FENCES (wood, metal, etc.) WILL BE PERMITTED. In laying out the plots at Levittown we have achieved a maximum of openness and parkline appearance. Fences will cut this up into small parcels and spoil the whole effect no matter how good-looking the fence material itself might be—and some of it is pretty terrible! This item is of prime importance.

7. Laundry can be hung in the rear but please use one of the revolving portable dryers. Old-fashioned clotheslines strung across a lawn look messy. And please don't leave laundry hanging out on Sundays or holidays when you and your neighbors are most likely to be relaxing on your rear lawn.

8. If your property backs on a road, the lot has been made 20 feet deeper than usual. This is so the rear 20 feet can be landscaped and screened, thereby protecting your privacy from passing automobiles and pedestrians. You must—and we're sure you'll want to—take care of this landscaping. With reasonable attention it will soon grow thick and high enough to give you complete privacy. This is the one and only place where shrub fencing is permitted to grow *higher* than 3 feet (see item 6 above). If you live on a corner plot, the same is true as regards the diagonal corner line connecting the sidewalks.

9. Mow your lawn and remove weeds at least *once a week* between April 15th and November 15th. Nothing makes a lawn—and a neighborhood—and a community —look shabbier than uncut grass and unsightly weeds. A lot of thought, work and money has gone into the preparation of your lawn. It will flourish if you take care of it—but it will quickly grow wild and unkempt if you don't.

10. If you live on a corner you cannot remove or add anything to the planting at the corner. If anything dies you may re-plant the same items if we don't. We go to special pains on corners and that's why we don't want them changed.

15

The Drive-In Culture of Contemporary America

Kenneth T. Jackson

Nothing has so transformed the landscape and architecture of America as the automobile. At the beginning of the twentieth century the automobile was a plaything of the rich, but by the end of World War II a majority of Americans owned automobiles, and the proportion has grown ever since. As more and more Americans purchased cars in the postwar decades, and as an increasing proportion of the nation's manufactured goods was transported by highway instead of rail, entirely new kinds of industries emerged to service an increasingly motorized society.

In this essay, Kenneth T. Jackson documents the tremendous impact of the automobile and truck on contemporary America. From the interstate highway system inaugurated during the Eisenhower administration to such innovations as shopping centers, motels, and service stations, "automobility" has done much to turn America into a service society. But, Jackson suggests, this thirty-year trend may be coming to an end. A countertrend has recently emerged, he tells us, in which central cities are increasingly being revitalized as living and shopping spaces, while the corporate consolidation of the gasoline, motel, and retail sales industries has led to the closing of independent service stations and many other artifacts of the early automobile age. If he is correct, the next decades may usher in yet another phase in America's constantly changing architectural landscape.

The postwar years brought unprecedented prosperity to the United States, as color televisions, stereo systems, frost-free freezers, electric blenders, and automatic garbage disposals became basic equipment in the middle-class American home. But the best symbol of individual success and identity was a sleek, air-conditioned, high-powered, personal statement on wheels. Between 1950 and 1980, when the American population increased by 50 percent, the number of their automobiles increased by 200 percent. In high school the most important rite of passage came to be the earning of a driver's license and the freedom to press an accelerator to the floor. Educational administrators across the country had to make parking space for hundreds of student vehicles. A car became one's identity, and the important question was: "What does he drive?" Not only teenagers, but also millions of older persons, literally defined themselves in terms of the number, cost, style, and horsepower of their vehicles. "Escape," thinks a character in a novel by Joyce Carol Oates. "As long as he had his own car he was an American and could not die."

Unfortunately, Americans did die, often behind the wheel. On September 9, 1899, as he was stepping off a streetcar at 74th Street and Central Park West in New York, Henry H. Bliss was struck and killed by a motor vehicle, thus becoming the first fatality in the long war between flesh and steel. Thereafter, the carnage increased almost annually until Americans were sustaining about 50,000 traffic deaths and about 2 million nonfatal injuries per year. Automobility proved to be far more deadly than war for the United States. It was as if a Pearl Harbor attack took place on the highways every two weeks, with crashes becoming so commonplace that an entire industry sprang up to provide medical, legal, and insurance services for the victims.

The environmental cost was almost as high as the human toll. In 1984 the 159 million cars, trucks, and buses on the nation's roads were guzzling millions of barrels of oil every day, causing traffic jams that shattered nerves and clogged the cities they were supposed to open up, and turning much of the countryside to pavement. Not surprisingly, when gasoline shortages created long lines at the pumps in 1974 and 1979, behavioral scientists noted that many people experienced anger, depression, frustration, and insecurity, as well as a formidable sense of loss.

Such reactions were possible because the automobile and the suburb have combined to create a drive-in culture that is part of the daily experience of most Americans. Because of unemployment and war, per capita motor-vehicle ownership was stable (at about 30 million vehicles) between 1930 and 1948, and as late as 1950 (when registrations had jumped to 49 million) an astonishing 41 percent of all American families and a majority of working-class families still did not own a car. Postwar prosperity and rising real wages, however, made possible vastly higher market penetration, and by 1984 there were about seventy motor vehicles for every one hundred citizens, and more cars than either households or workers. Schaeffer and Sclar have argued that high auto ownership is the result of real economic needs rather than some "love affair" with private transportation. Moreover, the American people have proven to be no more prone to motor vehicle purchases than the citizens of other lands. After World War II, the Europeans and the Japanese began to catch up, and by 1980 both had achieved the same level of automobile ownership that the United States had reached in 1950. In automotive technology, American dominance slipped away in the postwar years as German, Swedish, and Japanese engineers pioneered the development of diesel engines, front-wheel drives, disc brakes, fuel-injection, and rotary engines.

Although it is not accurate to speak of a uniquely American love affair with the automobile, and although John B. Rae claimed too much when he wrote in 1971 that "modern suburbia is a creature of the automobile and could not exist without it," the motor vehicle has fundamentally restructured the pattern of everyday life in the United States. As a young man, Lewis Mumford advised his countrymen to "forget the damned motor car and build cities for lovers and friends." As it was, of course, the nation followed a different pattern. Writing in the *American Builder* in 1929, the critic Willard Morgan noted that the building of drive-in structures to serve a motor-driven population had ushered in "a completely new architectural form."

THE INTERSTATE HIGHWAY

The most popular exhibit at the New York World's Fair in 1939 was General Motors' "Futurama." Looking twenty-five years ahead, it offered a "magic Aladdin-like flight through time and space." Fair-goers stood in hour-long lines, waiting to travel on a moving sidewalk above a huge model created by designer Norman Bel Geddes. Miniature superhighways with 50,000 automated cars wove past model farms en route to model cities. Five million persons peered eventually at such novelties as elevated freeways, expressway traffic moving at 100 miles per hour, and "modern and efficient city planning—breathtaking architecture—each city block a complete unit in itself (with) broad, one-way thoroughfares—space, sunshine, light, and air." The message of "Futurama" was as impressive as its millions of model parts: "The job of building the future is one which will demand our best energies, our most fruitful imagination; and that with it will come greater opportunities for all."

The promise of a national system of impressive roadways attracted a diverse group of lobbyists, including the Automobile Manufacturers Association, state-highway administrators, motor-bus operators, the American Trucking Association, and even the American Parking Association—for the more cars on the road, the more cars would be parked at the end of the journey. Truck companies, for example, promoted legislation to spend state gasoline taxes on highways, rather than on schools, hospitals, welfare, or public transit. In 1943 these groups came together as the American Road Builders Association, with General Motors as the largest contributor, to form a lobbying enterprise second only to that of the munitions industry. By the mid-1950s, it had become one of the most broad-based of all pressure groups, consisting of the oil, rubber, asphalt, and construction industries; the car dealers and renters; the trucking and bus concerns; the banks and advertising agencies that depended upon the companies involved; and the labor unions. On the local level, professional real-estate groups and home builders associations joined the movement in the hope that highways would cause a spurt in housing turnover and a jump in prices. They envisaged no mere widening of existing roads; but the creation of an entirely new superhighway system and the initiation of the largest peace-time construction project in history.

The highway lobby inaugurated a comprehensive public relations program in 1953 by sponsoring a national essay contest on the need for better roads. The winner of the $25,000 grand prize was Robert Moses, the greatest builder the world has yet known and a passionate advocate of the urban expressway. The title of his work was "How to Plan and Pay for Better Highways." As his biographer Robert A. Caro has noted, Moses was "the world's most vocal, effective and prestigious apologist for the automobile," and he did more than any other single urban official to encourage more hesitant officials to launch major road-building efforts in their cities.

The Cold War provided an additional stimulus to the campaign for more elaborate expressways. In 1951 the *Bulletin of the Atomic Scientists* devoted an entire issue to "Defense through Decentralization." Their argument was simple. To avoid national destruction in a nuclear attack, the United States should disperse existing large cities into smaller settlements. The ideal model was a depopulated urban core surrounded by satellite cities and low-density suburbs.

Sensitive to mounting political pressure, President Dwight Eisenhower appointed a committee in 1954 to "study" the nation's highway requirements. Its conclusions were foregone, in part because the chairman was Lucius D. Clay, a member of the board of directors of General Motors. The committee considered no alternative to a massive highway system, and it suggested a major redirection of national policy to benefit the car and the truck. The Interstate Highway Act became law in 1956, when Congress provided for a 41,000-mile (eventually expanded to a 42,500-mile) system, with the federal government paying 90 percent of the cost. President Eisenhower gave four reasons for signing the measure: current highways were unsafe; cars too often became snarled in traffic jams; poor roads saddled business with high costs for transportation; and modern highways were needed because "in case of atomic attack on our key cities, the road net must permit quick evacuation of target areas." Not a single word was said about the impact of highways on cities and suburbs, although the concrete thoroughfares and the thirty-five-ton tractor-trailers which used them encouraged the continued outward movement of industries toward the beltways and interchanges. Moreover, the interstate system helped continue the downward spiral of public transportation and virtually guaranteed that future urban growth would perpetuate a centerless sprawl. Soon after the bill was passed by the Senate, Lewis Mumford wrote sadly: "When the American people, through their Congress, voted a little while ago for a $26 billion highway program, the most charitable thing to assume is that they hadn't the faintest notion of what they were doing."

Once begun, the Interstate Highway System of the United States became a concrete colossus that grew bigger with every passing year. The secret of its success lay in the principle of nondivertibility of highway revenues collected from gasoline taxes. The Highway Trust Fund, as it was called, was to be held separately from general taxes. Although no less a person-

age than Winston Churchill called the idea of a nondivertible road fund "nonsense," "absurd," and "an outrage upon . . . common sense," the trust fund had powerful friends in the United States, and it easily swept all opposition before it. Unlike European governments, Washington used taxes to support the highway infrastructure while refusing assistance to railroads. According to Senator Gaylord Nelson of Wisconsin, 75 percent of government expenditures for transportation in the United States in the postwar generation went for highways as opposed to 1 percent for urban mass transit.

The inevitable result of the bias in American transport funding, a bias that existed for a generation before the Interstate Highway program was initiated, is that the United States now has the world's best road system and very nearly its worst public-transit offerings. Los Angeles, in particular, provides the nation's most dramatic example of urban sprawl tailored to the mobility of the automobile. Its vast, amorphous conglomeration of housing tracts, shopping centers, industrial parks, freeways, and independent towns blend into each other in a seamless fabric of concrete and asphalt, and nothing over the years has succeeded in gluing this automobile-oriented civilization into any kind of cohesion—save that of individual routine. Los Angeles's basic shape comes from three factors, all of which long preceded the freeway system. The first was cheap land (in the 1920s rather than 1970s) and the desire for single-family houses. In 1950, for example, nearly two-thirds of all the dwelling units in the Los Angeles area were fully detached, a much higher percentage than in Chicago (28 percent), New York City (20 percent), or Philadelphia (15 percent), and its residential density was the lowest of major cities. The second was the dispersed location of its oil fields and refineries, which led to the creation of industrial suburbs like Whittier and Fullerton and of residential suburbs like La Habra, which housed oil workers and their families. The third was its once excellent mass-transit system, which at its peak included more than 1,100 miles of track and constituted the largest electric inter-urban railway in the world.

The Pacific Electric Company collapsed in the 1920s, however, and since that time Los Angeles has been more dependent upon the private automobile than other large American cities. Beginning in 1942, the Los Angeles Chamber of Commerce, the automobile club, and elected officials met regularly to plan for a region-wide expressway network. They succeeded, and southern California's fabled 715 miles of freeways now constitute a grid that channels virtually all traffic and sets many communal boundaries. They are the primary form of transportation for most residents, who seem to regard time spent in their cars as more pleasurable than time walking to, waiting for, or riding on the bus. More than a third of the Los Angeles area is consumed by highways, parking lots, and interchanges, and in the downtown section this proportion rises to two-thirds. Not surprisingly, efforts to restore the region's public transportation to excellence have thus far failed. In 1976, for example, the state of California attempted to discourage single-passenger automobiles by reserving one lane in each direction on the Santa Monica Freeway for express buses and car pools. An emotional explosion ensued that dominated radio talk shows and television news, and Los Angeles's so-called "diamond lanes" were soon abolished.

More recently, southern California has followed the growing national enthusiasm for rail transit, and Los Angeles broke ground in 1984 for an 18-mile, $3.3 billion subway that will cut underneath the densely built, heavily trafficked Wilshire Boulevard corridor, cut through Hollywood, and end up in the residential San Fernando Valley. The underground will hopefully be the centerpiece of an eventual 160-mile network, second in size in the United States only to New York City's.

THE GARAGE

The drive-in structure that is closest to the hearts, bodies, and cars of the American family is the garage. It is the link between the home and the outside world. The word is French, meaning storage space, but its transformation into a multipurpose enclosure internally integrated with the dwelling is distinctively American.

In the streetcar era, curbs had been unbroken and driveways were almost unknown. A family wealthy enough to have a horse and carriage would have stored such possessions either in a public livery stable or in a private structure at the rear of the property. The owners of the first automobiles were usually sufficiently affluent to maintain a private stable. The first cars, therefore, which were open to the elements, often found lodging in a corner of the stable, side by side with the carriages they were soon to replace. These early accommodations for the automobile were often provided with gasoline tanks, for filling stations at the time were few and far between. This and the fact that cars often caught fire were good and sufficient reasons to keep the motor vehicles away from the family.

After World War I, house plans of the expensive variety began to include garages, and by the mid-1920s driveways were commonplace and garages had become important selling points. The popular 1928 *Home Builders* pattern book offered designs for fifty garages in wood, Tudor, and brick varieties. In affluent sections, such large and efficiently planned structures included housing above for the family chauffeur. In less pretentious neighborhoods, the small, single-purpose garages were scarcely larger than the vehicles themselves, and they were simply portable and prefabricated structures, similar to those in Quebec today, that were camouflaged with greenery and trellises. As one architect complained in 1924: "The majority of owners are really ashamed of their garages and really endeavor to keep them from view," and he implored his readers to build a garage "that may be worthy of standing alongside your house." Although there was a tendency to move garages closer to the house, they typically remained at the rear of the property before 1925, often with access via an alley which ran parallel to the street. The car was still thought of as something similar to a horse—dependable and important, but not something that one needed to be close to in the evening.

By 1935, however, the garage was beginning to merge into the house itself, and in 1937 the *Architectural Record* noted that "the garage has become a very essential part of the residence." The tendency accelerated after World War II, as alleys went the way of the horse-drawn wagon, as property widths more often exceeded fifty feet, and as the car became not only a status symbol, but almost a member of the family, to be cared for and sheltered. The introduction of a canopied and unenclosed structure called a "car port" represented an inexpensive solution to the problem, particularly in mild climates, but in the 1950s the enclosed garage was back in favor and a necessity even in a tract house. Easy access to the automobile became a key aspect of residential design, and not only for the well-to-do. By the 1960s garages often occupied about 400 square feet (about one-third that of the house itself) and usually contained space for two automobiles and a variety of lawn and wood-working tools. Offering direct access to the house (a conveniently placed door usually led directly into the kitchen), the garage had become an integrated part of the dwelling, and it dominated the front facades of new houses. In California garages and driveways were often so prominent that the house could almost be described as accessory to the garage. Few people, however, went to the extremes common in England, where the automobile was often so precious that living rooms were often converted to garages.

THE MOTEL

As the United States became a rubber-tire civilization, a new kind of roadside architecture was created to convey an instantly recognizable image to the fast-moving traveler. Criticized as tasteless, cheap, forgettable, and flimsy by most commentators, drive-in structures did attract

the attention of some talented architects, most notably Los Angeles's Richard Neutra. For him, the automobile symbolized modernity, and its design paralleled his own ideals of precision and efficiency. This correlation between the structure and the car began to be celebrated in the late 1960s and 1970s when architects Robert Venturi, Denise Scott Brown, and Steven Izenour developed such concepts as "architecture as symbol" and the "architecture of communication." Their book, *Learning from Las Vegas*, was instrumental in encouraging a shift in taste from general condemnation to appreciation of the commercial strip and especially of the huge and garish signs which were easily recognized by passing motorists.

A ubiquitous example of the drive-in culture is the motel. In the middle of the nineteenth century, every city, every county seat, every aspiring mining town, every wide place in the road with aspirations to larger size, had to have a hotel. Whether such structures were grand palaces on the order of Boston's Tremont House or New York's Fifth Avenue Hotel, or whether they were jerry-built shacks, they were typically located at the center of the business district, at the focal point of community activities. To a considerable extent, the hotel was the place for informal social interaction and business, and the very heart and soul of the city.

Between 1910 and 1920, however, increasing numbers of traveling motorists created a market for overnight accommodation along the highways. The first tourists simply camped wherever they chose along the road. By 1924, several thousand municipal campgrounds were opened which offered cold water spigots and outdoor privies. Next came the "cabin camps," which consisted of tiny, white clapboard cottages arranged in a semicircle and often set in a grove of trees. Initially called "tourist courts," these establishments were cheap, convenient, and informal, and by 1926 there were an estimated two thousand of them, mostly in the West and in Florida.

Soon after clean linens and comfortable rooms became available along the nation's highways, it became apparent that overnight travelers were not the only, or even the largest, pool of customers. Convenience and privacy were especially appealing to couples seeking a romantic retreat. A well-publicized Southern Methodist University study in 1935 reported that 75 percent of Dallas area motel business consisted of one man and one woman remaining for only a short stay. Whatever the motivation of patrons, the success of the new-style hotels prompted Sinclair Lewis to predict in 1920:

> Somewhere in these states there is a young man who is going to become rich. He is going to start a chain of small, clean, pleasant hotels, standardized and nationally advertised, along every important motor route in the country. He is not going to waste money on glit and onyx, but he is going to have agreeable clerks, good coffee, endurable mattresses and good lighting.

It was not until 1952 that Kemmons Wilson and Wallace E. Johnson opened their first "Holiday Inn" on Summer Avenue in Memphis. But long before that, in 1926, a San Luis Obispo, California, proprietor had coined a new word, "motel," to describe an establishment that allowed a guest to park his car just outside his room. New terminology did not immediately erase the unsavory image of the roadside establishments, however. In 1940 FBI Director J. Edgar Hoover declared that most motels were assignation camps and hideouts for criminals. Perhaps he was thinking of Bonnie and Clyde, who had a brief encounter with the law at the Red Crown Cabin Camp near Platte City, Missouri, one evening in July of 1933. Many of Hoover's "dens of vice" were once decent places that, unable to keep up, turned to the "hot pillow trade." Some Texas cabins, said the FBI director, were rented as many as sixteen times a night, while establishments elsewhere did business by the hour, with "a knock on the door when the hour was up."

Motels began to thrive after World War II, when the typical establishment was larger and more expensive than the earlier cabins. Major chains set standards for prices, services, and respectability that the traveling public could depend on. As early as 1948, there were 26,000 self-styled motels in the United States. Hard-won respectability attracted more middle-class families, and by 1960 there were 60,000 such places, a figure that doubled again by 1972. By that time an old hotel was closing somewhere in downtown America every thirty hours. And somewhere in suburban America, a plastic and glass Shangri La was rising to take its place.

Typical of the inner-city hotels was the Heritage in Detroit. The big bands once played on its roof, and aspiring socialites enjoyed crepethin pancakes. In 1975 a disillusioned former employee gestured futilely, "It's dying; the whole place is dying," as the famed hotel closed its doors. By 1984 about fifty historic establishments in downtown areas, such as the Peabody in Memphis, the Mayflower in Washington, the Galvez in Houston, the Menger in San Antonio, and the Biltmore in Providence, were reopening with antique-filled rooms and oak-paneled bars. But the trend remained with the standard, two-story motel.

THE DRIVE-IN THEATER

The downtown movie theaters and old vaudeville houses faced a similar challenge from the automobile. In 1933 Richard M. Hollinshead set up a 16-mm projector in front of his garage in Riverton, New Jersey, and then settled down to watch a movie. Recognizing a nation addicted to the motorcar when he saw one, Hollinshead and Willis Smith opened the world's first drive-in movie in a forty-car parking lot in Camden on June 6, 1933. Hollinshead profited only slightly from his brainchild, however, because in 1938 the United States Supreme Court refused to hear his appeal against Loew's Theaters, thus accepting the argument that the drive-in movie was not a patentable item. The idea never caught on in Europe, but by 1958 more than four thousand outdoor screens dotted the American landscape. Because drive-ins offered bargain-basement prices and double or triple bills, the theaters tended to favor movies that were either second-run or second-rate. Horror films and teenage romance were the order of the night, as *Beach Blanket Bingo* or *Invasion of the Body Snatchers* typified the offerings. Pundits often commented that there was a better show in the cars than on the screen.

In the 1960s and 1970s the drive-in movie began to slip in popularity. Rising fuel costs and a season that lasted only six months contributed to the problem, but skyrocketing land values were the main factor. When drive-ins were originally opened, they were typically out in the hinterlands. When subdivisions and shopping malls came closer, the drive-ins could not match the potential returns from other forms of investments. According to the National Association of Theater Owners, only 2,935 open-air theaters still operated in the United States in 1983, even though the total number of commercial movie screens in the nation, 18,772, was at a 35-year high. The increase was picked up not by the downtown and the neighborhood theaters, but by new multi-screen cinemas in shopping centers. Realizing that the large parking lots of indoor malls were relatively empty in the evening, shopping center moguls came to regard theaters as an important part of a successful retailing mix.

THE GASOLINE SERVICE STATION

The purchase of gasoline in the United States has thus far passed through five distinct epochs. The first stage was clearly the worst for the motorist, who had to buy fuel by the bucketful at a livery stable, repair shop, or dry goods store. Occasionally, vendors sold gasoline from small tank cars which they pushed up and down the streets. In any event, the automobile owner had to pour gasoline from a bucket through a funnel into his tank. The entire pro-cedure was inefficient, smelly, wasteful, and occasionally dangerous.

The second stage began about 1905, when C. H. Laessig of St. Louis equipped a hot-water heater with a glass gauge and a garden hose and turned the whole thing on its end. With this simple maneuver, he invented an easy way to transfer gasoline from a storage tank to an automobile without using a bucket. Later in the same year, Sylvanus F. Bowser invented a gasoline pump which automatically measured the outflow. The entire assembly was labeled a "filling station." At this stage, which lasted until about 1920, such an apparatus consisted of a single pump outside a retail store which was primarily engaged in other businesses and which provided precious few services for the motorist. Many were located on the edge of town for safety and to be near the bulk sta-tions; those few stations in the heart of the city did not even afford the luxury of off-street parking.

Between 1920 and 1950, service stations entered into a third phase and became, as a group, one of the most widespread kinds of commercial buildings in the United States. Providing under one roof all the functions of gasoline distribution and normal automotive maintenance, these full-service structures were often built in the form of little colonial houses, Greek Temples, Chinese pagodas, and Art Deco palaces. Many were local landmarks and a source of community pride. One car-toonist in the 1920s mocked such structures with a drawing in which a newcomer to town confused the gas station with the state capitol. Grandiose at the time, many of them molder today—deserted, forlorn structures with weeds growing in the concrete where gasoline pumps once stood. Their bays stand empty and silent, rendered that way by changing economics, changing styles, and changing consumer preferences.

After 1935 the gasoline station evolved again, this time into a more homogeneous entity that was standardized across the entire country and that reflected the mass-marketing techniques of billion-dollar oil companies. Some of the more familiar designs were innovative or memorable, such as the drumlike Mobil station by New York architect Frederick Frost, which featured a dramatically curving facade while conveying the corporate identity. Another popular service station style was the Texaco design of Walter Dorwin Teague—a smooth white exterior with elegant trim and the familiar red star and bold red lettering. Whatever the product or design, the stations tended to be operated by a single entrepreneur and represented an important part of small business in American life.

The fifth stage of gasoline-station development began in the 1970s, with the slow demise of the traditional service-station businessman. New gasoline outlets were of two types. The first was the super station, often owned and operated by the oil companies themselves. Most featured a combination of self-service and full-service pumping consoles, as well as fully equipped "car care centers." Service areas were separated from the pumping sections so that the two functions would not interfere with each other. Mechanics never broke off work to sell gas.

The more pervasive second type might be termed the "mini-mart station." The operators of such establishments have now gone full circle since the early twentieth century. Typically, they know nothing about automobiles and expect the customers themselves to pump the gasoline. Thus, "the man who wears the star" has given way to the teenager who sells six-packs, bags of ice, and pre-prepared sandwiches.

THE SHOPPING CENTER

Large-scale retailing, long associated with central business districts, began moving away from the urban cores between the world wars. The first experiments to capture the growing suburban retail markets were made by major department stores in New York and Chicago in the 1920s, with Robert E. Wood, Sears's vice president in charge of factories and retail stores, as the leader of the movement. A student of population trends, Wood decided in 1925 that motor-vehicle registrations had outstripped the parking space available in metropolitan cores, and he insisted that Sears's new "A" stores (their other retail outlets were much smaller) be located in low-density areas which would offer the advantages of lower rentals and yet, because of the automobile, be within reach of potential customers. With the exception of Sears's flagship store on State Street in Chicago (which was itself closed in 1983), Woods's dictum of ample free parking was rigorously followed throughout the United States. Early examples of the formula were the Pico Boulevard store in Los Angeles and the Crosstown store in Memphis. A revolution in retailing followed. Writing in the *American Builder* in 1929, the critic Willard Morgan found it natural that traffic congestion at the center would drive thousands of prospective customers to turn instead to suburban marketing centers.

Another threat to the primacy of the central business district was the "string street" or "shopping strip," which emerged in the 1920s and which were designed to serve vehicular rather than pedestrian traffic. These bypass roads encouraged city dwellers with cars to patronize businesses on the outskirts of town. Short parades of shops could already have been found near the streetcar and rapid transit stops, but, as has been noted, these new retailing thoroughfares generally radiated out from the city business district toward low-density, residential areas, functionally dominating the urban street system. They were the prototypes for the familiar highway strips of the 1980s which stretch far into the countryside.

Sears's big stores were initially isolated from other stores, while the retail establishments of highway strips were rarely unified into a coordinated whole. The multiple-store shopping center with free, off-street parking represented the ultimate retail adaptation to the requirements of automobility. Although the

Guinness Book of World Records lists the Roland Park Shopping Center (1896) as the world's first shopping center, the first of the modern variety was Country Club Plaza in Kansas City. It was the effort of a single entrepreneur, Jesse Clyde Nichols, who put together a concentration of retail stores and used leasing policy to determine the composition of stores in the concentration. By doing that, Nichols created the idea of the planned regional shopping center.

Begun in 1923 in a Spanish-Moorish style with red tile roofs and little towers—its Giralda Tower is actually a replica of the original in Seville—Country Club Plaza featured waterfalls, fountains, flowers, tree-lined walks, and expensive landscaping. As the first automobile-oriented shopping center, it offered extensive parking lots behind ornamented brick walls. Most buildings were two stories high, with the second-floor offices typically occupied by physicians, dentists, and attorneys, whose presence would help stimulate a constant flow of well-heeled visitors. An enormous commercial success, Country Club Plaza stood in organic harmony with the prairie surroundings, and it soon became the hub of Kansas City's business and cultural activities.

Nichols's Country Club Plaza generated considerable favorable publicity after it became fully operational in 1925, and by the mid-1930s the concept of the planned shopping center, as a concentration of a number of businesses under one management and with convenient parking facilities, was well known and was recognized as the best method of serving the growing market of drive-in customers. But the Great Depression and World War II had a chilling effect on private construction, and as late as 1946 there were only eight shopping centers in the entire United States. They included Upper Darby Center in West Philadelphia (1927); Suburban Square in Ardmore, Pennsylvania (1928); Highland Park Shopping Village outside Dallas (1931); River Oaks in Houston (1937); Hampton Village in St. Louis (1941); Colony in Toledo (1944);

Shirlington in Arlington, Virginia (1944); and Belleview Square in Seattle (1946). Importantly, however, they provided many of the amenities that shoppers would take for granted half a century later. In 1931, for example, Highland Park Village outside Dallas offered department, drug, and food stores, as well as banks, a theater, beauty and barber shops, offices, studios, and parking for seven hundred cars. The Spanish architecture was uniform throughout, and the rental charge included a maintenance fee to insure that the property was adequately cared for during the term of the lease.

The first major planned retail shopping center in the world went up in Raleigh, North Carolina, in 1949, the brainchild of Homer Hoyt, a well-known author and demographer best known for his sector model of urban growth. Thereafter, the shopping-center idea caught on rapidly in the United States and less rapidly in Canada, where the first shopping center—Dixie Plaza near Toronto—did not open until 1954. The most successful early examples, such as Poplar Plaza in Memphis, offered at least thirty small retailers, one large department store, and parking for five hundred or more cars. By 1984 the nation's 20,000 large shopping centers accounted for almost two-thirds of all retail trade, and even in relatively centralized cities like New York, Boston, and San Francisco downtown merchants adapted to the suburban shift. Easy facilities for parking gave such collections of stores decisive advantages over central city establishments.

The concept of the enclosed, climate-controlled mall, first introduced at the Southdale Shopping Center near Minneapolis in 1956, added to the suburban advantage. A few of the indoor malls, such as the mammoth Midtown Plaza in Rochester, New York, were located downtown, but more typical were Paramus Park and Bergen Mall in New Jersey; Woodfield Mall in Schaumburg outside Chicago; King's Plaza and Cross County outside Gotham; and Raleigh Mall in Memphis—all of which were located on outlying highways and all of which attracted shoppers from trading areas of a hundred square miles and more. Edward J. Bartolo, Sr., a self-made millionaire and workaholic, operated from a base in Youngstown, Ohio, to become the most prominent mall developer in the United States, but large insurance companies, especially the Equitable Life Assurance Society, increasingly sought high yields as shopping-center landlords.

During the 1970s, a new phenomenon—the super regional mall—added a more elaborate twist to suburban shopping. Prototypical of the new breed was Tyson's Corner, on the Washington Beltway in Fairfax County, Virginia. Anchored by Bloomingdale's, it did over $165 million in business in 1983 and provided employment to more than 14,000 persons. Even larger was Long Island's Roosevelt Field, a 180-store, 2.2 million square foot mega-mall that attracted 275,000 visitors a week and did $230 million in business in 1980. Most elaborate of all was Houston's Galleria, a world-famed setting for 240 prestigious boutiques, a quartet of cinemas, 26 restaurants, an olympic-sized ice-skating pavilion, and two luxury hotels. There were few windows in these mausoleums of merchandising, and clocks were rarely seen—just as in gambling casinos.

Boosters of such mega-malls argue that they are taking the place of the old central business districts and becoming the identifiable collecting points for the rootless families of the newer areas. As weekend and afternoon attractions, they have a special lure for teenagers, who often go there on shopping dates or to see the opposite sex. As one official noted in 1971: "These malls are now their street corners. The new shopping centers have killed the little merchant, closed most movies, and are now supplanting the older shopping centers in the suburbs." They are also especially attractive to mothers with young children and to the elderly, many of whom visit regularly to get out of the house without having to worry about crime or inclement weather.

In reality, even the largest malls are almost the opposite of downtown areas because they are self-contained and because they impose a uniformity of tastes and interests. They cater exclusively to middle-class tastes and contain no unsavory bars or pornography shops, no threatening-looking characters, no litter, no rain, and no excessive heat or cold. As Anthony Zube-Jackson has noted, their emphasis on cleanliness and safety is symptomatic of a very lopsided view of urban culture.

Despite their blandness, the shopping malls and the drive-in culture of which they are a part have clearly eclipsed the traditional central business districts, and in many medium-sized cities the last of the downtown department stores has already closed. The drive-in blight that killed them, like the Dutch Elm disease that ravaged Eastern towns in years past, has played hopscotch from one town to another, bringing down institutions that had once appeared invincible. The targets of this scourge, however, were not trees, but businesses, specifically the once-mighty department stores that anchored many a Main Street.

The most famous retailing victim of the drive-in culture thus far has been the stately J. L. Hudson Company of Detroit. It was a simple fact that all roads in the Motor City led to Hudson's. Featuring tall chandeliers, wood-paneled corridors, and brass-buttoned doormen, the 25-story full-square-block emporium at its height ranked with Macy's in New York and Marshall Field in Chicago as one of the country's three larges stores. After 1950, however, the once-proud store was choked by its own branches, all of them in outlying shopping centers. As soon as Hudson's opened Northland, its biggest suburban outlet and one of the earliest in the nation, sales downtown began to fall. They declined from a peak in 1953 of $153 million to $45 million in 1981. Finally, in 1981, the downtown landmark closed its doors for good. Hudson's was a victim of the product that made Detroit: the car.

In a Christmastime obituary for Detroit's most famous retailer, a WWJ radio commentator maintained that white flight to the suburbs, hastened by the Motor City's 1967 race riot, helped deal Hudson's a mortal blow. Actually, the 91-year-old store was killed by the free parking, easy accessibility, and controlled environment of the mega-malls.

By the 1960s, the primary rival to the shopping center as the locus of brief, informal communication and interaction had become the highway strip, with its flashing neon signs and tacky automobile showrooms. Especially in medium-sized cities, the vitality after dark is concentrated in the shopping malls or along the highway, not along Main Street.

A DRIVE-IN SOCIETY

Drive-in motels, drive-in movies, and drive-in shopping facilities were only a few of the many new institutions that followed in the exhaust of the internal-combustion engine. By 1984 mom-and-pop grocery stores had given way almost everywhere to supermarkets, most banks had drive-in windows, and a few funeral homes were making it possible for mourners to view the deceased, sign the register, and pay their respects without emerging from their cars. Odessa Community College in Texas even opened a drive-through registration window.

Particularly pervasive were fast-food franchises, which not only decimated the family-style restaurants but cut deeply into grocery store sales. In 1915 James G. Huneker, a raconteur whose tales of early-twentieth-century American life were compiled as *New Cosmopolis*, complained of the infusion of cheap, quick-fire "food hells," and of the replacement of relaxed dining with "canned music and automatic lunch taverns." With the automobile came the notion of "grabbing" something to eat. The first drive-in restaurant, Royce Hailey's Pig Stand, opened in Dallas in 1921, and later in the decade, the first fast-food franchise, "White Tower," decided that families touring in motorcars needed convenient meals

along the way. The places had to look clean, so they were painted white. They had to be familiar, so a minimal menu was standardized at every outlet. To catch the eye, they were built like little castles, replete with fake ramparts and turrets. And to forestall any problem with a land lease, the little white castles were built to be moveable.

The biggest restaurant operation of all began in 1954, when Ray A. Kroc, a Chicago area milkshake-machine salesman, joined forces with Richard and Maurice McDonald, the owners of a fast-food emporium in San Bernardino, California. In 1955 the first of Mr. Kroc's "McDonald's" outlets was opened in Des Plaines, a Chicago suburb long famous as the site of an annual Methodist encampment. The second and third, both in California, opened later in 1955. Within five years, there were 228 golden arches drive-ins selling hamburgers for 15 cents, french fries for 10 cents, and milkshakes for 20 cents. In 1961 Kroc bought out the McDonald brothers, and in the next twenty years this son of an unsuccessful realtor whose family came from Bohemia built an empire of 7,500 outlets and amassed a family fortune in excess of $500 million. Appropriately headquartered in suburban Oak Brook, Illinois, the McDonald's enterprise is based on free parking and drive-in access, and its methods have been copied by dozens of imitators. Late in 1984, on an interstate highway north of Minneapolis, McDonald's began construction of the most complete drive-in complex in the world. To be called McStop, it will feature a motel, gas station, convenience store, and, of course, a McDonald's restaurant.

Even church pews occasionally were replaced by the automobile. In early 1955, in suburban Garden Grove, California, the Reverend Robert Schuller, a member of the Reformed Church in America, began his ministry on a shoestring. With no sanctuary and virtually no money, he rented the Orange Drive-In movie theater on Sunday mornings and delivered his sermons while standing on top of the concession stand. The parishioners listened through speakers available at each parking space. What began as a necessity became a virtue when Schuller began attracting communicants who were more comfortable and receptive in their vehicles than in a pew. Word of the experiment—"Worship as you are . . . In the family car"—spread, the congregation grew, and in 1956 Schuller constructed a modest edifice for indoor services and administrative needs. But the Drive-in Church, as it was then called, continued to offer religious inspiration for automobile-bound parishioners, and in succeeding sanctuaries facilities were always included for those who did not want a "walk-in" church. By 1969 he had six thousand members in his church, and architect Richard Neutra had designed a huge, star-shaped "Tower of Power," situated appropriately on twenty-two acres just past Disneyland on the Santa Ana Freeway. It looked like and was called "a shopping center for Jesus Christ."

In 1980 a "Crystal Cathedral" was dedicated on the grounds. Designed by Philip Johnson, the $26 million structure is one of the most impressive and gargantuan religious buildings on earth. More than 125 feet high and 415 feet wide, its interior is a stunning cavern without columns, clad in over 10,000 panes of transparent glass. Yet the drive-in feature remains. Instead of separate services for his indoor and outdoor followers, Schuller broadcasts his message over the radio from an indoor/outdoor pulpit. At the beginning of each session, two 90-foot glass walls swing open so that the minister can be seen by drive-in worshippers. Traditionalists come inside the 3,000-seat "Crystal Cathedral," while those who remain in the "pews from Detroit" are directed to the announcement: "If you have a car radio, please turn to 540 on your dial for this service. If you do not have a radio, please park by the amplifiers in the back row." The appeal has been enormously successful. By 1984 Schuller's Garden Grove Community Church claimed to be the largest walk-in, drive-in church in the world. Its Sunday broadcasts were viewed by an estimated one million Californians and commanded the nation's highest ratings for religious programming.

THE CENTERLESS CITY

More than anyplace else, California became the symbol of the postwar suburban culture. It pioneered the booms in sports cars, foreign cars, vans, and motor homes, and by 1984 its 26 million citizens owned almost 19 million motor vehicles and had access to the world's most extensive freeway system. The result has been a new type of centerless city, best exemplified by once sleepy and out-of-the-way Orange County, just south and east of Los Angeles. After Walt Disney came down from Hollywood, bought out the ranchers, and opened Disneyland in 1955, Orange County began to evolve from a rural backwater into a suburb and then into a collection of medium and small towns. It had never had a true urban focus, in large part because its oil-producing sections each spawned independent suburban centers, none of which was particularly dominant over the others. The tradition continued when the area became a subdivider's dream in the 1960s and 1970s. By 1980 there were 26 Orange County cities, none with more than 225,000 residents. Like the begats of the Book of Genesis, they merged and multiplied into a huge agglomeration of two million people with its own Census Bureau metropolitan area designation—Anaheim, Santa Ana, Garden Grove. Unlike the traditional American metropolitan region, however, Orange County lacked a commutation focus, a place that could obviously be accepted as the center of local life. Instead, the experience of a local resident was typical: "I live in Garden Grove, work in Irvine, shop in Santa Ana, go to the dentist in Anaheim, my husband works in Long Beach, and I used to be the president of the League of Women Voters in Fullerton."

A centerless city also developed in Santa Clara County, which lies forty-five miles south of San Francisco and which is best known as the home of "Silicon Valley." Stretching from Palo Alto on the north to the garlic and lettuce fields of Gilroy to the south, Santa Clara County has the world's most extensive concentration of electronics concerns. In 1940, however, it was best known for prunes and apricots, and it was not until after World War II that its largest city, San Jose, also became the nation's largest suburb. With fewer than 70,000 residents in 1940, San Jose exploded to 636,000 by 1980, superseding San Francisco as the region's largest municipality. As the automobile-based circulation system matured, the county's spacious orchards were easily developed, and bulldozers uprooted fruit trees for shopping centers and streets. Home builders, encouraged by a San Jose city government that annexed new territory at a rapid pace and borrowed heavily to build new utilities and schools on the fringes of town, moved farther and farther into the rural outskirts. Dozens of semiconductor and aerospace companies expanded and built plants there. In time, this brought twice-daily ordeals of bumper-to-bumper traffic on congested freeways. The driving time of some six-mile commutes lengthened to forty-five minutes, and the hills grew hazy behind the smog. As Santa Clara County became a national symbol of the excesses of uncontrolled growth, its residents began to fear that the high-technology superstars were generating jobs and taxes, but that the jobs attracted more people, and the taxes failed to cover the costs of new roads, schools, sewers, and expanded police and fire departments.

The numbers were larger in California, but the pattern was the same on the edges of every American city, from Buffalo Grove and Schaumburg near Chicago, to Germantown and Collierville near Memphis, to Creve Couer and Ladue near St. Louis. And perhaps more important than the growing number of people living outside of city boundaries was the sheer physical sprawl of metropolitan areas. Between 1950 and 1970, the urbanized area of Washington, D.C., grew from 181 to 523

square miles, of Miami from 116 to 429, while in the larger megalopolises of New York, Chicago, and Los Angeles, the region of settlement was measured in the thousands of square miles.

Since World War II, the American people have experienced a transformation of the man-made environment around them. Commercial, residential, and industrial structures have been redesigned to fit the needs of the motorist rather than the pedestrian. Garish signs, large parking lots, one-way streets, drive-in windows, and throw-away fast-food buildings—all associated with the world of suburbia—have replaced the slower-paced, neighborhood-oriented institutions of an earlier generation. Some observers of the automobile revolution have argued that the car has created a new and better urban environment and that the change in spatial scale, based upon swift transportation, has formed a new kind of organic entity, speeding up personal communication and rendering obsolete the older urban settings. Lewis Mumford, writing from his small-town retreat in Amenia, New York, has emphatically disagreed. His prize-winning book, *The City in History*, was a celebration of the medieval community and an excoriation of "the formless urban exudation" that he saw American cities becoming. He noted that the automobile megalopolis was not a final stage in city development but an anticity which "annihilates the city whenever it collides with it."

There are some signs that the halcyon days of the drive-in culture and automobile are behind us. More than one hundred thousand gasoline stations, or about one-third of the American total, have been eliminated in the last decade. Empty tourist courts and boarded-up motels are reminders that the fast pace of change can make commercial structures obsolete within a quarter-century of their erection. Even that suburban bellwether, the shopping center, which revolutionized merchandising after World War II, has come to seem small and out-of-date as newer covered malls attract both the trendy and the family trade. Some older centers have been recycled as bowling alleys or industrial buildings, and some have been remodeled to appeal to larger tenants and better-heeled customers. But others stand forlorn and boarded up. Similarly, the characteristic fast-food emporiums of the 1950s, with uniformed "car hops" who took orders at the automobile window, are now relics of the past. One of the survivors, Delores Drive-In, which opened in Beverly Hills in 1946, was recently proposed as an historic landmark, a sure sign that the species is in danger.

GLOSSARY

Lewis Mumford (1895–1990): Social critic and writer whose works, such as *The Culture of Cities*, decry dehumanizing technology and call for a return to humanitarian and moral values.

Winston Churchill (1874–1965): British statesman, soldier, and author; Prime Minister during World War II.

Art Deco: A decorative and architectural style of the period 1925–1940, characterized by geometric designs, bold colors, and the use of plastic and glass.

Tract house: One of the numerous houses of similar design constructed on a tract of land.

IMPLICATIONS

Although we take automobiles, trucks, and SUVs for granted today, automobile ownership became commonplace only during the 1950s. Why do you think automobiles were so attractive to Americans in postwar America? Why do you think automobiles had such a dramatic impact on the American way of life?

PAST TRACES

Lyndon Johnson is remembered as a consummate power broker, but he was also a powerful liberal reformer whose guiding philosophy was the provision of equal opportunity for all Americans. This essay begins with excerpts from Johnson's commencement address at Howard University, the nation's most prestigious predominantly African American college. In it, Johnson clearly articulates his guiding philosophy.

Lyndon B. Johnson, Commencement Address at Howard University (1965)

Our earth is the home of revolution.

In every corner of every continent men charged with hope contend with ancient ways in pursuit of justice. They reach for the newest of weapons to realize the oldest of dreams: that each may walk in freedom and pride, stretching his talents, enjoying the fruits of the earth.

Our enemies may occasionally seize the day of change. But it is the banner of our revolution they take. And our own future is linked to this process of swift and turbulent change in many lands. But nothing, in any country, touches us more profoundly, nothing is more freighted with meaning for our own destiny, than the revolution of the Negro American.

In far too many ways American Negroes have been another nation: deprived of freedom, crippled by hatred, the doors of opportunity closed to hope.

In our time change has come to this nation too. Heroically, the American Negro—acting with impressive restraints—has peacefully protested and marched, entered the courtrooms and the seats of government, demanding a justice long denied. The voice of the Negro was the call to action. But it is a tribute to America that, once aroused, the courts and the Congress, the President and most of the people, have been the allies of progress.

Thus we have seen the high court of the country declare that discrimination based on race was repugnant to the Constitution, and therefore void. We have seen—in 1957, 1960, and again in 1964—the first civil rights legislation in almost a century. . . .

The voting rights bill will be the latest, and among the most important, in a long series of victories. But this victory—as Winston Churchill said of another triumph for freedom—"is not the end. It is not even the beginning of the end. But it is, perhaps, the end of the beginning."

That beginning is freedom; and the barriers to that freedom are tumbling. Freedom is the right to share, fully and equally, in American society—to vote, to hold a job, to enter a public place, to go to school. It is the right to be treated, in every part of our national life, as a man equal in dignity and promise to all others.

But freedom is not enough. You do not wipe away the scars of centuries by saying: Now, you are free to go where you want, do as you desire, and choose the leaders you please.

You do not take a man who, for years, has been hobbled by chains, liberate him, bring him to the starting line of a race, saying "you are free to compete with all the others," and still justly believe you have been completely fair.

Thus it is not enough to open the gates of opportunity. All our citizens must have the ability to walk through those gates.

This is the next and the more profound stage of the battle for civil rights. We seek not just freedom but opportunity—not just legal equity but human ability—not just equality as a right and a theory, but equality as a fact and a result.

For the task is to give twenty million Negroes the same chance as every other American to learn and grow—to work and share in society—to develop their abilities—physical, mental, and spiritual, and to pursue their individual happiness.

To this end equal opportunity is essential, but not enough. Men and women of all races are born with the same range of abilities. But ability is not just the product of birth. It is stretched or stunted by the family you live with, and the neighborhood you live in—by the school you go to, and the poverty or richness of your surroundings. It is the product of a hundred unseen forces playing upon the infant, the child, and the man.

This graduating class at Howard University is witness to the indomitable determination of the Negro American to win his way in American life.

The number of Negroes in schools of high learning has almost doubled in fifteen years. The number of nonwhite professional workers has more than doubled in ten years. The median income of Negro college women now exceeds that of white college women. And these are the enormous accomplishments of distinguished individual Negroes—many of them graduates of this institution.

These are proud and impressive achievements. But they only tell the story of a growing middle class minority, steadily narrowing the gap between them and their white counterparts.

But for the great majority of Negro Americans—the poor, the unemployed, the uprooted and dispossessed—there is a grimmer story. They still are another nation. Despite the court orders and the laws, the victories and speeches, for them the walls are rising and the gulf is widening. . . .

We are not completely sure why this is. The causes are complex and subtle. But we do know the two broad basic reasons. And we know we have to act.

First, Negroes are trapped—as many whites are trapped—in inherited, gateless poverty. They lack training and skills. They are shut in slums, without decent medical care. Private and public poverty combine to cripple their capacities.

We are attacking these evils through our poverty program, our education program, our health program and a dozen more—aimed at the root causes of poverty.

We will increase, and accelerate, and broaden this attack in years to come, until this most enduring of foes yields to our unyielding will.

But there is a *second* cause—more difficult to explain, more deeply grounded, more desperate in its force. It is the devastating heritage of long years of slavery; and a century of oppression, hatred and injustice.

For Negro poverty is not white poverty. Many of its causes and many of its cures are the same. But there are differences—deep, corrosive, obstinate differences—radiating painful roots into the community, the family, and the nature of the individual.

These differences are not racial differences. They are solely and simply the consequence of ancient brutality, past injustice, and present prejudice. They are anguishing to observe. For the Negro they are a reminder of oppression. For the white they are a reminder of guilt. But they must be faced, and dealt with, and overcome; if we are to reach the time when the only difference between Negroes and whites is the color of their skin.

Nor can we find a complete answer in the experience of other American minorities. They made a valiant, and largely successful effort to emerge from poverty and prejudice. The Negro, like these others, will have to rely mostly on his own efforts. But he cannot do it alone. For they did not have the heritage of centuries to overcome. They did not have a cultural tradition which had been twisted and battered by endless years of hatred and hopelessness. Nor were they excluded because of race or color—a feeling whose dark intensity is matched by no other prejudice in our society.

Nor can these differences be understood as isolated infirmities. They are a seamless web. They cause each other. They result from each other. They reinforce each other. Much of the Negro community is buried under a blanket of history and circumstance. It is not a lasting solution to lift just one corner. We must stand on all sides and raise the entire cover if we are to liberate our fellow citizens.

One of the differences is the increased concentration of Negroes in our cities. More than 73 per cent of all Negroes live in urban areas compared with less than 70 per cent of whites. Most of them live in slums. And most of them live together; a separated people. Men are shaped by their world. When it is a world of decay ringed by an invisible wall—when escape is arduous and uncertain, and the saving pressures of a more hopeful society are unknown—it can cripple the youth and desolate the man.

There is also the burden a dark skin can add to the search for a productive place in society. Unemployment strikes most swiftly and broadly at the Negro. This burden erodes hope. Blighted hope breeds despair. Despair brings indifference to the learning which offers a way out. And despair coupled with indifference is often the source of destructive rebellion against the fabric of society. . . .

Perhaps most important—its influence radiating to every part of life—is the breakdown of the Negro family structure. For this, most of all, white America must accept responsibility. It flows from centuries of oppression and persecution of the Negro man. It flows from the long years of degradation and discrimination which have attacked his dignity and assaulted his ability to provide for his family. . . .

Unless we work to strengthen the family—to create conditions under which most parents will stay together—all the rest: schools and playgrounds, public assistance and private concern—will not be enough to cut completely the circle of despair and deprivation.

There is no single easy answer to all these problems.

Jobs are part of the answer. They bring the income which permits a man to provide for his family.

Decent homes in decent surroundings and a chance to learn are part of the answer.

Welfare and social programs better designed to hold families together are part of the answer.

Care for the sick is part of the answer.

An understanding heart by all Americans is also part of the answer.

To all these fronts—and a dozen more—I will dedicate the expanding efforts of my administration. . . .

It is the glorious opportunity of this generation to end the one huge wrong of the American nation—and in so doing to find America for ourselves, with the same immense thrill of discovery which gripped those who first began to realize that here, at last, was a home for freedom.

All it will take is for all of us to understand what this country is and what it must become.

The Scripture promises: "I shall light a candle of understanding in thine heart, which shall not be put out."

Together, and with millions more, we can light that candle of understanding in the heart of America.

And, once lit, it will never go out.

16

The Vietnam War, the Liberals, and the Overthrow of LBJ

Allen J. Matusow

The Vietnam War dominated much of American life in the decade between 1964 and 1974. With an active draft supplying the bulk of the quarter of a million American troops and advisers fighting in Vietnam, three presidents—Kennedy, Johnson, and Nixon—sought to project American military power into southeast Asia in an effort to "contain communism."

Between 1954—when the United States assumed the role of supporter of the corrupt but anti-Communist South Vietnamese regime—and the early 1960s, American involvement in Vietnam was limited to small numbers of military and civilian advisers. But beginning in 1962, when President John F. Kennedy created the Green Berets, a special counterinsurgency force, American involvement in the region took the path of escalation. Slowly at first, but with increasing speed after the mid-1960s, the American military presence grew until daily reports from the war zone dominated the nightly television news.

As the war continued, with little evidence of success or purpose, growing numbers of Americans began to question the propriety of the war. At the same time, students and other Americans, including many church leaders, organized the most effective antiwar movement in American history. By the late 1960s, antiwar protest took on epic proportions as tens of thousands of Americans—men and women, young and old alike—demonstrated across the country to end the war and bring American troops home.

One of the Vietnam War's more famous casualties was President Lyndon Johnson. In the arrogance of his belief that he could convert the peasants of Vietnam into his image of upwardly mobile American farmers, Johnson escalated U.S. involvement on an unprecedented scale. Mindless of local conditions and the history of the

From *The Unraveling of America* by Allen J. Matusow (New York: Harper & Row, 1984), pp. 376–394. Copyright © 1984 by Allen J. Matusow. Reprinted by permission of HarperCollins Publishers.

Vietnamese people, Johnson and his advisers committed billions of dollars to a war that many military analysts agreed could not be won. As Allen J. Matusow shows in this essay, Johnson's arrogance cost him the support of American liberals and ultimately the presidency itself.

In April 1965, three months after Lyndon Johnson made his decision to bomb North Vietnam, Democratic Senator Wayne Morse of Oregon predicted that Johnson's war policy would send him "out of office the most discredited President in the history of the nation." Given the popularity of both the war and the president at the time, Morse's prophecy seemed absurd on its face. But, as Vietnam dragged on month after month, it did indeed become an acid eroding Johnson's political base, until in the end it destroyed his presidency. The first constituency to be alienated by Vietnam—and the most dangerous opponent of Johnson's war policy—proved to be the liberal intellectuals.

At first glance the split between the president and the intellectuals seemed surprising. He was, after all, attempting to govern in the liberal tradition not only in his conduct of domestic policy but in foreign affairs as well. They must hate him, he came to believe, not really for anything he did but because of who he was—a crude Texas cowboy without a Harvard degree. What he failed to understand was that his liberalism and theirs—apparently so similar in 1964—thereafter rapidly diverged, his remaining rooted in the ideas of the 1950s, theirs moving far beyond.

The root of the difficulty was the breakup of the Cold War consensus. In the 1950s, of course, liberal intellectuals typically had embraced the Cold War as a holy crusade, becoming in the process staunch defenders of the American way of life. Even after Sputnik in 1957, when the intellectuals began denouncing the nation for its materialism and complacency, they did so primarily to goad the people into greater sacrifice for the struggle against world Communism. The first sign of restlessness

began to appear around 1960. That was the year, for example, when Norman Podhoretz, a New York intellectual who had been a dutiful Cold War liberal but now felt the old ideas going stale, "going dead," became editor of the influential magazine *Commentary*. Daring to open his early issues to dissident voices, he discovered among the intellectuals who wrote for his magazine and read it "a hunger for something new and something radical." Radicalism was hardly the term to describe the outlook of the intellectuals in the Kennedy era, but they were more open to novelty, more willing to acknowledge the flaws in American society, than they had been for years. In 1963, when Kennedy and Kruschchev moved toward détente following the Cuban missile crisis, the international tension that for so long had sustained the Cold War mentality began to dissipate, the old obsession to bore. Liberal intellectuals supported Johnson's 1964 presidential campaign because they believed he shared not only their renewed commitment to social justice but their growing willingness to reach an accommodation with the Russians.

Strains in Johnson's relations with the liberals first appeared in February 1965 when Johnson launched his air war over North Vietnam. Immediately the *New Republic*, a leading journal of liberal opinion, and the Americans for Democratic Action (ADA), the leading liberal organization, condemned the bombing and called for a negotiated settlement. Johnson was perplexed by the criticism since he correctly believed that he was merely applying in Vietnam the doctrine of containment so recently espoused by the liberals themselves. He did not grasp that that doctrine had suddenly fallen from fashion. Among the prominent liberal intellectuals who attempted to account for the shifting views of their community were Hans Morgenthau, an academic specialist in foreign affairs, member of the ADA board, and an early and formidable war critic; Reinhold Niebuhr, the renowned theologian and a founder of ADA, ailing but still influential; Arthur Schlesinger, Jr., a historian, former White House aide of Kennedy and Johnson, half-hearted defender of the war in 1965, but a leading foe by 1966; John Kenneth Galbraith, the Harvard economist, Kennedy's ambassador to India, and in 1967 the ADA chairman; Richard Goodwin, a precocious speech writer for Johnson till September 1965, and a war critic by the following spring; and Richard Rovere, the prestigious political correspondent of *The New Yorker*, a late but important convert to the dove side of the war argument.

The liberal intellectuals did not apologize for their past support of the Cold War. So long as Communist parties everywhere had subordinated themselves to the malign purposes of the Soviet Union, every Communist gain threatened American security. But times had changed, the liberals said. The Communist world was now "polycentric" (many-centered), a situation resulting from the Sino-Soviet split and the emergence of conflicting national aspirations among Communist states. Wrote Schlesinger, "Communism is no longer a unified, coordinated, centralized conspiracy." According to Rovere, since Tito's break with Stalin in 1948, the U.S. should have known that "international Communism" was a myth, "that national interest was more powerful than ideology, and that while we might on occasion find it advisable to resist the outward thrust of certain Communist nations, it made absolutely no sense to have a foreign policy directed against an alliance that did not exist." In short, it was no longer necessary to oppose every Communist initiative on every part of the globe.

With the exception of Morgenthau, who favored recognizing spheres of influence, these intellectuals continued to advocate containing China. But they denied that the war in Vietnam followed logically from this policy. Secretary of State Dean Rusk's opinion to the contrary, China was not the enemy here. The war in South Vietnam, they argued, was primarily a civil war, pitting indigenous revolutionaries against the corrupt and repressive regime in Saigon. If the Communists won, Vietnam might well become a bulwark against the spread of Chinese influence in the region. As a practical matter, the U.S. could not win. Escalation on the ground in the South could easily be offset by the enemy and would do nothing to remedy the defects of the Saigon government. Bombing the North would merely strengthen the enemy's will to fight. If Johnson proceeded on the course of escalation, he would destroy the country he was trying to save or else provoke war with China.

The war, the liberals said, was not a result of American imperialism but a mistake of policy deriving from obsolete assumptions about international Communism. Unfortunately, it was a mistake not easily remedied. Liberals rejected unilateral withdrawal on the grounds that it would mean abandonment of America's friends in the South, a blow to U.S. prestige, and maybe even the rise at home of a new Joe McCarthy to exploit the frustrations attending defeat. The liberal solution was a negotiated settlement—the middle course, they called it. Stop the foolish bombing in the North, since Hanoi demanded it as a precondition for negotiations. Convince Ho Chi Minh that the U.S. could not be dislodged by force. Offer the Vietcong a seat at the conference table and a role in the postwar political life of South Vietnam. It was possible, of course, that negotiations would fail. In that event, said Galbraith, "We must be prepared to defend for the time being the limited areas that are now secure." Indeed, on close inspection, it turned out that the liberals were waist deep in the Big Muddy along with LBJ and were no more certain than he of getting back to shore. The difference was that they thought the war was all a big mistake, and he was there on principle.

As opposition to the war among the intellectuals mounted, so did their impatience with the administration's response to the great racial and urban crisis that was tearing the country apart. As they never would have done during the American celebration that had characterized the heydey of the Cold War, liberals were now earnestly discussing the menace of corporate monopoly, redistribution of income, and a Marshall Plan for the cities. In its January 1967 issue *Commentary* ran both a long article by Theodore Draper attacking Johnson's foreign policy for its "willingness to use and abuse naked military power" and an essay by the Keynesian economist Robert Lekachman summarizing the case of many liberal intellectuals against the president's domestic policies. Lekachman wrote:

> Possibly Mr. Johnson went just about as far as a conservative politician in a conservative, racist country could have gone. The Great Society has distributed the nation's income even less equally than it was distributed before 1960. It has enlarged the prestige and influence of the business community. It has lost its token bouts with racism and poverty. The Great Society, never a giant step beyond the New Deal which was President Johnson's youthful inspiration, has ground to a halt far short of a massive attack on urban blight, far short of the full integration of Negroes into American society, and far short of a genuine assault upon poverty and deprivation.

Where liberal intellectuals led, liberal politicians usually followed. But politicians skeptical of the war in Vietnam initially hesitated to tangle with a president to whom most were bound by ties of party loyalty and whose vindictive character was legend. In 1965 even senators held their tongues, excepting of course Oregon's Wayne Morse and Alaska's Ernest Gruening, the lone opponents of the 1964 Gulf of Tonkin Resolution. Among those who privately worried but publicly acquiesced in Johnson's war policy were Senators Mike Mansfield, George McGovern, Frank Church,

Joseph Clark, Eugene McCarthy, and J. William Fulbright. Fulbright was the pivotal figure. If he moved into the open against Johnson, the rest would follow.

A senator from the ex-Confederate state of Arkansas, Fulbright was a gentleman of inherited wealth, excellent education, and illiberal record on matters of race and social reform. But for more than twenty years, on matters of foreign policy, Fulbright had been the leading spokesman in Congress for the views of the liberal community. Though he had had his share of arguments with presidents, he was by nature a contemplative rather than a combative man, a Senate club member who played by the rules. Fulbright's early opinions on Vietnam were hardly heretical. In March 1964, in a wide-ranging speech attacking Cold War mythology, he paused over Vietnam long enough to make a few hawkish observations. The allies were too weak militarily to obtain "the independence of a non-Communist South Vietnam" through negotiations, he said. The only "realistic options" were to hasten the buildup of the regime in the South or to expand the war, "either by the direct commitment of large numbers of American troops or by equipping the South Vietnamese Army to attack North Vietnamese territory." In August 1964 Fulbright sponsored the Gulf of Tonkin Resolution, which gave Johnson authority to expand the war.

For reasons unknown, Fulbright had second thoughts about escalation once it actually began. Publicly in the spring of 1965 he backed Johnson's policy, though he called for a temporary bombing halt to induce Hanoi to negotiate. Privately, he warned his old friend in the White House against waging war on North Vietnam and tempted him with the vision of a Communist Vietnam hostile to China. Johnson seemed bored by Fulbright's conversation. Fulbright gave a Senate speech in June that both criticized the bombing and praised Johnson's statesmanship. In July Johnson began the massive infusion of ground troops into South Vietnam.

Fulbright's first real attack on the Johnson administration was occasioned not by Vietnam but by policy in the Dominican Republic. In April 1965 Johnson sent U.S. troops into the midst of a developing civil war, ostensibly to protect Americans but really to prevent a possible Communist takeover. Fulbright brooded over this intervention, held secret hearings on it, and finally in September delivered a powerful Senate speech attacking the administration's conduct as ruthless and lacking in candor. The president promptly ended all pretense of consulting the chairman of the Foreign Relations Committee and cut him socially.

As Fulbright edged toward open rebellion on the issue of the war, so did the other Senate doves, almost all of whom were liberal Democrats. This was probably one reason why Johnson halted the bombing of North Vietnam on Christmas Eve, 1965, and launched a well-advertised peace offensive allegedly to persuade Hanoi to negotiate. The State Department moved closer to Hanoi's conditions for negotiations in early January, and both sides scaled down ground action in South Vietnam. Diplomats in several capitals worked to bring the wary antagonists together. But on January 24, 1966, Johnson hinted to a group of congressional leaders that he might soon resume the bombing. Two days later fifteen senators, all of them liberal Democrats, sent a letter to Johnson urging him to continue the pause. Fulbright and Mansfield did not sign but were on record with similar views. On January 29, Johnson ordered the air attack to recommence. The episode convinced many liberals that Johnson's talk about peace masked his private determination to win total military victory.

In February 1966 Fulbright held televised hearings on the war. The scholar-diplomat George Kennan and the retired general James Gavin argued the case against it on grounds of American self-interest. Dean Rusk and General Maxwell Taylor parried the thrusts of liberal committee members now openly critical of Johnson's policy. Neither side drew blood in debate, but by helping legitimize dissent, the Fulbright hearings were a net loss for Johnson. Fulbright, meantime, was reading, talking to experts, and rethinking first principles. In the spring of 1966 he took to the lecture platform to hurl thunderbolts at orthodoxy. Revised and published as a book later in the year, Fulbright's lectures were a critique of American foreign policy far more advanced than any yet produced by the liberal academicians.

"Gradually but unmistakably America is showing signs of that arrogance of power which has afflicted, weakened, and in some cases destroyed great nations in the past," Fulbright said. Harnessing her might to a crusading ideology, America had overextended herself abroad and was neglecting vital tasks at home. Americans meant well overseas, Fulbright conceded, but they often did more harm than good, especially in the Third World. A conservative people, Americans supported necessary social revolutions in traditional societies only if they were peaceful, that is, in "our own shining image." To violent revolutions, which "seem to promise greater and faster results," Americans reacted with automatic hostility or panic. Fulbright was hardly an apologist for revolutions, but neither would he oppose them, even if they were led by Communists. Fulbright dared to find much that was praiseworthy in Castro's Cuba and even extended sympathy to the aims of the Chinese revolutionaries, whose regime he would recognize de facto. In Vietnam, he said, the U.S. had blundered into a war against Communism in the only country in the world "which won freedom from colonial rule under communist leadership." Fulbright favored a negotiated settlement that would provide self-determination for South Vietnam through the mechanism of a referendum.

President Johnson had expected his main trouble to come from hawks who wanted to escalate faster than he did. Stung by the sweeping attacks of Fulbright and other doves, he resorted to a scoundrel's last refuge. Before a friendly audience of Democratic politicians in

Chicago mid-May 1966, Johnson defended the war as a patriotic effort to secure lasting peace by punishing aggression and then said, "There will be some 'Nervous Nellies' and some who will become frustrated and bothered and break ranks under the strain, and some will turn on their leaders, and on their country, and on our own fighting men. . . . But I have not the slightest doubt that the courage and the dedication and the good sense of the wise American people will ultimately prevail." The attack failed to silence the critics. The majority of the people still backed the war, but not with the passion aroused by wars of the past. Fulbright continued to assault the premises of American foreign policy and, indirectly, the president who was acting on them. Confronted with irreconcilable views of world politics, members of the liberal public in ever-increasing numbers deserted the president and sided with the senator.

To make matters worse for Johnson, he faced a personal as well as an intellectual challenge to his party leadership. When Robert Kennedy emerged from mourning in early 1964, he discovered a remarkable fact. Despite his squeaky voice, diffident public manner, private shyness, and reputation as a ruthless backroom operator, he was the sole beneficiary of his brother's political estate. In him resided the hopes of millions who believed the myth of Camelot and longed for a Kennedy restoration. Robert Kennedy believed the myth himself and shared the longing. Lyndon Johnson, however, despised Kennedy personally and made himself the great obstacle to the younger man's ambitions. After Johnson denied him the vice-presidential nomination in 1964, Kennedy repaired to New York, where he successfully ran for the Senate. Soon there grew up around him what the political columnists called the Kennedy party—Kennedy loyalists still in the bureaucracy, some senators, New Frontiersman out of favor, and lesser politicians, lawyers, and professors scattered around the country. Most of the Kennedy loyalists were liberals, but by no means all liberals were Kennedy loyalists.

Robert Kennedy, after all, had been an ally of Joe McCarthy, an advocate of wiretapping, too zealous a pursuer of the Teamster chief Jimmy Hoffa, and a frequent offender of liberal sensibilities. But liberals unhappy with Johnson needed a popular leader, and Kennedy needed to broaden his party base. The one issue guaranteed to bring them together was Vietnam.

The issue posed problems for Kennedy. As a Cabinet officer, he had been an enthusiastic student of guerrilla warfare and a strong supporter of his brother's counterinsurgency program in South Vietnam. When Johnson escalated in 1965, Kennedy questioned less the attempt to rescue South Vietnam by force of arms than the tendency to subordinate political to military considerations in fighting the war. Speaking at the graduation ceremony of the International Police Academy in July, he said, "I think the history of the last 20 years demonstrates beyond doubt that our approach to revolutionary war must be political—political first, political last, political always." To avoid offending Johnson, he excised from his prepared text the view that "victory in a revolutionary war is won not by escalation but by de-escalation." Kennedy waited one whole year after escalation before putting real distance between his position and Johnson's. It bothered Kennedy that, when Fulbright asked Rusk during the television hearings of February 1966 to state the options other than "surrender or annihilation" that he was offering the Vietcong, Rusk had replied, "They do have an alternative of quitting, of stopping being an agent of Hanoi and receiving men and arms from the North." The war could go on forever if this was the American requirement for peace. So Kennedy decided to propose another option. On February 19, 1966, he became the first senator to suggest a negotiated settlement that would give the Vietcong "a share of power and responsibility"—in what he did not say. Assuming he meant the government of Vietnam, the administration dismissed the idea contemptuously. Kennedy's proposal, said Vice

President Humphrey, would be like putting "a fox in the chicken coop" or "an arsonist in a fire department." Kennedy spent the next week clarifying and qualifying, and though he retreated some, he was clearly moving toward the peace wing of his party.

Strange things were happening to Bobby Kennedy. Perhaps prolonged grief deepened his social sympathies, perhaps he was trying in his own life to vindicate his brother's legend—or outdo it. Whatever the cause, Kennedy plunged into the currents of change that were swirling through America in the mid-1960s, currents that were altering the perspective of liberalism and passing Johnson by. Kennedy opened a running dialogue with students, made a friend of Tom Hayden, felt the yearnings of the poor and the black for power and dignity, and took unnecessary political risks. Blood donations for the Vietcong? Burial for a Communist war hero in Arlington Cemetery? Why not? he asked. Kennedy went to South Africa in mid-1966 to aid the opponents of apartheid. He attacked administration witnesses at Senate hearings in August for unresponsiveness to the poor. He flew to California to stand with Cesar Chavez in his fight to unionize the grape pickers. A man who risked his life scaling mountains and defying tropical storms on the Amazon, Kennedy was becoming an existentialist in politics, defining himself in action and moving where his heart told him to go.

As Kennedy and Johnson edged closer toward political combat, their personal relations worsened. In February 1967 *Newsweek* erroneously reported that Kennedy had brought back from a recent trip to Paris a peace feeler from Hanoi. The story enraged Johnson, who, believing it was planted by Kennedy, called him to the White House for a tongue lashing. According to *Time*'s colorful account, Johnson told Kennedy, "If you keep talking like this, you won't have a political future in this country within six months," warned him that "the blood of American boys will be on your hands," and concluded, "I never want to see you again." Uncowed,

Kennedy called Johnson an s.o.b and told him, "I don't have to sit here and take that—." Whether Kennedy really used vulgarity was a matter of some dispute, but there was no doubt that the gist of the conversation had been accurately reported. Less than a month later (March 2, 1967) Kennedy gave a major Senate speech calling for a halt to the bombing and a compromise settlement through negotiations. A few party malcontents, especially in the liberal wing, permitted themselves a small hope that maybe the crown prince of the Democratic party would claim his inheritance sooner than expected.

In the summer of 1967 gloom descended on the camp of the liberals. In August Johnson sent 45,000 more troops to Vietnam and asked for higher taxes to finance the war. And, though Defense Secretary Robert McNamara himself voiced public criticism of the bombing, day after day the bombs continued to fall. Liberals who had once viewed it merely as politically stupid watched in horror as the carnage mounted and now pronounced the war morally wrong as well. Meanwhile domestic insurrectionaries were gutting great American cities, the War on Poverty was bogging down, and the long-awaited white backlash finally arrived. Among those surrendering to despair that summer was Senator Fulbright. Speaking to the American Bar Association in August, he said, "How can we commend democratic social reform to Latin America when Newark, Detroit, and Milwaukee are providing explosive evidence of our own inadequate efforts at democratic social reform? How can we commend the free enterprise system to Asians and Africans when in our own country it has produced vast, chaotic, noisy, dangerous and dirty urban complexes while poisoning the very air and land and water?" Fulbright called the war "unnecessary and immoral" and blamed it for aggravating grave domestic problems. The country "sickens for lack of moral leadership," he said, and only the idealistic young may save us from the "false and dangerous dream of an imperial destiny."

Fulbright's charges about the damage done at home by the war were confirmed in the autumn. Driven by hatred of the war, new left students began acting out their guerrilla fantasies, and major campuses were threatened by chaos. No less disturbing to liberals was the fever of discontent rising in intellectual circles. Some of the nation's most brilliant writers and artists were concluding, as had their counterparts in France during the Algerian war, that they now had no choice but to resist the state.

From the beginning a minority of the nation's intellectual elite—call them radicals—saw the war as more than a blunder in judgment. Most of these radicals had life histories punctuated by episodes of dissent but had stayed aloof from politics during the Cold War. Vietnam brought them back to political awareness and gave focus to their inchoate alienation. To people like the novelists Norman Mailer and Mary McCarthy, the critics Susan Sontag and Dwight Macdonald, *New York Review of Books* editor Robert Silvers, the linguist Noam Chomsky, the anarchist writer Paul Goodman, and the poet Robert Lowell, America appeared to be in the hands of a technological elite that was debauching the American landscape and lusting after world dominion. Morally revolted by the imperial war against the peasants of Vietnam, the radicals found traditional politics insufficient to express their opposition. The war was a matter of conscience, and good men would act accordingly.

Their first impulse was to avoid complicity with the crime. Thus when Johnson invited a group of writers and artists to participate in a White House Festival of the Arts in June 1965, Robert Lowell refused to come. Scion of a distinguished American family, perhaps the best of living American poets, and a draft resister in World War II, Lowell sent a letter to the president, saying, "Every serious artist knows that he cannot enjoy public celebration without making subtle public commitments. . . . We are in danger of imperceptibly becoming an explo-

sive and suddenly chauvinistic nation, and we may even be drifting on our way to the last nuclear ruin. . . . At this anguished, delicate and perhaps determining moment, I feel I am serving you and our country best by not taking part." Robert Silvers took the lead in circulating a statement in support of his friend Lowell and in two days attracted the signatures of twenty of the nation's most prominent writers and artists, among them Hannah Arendt, Lillian Hellman, Alfred Kazin, Dwight Macdonald, Bernard Malamud, Mary McCarthy, William Styron, and Robert Penn Warren. Johnson was so angry at "these people," these "sonsofbitches" that he almost canceled the festival.

By 1967 the radicals were obsessed by the war and frustrated by their impotence to affect its course. The government was unmoved by protest, the people were uninformed and apathetic, and American technology was tearing Vietnam apart. What, then, was their responsibility? Noam Chomsky explored this problem in February 1967 in the *New York Review*, which had become the favorite journal of the radicals. By virtue of their training and leisure, intellectuals had a greater responsibility than ordinary citizens for the actions of the state, Chomsky said. It was their special responsibility "to speak the truth and expose lies." But the "free-floating intellectual" who had performed this function in the past was being replaced by the "scholar-expert" who lied for the government or constructed "value-free technologies" to keep the existing social order functioning smoothly. Chomsky not only enjoined the intellectuals once again "to seek the truth lying behind the veil of distortion"; he concluded by quoting an essay written twenty years before by Dwight Macdonald, an essay that implied that in time of crisis exposing lies might not be enough. "Only those who are willing to resist authority themselves when it conflicts too intolerably with their personal moral code," Macdonald had written, "only they have the right to condemn." Chomsky's article was immediately recognized as an important intellectual event. Along with the radical students, radical intellectuals were moving "from protest to resistance."

The move toward resistance accelerated through 1967. Chomsky announced in the *New York Review* that for the second consecutive year he was withholding half his income taxes to protest the war. Paul Goodman invited federal prosecution by acknowledging his efforts to aid and abet draft resistance. Mary McCarthy, back from a trip to Vietnam, said that "to be in the town jail, as Thoreau knew, can relieve any sense of imaginary imprisonment." On the cover of its issue of August 24, 1967, the *New York Review* put a diagram of a Molotov cocktail, while inside Andrew Kopkind, in the midst of dismissing Martin Luther King for having failed to make a revolution, wrote, "Morality, like politics, starts at the barrel of a gun." (Some intellectuals never forgave the *New York Review* for that one.) On October 12, 1967, the *New York Review* published a statement signed by 121 intellectuals and entitled "A Call to Resist Illegitimate Authority." The statement denounced the war on legal and moral grounds and pledged the signers to raise funds "to organize draft resistance unions, to supply legal defense and bail, to support families and otherwise aid resistance to the war in whatever ways may seem appropriate."

A few days later Stop the Draft Week began. This was an event whose possibilities excited radical intellectuals as well as radical students. Paul Goodman kicked the week off with a speech at the State Department before an audience of big business executives. "You are the military industrial of the United States, the most dangerous body of men at the present in the world," Goodman declaimed. On Friday, October 20, 1967, Lowell and Mailer spoke on the steps of the Justice Department prior to the efforts of the Reverend William Sloane Coffin to deliver to the government draft cards collected from draft resisters across the country earlier in the week. (This occasion provided evidence for later federal charges of criminal

conspiracy against Coffin, Dr. Benjamin Spock, and three other antiwar activists.) Saturday began with speeches at the Lincoln Memorial ("remorseless, amplified harangues for peace," Lowell called them), and then the march across the bridge toward the Pentagon. Lowell, Mailer, and Macdonald, described by Mailer as "America's best poet? and best novelist??, and best critic???," walked to the battle together. Lowell wrote of the marchers that they were

> . . . like green Union recruits
> for the first Bull Run, sped by photographers,
> the notables, the girls . . . fear, glory, chaos,
> rout . . .
> our green army staggered out on the miles-long
>   green fields,
> met by the other army, the Martian, the ape, the
>   hero,
> his new-fangled rifle, his green new steel helmet.

At the Pentagon Mailer was arrested, much to his satisfaction, but Lowell and Macdonald failed of their object. Noam Chomsky, also present, had not intended to participate in civil disobedience, feeling its purpose in this occasion too vague to make a point. Swept up by the events of the day, Chomsky found himself at the very walls of the fortress, making a speech. When a line of soldiers began marching toward him, he spontaneously sat down. Chomsky spent the night in jail with Mailer.

In his brilliant book *The Armies of the Night*, Mailer probed for the meaning of these apocalyptic events. For him the siege of the Pentagon was a rite of passage for the student rebels, for the intellectuals, for himself. The few hundred fearful youths who sat on the Pentagon steps till dawn on Sunday were a "refrain from all the great American rites of passage when men and women manacled themselves to a lost and painful principle and survived a day, a night, a week, a month, a year." The battle at the Pentagon was a pale rite of passage, he thought, compared to that of the immigrants packed in steerage, Rogers and

Clark, the Americans "at Sutter's Mill, at Gettysburg, the Alamo, the Klondike, the Argonne, Normandy, Pusan." But it was a true rite of passage nonetheless, the survivors having been reborn and rededicated to great purpose. On departing from jail Sunday morning, Mailer felt as Christians must "when they spoke of Christ within them." For Mailer and many other radical intellectuals, American institutions seemed so illegitimate that a moral man could find redemption only in resisting them. As for the liberals, they could only wonder what would happen to America if Lyndon Johnson was not stopped.

Signs of a liberal revolt against Johnson's renomination were plentiful in the fall of 1967. Reform Democrats in New York, the liberal California Democratic Council, party factions in Minnesota, Michigan, Wisconsin, and elsewhere were preparing to oppose him. In late September the ADA national board implicitly came out against him by promising to back the candidate who offered "the best prospect for a settlement of the Vietnam conflict." The *New Republic* explicitly rejected his candidacy in an editorial that same week. And Allard Lowenstein, thirty-eight-year-old liberal activist and ADA vice-chairman, opened an office in Washington and began organizing a movement on campuses, in the peace movement, and among dissident Democratic politicians to "dump Johnson."

Lowenstein wanted Robert Kennedy to be his candidate. And the existentialist Bobby was tempted. Kennedy worried about the frustration building up in the antiwar movement and had himself come to view the war as morally repugnant. "We're killing South Vietnamese, we're killing women, we're killing innocent people because we don't want to have the war fought on American soil, or because they're 12,000 miles away and they might get 11,000 miles away," he said on *Face the Nation* late in November 1967. But Bobby the professional hated losing, and in his view he could not defeat Johnson in a fight for the nomination, and neither could anybody else. On that same

TV program he stated flatly that he would not be a candidate. If he were, he said, "it would immediately become a personality struggle," and the real issues would be obscured. Asked about some other Democrat, such as Senator Eugene McCarthy of Minnesota, taking on the president, Kennedy replied, "There could be a healthy element in that." He would endorse neither Johnson nor McCarthy but support whoever was the eventual party nominee.

Eugene McCarthy had become convinced that someone would have to raise the issue of the war in the party primaries in 1968. When Kennedy and other leading doves rejected Lowenstein's pleas to be the candidate, McCarthy agreed to run. Explaining his purpose at a press conference on November 30, 1967, he said, "There is growing evidence of a deepening moral crisis in America—discontent and frustration and a disposition to take extralegal if not illegal actions to manifest protest. I am hopeful that this challenge . . . may alleviate at least in some degree this sense of political helplessness and restore to many people a belief in the processes of American politics and of American government." In other words, McCarthy was offering his candidacy as an alternative to radicalism.

Only an unusual politician would undertake what no one else would dare. In truth McCarthy, who had spent eight months of his youth as a novice in a Benedictine monastery, was in the political world but not of it. He was a senator bored by the Senate, an office seeker who distained intrigue and self-advertisement, a professional who valued honor more than influence. In recent years he had seemed more interested in Thomistic theology and writing poetry than in the business of government. His career, it appeared, would not fulfill its early promise. But the political crisis in the United States in late 1967 provided McCarthy with an opportunity perfectly suited to his self-conception. Like his hero Thomas More, he would play the martyr in a historic confrontation between conscience and power.

McCarthy's candidacy prospered beyond anyone's expectation, even his own. Though Johnson's rating on the Gallup poll was only 41 percent in November, the professionals were mesmerized by the cliché that no president could be denied renomination by his own party. The war was the biggest cause of Johnson's unpopularity. Hawks and doves disagreed on how best to end the war but otherwise had much in common: both disliked the war, wanted its early termination, and tended to blame Lyndon Johnson for dragging it on. It was the public's declining confidence in Johnson's ability to conclude the war that made him vulnerable to McCarthy's candidacy.

What little confidence still existed in the president's war leadership was shattered on January 31, 1968, when the Vietnamese Communists launched a massive attack in the midst of a truce called for the Tet holiday. Sixty-seven thousand enemy troops invaded more than one hundred of South Vietnam's cities and towns. The allies recaptured most urban areas after a few days and inflicted huge casualties on the attackers. But the Tet Offensive had astounded military men by its scope and daring. It showed that no place in South Vietnam was secure, not even the American embassy, whose walls had been breached in the first hours of the attack. And it temporarily derailed the pacification program in the countryside by drawing allied troops into the cities. Coming after recent administration assurances that the war was being won, the Tet Offensive dealt Johnson's credibility its crowning blow. When he and the U.S. commander in Vietnam, General William Westmoreland, issued victory statements after the offensive ended, few took them seriously, though militarily they were right. The chief political casualty of the Tet Offensive, therefore, was Lyndon Johnson.

In the six weeks after Tet, such pillars of establishment opinion as Walter Cronkite, *Newsweek*, the *Wall Street Journal*, and NBC News gave way and called for de-escalation. High officials in the government finally dared express their private doubts about the war to the president. The Gallup poll reported a seismic shift in public opinion: in February self-described hawks had outnumbered doves 60 percent to 24 percent; in March it was hawks 41 percent, doves 42 percent. And on March 10, two days before the New Hampshire primary, the *New York Times* set off waves of national anxiety by reporting a secret request from the generals to the president for 206,000 more troops for the war.

Meanwhile, in New Hampshire, the first primary state, McCarthy was proving an eccentric candidate. A lazy campaigner, he often did not return phone calls, would not court potential contributors, and avoided local politicians. His manner on the stump was uninspired, and even his references to the war were low-key. (McCarthy opposed unilateral withdrawal and advocated a negotiated settlement.) But McCarthy had an insight denied to his detractors: he mattered less in this campaign than the movement he represented. At the climax of the campaign there were so many student volunteers in the tiny state (3,000, or one for every 25 Democratic voters) that McCarthy's lieutenants begged potential workers to stay home. Scrubbed and shaven, the students ran a canvassing operation that was the envy of the professionals. Even McCarthy's peculiar style proved to be an asset. At a time when the country was fed up with politicians, shrill voices, and the hard sell, there was something reassuring in McCarthy's unhurried, dignified manner. He did not frighten people. He seemed safe.

Governor John W. King, one of the inept managers of Johnson's write-in campaign in New Hampshire, said in the beginning that McCarthy would get 5 percent of the vote. McCarthy himself predicted 30 percent. On March 12, 1968, 49 percent of New Hampshire's Democratic voters wrote in the name of the president of the United States, and 42 percent marked their ballots for a senator of whom days before few had heard. Poll data showed that more McCarthy voters in

New Hampshire were hawks than doves. McCarthy's remarkable showing, then, was not a victory for peace, merely proof that Lyndon Johnson, who could neither pacify the ghetto, speak the plain truth, lick inflation, nor above all end the war, was a mighty unpopular president indeed.

McCarthy had done more than demonstrate Johnson's vulnerability. As he had hoped, his candidacy drained off some of the discontent flowing into illegal protest. Thousands of students who might otherwise have joined SDS got "clean for Gene." Intellectuals who had flirted with resistance a few months before became the senator's avid fans. McCarthy's traveling companion through much of New Hampshire was Robert Lowell—a symbolic relationship whose significance was probably lost on neither of these famous poets.

It had been a hard winter for Robert Kennedy. He realized after the Tet Offensive that his refusal to run had been a mistake. Throughout February 1968, while McCarthy's New Hampshire campaign was getting started, Kennedy and his advisers wrestled again with the problem of his candidacy. Kennedy was ready to go early in March and set in motion machinery for a campaign. But still he found reason to delay a public announcement. By the time he declared on March 16, 1968, the results of the New Hampshire primary had already electrified the country. Much of the constituency that would have been his now belonged to McCarthy. Lyndon Johnson, however, took Kennedy's candidacy more seriously than McCarthy's. He knew, even if the students did not, that Kennedy was the one man in the party who might beat him.

McCarthy refused to set aside for Kennedy and moved on to the Wisconsin primary, whose date was April 2. Early in March the president's men in Wisconsin had been confident of victory. But McCarthy arrived with more students, money, and prestige than he had had in New Hampshire, and by mid-month the Johnson managers knew their man was in trouble. On March 28 Postmaster Larry O'Brien,

an old political pro, returned from a look around the state to tell Johnson that his cause there was hopeless.

While the political storms raged around them, Johnson and his advisers were deep into a momentous review of war policy. General Earl Wheeler, chairman of the Joint Chiefs of Staff, had blundered in late February when he privately requested 206,000 additional troops for Vietnam. Since General Westmoreland was in no danger of being overrun, there was never much chance that Johnson would dispatch massive reinforcements. The tax money to pay for escalation was not there, and neither was the political support. Wheeler's request had one unintended result. By asking so much, it forced policy makers to resolve the basic ambiguity that had characterized America's policy since 1965. Militarily, Johnson had been seeking victory over the Vietcong. Diplomatically, he paid lip service to a negotiated settlement, which implied compromise. Since his generals were in effect telling him that they needed more troops than he could furnish to win, Johnson had no choice now except to opt for negotiation. Accounts differ on how Johnson reached this conclusion in March 1968. But in the end those of his advisers urging some steps in the direction of de-escalation prevailed. On March 31 Johnson went on television to announce that he was stopping the bombing over most of North Vietnam and would end it entirely if Hanoi demonstrated comparable restraint. Johnson called on the North Vietnamese to respond to his partial bombing halt by accepting his invitation to negotiate. A few days later they did so.

Johnson announced another decision in this speech. For some time he had been dropping hints among friends and advisers that he might not run in 1968. Only at the last minute did he determine not to make his 1968 State of the Union Message the occasion for announcing his retirement. But his mood seemed to change after that, and he took steps to organize a re-selection campaign. Even after the ambush in New Hampshire, Johnson authorized Larry

O'Brien to meet with cabinet officers and give them marching orders for the political battle ahead.

Though most Johnson intimates believed he would run, he had compelling reasons not to. Exhausted, haunted by fear of another heart attack, bitter at the vilification he had suffered, the man had had enough. "The only difference between the [John F.] Kennedy assassination and mine," he said in this period, "is that I am alive and it has been more tortuous." There were other reasons too. Politically he faced a Congress opposed to his programs, a public that had lost confidence in his leadership, a defeat at the hands of McCarthy in the Wisconsin primary, and an uncertain contest with Robert Kennedy. On the diplomatic front, he wished to take a step toward peace, which his opponents, domestic and foreign, would probably dismiss as insincere if he remained a potential candidate. In his speech of March 31, Johnson spoke of "division in the American house" and declared his intention to keep the presidency above partisanship in this election year. "Accordingly," he told a stunned nation, "I shall not seek, and I will not accept, the nomination of my party for another term as your President." The liberals, with an assist from the peace movement, the attackers of Tet, and war-weariness, had dumped Johnson.

GLOSSARY

Nikita Kruschchev: Soviet leader during the early to mid-1960s.

Sino-Soviet split: The rift between Chinese and Soviet communism in the late 1940s and early 1950s that led both nations to adopt separate national and international policies.

Gulf of Tonkin Resolution: A 1964 Congressional resolution authorizing military action in southeast Asia, the legal basis for the escalation of the Vietnam War.

IMPLICATIONS

In this essay, Matusow shows how the Vietnam war marked the downfall of Johnson and his Great Society program of domestic reform. How do you explain Johnson's increasingly inflexible commitment to the Southeast Asian war when it meant the destruction of his domestic reform program?

PAST TRACES

The passage of the Civil Rights and Voting Rights Acts in 1964 and 1965 mandated an end to racial discrimination in the United States. But social practice ran well behind the law in the United States during the 1960s and 1970s. In education, for example, public schools reflected the segregated nature of the neighborhoods from which they drew their students. Determined to correct this situation, federal courts ordered the busing of students to equalize the racial makeup of local schools. Responding to the prospect of having their children transported to distant schools, many parents aggressively protested the very idea of school busing. This essay is introduced by an account of life inside a local school during one of the most vocal and dramatic of these protests—that in South Boston, Massachusetts, in 1975. Written from the perspective of teachers and administrators, it reveals the tensions and anxieties associated with readjusting the racial balance in America.

Ione Malloy, Southie Won't Go (1975)

From my homeroom window I watched the school buses empty one by one, while an administrator, Mr. Gizzi, checked each student's class program to see whether the student belonged at the high school. As I watched, a girl's piercing screams rose from the front lobby. Troopers began running toward the building. Trooper squad cars blocked off G Street down the hill so the buses couldn't move. Mr. Gizzi stayed with the buses. Over the intercom the secretary's voice cried, "We need help here on the second floor. Please send help to the office." Isolated on the second floor in the front corner of the building, in a small room attached to two adjoining rooms, I again felt the terror of not knowing what was coming from what direction, feeling unable to protect myself or the students from an unidentified danger.

I have never had a desire to flee, just to protect the students, though I don't like the feeling of being trapped. I closed the door, turned out the lights, and told my homeroom students we would stay there and help each other. We waited—two white girls, Kathryn and Becky; James, a small, long-haired white boy; and Jeffrey, a black. In a few minutes the door opened. The gym teacher, carrying an umbrella, stood there with a trooper, their faces anxious. "Have you seen Jane?" they asked, then hurried away. What had happened? Why was the teacher carrying an umbrella? Who was Jane, and where might she have gone, we wondered, but there was no chance to ask. They had already shut the door behind them.

Then came a call for all teachers not assigned to homerooms to report to the front lobby. The call was repeated several times.

About forty minutes later, I was amazed when, from my window, I saw the last bus empty. Several minutes later the intercom announced that the school day would begin. Students should proceed to their first class. Instead, everyone just sat, afraid to move, paralyzed by the unknown.

There were only twenty minutes left in the first class, senior English. The seniors were upset. There had been fights in the South Cafeteria, in the third floor lavatory, and in room 303 on the third floor down the hall, they told me. Because the fights had broken out simultaneously, the seniors felt they had been planned. Just then the intercom requested custodians to report to the third floor lavatory and to the South Cafeteria. "To clean up the blood," the seniors explained.

Although the seniors wanted to discuss the fights, I said we would first take a quick, objective, one-word teat. I was a little angry. It was better to get their minds focused on something else. In the few remaining minutes, I let them take the Luscher color preference test and talk about the correlation of color with personality. Most of them chose yellow, red, or blue in their color preference. They are a good class.

When I passed room 303 a few minutes later, the students were pushing at the door to get out. A trooper was holding them in. I told two boys at the door to go in and help their teacher. They asked, "Help *her*?" It hadn't occurred to them that she might need their help. Jack Kennedy, administrator, passed me in the corridor, his face white and drained. I stopped in the teachers' room

to comb my hair. My face in the mirror looked ghastly. It must take the body time to recover its equilibrium, even after the mind has composed itself.

As I walked around the school, and felt the mood of the school, I thought, "This school is DEATH. The mood of the school is black."

The troopers were happy, however, I was surprised to see. One said, "This is more like it. It gets the old adrenalin going."

My sophomores, a mixed class of black and white students, also wanted to talk about the incidents. They explained how the fight before school had started at the front lobby door. A black girl and a white boy were going through the front lobby—the boy first. He let the door slam on her. She screamed; a black male jumped to her defense, and the fight was on. A trooper pushed a white boy back over a desk and dislocated his shoulder. A black student on the stairs started screaming insults at the white students—among them Michael Faith—and Faith lunged for him. Fights broke out everywhere in the lobby. Students rushed down from the classrooms, or out of their homerooms to aid the secretaries when they called for help on the intercom.

Anne was upset because a trooper in the cafeteria had grabbed a black girl and called her "nigger." "Nobody calls me 'nigger.'" Anne said. "My friend got her comb and got a piece of his red meat."

I played dumb and, for the benefit of white students, said, "But I hear black kids call each other 'nigger,' and they don't seem to mind." Anne said, "Nobody's called me 'nigger.' I don't care who he is." Louis, a black student who has come to school regularly in a taxi even when Atkins called for a boycott, sat back confidently in his fine pressed suit and said, "It's all right when another black person calls me a 'nigger,' but not a white person. Then it's an insult. If I don't know a person and he calls me 'nigger,' I don't say anything until I find out how he feels about me."

Anne said, "I hate this school. I don't never want to come back."

I concluded, "We all need more understanding." . . .

There was a faculty meeting after school. Dr. Reid took the toll of casualties and names involved in fights. Unconsciously he wiped his brow with the classic tragic sweep of his hand and said, "I don't know what we can do. We were all at our posts doing our jobs. But if a youngster will insult and another responds with his fists, there's nothing we can do—except encourage them to watch their mouths and language."

Dr. Reid announced he would like to have an honor roll assembly for sophomores. Mrs. Marie Folkart, the oldest, most respected member of the faculty, raised her hand: She hoped he wouldn't have an assembly. Usually very deferential to her, he disagreed, "I don't know about that. I think maybe we should."

The assembly, the first this year, is scheduled for Friday, a day when attendance is the lowest. . . .

The sophomore assembly convened as planned. Classes filed to assigned seats room by room without incident. Troopers lined the auditorium. The mood was ugly.

Dr. Reid entered from the rear of the hall. As he moved down the center aisle to the stage, he urged the students to stand. He stopped at my class. Martin

wouldn't stand because Siegfried, behind him, wouldn't. Then James sat down—later, he told me, because the black kids—Martin and Siegfried—wouldn't stand. Dr. Reid insisted, and I insisted, but Martin refused. Dr. Reid proceeded on. Again I thought, "This school is death."

After the pledge of allegience to the flag, Dr. Reid lectured on the courtesy of standing when a guest comes to one's home. A few students snickered. When he alluded to the troopers, the black boys in the row behind me yelled, "Get them out." Then Dr. Reid outlined the sports plan for the winter and told the assembly, "We will be together for the year. After that I don't know. But we're here, and we had better make the best of it. And let's have a little courtesy toward one another. Let's treat each other with respect and watch what we say to one another—treat each other with a little kindness. A smile goes a long way if someone accidentally bumps you, instead of pushing back." The students listened respectfully.

Then, as both black and white students crossed the stage to accept their honor roll cards from Dr. Reid, the assembly applauded.

Students left the auditorium room by room.

During the day, girl students traveled the school in roving gangs of blacks and whites, bursting out of classes at any provocation, spreading consternation among the police. "They're in holiday mood," I told the police, dismayed at the prospect of chasing pretty girls back to classrooms.

At the end of the day in homeroom, I told Martin, "Dr. Reid has put his life on the line about desegregation because it is the law. His house in South Boston is guarded. Then he asks you to stand in the assembly, and you refuse. He is your friend, the friend of all of us, and you should know that." James said to Martin, "That's right, Dr. Reid has guards."

A neighborhood crowd chanted at Dr. Reid outside the school this morning. . . .

A librarian at the Boston Public Library in Copley Square told me there are enough kids in the library all day to have school there. He doesn't know where they come from. . . .

The number of troopers in the building was increased instead of decreased, contrary to what the troopers had anticipated Friday when I talked to them.

The two black boys—Martin and Jeffrey—and one white girl, Kathryn, were present in my homeroom today. Expecting a boycott, I was surprised to see any white students in school until I learned that a walkout of white students was anticipated at 9:45 A.M., when the parents, now gathering on the sidewalk, planned to walk in to protest the presence of steel combs in the school.

Walkers (or white students) were permitted to leave by the side doors, if they preferred, so as not to be identified and, perhaps, intimidated by the now divided community. In South Boston families once friends are now enemies, since half support the antibusing boycott and the other half feel they have to educate their children.

Television cameras recorded Dr. Reid facing the protesters outside the building in the morning sunshine. He told them, "The black parents have elected no biracial council; the white students have elected none; the white parents have elected none. And frankly, the number of fights last week made me afraid."

In class Anne described the walkout. "The white kids said, 'See you Tuesday, niggers.' If the black kids had a walkout, I'd go, too. The white kids have to go, or they'll get beaten up. " Gretchen, a diligent and intelligent white student, who had attended the advanced classes of the New York public schools, listened. I give her extra reading and reports because she is highly motivated. Besides Gretchen, there were five black students in the class.

I left school at the end of the day by the front lobby staircase, passing the Greek frieze laboriously painted by the art teachers in neutral dark brown last September before school began. The frieze had been nightly mutilated with spray paint and daily repaired by the art department, until finally they gave up. The frieze is now hideous: The faces are black blobs, or white blobs, or faceless with black holes for eyes. Looking at them, one teacher shuddered, "The hatred is getting to me."

17

After Civil Rights: The African American Working and Middle Classes

Robin D. G. Kelley

The passage of civil rights legislation in the mid-1960s signaled the end of racial segregation that had been a fact of American life since the Civil War. With comprehensive voting and civil rights legally secured, most white Americans congratulated themselves for having solved the nation's long-standing "race problem." All Americans, they felt, now had equal opportunities for education, employment, advancement, and success. As the 1970s progressed and passed into the 1980s, mainstream America became much more concerned about the faltering economy than about the condition of its African American counterparts.

But while federal legislation was a crucial step forward, it failed to bring about immediate changes in African American economic life. By the mid-1970s, it had become increasingly obvious to many observers that the economic conditions of African American life had changed but little. While a small middle class had benefited from antidiscriminatory legislation and had gained educations and well-paying jobs during the 1970s and 1980s, the majority of African Americans continued to find themselves frozen into low-status and low-paying jobs with little security. During the 1970s and 1980s, for example, the unemployment rate of black teens was more than twice that of whites.

Making conditions even worse, the late 1970s and early 1980s witnessed the end of America's post–World War II economic boom. Foreign competition and the increasing use of cheap, overseas labor joined with the mounting costs of the Vietnam war and the nation's burgeoning welfare state to drive the American economy into a downward spiral that, by the 1980s, would find it at its lowest point since the Great Depression. This economic downturn had an especially detrimental impact on the African American working class, as Robin D. G. Kelley demonstrates in this essay.

From *To Make Our World Anew: A History of African Americans* edited by Robin D. G. Kelly and Earl Lewis (New York: Oxford University Press, 2000). Copyright © 2000 by Oxford University Press, Inc. Reprinted by permission of the publisher.

Despite affirmative action policies that had placed black workers on many payrolls for the first time, when layoffs began, as the last hired, African Americans became the first fired. Even middle-class blacks discovered that their access to education seldom took them as far as their white counterparts. As Kelley notes, by the 1980s, it was apparent to African American leaders that "a new freedom movement was needed."

INNER CITY BLUES: URBAN POVERTY IN THE SEVENTIES

North Lawndale was once a thriving Chicago community made up of European immigrants and U.S.-born whites and blacks. A community of working-class neighborhoods, North Lawndale before 1970 was home to people who worked for International Harvester, Western Electric, Sears Roebuck, Zenith, Sunbeam, or any one of several other factories and retail outlets in the area. By 1980, most of these firms had closed up shop, leaving empty lots and burned-out buildings in their wake. The dominant retail outlets by the early eighties were bars and liquor stores. In less than a generation, North Lawndale's economy had evaporated, leaving fifty-eight percent of its able-bodied workers unemployed and half of its population on welfare. As jobs disappeared, so did most of the white and black middle-class residents. Once a thriving industrial hub, North Lawndale became one of the poorest black ghettos in Chicago.

The story of North Lawndale was repeated in almost every major city in the United States after 1970. What are the reasons for such economic devastation? Why has the collapse of the urban economy had such a profound impact on African Americans? To answer these questions, we need to first acknowledge that the economies under the free enterprise system have always had their ups and downs. Sometimes manufacturers produce more than the market can absorb, which not only results in lower prices but leads many companies to fire excess workers. Other times new technology intended to make production faster and more efficient leads to layoffs or reduced wages

because new machinery often requires workers with less skill. These and other worldwide economic conditions have caused the U.S. economy to swing between economic surges and periods of economic recessions or outright depressions. And in virtually every case of recession, African-American workers were the "last hired and first fired."

But by the mid-seventies, parts of the U.S. economy appeared to be in a permanent crisis. Ironically, just as programs were being implemented to correct racial imbalances in the workplace, and laws barring discrimination in hiring were being enforced a little more vigorously than before, much of the manufacturing part of the economy began a downward cycle from which it never seemed to recover. Even if protection for black workers improved slightly, changes in the global economy created massive unemployment and led to an expansion of poverty among African Americans not seen since the Great Depression of the thirties.

A series of events and policies during the early seventies contributed to the decline of the U.S. economy, especially its heavy industry—steelmaking and the manufacture of automobiles, tires, textiles, and machines of various kinds. In 1973, the Organization of Petroleum Exporting Countries (OPEC), an alliance of mostly Arab oil-producing countries that joined together in 1960 to reduce competition and set higher oil prices, declared an embargo on oil shipments to the United States and Western Europe to protest Israel's war with its Arab neighbors. Because the United States had become dependent on foreign oil supplies, the embargo had a devastating impact on the economy, making it difficult for individual consumers and big business to obtain inexpensive fuels. Plants shut down in large numbers. In 1974 alone, sales and manufacturing of American automobiles declined drastically, unemployment nearly doubled, and inflation more than doubled. Over the next ten years the economy never really recovered; the value of imported manufactured goods from places like Japan and Western Europe grew from less than fourteen percent of the U.S. domestic economy in 1970 to almost forty percent in 1979, while at the same time inflation sharply increased. With increased inflation came a steady loss in the standard of living for all Americans.

President Nixon tried to control inflation, but his policies actually made matters worse, especially for the poor. First, in August 1971 he temporarily froze wages, prices, and rents. But because prices and rents were already high, those earning low wages found themselves in the same situation as before. Second, Nixon placed a tariff on Japanese-made cars. This was intended to reduce competition between Japanese auto manufacturers and American manufacturers, but all it did was increase the price of otherwise affordable Japanese economy cars. American-made cars, for the most part, were still rather expensive and tended to use more gas than foreign cars. And in an economy in which oil prices were rising faster than just about any other item, cars that required less gas continued to be popular in the United States.

In spite of Nixon's measures, inflation continued to rise rapidly and low wages and growing unemployment made it impossible for large numbers of consumers to buy American products, no matter how much the government tried to protect the market with tariffs. Moreover, massive military spending exacerbated the country's economic woes. It dramatically increased the national debt and redirected much-needed investment away from roads, schools, and industries unrelated to the military buildup. Just months before President Nixon signed a peace agreement withdrawing U.S. troops from Vietnam, the national deficit had grown to $40 billion.

President Gerald Ford continued Nixon's economic policies, and when Democrat Jimmy Carter took over the Presidency in 1976, the situation for African Americans improved only slightly. He appointed Patricia Harris, an African-American woman, as Secretary of Housing and Urban Development, and Andrew Young, a black veteran of the civil rights movement, as ambassador to the United Nations. The Carter administration did little to lessen unemployment, and the jobless rate for African Americans increased during his first two years in office. Like the Republican presidents before him, Carter gave corporations a big tax cut, reduced financial aid to black colleges and universities, provided minuscule support for the nation's declining cities, and slashed federal spending for social programs—notably welfare, free lunch programs for children, and health, services. He even backpedaled on his promise to reduce defense spending: the military budget for 1978 reached $111.8 billion, the highest level in U.S. history up to that point.

The creation of multinational corporations in the post–World War II era was the most important change in the new global economy. These multinational corporations no longer had a stake in staying in a particular country or region. Instead, they moved their firms wherever labor and taxes were cheaper, pollution laws were less stringent, and labor unions were either weak or nonexistent. Some manufacturers moved from the Midwest and Northeast to the southern United States in search of cheaper labor with weaker unions, although the South hardly experienced an economic boom during the seventies. The more common trend was for big companies to set up shop in countries like Mexico, Brazil, and South Africa, leaving in their wake empty American factories and huge numbers of unemployed workers. By 1979, for example, ninety-four percent of the profits of the Ford Motor Company and sixty-three percent of the profits from Coca-Cola came from overseas operations. Between 1973 and 1980, at least four million U.S. jobs were lost when firms moved their operations to foreign countries. And during the decade of the seventies, at least 32 million jobs were lost as a result of shutdowns, relocations, and scaling-back operations.

The decline of manufacturing jobs in steel, rubber, auto, and other heavy industries had a devastating impact on black workers. Although black joblessness had been about twice that of whites since the end of World War II, black unemployment rates increased even more rapidly, especially after 1971. During these economic downturns, white unemployment tended to be temporary, with a higher percentage of white workers returning to work. For blacks, layoffs were often permanent. While the number of unemployed white workers declined by 562,000 between 1975 and 1980, the number of black unemployed *increased* by 200,000 during this period—the widest unemployment gap between blacks and whites since the government started keeping such statistics.

The loss of well-paying industrial jobs affected not only African Americans but the entire working class. Some workers looked to labor unions affiliated with the AFL-CIO to battle factory closures and wage reductions. At the height of the recession in the seventies, however, most labor unions were on the defensive, fighting desperately to hold on to the gains they had made a decade earlier. To make matters worse, many black industrial workers felt that white labor leaders were not very responsive to their needs. These leaders did not actively promote African Americans to leadership positions within the unions. In 1982, for example, the AFL-CIO's thirty-five member Executive Council had only two black members, a figure that fell far short of representing actual black membership. Indeed, African Americans tended to have higher rates of participation than whites in union activities: by 1983, more than twenty-seven percent of black workers were union members, compared to about nineteen percent of white workers.

Politically, the AFL-CIO leadership took stands that openly went against the interests of the majority of black workers. In 1972 George Meany supported Nixon's bid for the Presidency, which was interpreted by black rank-and-file members as a clear sign that the AFL-CIO was deserting African Americans. In response, a group of black trade union activists formed the Coalition of Black Trade Unionists (CBTU) in 1972. Under the leadership of veteran labor organizer William Lucy, secretary-treasurer of the American Federation of State, County, and Municipal Employees (AFSCME), the CBTU not only condemned the Nixon administration for what it felt were racist policies but also attacked AFL-CIO president George Meany for endorsing Nixon. The CBTU also issued a statement critical of union leaders who did not actively oppose discrimination and support minority and rank-and-file efforts to have a greater voice in the affairs of the union.

The loss of manufacturing positions was accompanied by an expansion of low-wage service jobs. The more common service jobs included retail clerks, janitors, maids, data processors, security guards, waitresses, and cooks—jobs with little or no union representation. Not everyone who was laid off in the seventies and eighties got these kinds of jobs, and those who did experienced substantial reductions in their income. Many of these new service jobs paid much less than manufacturing jobs. They tended to be part-time and offered very little in the way of health or retirement benefits.

Black men and women who were laid off from auto plants and steel mills in the Midwest and South suddenly found themselves working at fast food and sanitation jobs to make ends meet. Young people entering the job market for the first time quickly discovered that the opportunities their parents once had were fading quickly. Many African-American youths without the option to go to college chose the military as an alternative to low-wage service work. As the United States pulled out of Vietnam, the military became one of the biggest employers of African Americans: the percentage of blacks in the armed forces rose from eighteen percent in 1972 to thirty-three percent in 1979.

These dramatic changes in the economy meant greater poverty for African Americans. One of the most striking features of the seventies was the widening income gap between blacks and whites. At the beginning of the decade, African Americans in the northeastern United States made about seventy-one cents for every dollar whites made; by 1979 that ratio dropped to fifty-eight cents. In 1978, 30.6 percent of black families earned income below the official poverty line, compared with 8.7 percent of white families.

Black women and children were the hardest hit by the economic crisis. Hemmed in by limited job opportunities, more and more working-class black women found themselves having to raise children without the benefit of a spouse to help pay the bills or participate in child care. The number of black homes without male wage earners rose from twenty-two percent in 1960 to thirty-five percent in 1975. Since black women, especially those in their teens and twenties, were the lowest paid and had the highest unemployment rate, it is not an accident that black single-mother households headed the list of families below the poverty line. In 1969, fifty-four percent of all black families below the poverty line were headed by women; in 1974 this figure rose to sixty-seven percent.

Several politicians and academics blame the rising number of "female-headed households" for the decline of inner cities and the rise of black crime and violence. This crisis of the black family, they argue, is new and unprecedented. They insist that the inability of single mothers to control and discipline their children, combined with the lack of male role models, has led to a whole generation of out-of-control youth. But a lot of these claims are based on misinformation. First of all, single-mother families are not a uniquely "black" crisis; between 1970 and 1987 the birth rate for white unwed mothers rose by seventy-seven

percent. Second, out-of-wedlock births are not entirely new to African-American communities. Studies have shown that at least since the days of slavery black women are more likely than white women to bear children outside of marriage and to marry at later ages, after becoming mothers. Part of the reason has to do with the fact that black families have tended not to ostracize women for out-of-wedlock births.

Why have the number of female-headed households grown, and what impact has it had on the social and economic fabric of black communities? First, the declining number of employed black men has contributed to the growth of single-parent households. Aside from a rapid increase in permanently unemployed black men who suddenly cannot support their families as they had in the past, black men have a higher chance of dying young than any other male population in the United States. They are more often victims of occupational accidents, fatal diseases, and homicides than other men. And throughout the seventies and eighties, the black male prison population increased threefold; by 1989, twenty-three percent of black males ages twenty to twenty-nine, or almost one out of every four, were either behind bars or on legal probation or parole. Another important factor is that African Americans have a higher divorce and separation rate than whites. High unemployment for black males certainly contributes to marital instability among poor families, but welfare policies also play a major role. In at least twenty-five states, two-parent families are ineligible for Aid to Families with Dependent Children (AFDC), and in many cases black men have to leave the household in order for the women and children to have access to welfare and Medicaid.

Although single-parent families (including those run by males) tended to suffer more than two-parent families because they lacked a second wage earner, the structure of the family was not the *cause* of poverty. Most of these households were poor not because the women were unmarried but because of the lack of employment opportunities for women, lower levels of education, and the gross inequality in wages as a result of race and sex discrimination. One study shows, for example, that while seventy-five percent of unemployed black women heading families were poor in 1977, only twenty-seven percent of employed black women heading families were poor. Besides, the vast majority of women who ended up as single parents were poor *before* they had children or experienced divorce, separation, or the death of their husband.

Finally, single-parent families are not always the product of economic deprivation. Oftentimes they reflect the efforts of black women to escape abusive situations and to raise their children in a more supportive environment. As Barbara Omolade, an African-American scholar and activist, explained it: "My children and other children of Black single mothers are better people because they do not have to live in families where violence, sexual abuse, and emotional estrangement are the daily, hidden reality. . . . In a society where men are taught to dominate and women to follow, we all have a lot to overcome in learning to build relationships, with each other and with our children, based on love and justice. For many Black single mothers, this is what the struggle is about."

Because many families headed by single women are poor, they frequently must turn to welfare to survive. The amount of financial support available to welfare recipients in most states barely allowed families to make ends meet. In a recent study of welfare in the eighties, for example, one researcher met a divorced mother of two whose combined cash aid and food stamps amounted to a mere twelve dollars per day. "This is probably about the lowest point in my life," she admitted, "and I hope I never reach it again. Because this is where you're just up against a wall. You can't make a move. You can't buy anything that you want for your home. You can't go on vacation. You can't take a weekend off and go see things

because it costs too much." The stigma attached to welfare made matters worse. Using food stamps often brought stares and whispers of disgust from clerks and consumers standing by.

The majority of single black mothers who received welfare during the eighties, however, did so for an average of only six months, and most had to supplement aid with odd jobs in order to make ends meet. Besides, not all poor African Americans received public assistance, nor were they the primary beneficiaries of welfare. In 1991, sixty-one percent of all people on welfare were white. Blacks, by comparison, made up only thirty-three percent of welfare recipients. And many who did qualify for some form of public assistance did not always receive it. A 1979 study revealed that seventy percent of all unemployed blacks never received any unemployment benefits; more than half of all poor black households received no AFDC or General Assistance; half of all black welfare households received no Medicaid coverage and fifty-eight percent of all poor black households received benefits from only one or two of the seven income programs available to assist the poor. There are many reasons why a substantial number of poor people did not receive full benefits. In some cases, the lengthy application process discouraged applicants; in other instances, computer errors, misplaced files, or unsympathetic or ill-informed case workers were to blame. But in many cases, black men and women living below the poverty line were simply too proud to accept welfare.

LIVING THE DREAM? THE BLACK MIDDLE CLASS

To the residents of Philadelphia, July 1976 must have felt like the hottest month in that city's history. Throngs of people from all over the country and throughout the world invaded the "City of Brotherly Love" to celebrate the 200th birthday of the Declaration of Independence. Waving overpriced flags and wearing red, white, and blue outfits, they came to examine the famous crack in the Liberty Bell and see firsthand the document that announced the beginning of this country's democratic journey.

In the neighborhoods just north, west, and south of the celebrations, a growing number of jobless and working-poor African Americans were fighting to survive. While the patriotic celebrations of the moment cast a shadow over Philadelphia's dark ghettos, hiding much of the recent devastation that would characterize the next two decades, a group of African-American leaders was trying to get the bicentennial committee to acknowledge the black presence in the past two hundred years of history. The fact that the majority of Africans in America were still slaves when the Declaration of Independence was signed made many bicentennial organizers uncomfortable. Instead, they tried to integrate the celebrations by highlighting black achievement in business, politics, the arts and entertainment, sciences, and education.

By emphasizing black achievement and paying less attention to the crumbling ghettos in earshot of the Liberty Bell, the organizers of the bicentennial were not being entirely dishonest. Just as the majority of African Americans experienced immense poverty, segregation, violence, and rising racism, some black professionals and entrepreneurs were reaping the fruits of integration. Of course, there had always been middle- land upper-class blacks, but in the past they succeeded in a segregated economy, lived in segregated neighborhoods, and had to operate in an atmosphere of outright racial discrimination. Although discrimination did not disappear entirely, the civil rights struggles of the previous two decades helped usher in affirmative action programs that gave minorities and women preference in hiring and college admission to compensate for past and present discrimination.

"We were all . . . children of the civil rights movement: the nation had changed its laws and, in some respects, its ways during our childhoods and adolescences. We were living the opportunities for which generations of black folk had fought and died. Walking paths wet with the blood of our martyrs, we felt an uneasy fear that taking advantage of those opportunities was changing us."

These words were written in 1991 by Yale law professor and best-selling author Stephen L. Carter. Carter exemplifies what it meant for a generation of young people to live the American Dream. A graduate of Yale Law School, Carter turned out to be a gifted legal scholar and talented writer. In another era, a black person of his considerable talents might not have had the chance to attend Yale or to accept a major professorship at his alma mater. But affirmative action policies and an aggressive recruitment effort to attract African Americans to the school opened doors for him that had been closed to previous generations. He is clearly one of those who "made it." Between his salaries, royalties on his book sales, and fees for speaking engagements, Professor Carter makes more than enough money to live a comfortable middle- or upper-middle-class existence.

And yet, Carter is somewhat ambivalent about how his success and the particular road he had to take to achieve it has changed him and other black professionals. Everywhere he turned, his white colleagues hinted that he did not make it on his own merit; that every college and every law firm opened doors to him because he was black, not because he was good. Some days be believed this argument. Other days he felt enraged that so many of his colleagues viewed him as the representative of a race rather than as an individual. Occasionally he convinced himself that his success was entirely the result of his own initiative and hard work. Indeed, there were moments when Carter believed that the old racial barriers of the past had been completely destroyed. But just when life seemed good, the handsomely attired and articulate scholar would be reminded of his race. "When in New York, for example, if I am traveling with a white person, I frequently swallow my pride and allow my companion to summon the taxi as I hang back—for to stand up for my rights and raise the arm myself would buy only a tired arm and no ride. For a black male, blue jeans in New York are a guarantee of ill-treatment. There are the jewelry-store buzzers that will not ring, the counter clerks who will not say 'Sir,' the men's departments with no staff to be found."

Carter's mixed feelings about his success are characteristic of a rapidly expanding class of black urban and suburban professionals who came of age during the fifties and sixties. Their numbers increased substantially during the seventies. In 1970, 15.7 percent of black families had incomes over $35,000; by 1986 the percentage had grown to 21.2 percent. Likewise, black families earning more than $50,000 almost doubled, increasing from 4.7 percent in 1970 to 8.8 percent in 1986. And like Carter, their rapid success can be partially attributed to antidiscrimination laws and affirmative action programs first established in the sixties and expanded under President Jimmy Carter during the mid- to late-seventies.

The roots of recent affirmative action policies can be traced to the Civil Rights Act of 1964 and the establishment of the Equal Employment Opportunity Commission (EEOC) and the Office of Federal Contract Compliance (OFCC). Both of these agencies were created to monitor employment discrimination and enforce the law. Unfortunately, the staff at the EEOC and the OFCC was small relative to the number of cases it received each year.

While lack of personnel within these institutions has led to a huge backlog of cases and limited their effectiveness, the EEOC, especially, has put pressure on firms to hire more women and minorities. For example, in 1973 the EEOC successfully sued the U.S. Steel Corporation for failing to promote black workers at its Fairfield, Alabama, plant. The court ordered U.S. Steel to expand job opportunities for its African-American workers. The EEOC discovered blatant incidents of white workers with less seniority being promoted

to better jobs—mainly skilled machinist, clerical, technical, and managerial occupations. The court ruling required equal hiring of black and white apprentices and black and white clerical and technical employees until African Americans held about a quarter of these jobs.

Soon thereafter, the Detroit Edison Company was fined $4 million in punitive damages for discriminating against African-American employees, and a Detroit union local of the Utility Workers of America (UWA) was slapped with a $250,000 fine. The suit was initiated by a group of black Detroit Edison workers after the UWA and the International Brotherhood of Electrical Workers refused to file their grievance for them. Their primary complaint was that Detroit Edison employed very few black workers, turned down a large number of qualified black applicants, and kept blacks in the lowest-paid jobs. The judge in the case ordered the company to increase the proportion of black employees from eight percent to thirty percent and to set hiring guidelines that would ultimately place more black workers in higher-paying jobs with more authority.

Affirmative action policies were also responsible for briefly increasing black enrollment at major colleges and universities starting in the late sixties. Black enrollment rates rose from twenty-seven percent in 1972 to thirty-four percent in 1976, before dropping steadily during the next decade. Many leading black scholars and corporate leaders who came of age in the 1950s and sixties benefited from affirmative action initiatives. Because such policies were more strongly enforced at the federal, state, and municipal levels, African Americans employed in the public sector gained the most. By 1970, twenty-eight percent of all employed African Americans held government jobs, and approximately sixty percent of all black professional workers were employed by governmental bodies. This is particularly striking when we consider that in 1970 African Americans held only one percent of the managerial and administrative jobs in manufacturing. Thus, the expansion of public sector jobs for minorities has been largely responsible for the growth of the black middle class.

However, the inclusion of African Americans in public sector jobs and managerial positions did not always translate into big salary increases. Many black families reporting middle-class incomes were often the result of two parents working full-time for fairly low or moderate wages. Besides, in 1979, eighteen percent of all black female managers and thirteen percent of all black male managers actually earned wages below the poverty line. Many middle-class black families who had purchased suburban homes during the seventies lived from paycheck to paycheck; one layoff could mean the loss of their home. In fact, all economic indicators show that middle-class blacks, on average, possess substantially less "wealth" (savings, money invested in buying a home, stocks, bonds, retirement accounts, etc., minus debts) than middle-class whites who earn the same income.

Much of African-American wealth is concentrated in the hands of independent entrepreneurs, some of whom also benefited from affirmative action initiatives to provide more minority firms with government contracts and loans. The purpose of such programs was not to provide a handout to struggling businesses. Rather, they sought to rectify policies that had kept minority firms from obtaining government contracts in the first place and to improve the economic status of all African Americans by establishing a strong foundation for "black capitalism." The Nixon administration, for example, created several subsidy programs to assist black businesses, including the Office of Minority Business Enterprise, the Manpower Development and Training Program, and the Minority Enterprise Small Business Investment Company. Although these programs might have been effective if properly funded, they were never given much of a chance: after Ronald Reagan was elected

President in 1980, virtually all of these programs were cut back.

Between 1972 and 1977, the number of black-owned firms and their proportion of total industry revenue declined for the most part. The number of black-owned auto dealerships fell by twenty-four percent; black-owned hotel and lodging facilities dropped by twenty-one percent; and the number of food and eating establishments declined by ten percent. In 1977, black-owned firms made up only three percent of all businesses in' the country. By 1980, more than eighty percent of all black-owned firms did not have a single paid employee aside from the owner, and at least one-third of these firms failed within twelve months of opening.

Competition with other businesses only partly explains the failure of certain black-owned ventures. Black entrepreneurs have had more difficulty securing loans for their businesses than their white counterparts. A recent survey of five hundred black entrepreneurs with an annual revenue of $100,000 or more revealed that ninety percent had been turned down by banks when they applied for business loans. Of those surveyed, seventy percent had to rely on personal savings to finance their business. Often, black business people have to turn to black-owned community banks for help.

Not all black business suffered during the seventies recessions and Reagan-era cutbacks. On the contrary, the last decades of the twentieth century are filled with remarkable stories of black entrepreneurship. One rising corporate star during the seventies was Naomi Sims, a high-fashion model originally from Oxford, Mississippi. After earning a degree in psychology from New York University and studying at the Fashion Institute of Technology, Sims quickly emerged as one of the most popular black women models in the country, making several magazine-cover and television appearances. In 1973, she helped develop a new fiber for a line of wigs and founded the Naomi Sims

Collection, selling cosmetics and hair-care products nationwide. By 1977, her firm reported annual revenues of about four million dollars.

Reginald F. Lewis's road to success was a bit more traditional. Born in Baltimore, Maryland, Lewis was helped by affirmative action policies that enabled him to earn a law degree from Harvard in 1968. After working for one of New York's most prestigious corporate law firms, Lewis, with fellow attorney Charles Clarkson, started his own law firm on Wall Street in 1970. His firm helped minority-owned businesses obtain financing and structure deals. In 1983, Lewis launched the TLC Group, an aggressive investment firm with the specific purpose of acquiring companies. And acquire he did: in 1984 TLC bought McCall's Pattern Company (a manufacturer of sewing patterns) for $25 million—and sold it for $90 million three years later. Then in 1987, the TLC Group made history by purchasing BCI Holdings, the former international division of the Chicago-based Beatrice Foods. Comprised of sixty-four companies operating in thirty-one countries, BCI Holdings manufactured and distributed a wide range of food products, including ice cream, meats, chocolates, and soft drinks. Lewis's firm paid $985 million for BCI Holdings, making it the largest leveraged buyout of an overseas operation in the history of American business up to that time.

The year before Lewis's death in 1993, TLC Beatrice had revenues of $1.54 billion and Lewis himself had amassed assets of more than $300 million, making him the wealthiest African American in U.S. history.

Perhaps the best-known black millionaire is publishing magnate John H. Johnson, founder of *Ebony* and *Jet* magazines. Born in Arkansas in 1918, he migrated to Chicago with his mother at age fifteen. While working for the black-owned Supreme Liberty Life Insurance Company in 1942, twenty-four-year-old Johnson decided to launch *Negro Digest*, a small magazine summarizing longer articles for

and about African Americans. Raising the money was hard. "Most people had seen *Reader's Digest* and *Time*," he recalled, "but nobody had seen a successful black commercial magazine. And nobody was willing to risk a penny on a twenty-four-year-old insurance worker." That is, except for the Citizens Loan Corporation of Chicago, one of the few financial institutions willing to loan money to African Americans. They loaned him $500, but only after Johnson's mother offered to put up all of her new furniture as collateral. It was a good investment, for within eight months of its founding *Negro Digest* was selling fifty thousand copies a month nationally. Three years later, Johnson launched *Ebony* magazine, a photo magazine modeled after *Life*. By 1991, the Johnson companies reported total gross sales of $252 million. According to *Forbes* magazine, Johnson headed one of the four hundred richest families in the United States.

The combination of higher incomes and the dismantling of legal segregation enabled many rising middle-class black families to flee collapsing ghettos and move out to the suburbs or to lavish townhouses and brownstones in wealthy urban communities. The trend is reflected in the rapid suburbanization of the African-American population during the seventies and eighties: between 1970 and 1986, the black suburban population grew from 3.6 million to 7.1 million. Although they often left behind deteriorating neighborhoods, a growing drug economy, and a rapidly expanding army of unemployed men and women, most blacks could not escape bigotry. To their surprise, some middle-class black families who moved into predominantly white suburbs discovered burning crosses on their lawns, hate mail, and letters from property owners' associations concerned that their presence would lower property values.

Potential black homebuyers also had to deal with real estate agents who deliberately steered them to poorer, predominantly black neighborhoods, and with financial institutions that blatantly discriminated against African Americans. The evidence of discrimination against African Americans in housing is overwhelming. Numerous studies conducted in major metropolitan areas since the sixties demonstrated that real estate agents frequently showed black home buyers different properties, withheld information, or simply lied about the status of the property in question. This practice of steering black home buyers toward nonwhite neighborhoods is a form of discrimination known as "redlining." Similarly, a massive study of ten million applications to savings and loan associations between 1983 and 1988 revealed that the rejection rate for blacks applying for home mortgages was more than twice that of whites, and that high-income African Americans were rejected more than low-income whites.

What is clear from such stories of discrimination is that the dismantling of legal barriers to segregation has not been completely effective. Indeed, by some measures racial segregation has increased in the urban North during the last three decades. Despite evidence that middle- and upper-income African Americans were the greatest beneficiaries of integration, it is interesting to note that in some major cities African Americans earning more than $50,000 were as segregated as those making less than $2,500 annually. Of course, in a few cases middle-class blacks have chosen predominantly black suburban enclaves in well-to-do communities such as Prince George's County, Maryland (just outside of Washington, D.C.), or sections of Westchester County, a community north of New York City. Their decision is understandable given the history of violence and discrimination directed at African Americans who try to integrate all-white suburban communities. But fear of racist attacks and the desire for respectful neighbors indicate the narrowness of choices that are offered to blacks compared to whites.

School integration, another component of African Americans' desire to reach for the American Dream, quickly became one of the most contested racial battlefields during the post–civil rights era. A quarter of a century after the landmark case of *Brown v. Board of Education of Topeka, Kansas* (1954), the nation's public schools looked as segregated as they had ever been. Although black children made up about one-fifth of the total public school enrollment, almost two-thirds went to schools with at least fifty percent minority enrollment. This pattern is even more striking in major cities, where African-American children attended underfunded public schools while many white students, often the children of urban professionals, have deserted the public school system for private institutions. By 1980, for example, whites made up only four percent of public school enrollment in Washington, D.C., eight percent in Atlanta, nine percent in Newark, and twelve percent in Detroit.

Drastic measures were needed to remedy this situation, especially since middle-class families who had migrated to the suburbs took precious tax dollars needed to run city schools. With fewer well-paid, property-owning families living in urban areas, the property taxes so essential to funding education and other city services declined considerably. Under pressure from black families who wanted to send their children to better-funded schools in the suburbs and civil rights groups that believed the nation should live up to the *Brown* decision, school boards across the country tried to achieve racial balance by busing students to schools in different neighborhoods.

The nation was sharply divided over the issue of busing. President Nixon vehemently opposed court-ordered busing, officials in the Department of Health, Education and Welfare thought it was a good idea, and the Supreme Court remained unsure whether it was constitutional or not. The clearest expression of resistance to mandatory busing came from white parents who believed the addition of black children from the inner city would bring down the quality of education. Indeed, in some cities busing programs were met with militant protests that frequently led to violence. Throughout the early to mid-seventies, organized resistance erupted in cities throughout the country, including Pontiac, Michigan; Louisville, Kentucky; Pasadena, California; and Kansas City, Missouri. The best-known clashes were in Boston, where most public schools had been racially segregated until an NAACP-led campaign won a court order in 1975 to bus children from predominantly black and poor Roxbury to Charlestown, a largely working-class Irish community. Over the course of the next three years, Boston police were called in to protect black children from white mobs screaming racial epithets and occasionally throwing bricks and fists.

The Boston busing controversy died down by the early eighties, partly because liberal black and white politicians created a coalition that elected more supporters of integration to the city council and to the Board of Education. Besides, proponents of school integration could hardly claim a victory. By 1980, white flight to the suburbs and a decrease in the use of busing by conservative judges caused a resegregation of most big city school systems.

In the area of higher education, the backlash against affirmative action policies and financial aid for minorities took on many forms. During the late seventies and through the eighties, the number of reported racial assaults and acts of intimidation against blacks on college campuses showed a marked increase. The specific cases are chilling.

At Wesleyan University in 1981, black students found racist graffiti and flyers riddled with epithets and threats, including a leaflet advertising a fraternity "dedicated to wiping all goddamned niggers off the face of the earth." Ten years later, a white sorority at the University of Alabama hosted a party at which pledges painted their faces black and dressed as pregnant welfare mothers. Usually white backlash is much more subtle. One black college administrator vividly described the attitudes of white freshmen toward African Americans at

his university: "Somebody will have the idea that the dorm is exclusively theirs, so therefore we can't have these 'germy, diseasey, dirty, filthy,' black kids live in their dormitory. . . . Black kids are seen as a gang now. They must be on drugs or crazy or something."

By far the most devastating form of white backlash in higher education was the partial dismantling of affirmative action initiatives. In the case of *Regents of the University of California v. Bakke* (1978), Allan Bakke, an unsuccessful white applicant, claimed that he was discriminated against because the University of California, Davis, admitted African Americans with lower test scores than his in order to meet their quota of minority students. The Supreme Court ruled that Bakke had been unfairly denied admission to the medical school. The court did not overturn all forms of affirmative action, but it did argue that quotas—setting aside a specific number of slots for designated groups—were unconstitutional. The medical school's denial of admission to Bakke in order to increase the number of minority students was regarded by the court's majority opinion as "reverse discrimination."

Although Bakke won the case, the unspoken facts behind U.C. Davis's admissions policy call into question the court's opinion that he was a victim of reverse discrimination. First, the sons and daughters of influential white families—potential donors or friends of the dean of the medical school—were also admitted over Bakke despite lower test scores. As had been the case historically, the dean controlled a handful of slots to admit special cases. Second, most minority applicants had higher scores than Bakke. This is an important fact, for the Bakke case left many observers with the incorrect impression that U.C. Davis admitted unqualified minorities. Most importantly, the decision was a major setback for efforts to achieve racial equality through social policy. Justice Thurgood Marshall, the first African American to serve on the Supreme Court, dissented from the majority opinion. Marshall, who viewed the Bakke decision as a tragedy, did not believe that America was even close to becoming a color-blind society. "The dream of America as a great melting pot," he wrote in his dissenting opinion in the Bakke case, "has not been realized for the Negro; because of his skin color he never even made it into the pot."

Most African Americans who stood at the threshold of the Reagan era knew they had entered the worst of times. *Equal opportunity*, *welfare*, *civil rights*, and *Black Power* became bad words in the national vocabulary. Most white Americans believed they had given all they could give, and that any form of government support would be nothing more than a handout. A small but growing contingent of black conservatives agreed. And if this was not enough, the crumbling cities that African Americans and other minorities had inherited turned out not to be the utopia they had hoped for. They were dangerous, difficult places where racist police officers still roamed and well-paying jobs fled the city limits. Despite the rising number of black mayors, it became clear by the eighties that a new freedom movement was needed.

GLOSSARY

AFL-CIO: American Federation of Labor and Congress of Industrial Organizations, the nation's largest union organization.

George Meany (1894–1980): American labor leader who exerted great political influence as the first president of the American Federation of Labor and the Congress of Industrial Organizations (1955–1979).

Aid to Families with Dependent Children: A federally sponsored welfare program.

IMPLICATIONS

In this essay, Kelley discusses the differing impacts that the civil rights "revolution" of the 1960s and the economic dislocations of the 1970s had on African American life. Do you think that passage of the Civil Rights Acts solved the problems of race in America? What do you think civil rights legislation accomplished?

PAST TRACES

The economic boom of the late 1980s combined with greatly increased access to higher education to create a new phenomenon: young urban professionals, or Yuppies. Commanding substantial salaries, yuppies developed a distinctive, fast-paced lifestyle focused around high-priced and prestigious consumer goods. This essay is introduced by an early account of the new yuppie lifestyle.

Patricia Morrisroe, Yuppies—The New Class (1985)

It's a Saturday night at 96th and Broadway. Inside the new Caramba!!! everybody's drinking frozen maragaritas and talking real estate, while outside on the traffic strip, a derelict swigs Wild Turkey and shouts obscenities. By 11 P.M., he's sound asleep on the bench, but the crowd at Caramba!!! is still going strong.

"These are the most lethal maragaritas in Manhattan," says a man in a blue pinstriped suit by Polo. He staggers out of the restaurant and into David's Cookies next door. "Get the double-chunk chocolate chip," says his girl-friend, who is window-shopping at Pildes Optical.

At the newsstand across the street, a middle-aged woman buys the Sunday *Times* and looks at the dozens of young professionals spilling out of Caramba!!! "Yuppies," she shouts. "Go home!"

But they are home. Ads in the *Times* tout the Upper West Side as "Yuppie Country," and Amsterdam is being called "Cinderella Avenue." According to a study of the years 1970 through 1980 by New York's Department of City Planning, 7,500 people between the ages of 25 and 44 flooded the area between West 70th and 86th Streets. That age-group now makes up 47 percent of the population there. At the same time, the number of singles went up by 31 percent, while the number of families dropped 24 percent. "You want to know who's moving into the West Side?" says a woman who owns an antiques store on Amsterdam Avenue. "It's the young, the rich, and the restless."

Some older West Siders blame the newcomers for the skyrocketing rents and the uprooting of local merchants. They deplore the cuteness of Columbus Avenue and the hordes of tourists who congest the sidewalks. They worry that the neighborhood's solid middle class values will be replaced by the yuppie version of the West Side Dream: a pre-war apartment with a Food Emporium around the corner.

They can't relate to the 30-year-old on Central Park West who takes her husband's shirts to the East Side because she can't find a "quality" laundry in the neighborhood. Or to the tenants at the Sofia on West 61st Street, 50 percent of whom bought their apartments after seeing a model of the bathroom. ("They're big and very Deco," says Richard Zinn, the building's director of sales.)

The Columbia, a condominium on West 96th Street, has been called the "Yuppie Housing Project" by locals who can't believe anyone would *pay* to live on Broadway. "Didn't anyone tell these people it's a *commercial* street?" says an elderly man who is buying Rice Krispies at the Red Apple on the corner. "If I had the money for a condo, I'd move to Florida."

One third of the Columbia's units were bought by lawyers; the average income per apartment is $100,000. "It's a nice first home for couples on their way up," says developer Arthur Zeckendorf, who worked with his father, William, to build the Columbia. Once they've made it, they can move to the Park Belvedere, a condominium on West 79th Street also built by the Zeckendorfs. Sold for an average of $400 per square foot, it has attracted a better-off buyer. "I looked at the Columbia," says a 27-year-old Wall Street bond trader, "but the neighborhood was just too borderline for me." So he bought an apartment in one of the Belvedere's towers and persuaded a friend to buy one, too. "It's a great deal," he says of his $400,000 one-bedroom.

Many West Side co-ops are besieged by Wall Street financiers who use their bonuses to make down payments.

"The last five apartments in my building went to investment bankers," says a woman who owns a co-op on West End Avenue. "I want to protect my property, so it's good to have people with money move in. But I worry about the population in the next ten years. Are you going to need an MBA to get into Zabar's?" . . .

Yet for all the money being poured into the neighborhood, some of the new West Siders have a decidedly old-fashioned point of view. For every yuppie who dreams about moving from Broadway to Central Park West there are others who chose the West Side because it seemed unpretentious. "I always hated everything the East Side represented," says 33-year-old Joe Powers in between feeding mashed carrots to his five-month-old son, Mark. "The West Side always seemed to have less airs about it. To me, it's Zabar's and Fairway. Not Rúelles and Pasta & Cheese." . . .

Ten blocks uptown, 31-year-old Richard Conway is setting up his VCR to tape Jacqueline Bisset in *Anna Karenina*. A vice-president at a Wall Street investment firm, Conway recently bought a twelfth-floor five-room co-op at 106th Street and Riverside Drive. In the past fifteen years, Conway has moved from Greenwich to Harvard to Third Avenue to Yale to Chelsea, and now to Duke Ellington Boulevard.

"This is not a yuppie neighborhood," says Conway, uncorking a bottle of white wine. "That's what I like about it. In my building, we have a wonderful mix of people. The head of the co-op board is a musical director, and we've got artists and writers and movie producers."

When Conway decided to buy a co-op, he wanted to look only north of West 96th Street. "I think a lot of the glamour is gone from the East Side," he says. "Besides, I considered it boring and staid, too much like Greenwich. I like living in a neighborhood that's ethnically diverse. Broadway has a lot of bodegas and mom-and-pop stores. To me, that's nice."

From his living room, Conway has a spectacular view of the Hudson. From the opposite end of the apartment, in the dining room, he can see a cityscape of charming turn-of-the-century brown-stones. "I wonder how long they'll last," he says. "It's ironic, but everything I like about the neighborhood will probably disappear. And unfortunately, the reason is that people like me are moving into it." . . .

[Lawyer Jay] Zamansky, who grew up in Philadelphia, now makes his home in a renovated SRO next door to the Salvation Army senior citizen's home on West 95th Street. "I really wanted a place where I could establish roots," he says. Constructed around the turn of the century, the building has 30 apartments, most of which are inhabited by young professionals. "We're a real unique building," he explains. "In the summer, we have barbecues, and when our first co-op baby was born, everybody was thrilled."

Zamansky bought this apartment, a duplex with a roof garden, for a little over $100,000. "I'm real proud of it," he says. "It's the consummate bachelor pad." The ceiling is painted black, with lots of track lighting. "I met an interior designer at the Vertical Club," he explains, "and she helped me with the overall concept."

But Zamansky says he doesn't want to be the kind of person who does nothing but "work, eat at restaurants, and go to a health club. I really want to be a part of this neighborhood," he says. "I

attend community-board meetings, and I registered voters in front of Zabar's. I even went into the Salvation Army's old people's home and registered senior citizens. They were just so glad to see a young face that I don't think they cared how they voted. By the way, I'm a Republican. I think it's important to put that in the article.

"I'm also very pro-development," he adds. "It makes me angry when people criticize a lot of the changes. The displacement is unfortunate, but where are we supposed to live? We have rights. We pay taxes. Whether people realize it or not, we're real assets to this community."

Twenty-nine-year-old Paula Handler, who lives with her husband in a three-bedroom apartment in the Eldorado on Central Park West between 90th and 91st Streets agrees. "These big pre-war buildings need young blood," she says. "The old people can't maintain their apartments. They resist everything, from redoing the lobby to putting in new windows. The problem is they can't switch their rental mentalities into a co-op mode."

The Handlers moved from the East Side to the Eldorado a year ago. "Frankly, I didn't know anything about Central Park West," says Paula. "I mean, I knew the Dakota, but the Eldorado? What? All I knew was that I wanted space, and I wanted old. Old is chic."

"Originally, I said no to the West Side," says Scott, a quiet man who is involved in commercial real estate.

"That's right, he did," Paula says. "He didn't like it because it was dirty and nobody we knew lived there. But I fell in love with this apartment. It was a total wreck, but it was me. We gave them an offer the minute we saw it. We even offered more than they asked because we wanted it so much."

The Handlers put in two new bathrooms and a new kitchen, and redid the plumbing and wiring. Today, the apartment, which faces the park, is completely renovated. "See what I mean about new blood?" Paula says. "It doesn't take money. It just takes creativity."

Six floors above the Handlers, Linda and Mark Reiner also had to redo their apartment completely. "It was considered the worst disaster in the building," Linda says. "The walls, which were painted magenta, royal blue, and orange, were falling down. But we really wanted to live here. We recognized how the West Side was growing, and we wanted to be a part of that."

Two years ago, they moved from a house in Hewlett Harbor, where Mark Reiner had a medical practice. "It was a risk giving up everything," he says, "but Hewlett Harbor was very sterile and uniform.

"That's why we didn't want the East Side," adds Linda, who until recently was a practicing psychologist. "Now I sell real estate," she says. "I became addicted to it while we were looking for this apartment." The au pair brings their two-year-old son into the living room to say good night. "You wouldn't believe the children's playground in the park," Linda says. "You can barely get a place for your kid in the sandbox."

"Everybody wants to come here," says Mark. "There's nothing more exciting than living in a neighborhood in transition. It's sad, because a lot of people who live here can't afford to shop in the stores. But they're being pushed out of Manhattan, not just the West Side."

"The West Side makes you feel the difference between the haves and the have-nots," says Linda, who is dressed in a silk Chanel shirt, black pants, and pumps. "Right in our building, there's a real schism between the pre-conversion and post-conversion people. A new breed is taking over, and there's a lot of hostility. People are separated by age and economic class. The senior citizens got insider prices so low that there's a lot of resentment on all sides. At a recent meeting, one elderly person shouted, 'Well, I'm not rich like you.' But what can you do?"

"Basically, we're very optimistic," Mark says. "We feel good about the changes. The neighborhood is going to continue to improve."

Linda nods. "Definitely," she says. "For the West Side, there's no turning back."

18

·····························

The Insidious Cycle of
Work and Spend

Juliet B. Schor

Beginning in the 1980s and building to a fever pitch during the 1990s, Americans embarked on the largest spending spree in the nation's history. Taking advantage of easy credit, falling interest rates, two-income households, and rising wages, working- and middle-class men and women began to emulate the lifestyles of the wealthy and famous. No longer content with modest homes, people throughout the country began to purchase new and expensive houses that were designed to look like the mansions of the wealthy. Families leased prestigious cars and newly popular sport utility vehicles for fill their three-car garages. New and renovated shopping malls mushroomed everywhere, often anchored by high-end prestige stores, such as Nieman-Marcus, Lord and Taylor, and Saks Fifth Avenue, all catering to the newly developed upscale tastes of middle-class consumers. As the economy peaked in the late 1990s, advertising and television commercials made it appear that all Americans were striving to live like the rich and famous.

Although often portrayed by the media as a new phenomenon, this combination of materialism and consumerism had a long pedigree, stretching back at least to the 1920s. It was during the post–World War I era that businesses began to employ advertising to induce people to buy their products and created consumer credit to give Americans the means to pay for their purchases. Despite sometimes drastic swings in the national economy, consumerism has been a large part of American life ever since. In fact, today consumer indebtedness is at a record high and shows no signs of subsiding. With consumer spending accounting for two-thirds of the nation's gross domestic product, middle-class consumption has literally driven the post-industrial economy.

This affluence has come at a price, however. As economist Juliet B. Schor shows in this essay, Americans have committed themselves to long working hours, little time for leisure and family life, and a frenetic pace of life in order to support their consumption-driven lifestyles. As Schor notes, the more Americans become committed to consumerism, the more difficult it becomes for them to choose other ways of life.

....

SHOP 'TIL YOU DROP

We live in what may be the most consumer-oriented society in history. Americans spend three to four times as many hours a year shopping as their counterparts in Western European countries. Once a purely utilitarian chore, shopping has been elevated to the status of a national passion.

Shopping has become a leisure activity in its own right. Going to the mall is a common Friday or Saturday night's entertainment, not only for the teens who seem to live in them, but also for adults. Shopping is also the most popular weekday evening "out-of-home-entertainment." And malls are everywhere. Four billion square feet of our total land area has been converted into shopping centers, or about 16 square feet for every American man, woman, and child. Actually, shopping is no longer confined to stores or malls but is permeating the entire geography. Any phone line is a conduit to thousands of products. Most homes are virtual retail outlets, with cable shopping channels, mail-order catalogues, toll-free numbers, and computer hookups. We can shop during lunch hour, from the office. We can shop while traveling, from the car. We can even shop in the airport, where video monitors have been installed for immediate on-screen purchasing.

Some of the country's most popular leisure activities have been turned into extended shopping expeditions. National parks, music concerts, and art museums are now acquisition opportunities. When the South Street Seaport Museum in New York City opened in the early 1980s as a combination museum-shopping center, its director explained the commercialization as a bow to reality: "The fact is that shopping is the chief cultural activity in the United States." Americans used to visit Europe to see the sights or meet the people. Now "Born to Shop" guides are replacing Fodor and Baedeker, complete with walking tours from Ferragamo to Fendi. Even island paradises, where we go "to get away from it all," are not immune: witness titles such as *Shopping in Exciting Australia and Papua New Guinea.*

Debt has been an important part of the shopping frenzy. Buying is easier when there's no requirement to pay immediately, and credit cards have seduced many people beyond their means: "I wanted to be able to pick up the tab for ten people, or take a cab when I wanted. I thought that part of being an adult was being able to go to a restaurant, look at the menu, and go in if you like the food, not because you're looking at the prices." This young man quickly found himself with $18,000 of credit card debt, and realized that he and his wife "could have gone to Europe last year on [the] interest alone." For some people, shopping has become an addiction, like alcohol or drugs. "Enabled" by plastic, compulsive shoppers spend money they don't have on items they absolutely "can't" do without and never use. The lucky ones find their way to self-help groups like Debtors Anonymous and Shopaholics Limited. And for every serious compulsive shopper, there are many more with mild habits. Linda Weltner was lucky enough to keep her addiction within manageable financial bounds, but still her "mindless shopping" grew into a "troubling preoccupation . . . which was impoverishing [her] life."

The "shop 'til you drop" syndrome seemed particularly active during the 1980s, a decade popularly represented as one long buying spree. In the five years between 1983 and 1987, Americans purchased 51 million microwaves, 44 million washers and dryers, 85 million color televisions, 36 million refrigerators and freezers, 48 million VCRs, and 23 million cordless telephones—all for an adult population of only 180 million.

Much has, with some justification, been made of the distinctiveness of the decade. The rich made an important social comeback. Not since the 1920s had the country been so tolerant of unrestrained materialism and greed. But in other ways the 1980s were not unique. The growth of personal consumption—the hallmark of 1980s culture—is nothing new. Modern consumerism harkens back to at least the 1920s. The growth of expenditures was temporarily derailed by the Depression and the war but was on track again by the 1950s. Since then, the nation has been feeding on a steady diet of single-family houses, cars, household appliances, and leisure spending. The average American is consuming, in toto, more than twice as much as he or she did forty years ago. And this holds not only for the Gucci set but all the way down the income scale. Nearly everyone participated in the postwar consumption boom. Compared with forty years ago, Americans in every income class—rich, middle class, and poor—have about twice as much in the way of income and material goods.

Of course, the consumer boom of the 1980s *has* been different from the earlier decades in one important way—consumerism has been far more an affair of the affluent—the top 20 or 40 percent of the population. Income became far less equally distributed during this decade, and many people, especially those in the bottom quarter of the population, have experienced substantial declines in their standard of living. Others have maintained their incomes only by working longer hours. Had hours not risen, the average American worker's annual earnings would have been lower at the close of the decade than when it began. Still, declining wages have been mainly a phenomenon of the last ten years. From the longer vantage point of the "golden age" of the 1950s, 1960s, and 1970s, the depth and breadth of American affluence comes clearly into view.

Housing expenditures—the largest item in most family budgets—clearly reflect the country's growing wealth. In the 1950s, when developer William Levitt created Levittowns for ordinary American families, his standard house was 750 square feet. In 1963, the new houses were about twice as large; and by 1989, the average finished area had grown to almost three times the Levittown standard—2,000 feet. At the same time, fewer people were living in these dwellings. The typical 1950s family of four has shrunk to an average of 2.6 persons, so that each individual now has as much space as an entire family of four occupied in 1950. Fifty years ago, only 20 percent of all houses had more rooms than people living in them; by 1970, over 90 percent of our homes were spacious enough to allow more than one room per person. The size and quality of the American housing stock has not been replicated anywhere else on earth.

Houses are not only bigger, they are also more luxuriously equipped. As late as 1940, 30 percent still had no running water, and 40 percent were without flush toilets. Today virtually all houses have both, and three-quarters of single-family dwellings have two or more bathrooms. In 1940, less than 45 percent of homes had electric refrigerators. Now all do. Americans also acquired vacuum cleaners, toasters, irons, radios, and washing machines. Forty years ago, fewer than 5 percent of U.S. homes had air-conditioners, dishwashers, and clothes dryers. Now two-thirds have air-conditioning (a majority with centralized systems), microwaves, and dryers, and almost half have dishwashers. Only a quarter of homes had kitchen ranges in 1953; now all do.

More of us also own our own homes. The difficulties young people have had buying houses in the 1980s notwithstanding, overall rates of home ownership have risen impressively—from 44 percent in 1940, to 55 percent in 1950, to 64 percent in 1989. Homeownership rates for two-person households are even higher—just over 70 percent. Ownership of motor vehicles has also grown: in 1935, 55 percent of families had a car; today, 88 percent of households have a motor vehicle, and the average number of vehicles per household is two. Over 90 percent of all households also have color televisions and 80 percent have VCRs. In addition to VCRs and microwaves, Americans are buying many more services—like foreign travel, restaurant meals, medical attention, hair and skin care, and products of leisure industries such as health clubs or tennis lessons. Overall, per-capita service expenditures have risen 2.6 times since 1950—even more than consumer expenditures as a whole.

The consumerism of the postwar era has not been without its effects on the way we use our time. As people became accustomed to the material rewards of prosperity, desires for leisure time were eroded. They increasingly looked to consumption to give satisfaction, even meaning, to their lives. In both the workplace and the home, progress has repeatedly translated into more goods and services, rather than more free time. Employers channel productivity increases into additional income; housewives are led to use their labor-saving appliances to produce more goods and services. Consumerism traps us as we become habituated to the good life, emulate our neighbors, or just get caught up in the social pressures created by everyone else's choices. Work-and-spend has become a mutually reinforcing and powerful syndrome—a seamless web we somehow keep choosing,' without even meaning to.

THE CREATION OF DISCONTENT

I never knew how poor I was until I had a little money.

—a banker

There is no doubt that the growth of consumption has yielded major improvements in the quality of life. Running water, washing machines, and electrical appliances eliminated arduous, often backbreaking labor. Especially for the poor women who not only did their own housework, but often someone else's as well, the transformation of the home has been profoundly liberating. Other products have also enhanced the quality of life. The compact disc raises the enjoyment of the music lover; the high-performance engine makes the car buff happy, and the fashion plate loves to wear a designer suit.

But when we add up all the items we consume, and consider the overall impact, rather than each in isolation, the picture gets murkier. The farther we get from the onerous physical conditions of the past, the more ambiguous are the effects of additional commodities. The less "necessary" and more "luxurious" the item, the more difficult it is automatically to assume that consumer purchases yield intrinsic value.

We do know that the increasing consumption of the last forty years has not made us happier. The percentage of the population who reported being "very happy" peaked in 1957, according to two national polls. By the last years these polls were taken (1970 and 1978), the level of "very happy" had not recovered, in spite of the rapid growth in consumption during the 1960s and 1970s. Similar polls taken since then indicate no revival of happiness.

Despite the fact that possessions are not creating happiness, we are still riding the consumer merry-go-round. In fact, for some Americans the quest for material goods became more intense in the last decade: according to the pollster Louis Harris, "by the mid-1980s, the American people were far more oriented toward economic growth and materialism than before. Most significant, young people were leading the charge back to material values."

Materialism has not only failed to make us happy. It has also bred its own form of discontent—even among the affluent. Newspaper and magazine articles chronicle the dissatisfaction. One couple earning $115,000 tallied up their necessary expenses of $100,000 a year and complained that "something's gone terribly wrong with being 'rich.'" An unmarried Hollywood executive earning $72,000 worried about bouncing checks: "I have so much paid for by the studio—my car, my insurance, and virtually all food and entertainment—and I'm *still* broke." Urbanites have it especially hard.

As one New York City inhabitant explained, "It's incredible, but you just can't live in this city on a hundred thousand dollars a year." According to the *New York Times*, the fast lane is not all it's cracked up to be, and Wall Streeters are "Feeling Poor on $600,000 a Year." "When the Joneses they are keeping up with are the Basses . . . $10 million in liquid capital is not rich."

Whatever we think of these malcontents—whether we find them funny, pathetic, or reprehensible—we must acknowledge that these feelings are not confined to those in the income stratosphere. Many who make far less have similar laments. Douglas and Maureen Obey earn $56,000 a year—an income that exceeds that of roughly 70 percent of the population. Yet they complain that they are stretched to the breaking point. Douglas works two jobs "to try to keep it all together. . . . I feel I make a fairly good income that should afford a comfortable lifestyle, but somehow it doesn't. . . . [I'm] in hock up to my eyeballs." The Obeys own their home, two cars, a second rental property, and a backyard pool.

Complaints about life style have been particularly loud among the baby-boom generation. One writer explained a state of mind shared by many in her generation: she was convinced she would not achieve the comfortable middle-class life style enjoyed by her parents (four-bedroom house, two-car garage, private schools for the children, and cashmere blankets at the bottom of the beds): "I thought bitterly of my downward mobility . . . and [had] constant conversations with myself about wanting . . . a new couch, a weekend cottage, a bigger house on a quieter street." Eventually she realized that more money was not the answer, Her needs were satisfied. As she acknowledged: "Discontent was cheating me of the life I *had*."

CAPITALISM'S SQUIRREL CAGE

This materialism (and its attendant discontent) is taken for granted. It is widely believed that our unceasing quest for material goods is part of the basic makeup of human beings. According to the folklore, we may not like it, but there's little we can do about it.

Despite its popularity, this view of human nature is wrong. While human beings may have innate desires to strive toward something, there is nothing preordained about material goods. There are numerous examples of societies in which *things* have played a highly circumscribed role. In medieval Europe, there was relatively little acquisitiveness. The common people, whose lives were surely precarious by contemporary standards, showed strong preferences for leisure rather than money. In the nineteenth- and early twentieth-century United States, there is also considerable evidence that many working people exhibited a restricted appetite for material goods. Numerous examples of societies where consumption is relatively unimportant can be found in the anthropological and historical literature.

Consumerism is not an ahistorical trait of human nature, but a specific product of capitalism. With the development of the market system, consumerism "spilled over," for the first time, beyond the charmed circles of the rich. The growth of the middle class created a large group of potential buyers and the possibility that mass culture could be oriented around material goods. This process can be seen not only in historical experiences but is now going on in places such as Brazil and India, where the growth of large middle classes have contributed to rampant consumerism and the breakdown of longstanding values.

In the United States, the watershed was the 1920s—the point at which the "psychology of scarcity" gave way to the "psychology of abundance." This was a crucial period for the development of modern materialist culture. Thrift and sobriety were out; waste and excess were in. The nation grew giddy with its exploding wealth. Consumerism blossomed—both as a social ideology and in terms of high rates of real spending. In the midst of all this buying, we can discern the origins of modern consumer discontent.

This was the decade during which the American dream, or what was then called "the American standard of living," captured the nation's imagination. But it was always something of a mirage. The historian Winifred Wandersee explains:

> It is doubtful that the average American could have described the precise meaning of the term "American standard of living," but nearly everyone agreed that it was attainable, highly desirable, and far superior to that of any other nation. Its nature varied according to social class and regional differences, but no matter where a family stood socially and financially, it was certain to have aspirations set beyond that stance. This was the great paradox posed by the material prosperity of the twentieth century: prosperity was conspicuously present, but it was always just out of reach, for nearly every family defined its standard of living in terms of an income that it hoped to achieve rather than the reality of the paycheck.

The phenomenon of yearning for more is evident in studies of household consumption. In a 1928 study of Yale University faculty members, the bottom category (childless couples with incomes of $2,000) reported that their situation was "life at the cheapest and barest with nothing left over for the emergencies of sickness and childbirth." Yet an income of $2,000 a year put them above 60 percent of all American families. Those at the $5,000 level (the top 10 percent of the income distribution) reported that they "achieve nothing better than 'hand to mouth living.'" At $6,000, "the family containing young children can barely break even." Yet these were the top few percent of all Americans. Even those making $12,000—a fantastic sum in 1928—complained about items they could not afford. A 1922 Berkeley study revealed similar sentiments of discontent—despite the facts that all the families studied had telephones, virtually all had purchased life insurance, two-thirds owned their own homes and took vacations, over half had motor cars, and nearly every family spent at least a little money on servants or house-cleaning help.

The discontent expressed by many Americans was fostered—and to a certain extent even created—by manufacturers. Business embarked on the path of the "hard sell." The explosion of consumer credit made the task easier, as automobiles, radios, electric refrigerators, washing machines—even jewelry and foreign travel—were bought on the installment plan. By the end of the 1920s, 60 percent of cars, radios, and furniture were being purchased on "time." The ability to buy without actually having money helped foster a climate of instant gratification, expanding expectations, and, ultimately, materialism.

The 1920s was also the decade of advertising. The admen went wild: everything from walnuts to household coal was being individually branded and nationally advertised. Of course, ads had been around for a long time. But something new was afoot, in terms of both scale and strategy. For the first time, business began to use advertising as a psychological weapon against consumers. "Scare copy" was invented. Without Listerine, Postum, or a Buick, the consumer would be left a spinster, fall victim to a crippling disease, or be passed over for a promotion. Ads developed an association between the product and one's very identity. Eventually they came to promise everything and anything—from self-esteem, to status, friendship, and love.

The psychological approach responded to the economic dilemma business faced. Americans in the middle classes and above (to whom virtually all advertising was targeted) were no longer buying to satisfy basic needs—such as food, clothing and shelter. These had been met. Advertisers had to persuade consumers to acquire things they most certainly did not need. In the words of John Kenneth Galbraith, production would have to "create the wants it seeks to satisfy." This is exactly what manufacturers tried to do. The normally staid AT&T attempted to transform the utilitarian telephone into a luxury, urging families to buy "all the telephone facilities that they can conveniently use, rather than the smallest amount they can get along with." One ad campaign targeted fifteen phones as the style for an affluent home. In product after product, companies introduced designer colors, styles, even scents. The maid's uniform had to match the room decor, flatware was color-coordinated, and Kodak cameras came in five bird-inspired tints—Sea Gull, Cockatoo, Redbreast, Bluebird, and Jenny Wren.

Business clearly understood the nature of the problem. It even had a name—"needs saturation." Would-be sellers complained of buyers' strike and organized a "Prosperity Bureau," urging people to "Buy Now." According to historian Frederick Lewis Allen: "Business had learned as never before the importance of the ultimate consumer. Unless he could be persuaded to buy and buy lavishly, the whole stream of six-cylinder cars, super heterodynes, cigarettes, rouge compacts, and electric ice boxes would be dammed up at its outlets."

But would the consumer be equal to her task as "the savior of private enterprise"? The general director of General Motors' Research Labs, Charles Kettering, stated the matter baldly: business needs to create a "dissatisfied consumer"; its mission is "the organized creation of dissatisfaction." Kettering led the way by introducing annual model changes for GM cars—planned obsolescence designed to make the consumer discontented with what he or she already had. Other companies followed GM's lead. In the words of advertising historian Roland Marchand, success now depended on "the nurture of qualities like wastefulness, self-indulgence, and artificial obsolescence." The admen and the businessmen had to instill what Marchand has called the "consumption ethic," or what Benjamin Hunnicutt termed "the new economic gospel of consumption."

The campaign to create new and unlimited wants did not go unchallenged. Trade unionists and social reformers understood the long-term consequences of consumerism for most Americans: it would keep them imprisoned in capitalism's "squirrel cage." The consumption of luxuries necessitated long hours.

Materialism would provide no relief from the tedium, the stultification, the alienation, and the health hazards of modern work; its rewards came outside the workplace. There was no mystery about these choices: business was explicit in its hostility to increases in free time, preferring consumption as the *alternative* to taking economic progress in the form of leisure. In effect, business offered up the cycle of work-and-spend. In response, many trade unionists rejected what they regarded as a Faustian bargain of time for money: "Workers have declared that their lives are not to be bartered at any price, that no wage, no matter how high can induce them to sell their birthright. [The worker] is not the slave of fifty years ago. . . . he [sic] reads . . . goes to the theater . . . [and] has established his own libraries, his own educational institutions. . . . And he wants time, time, time, for all these things."

Progressive reformers raised ethical and religious objections to the cycle of work-and-spend. Monsignor John A. Ryan, a prominent Catholic spokesman, articulated a common view:

> One of the most baneful assumptions of our materialistic industrial society is that all men should spend at least one-third of the twenty-four hour day in some productive occupation. . . . If men still have leisure [after needs are satsfied], new luxuries must he invented to keep them busy and new wants must be stimulated . . . to take the luxuries off the market and keep the industries going. Of course, the true and rational doctrine is that when men have produced sufficient necessaries and reasonable comforts and conveniences to supply all the population, they should spend what time is left in the cultivation of their intellects and wills, in the pursuit of the higher life.

The debates of the 1920s clearly laid out the options available to the nation. On the one hand, the path advocated by labor and social reformers: take productivity growth in the form of increases in free time, rather than the expansion of output; limit private consumption, discourage luxuries, and emphasize public goods such as education and culture. On the other hand, the plan of business: maintain current working hours and aim for maximal economic growth. This implied the encouragement of "discretionary" consumption, the expansion of new industries, and a culture of unlimited desires. Production would come to "fill a void that it has itself created."

It is not difficult to see which alternative was adopted. Between 1920 and the present, the bulk of productivity advance has been channeled into the growth of consumption. Economist John Owen, has found that between 1920 and 1977, the amount of labor supplied over the average American's lifetime fell by only 10 percent; and since 1950, there has even been a slight increase. The attitude of businessmen was crucial to this outcome. As employers, they had strong reasons for preferring long hours. As sellers, they craved vigorous consumption to create markets for their products. Labor proved to be no match for the economic and political power of business.

Finally, we should not underestimate the appeal of consumption itself. The working classes and the poor, particularly those migrating from Europe or the rural United States, grew up in conditions of material deprivation. 'The array of products available in urban America was profoundly alluring, at times mesmerizing. For the middle classes, consumption held its own satisfactions. Designer towels or the latest GM model created a sense of privilege, superiority, and well-being. A Steinway "made life worth living." Once the Depression hit, it reinforced these tendencies. One of its legacies was a longlasting emphasis on finding security in the form of material success.

THE PITFALLS OF CONSUMERISM

The consumerism that took root in the 1920s was premised on the idea of *dis*satisfaction. As much as one has, it is never enough. The implicit mentality is that the next purchase will yield happiness, and then the next. In the words of the baby-boom writer, Katy Butler, it was the new couch, the quieter street, and the vacation cottage. Yet happiness turned out to be elusive. Today's luxuries became tomorrow's necessities, no longer appreciated. When the Joneses also got a new couch or a second home, these acquisitions were no longer quite as satisfying. Consumerism turned out to be full of pitfalls—a vicious pattern of wanting and spending which failed to deliver on its promises.

The inability of the consumerist life style to create durable satisfaction can be seen in the syndrome of "keeping up with the Joneses." This competition is based on the fact that it is not the absolute level of consumption that matters, but how much one consumes relative to one's peers. The great English economist John Maynard Keynes made this distinction over fifty years ago: "[Needs] fall into two classes—those which are absolute in the sense that we feel them whatever the situation of our fellow human beings may be, and those which are relative only in that their satisfaction lifts us above, makes us feel superior to, our fellows." Since then, economists have invented a variety of terms for "keeping up with the Joneses": "relative income or consumption," "positional goods," or "local status." A brand-new Toyota Corolla may be a luxury and a status symbol in a lower-middle-class town, but it appears paltry next to the BMWs and Mercedes that fill the driveways of the fancy suburb. A 10-percent raise sounds great until you find that your co-workers all got 12 percent. The cellular phone, fur coat, or _ (fill in the blank) gives a lot of satisfaction only before everyone else has one. In the words of one 1980s investment banker: "You tend to live up to your income level. You see it in relation to the people of your category. They're living in a certain way and you want to live in that way. You keep up with other people of your situation who have also leveraged themselves."

Over time, keeping up with the Joneses becomes a real trap—because the Joneses also keep up with you. If everyone's income goes up by 10 percent, then relative positions don't change at all. No satisfaction is gained. The more of our happiness we derive from comparisons with others, the less additional welfare we get from general increases in income—which is probably why happiness has failed to keep pace with economic growth. This dynamic may be only partly conscious. We may not even be aware that we are competing with the Joneses, or experience it as a competition. It may be as simple as the fact that exposure to their latest "life-style upgrade" plants the seed in our own mind that we must have it, too—whether it be a European vacation, this year's fashion statement, or piano lessons for the children.

In the choice between income and leisure, the quest for relative standing has biased us toward income. That's because status comparisons have been mostly around commodities—cars, clothing, houses, even second houses. If Mrs. Jones works long hours, she will be able to buy the second home, the designer dresses, or the fancier car. If her neighbor Mrs. Smith opts for more free time instead, her two-car garage and walk-in closet will be half empty. As long as the competition is more oriented to visible commodities, the tendency will be for both women to prefer income to time off. But once they both spend the income, they're back to where they started. Neither is *relatively* better off. If free time is less of a "relative" good than other commodities, then true welfare could be gained by having more of it, and worrying less about what the Joneses are buying.

It's not easy to get off the income treadmill and into a new, more leisured life style. Mrs. Smith won't do it on her own, because it'll set her back in comparison to Mrs. Jones. And Mrs. Jones is just like Mrs. Smith. They are trapped in a classic Prisoner's Dilemma: both would be better off with more free time; but without cooperation, they will stick to the long hours, high consumption choice. We also know their employers won't initiate a shift to more leisure, because they prefer employees to work long hours.

A second vicious cycle arises from the fact that the satisfactions gained from consumption are often short-lived. For many, consumption can be habit forming. Like drug addicts who develop a tolerance, consumers need additional hits to maintain any given level of satisfaction. The switch from black and white to color television was a real improvement when it occurred. But soon viewers became habituated to color. Going back to black and white would have reduced well-being, but having color may not have yielded a permanently higher level of satisfaction. Telephones are another example. Rotary dialing was a major improvement. Then came touch-tone, which made us impatient with rotaries. Now numbers are preprogrammed and some people begin to find any dialing a chore.

Our lives are filled with goods to which we have become so habituated that we take them for granted. Indoor plumbing was once a great luxury—and still is in much of the world. Now it is so ingrained in our life style that we don't give it a second thought. The same holds true for all but the newest household appliances—stoves, refrigerators, and vacuum cleaners are just part of the landscape. We may pay great attention to the kind of automobile we drive, but the fact of having a car is something adults grew accustomed to long ago.

The process of habituation can be seen as people pass through life stages—for example, in the transition from student life to a first job. The graduate student makes $15,000 a year. He has hand-me-down furniture, eats at cheap restaurants, and, when traveling long distances, finds a place in someone else's car. After graduation, he gets a job and makes twice as much money. At first, everything seems luxurious. He rents a bigger apartment (with no roommates), buys his own car, and steps up a notch in restaurant quality. His former restaurant haunts now seem unappetizing. Hitching a ride becomes too inconvenient. As he accumulates possessions, the large apartment starts to shrink. In not too many years, he has become habituated to twice as much income and is spending the entire $30,000. It was once a princely sum, which made him feel rich. Now he feels it just covers a basic standard of living, without much left over for luxuries. He may not even feel any better off. Yet to go back to $15,000 would be painful.

Over time, further increases in income set in motion another round of the same. He becomes dissatisfied with renting and "needs" to buy a home. Travel by car takes too long, so he switches to airplanes. His tastes become more discriminating, and the average price of a restaurant meal slowly creeps upward. Something like this process is why Americans making $70,000 a year end up feeling stretched and discontented.

Of course, part of this is a life-cycle process. As our young man grows older, possessions like cars and houses become more important. But there's more to it than aging. Like millions of other American consumers, he is becoming addicted to the accoutrements of affluence. This may well be why the doubling of per-capita income has not made us twice as well off. In the words of psychologist Paul Wachtel, we have become an "asymptote culture . . . in which the contribution of material goods to life satisfaction has reached a point of diminishing returns. . . . Each individual item seems to us to bring an increase in happiness or satisfaction. But the individual increments melt like cotton candy when you try to add them up."

These are not new ideas. Economists such as James Duesenberry, Edward Schumacher, Fred Hirsch, Tiber Scitovsky, Robert Frank, and Richard Easterlin have explored these themes. Psychologists have also addressed them, providing strong support for the kinds of conclusions I have drawn. My purpose is to add a dimension to this analysis of consumption which has heretofore been neglected—its connection to the incentive structures operating in labor markets. The consumption traps I have described are just the flip side of the bias toward long hours embedded in the production system. We are not merely caught in a pattern of spend-and-spend—the problem identified by many critics of consumer culture. The whole story is that we work, and spend, and work and spend some more.

CAUSES OF THE WORK-AND-SPEND CYCLE

The irony in all the consuming Americans do is that, when asked, they reject materialist values. The Gallup Poll recently asked respondents to choose what was most important to them—family life, betterment of society, physical health, a strict moral code, and so on. Among a list of nine, the materialist option—"having a nice home, car and other belongings"—ranked *last*. In a second survey, respondents ranked "having nice things" twenty-sixth in a list of twenty-eight. (Only opposing abortion and being free of obligations were less popular.) Over two-thirds of the population says it would "welcome less emphasis on money." Yet behavior is often contrary to these stated values. Millions of working parents see their children or spouses far less than they should or would like to. "Working" mothers complain they have no time for themselves. Volunteer work is on the decline, presumably because people have little time for it. Employed Americans spend long hours at jobs that are adversely affecting their health—through injury, occupationally induced diseases, and stress. My explanation for this paradoxical behavior is that people are operating under a powerful set of constraints: they are trapped by the cycle of work-and-spend.

Work-and-spend is driven by productivity growth. Whether the annual increment is 3 percent, as it was for much of the postwar period, or less, as it has been in recent years, growth in productivity provides the chance either to raise income or to reduce working hours. This is where the cycle begins, with the employer's reaction to the choice between "time and money." Usually a company does not offer this choice to its employees but unilaterally decides to maintain existing hours and give a pay increase instead. As we have seen, for forty years, only a negligible portion of productivity increase has been channeled into free time. Using productivity to raise incomes has become the firmly entrenched "default option."

One might imagine that where wages are set by collective-bargaining agreements employees would have more of a say in the choice between income and time. But less than 20 percent of the workforce is unionized. Furthermore, as union negotiators will attest, employers are frequently fiercely resistant to granting concessions on hours and jealously guard the authority to set schedules. But even if a firm is willing, the reduced worktime option it offers will often be worth less (in dollar terms) than a straight pay increase, because of the extra costs incurred, such as additional fringe benefits for new employees. The company will try and force the employees to bear the expenses associated with shorter working hours. So even with collective bargaining, the choice will be skewed against shorter hours.

Once a pay increase is granted, it sets off the consumption cycles I have described. The additional income will be spent, (The personal savings rate is currently only 4.5 percent of disposable income.) The employee will become habituated to this spending and incorporate it into his or her usual standard of living. Gaining free time by *reducing* income becomes undesirable, both because of relative comparisons (Joneses versus Smiths) and habit formation. The next year, when another increase in productivity occurs, the process starts again. The company offers income, which the employee spends and becomes accustomed to. This interpretation is consistent with the history of the last half-century. Annual productivity growth has made possible higher incomes or more free time. Repeatedly, the bulk of the productivity increase has been channeled into the former. Consumption has kept pace.

What drives this cycle of work-and-spend? One view—that of neoclassical economic theory—contends that it is motivated by the choices of workers. Workers have prior (and fixed) attitudes about how valuable income is to them and how much they dislike work. On the basis of these attitudes they select the number of hours they want to work. Firms are passive and willing to hire workers for whatever quantity of hours they choose. By this account, if factory workers in the nineteenth century toiled twelve, fourteen, or sixteen hours a day, it was because they "preferred" this schedule above all others. If U.S. workers have added a month onto their annual worktime, it is because they want the extra income. Attempts to limit hours of labor will make employees worse, not better off. Invariably, *workers get what they want.*

I turn the neoclassical analysis on its head, arguing that *workers want what they get*, rather than get what they want. My starting point is firms rather than individual workers. Firms set the hours they require of their employees. Associated with those hours is a level of income that determines workers' consumption level. As a result of habit formation and relative status considerations, people develop preferences to accommodate that level of spending. Attitudes toward consumption are not preordained but are actually formed in the process of earning and consuming itself. These two interpretations—workers get what they want or want what they get—are the polar cases. According to neoclassical theory, attitudes toward consumption are independent of the actual experience of spending, and firms are passive. In my interpretation, firms set hours and workers do most of the adjusting.

ASSESSING THE NEOCLASSICAL VIEW

The crux of the neoclassical story is that workers determine hours. But do they? Not according to the evidence. Every study I have seen on this topic has found that workers lack free choice of hours. They are limited in both how much and how little they can work. In one survey of male heads of households, 85 percent reported that they did not have free choice of hours. A second study (of married men) again found that 85 percent were faced with the choice of either no job or a job at hours that were not those they would choose. The men wanted shorter hours, but all the jobs were full-time. The other existing studies report consistent results: workers face constraints on their hours of work. Indeed, institutionalist labor economists (oriented to the "real world") have long maintained that firms choose hours, giving employees a take-it-or-leave-it option. Now this institutionalist view is backed up by statistical evidence.

These findings do not imply that workers have *no* freedom in the matter of working hours. Moonlighting and retirement are options. And hours differ across occupations and industries, so that workers can quit their jobs to find alternate schedules. But the research shows that for most workers these adjustments are not sufficient to eliminate *binding* constraints on hours. As the economist Paul Samuelson noted years ago: "In contrast with freedom in the spending of the money we earn, the modern industrial regime denies us a similar freedom in choosing the work routine by which we earn those dollars." The failure of the neoclassical approach is rooted in its assumption that there is always full employment and that workers' choices are sovereign. As I have argued, this characterization is mistaken. Competition in labor markets is typically skewed in favor of employers: it is a buyer's market. And in a buyer's market, it is the sellers who compromise. Competition for labor is not strong enough to ensure that workers' desires are always satisfied. This is part of why firms are able to set working hours, even when they entail binding constraints on workers.

The second major point of difference between my approach and the neoclassical involves the nature of preferences. Neoclassical economists point to worker attitudes as evidence that the market is delivering the hours they want. Results from a 1985 survey are typical: asked whether they would prefer more, fewer, or just the hours they were currently working, accompanied by commensurate changes in income, about two thirds of workers reported satisfaction with their current hours/income choice.

This evidence may sound compelling. But imagine, for a moment, what the responses would be like in the light of my interpretation, and workers want what they get. *The results would look just the same,* in the sense that majorities would express satisfaction with their current hours. The standard survey evidence is perfectly consistent with both views.

A great deal of psychological evidence casts doubt, however, on the neoclassical interpretation. Psychologists find that people tend to "adapt" to their environments: that is, their preferences adjust over time. The fact that large numbers of people say they are contented with their working hours (or job conditions) may reveal that they are tractable, not that their deeper desires have been fulfilled.

One type of evidence that can differentiate between the two interpretations is forward-looking surveys—questions about trading off future income for leisure. Here workers express markedly different views. In a 1978 Department of Labor study, 84 percent of respondents said that they would like to trade off some or all of future income for additional free time. Nearly half (47 percent) said they would trade *all* of a 10-percent pay raise for free time. Only 16 percent opted for the money with no increase in time off.

These findings support a key feature of the work-and-spend cycle—the difference in attitudes toward current and future income. As with all the previous surveys, this group was unwilling to give up its current income (only a small percentage chose that option). Presumably they had become materially or psychologically attached to their existing standard of living. But the desire to consume out of future income was far less compelling, a fact consistent with recent psychological research. In the neoclassical interpretation, there is no explanation for this asymmetry.

Because this study was conducted over ten years ago, we can check to see whether the stated preferences were actually validated. Did 84 percent of the population gain the free time they said they wanted? As we know, they did not. In fact, they lost free time. Of course, what has happened since 1978 is complicated. Some workers, particularly younger less-educated men, have lost purchasing power since 1978. Others have had stagnant incomes. But leisure time did not even increase among those with gains in income. In fact, hours increased substantially for those groups who both did well in the labor market and expressed the strongest desires for more time off—women and people in the higher-paid occupational categories. In 1989, when a similar survey was taken, the results indicated that forward-looking preferences for leisure are still strong. Eight out of ten Americans declared that they would sacrifice career advancement in order to spend more time with their families.

This evidence hardly settles the issue. Many more studies and surveys are necessary, particularly to track working hours and preferences over time. However, the findings do cast doubt on the sanguine view of labor/leisure choices which dominates the economic discourse. It is clear that we can no longer rely on the simple assumption that labor and product markets provide optimal outcomes, in response to what people want and need. The interaction between what we want and what we get is far more complicated.

THE SOCIAL NATURE OF WORK-AND-SPEND

Part of the power of the work-and-spend cycle is its social pervasiveness. Although individuals are the proximate decision makers, their actions are influenced and constrained by social norms and conventions. The social character of the cycle of work-and-spend means that individuals have a hard time breaking out of it on their own. This is part of why, despite evidence of growing desires for less demanding jobs and disillusionment with "work-and-spend," hours are still rising.

To see the difficulties individuals have in deviating from the status quo, consider what would happen to an ordinary couple who have grown tired of the rat race. John and Jane Doe, like nearly half of all Americans, want more time to spend with their children and each other. What will happen if they both decide to reduce their hours by half and are willing to live on half their usual earnings?

The transition will be most abrupt for John. Few men work part-time, with the exception of teens, students, and some seniors. Among males aged twenty-five to forty-four, virtually none (a meager 2.5 percent) voluntarily choose part-time schedules. Most report that they are not able to reduce their hours of work at all. And of those who do have the freedom to work fewer hours, it is likely that only a small percentage can reduce hours by as much as half. Unless John has truly unusual talents, his employer will probably refuse to sanction a change to part-time work. Chances are he'll have to find a new job.

Given the paucity of part-time jobs for men, John's choices will be limited. It will be almost impossible to secure a position in a managerial, professional, or administrative capacity. Most part-time jobs are in the service sector. When he does land a job, his pay will fall far short of what he earned in full-time work. The median hourly wage rate among male workers is about $10.50, with weekly earnings of $450. As a part-time worker paid by the hour, his median wage will be about $4, or $80 a week. He will also lose many of the benefits that went with his full-time job. Only 15 percent of part-time workers are given health insurance. The total income loss John will suffer is likely to exceed 80 percent. Under these conditions, part-time work hardly seems feasible.

The social nature of John's choice is revealed by the drama of his attempt to go against the grain. Since few adult men choose part-time work, there is almost none to be had. The social convention of full-time work gives the individual little choice about it. Those who contemplate a shift to part-time will be deterred by the economic penalty. There may even be many who would prefer shorter hours, but they will exert very little influence on the actual choices available, because their desires are latent. Exit from existing jobs—one channel for influencing the market—is not available, because they cannot find part-time jobs to exit to. Unless people begin to speak up and collectively demand that employers provide alternatives, they will probably remain trapped in full-time work.

Jane's switch to part-time will be less traumatic. She will find more job possibilities, because more women work part-time. Her earnings loss will be less, because women are already discriminated against in full-time work. (The median hourly wage for women working part-time is almost three-quarters of the full-time wage, compared with one-half for men.) If Jane can get health insurance through John's employment, part-time work may be feasible. But a great deal depends on his earnings and benefits. Even under the best of assumptions, Jane will have to forgo a wide variety of occupations, including most of those with the best pay and working conditions. She will most likely be relegated to the bottom part of the female labor market—the service, sales, and clerical jobs where the majority of women part-timers reside. Social convention and the economic incentives it creates will reproduce inequalities of gender. Despite their original intentions, Jane, rather than John, will end up in part-time employment.

These are the obstacles on the labor market side—low wages, few benefits, and severe limitations on choice of occupations. The dominance of full-time jobs also has effects on the consumption side. Imagine that Jane and John still want to cut back their hours, even under the adverse circumstances I have described. Their income will now be very low, and they will be forced to economize greatly on their purchases. This will affect their ability to fit in socially. As half-time workers, they will find many social occasions too expensive (lunches and dinners out, movies). At first, friends will be understanding, but eventually the clash in life styles will create a social gap. Their children will have social difficulties if they don't have access to common after-school activities or the latest toys and clothes. They'll drop off the birthday party circuit because they can't afford to bring gifts. We can even see these pressures with full-time workers, as parents take on extra employment to live up to neighborhood standards. After her divorce Celeste Henderson worked two jobs to give her children the things their schoolmates had. Ms. Henderson's daughter says her mother "saved her the embarrassment of looking poor to the other children." For a family with only part-time workers, the inability to consume in the manner of their peers is likely to lead to some social alienation. Unless they have a community of others in similar circumstances, dropping down will include an element of dropping out. Many Americans, especially those with children, are not willing to risk such a fate.

Even with careful budgeting, a couple like the Does may have trouble procuring the basics (housing, food, and clothing), because the U.S. standard of living is geared to at least one full-time income and, increasingly, to two. Rents will be high relative to the Does' income. In part, this is because of price increases in the last decade. But there is also a more fundamental impediment. As I have argued, contemporary houses and apartment are large and luxurious. They have indoor plumbing, central heating, stoves, and refrigerators. They have expensive features such as closets, garages, and individual bedrooms. In our society, housing must conform to legal and social conventions that define the acceptable standard of housing. The difficulty is that the social norm prevailing in the housing market is matched to a full-time income (or incomes). It is not only that the cost of living is high these days. It is also that bare-bones housing, affordable on only half a salary, is rare. Even if the Does were willing to go without closets, garages, and central heating in order to save money, they would be hard-pressed to find such a dwelling.

This problem is common to many goods and services. In an economy where nearly everyone works full-time, manufacturers cater to the purchasing power of the full-time income. There is a limited market for products that are desired only by those with half an income. A whole range of cheap products are not even available. Only the better-quality goods will be demanded, and hence only they will be produced. We can see this phenomenon in the continual upscaling of products. We've gone from blender to Cuisinart, from polyester to cotton, from one-speed Schwinn to fancy trail bike. Remember the things that were available forty years ago but have disappeared? The semiautomatic washing machine. The hand-driven coffee grinder. The rotary dial telephone. For those who are skeptical about this point, con-sider the markets of poor countries. In India, one can find very cheap, low-quality clothing—at a fraction of the price of the least expensive items in the United States. Semiautomatic washers and stripped-down cars are the norm. On a world scale, the American consumer market is very upscale, which means that Americans need an upscale income to partici-pate in it.

The strength of social norms does not mean that the nature of work cannot be changed. Part-time employment *could* become a viable option for larger numbers of people. But the existence of social norms suggests that change will not come about, as the neoclassical econo-mist predicts, merely through individuals exer-cising their preferences in the market. Where Prisoner's Dilemmas and vicious cycles exist, change requires intervention on a social level—from government, unions, professional associa-tions, and other collective organizations.

GLOSSARY

Tract house: One of numerous houses of similar design constructed on a tract of land.

John Kenneth Galbraith (1908–): Canadian-born American economist, writer, and diplomat who served as U.S. ambassador to India (1961–1963). His best-known works include *The Great Crash* (1955) and *The Affluent Society* (1958).

IMPLICATIONS

At a national level, the late 1980s and early 1990s witnessed near-record economic pros-perity in America. But, as Schor reveals, this prosperity was purchased at the price of dual wage-earning families, long working hours, and an often frantic pace of life. Why do you think so many Americans accepted the "squir-rel cage" existence that Schor describes? What do you think the personal and economic conse-quences would be if Americans worked fewer hours and spent less money on consumer goods?